SCHOOL OF RACISM

CATHERINE LAROCHELLE

SCHOOL
OF RACISM

A Canadian History, 1830–1915

Translated by S.E. Stewart

UNIVERSITY OF MANITOBA PRESS

School of Racism: A Canadian History, 1830–1915
© University of Manitoba Press 2023
Originally published as *L'école du racisme:*
La construction de l'altérité à l'école québécoise © Presses de l'université
de Montréal 2021

27   26   25   24   23   1   2   3   4   5

University of Manitoba Press
Winnipeg, Manitoba, Canada
Treaty 1 Territory
uofmpress.ca

Cataloguing data available from Library and Archives Canada
ISBN 978-1-77284-053-7 (PAPER)
ISBN 978-1-77284-055-1 (PDF)
ISBN 978-1-77284-056-8 (EPUB)
ISBN 978-1-77284-054-4 (BOUND)

Cover illustration from *L'Enseignement primaire*, 36th year, no. 10
[1915], reprinted from American *Life* magazine.
Cover design by David Drummond
Interior design by Jess Koroscil

Printed in Canada

This book has been published with the help of a grant from the
Federation for the Humanities and Social Sciences, through the Awards
to Scholarly Publications Program, using funds provided by the
Social Sciences and Humanities Research Council of Canada.

The University of Manitoba Press acknowledges the financial support for
its publication program provided by the Government of Canada through
the Canada Book Fund, the Canada Council for the Arts, the Manitoba
Department of Sport, Culture, and Heritage, the Manitoba Arts Council,
and the Manitoba Book Publishing Tax Credit.

Funded by the Government of Canada | Canadä

Contents

Author's Note

In this book, many quotations from the French-language academic literature have been translated into English. However, I have preserved the French-language versions of quotations from documents of the historical period under study, since I consider that necessary to the book's intellectual intent. The juxtaposition of excerpts from the work of francophone and anglophone writers obliges us to note to what extent the world views of Quebec's and Canada's two linguistic communities are similar. In dealing with a historiography that tends to highlight the differences between these two groups, I wanted to demonstrate the shared responsibility of francophones and anglophones for the transmission of racism in the schools of Quebec and Canada. Unless otherwise indicated, all translations are from Sue Stewart.

Given that this book's central theme is how Canada's schools constructed racism, and how generations of children learned this in turn, quotations taken from historical archives include many offensive words and phrases. These terms refer of course to ideological social constructions, not objective realities. Studying the deployment of such constructions is crucial to understanding racism—both historical and contemporary—including the violence associated with it. Generally, when referring to the real groups and populations that these terms targeted, I use words that are accepted today, such as Indigenous Peoples, Arab and Muslim communities, and the world's diverse Black populations. However, the social construction refers occasionally to a group so vast or so imaginary that I have been obliged to keep the original term, that is to say, the term associated with a specific social construction.

When quoting historical documents, I have retained the antiquated spelling (e.g., *enfans*, *serpens*, etc.) and the use of capital letters as it appeared in the original without signalling the error. In the case of quotations from students' homework, however, I include [*sic*] when the errors are those of the children.

Introduction

To define difference is to tame otherness. It is to assign
to the other their place, their function. And to require, in addition,
a recognition of the gap maintained between who sets the norm
and who must conform to it.

MADELEINE OUELLETTE-MICHALSKA[1]

The 2018–19 school year. Montreal, Quebec. Two of my children are in primary school, in the third grade. At the first parent-teacher meeting, one of the teachers explains that our children will be introduced to two new subjects that year: science and the social sciences. In the first case, they will learn about problems, experimentation, and the hypothesis. In the social sciences, they will hear stories about "*les Amérindiens*" (Amerindians, a term that is first used in French in the mid-twentieth century). The teacher then adds that the children are especially fond of these stories because they take them into another world, a little like "stories about dragons and fairies." Some of the parents, as shocked as I was, wanted to know whether the children would be informed of the present-day existence of First Nations (and took offence at the comparison to dragons and fairies). The answer was that it is not part of the third-grade program.

At the end of the school year, while sorting out my children's copybooks, Duo-Tangs, and other loose-leaf sheets, I came across an exercise that staggered me. The photocopied workbook accompanying it, entitled *Les Amérindiens*, was illustrated with the drawing of an "Indigenous" girl sitting cross-legged before a wigwam. The very childish illustration was replete with stereotypes—feathers in her hair, a bow, a painted face, hand on her heart, a homogenized décor from no particular period, and the features of a White person. What nation does she represent? In what century does she live? These questions go unanswered. The homework assignment that caught my attention was a composition—the students were asked to write a letter to their teacher, "putting themselves in the place of a Native American." The children could choose between "an Iroquoian and an Algonquin." In their letter, they must describe their dwelling, their environment, and the activities they engage in, depending on whether they are "a girl or a boy," and conclude by inviting the teacher to pay a visit to their era. There I was faced with the centuries-old practice of "playing Indian," 2019 version.

Alterity as staged and recounted by Quebec's educational institutions is at the centre of this book. In addition to questioning the narrative field of "make-believe" and the discourse imposed by representation, the objects of analysis are the contours of the appropriation of such figures of otherness by Québécois students. The representation of otherness raises the issue of the very thin line between being open to the world and appropriating that world for purposes of identity. The interest manifested in different peoples on our planet in the educational discourse goes hand in hand with the formation of our collective identity in Canada. In this connection, the study of historical representations of otherness makes it possible to see the nation-building narrative in a new light. Cannibals, caravans under the burning desert sun, and "Savages of the American West" were some of the exotic images offered to Québécois children who attended school in the nineteenth century. A tool of socialization, the school was also a window on the world and a place to learn stereotypes.

Teaching Racism

The questions guiding this exploration of history are the following: What representations of Others[2] were offered to Quebec students from 1830 to 1910? Were they vectors for the construction of a national identity? What codes of difference became symbolized in educational institutions? Which ideologies were Canadian teachers drawing on? How did the children and youth belonging to the majority group appropriate alterity? What recreational and educational functions did alterity fulfill in the lives of these young Canadians? Which stereotypes were broadly disseminated by educational institutions? The answers to these questions will cast light on how generations of Québécois students learned racism. Obviously, it will not be a matter of determining the truth of these representations of Others but rather of knowing how they functioned in the school curriculum. Studying representations of alterity allows for a better understanding of the society that produces or disseminates them by observing how that society defines itself in relation to what it places outside its boundaries.

My research objective aligns with a movement that questions the conditions for manufacturing White Canadian identities. To date, the historiography has stressed "internal" conditions and the peculiar and contingent character of identity building, while often ignoring the racial assumption. In this case, it is a matter of enriching the historiography by studying contrasts in the alterities that throw this identity formation into relief, while openly addressing the question of race and illustrating the central role played by the representation of Indigenous individuals in the process of building this identity. The study also enables a better appreciation of the common elements, divergences, and reciprocal influences in the francophone and anglophone discourses on alterity. In shedding light on the cultural discourse shared by Quebec's two largest communities, I reassess, downward, the impact of the differences normally assumed to exist between the two White Canadian identities.

Alterity is constructed of different discourses to be found in a variety of institutions—newspapers, literary works, parliamentary

debates, the advertising industry, and so on. There are many reasons
for choosing educational institutions as the territory for enquiry. First,
the period under study corresponds to the development of public
education in Canada. The school's discourse could then reach more
and more individuals, which made the school one of the principal institutions through which stereotypes were disseminated. In addition, the
educational framework could give the representations an aura of truth
that would make them all the more influential. And then, studying
the school makes it possible to understand which forms of knowledge
were considered to be necessary and relevant by the governmental and
religious elites, and also how scientific findings were democratized and
simplified so as to be taught to children. The school was a prime site of
socialization; along with the family and the Church, it was the place of
identity formation, both individual and collective.

The chosen methodology takes in the entire educational institution, with all its subjects, activities, and actors. Existing research on the
ideology at work in schools has effectively been confined for too long
to studies of particular disciplines, most often history or geography.
The study of the various disciplines and school activities reveals the
multiplicity of discourses disseminated and reinforced by the schools,
their interactions and paradoxes. This approach places the educational
institutions, rather than the scholarly disciplines, at the centre of the
historical enquiry and allows for an overall view of the normative
meta-discourse transmitted through the school—studies that take this
broader perspective are rare.

The period under study begins in the 1830s and ends in the decade
of the 1910s. In Lower Canada, the 1830s stand out for the first major
steps to be taken in the development of public education. Following
a significant increase in school attendance, resulting from the establishment in the early 1830s of schools run by trustees, attendance grew
steadily from 1840 to 1860. This period saw the establishment of an
educational system that would last for over a century, into the mid-1900s.
The increase in attendance resulted from the democratization of public

education. The period under study therefore corresponds to that of a gradual normalization of the school experience for children in Quebec.

Further, between the 1830s and 1910s, the world order was overturned by the rapid expansion of the Euro-American empires. In Canada, specifically, the second half of the nineteenth century was marked by the conquest of land in the west of the continent. This period also coincides with the development of anthropology, scientific racism, human zoos, and the concept of the "civilizing mission," all of which greatly influenced the definition and representation of otherness in Euro-American societies. Imperialism pervaded popular culture in Europe and America in the century's last decades. In the period chosen it is possible to observe how these phenomena influenced the representation of human differences as conveyed in schools throughout the nineteenth century.

The period ends in the 1910s for many reasons. From the end of the nineteenth century, the school discourse was increasingly infused with nationalism, and so the identity constructed in relation to the Other evolved and became more specifically national. The heightened nationalism altered the methods and context of delivering the narrative of alterity. It was not so much a modification of the representations' nature that produced this alteration as it was a paradigm shift in the presentation of otherness. The nationalist influence could also be seen in the missionary propaganda circulated to schoolchildren. The First World War would have consequences for defining the Canadian and Québécois national identity but also for concepts of civilization and barbarity, concepts that were central to the world view of the previous century.

To a large extent, my study applies to the Canadian context as a whole, in particular for the first decades under study. Many school textbooks used by Quebec's anglophones were also to be found in Ontario schools. In addition, Quebec's French-language texts were often sent to francophone communities elsewhere in Canada when they were no longer being used in Quebec. Within that larger context, the specific geographical frame of my research is the educational territory of Lower Canada and the Province of Quebec. These well-defined boundaries allowed me to assemble a collection of sources that are cohesive and easily identified. Nonetheless, my interpretations apply only to Quebec's White school population. If we know that the school texts being analyzed here could also have been found on the desks of Indigenous and Black students, subsequent studies, if the archives allow them, should be conducted to determine how this racist knowledge was taught and appropriated in the schools those children attended. For example, the violence inherent in the representation of the "Indians" in these texts had a completely different resonance in the Indigenous context. In that case, alterity did not serve to build a "civilized White" identity as a mirror image of the "Savage's barbaric identity." The fact of presenting the Indian as the principal figure of the Other to Indigenous children certainly contributed to the acculturation and humiliation of Indigenous people.[3] In this regard, my research conclusions cannot be applied to the Indigenous context any more than to the educational experience of any non-White children. As has been demonstrated in multiple works dealing with the education of girls in Quebec or Black and Indigenous children in Canada, the dehumanization, stereotyping, and educational limitations placed on these groups by the school were simultaneously rejected, worked around, and internalized by these students.[4]

Throughout the book, when reference is made to an archive or a historical argument, I use words relating to figures of otherness without quotation marks. These terms are derived from ideological social constructs and not from objective realities. As Emma LaRocque describes it, "There is little resemblance between the colonizer's Indian and the real human beings who are indigenous to this land."[5] Most often, to evoke real groups who have inspired these images—for the most part fantasies—I use words that refer to their current designation, such as Indigenous nations, First Peoples, the Arab Muslim communities, and Black populations.[6] These designations serve to remind the reader that the colonial imagery was contemporaneous with the real presence of these groups at the time.

In taking an interest in the representation of otherness in educational institutions, it quickly became apparent to me that, rather than looking for a figure of the Other that would present itself as such—and would be named as such—what I should be uncovering is a process of constructing alterity. As François Hartog writes, "The question is to perceive how [the narrator, here the educational institution] 'translates' the other and how [it] makes the person addressed believe in the other [it] is constructing. In other words, it will be a matter of noticing a rhetoric of otherness at work in the text, identifying some of its figures and deconstructing some of its procedures; in short, pulling together the rules of operation for fabricating the Other."[7] These rules are what I am attempting to explain in this book.

In a text entitled "La construction de l'Autre. Approches culturelles et socio-historiques" (Constructing the other. Cultural and socio-historical approaches), Hans-Jürgen Lüsebrink defines a methodological approach specific to analyzing otherness that corresponds exactly to the process I have undertaken: "An intercultural analysis of the exotism phenomenon, and of other devices for representing the Other, can be based on three methodological approaches that are systematically inter-woven—the *semiological analysis* of the forms of representation that make up [these devices]; the *sociocritical analysis* [of the] ideological and social anchors [for this representation of the Other]; and the *interdiscursive analysis* of the discourse networks into which a given text becomes integrated and in which it acquires meaning."[8] The methodology's first aspect, semiological analysis, aims to understand the construction of the language of alterity by studying the descriptions and statement patterns for the different figures and the repeated semantic fields. This purely textual analysis is coupled with attention to the insertion of representations of the Other into the entirety of discourse governing the social perception of difference: "Analyzing the construction of the Other, far from simply putting together a 'theme' or an 'image,' or even an assemblage of stereotypical features, largely surpasses, principally through levels of sociocritical and discursive analysis, the domain of a type of precise discourse, whether in literature, cinema, advertising or politics. . . . [An intercultural critique] locates a given text that was first studied for its semantic registers and narrative logic in a variable, historically determined network of ideological and discursive formations that represent, in this instance, figures of alterity."[9] The interdiscursive and sociocritical dimensions of the analysis are established through the study of multisemic discourses that travel through the educational institutions and shape their representation of Others—discourses that are academic, literary, religious, national, imperial, racist, and moral. How the transmitted knowledge has been contextualized is essential to understanding the construction of alterity: Who produces this knowledge? How did it end up in the educational discourse? What changes did it undergo in order to be aligned with the teaching community's objectives?

A large number of archival materials were consulted in carrying out this intercultural analysis of manufacturing otherness in Quebec schools. Studying school textbooks is of course crucial, but to enrich and optimize the study, such a book should be placed in the larger teaching context. In particular, this makes it possible to confirm its use and analyze complementary or competing discourses that a school disseminated by other means: for example, in missionary propaganda.

This research is based first of all on an exhaustive perusal of eighty-seven textbooks published in Quebec and Canada.[10] Drawing inspiration from research carried out in other countries, I chose to examine the rhetorical construction of alterity by studying teaching texts for different school subjects. The corpus is thus made up of twenty-five textbooks of geography, eight of Canadian history, thirty-four for teaching French, sixteen for teaching English, three for teaching English or French as a second language, and one on multiple topics.[11]

The corpus is rounded out with a large number of very varied documents—teachers' notes, study plans, homework and composition notebooks, student newspapers, minutes of debating societies, programs for drama productions, reports of school visitors, scripts of school plays, minutes of organizations responsible for Sunday schools, documents regarding the participation of Quebec schools in world fairs (Paris 1878, Chicago 1893, Paris 1900), glass photographic plates (the forerunners of slides), and so on. The corpus includes much published material from the *Journal de l'instruction publique* (1857–1879), *Journal of Education* (1857–1879), *L'Enseignement primaire* (1881–1915), *The Educational*

Record of the Province of Quebec (1881–1915), *Le Couvent* (1886–1899),[12] and Canadian papers related to the Œuvre de la Sainte-Enfance/Holy Childhood Association.

The book is divided into six chapters. The first presents my study's theoretical underpinnings. Following a detour into the philosophies of Emmanuel Levinas and Jean-Paul Sartre on the significance of the face and the gaze in relating to others, I explore the uses and functions of alterity. To trace the contours of the codes of difference constructed by Quebec's educational institutions, a number of theoreticians' works were consulted, in particular those of Sara Ahmed, Emma LaRocque, Iris Marion Young, and Stuart Hall.

The next three chapters explore the inroads made by alterity into educational discourse by noting all its manifestations, as inconsistent as they might seem at times. In these chapters, I demonstrate how the school produces otherness, how the knowledge thus offered draws on the hegemonic discourse of the day, and how it changes between the mid-nineteenth century and the First World War, as the sciences and the socio-political context of Canadian society evolved. I examine the construction of difference and the ways in which the boundary, always permeable, is erected between Us and the Other. This boundary is socio-cultural (civilization, customs), bodily (race, slavery), and political (freedom, domination). How is the boundary defined and how does alterity, thus acknowledged, then look? Who are the Others, or, rather, who is Other? These chapters analyze the rhetorical processes used to tip a society or an individual into otherness. I pay attention to the functions that the presence of the Other serves in school. Categorizing people in a thousand and one ways is necessary to affirming and maintaining a hierarchy of peoples that favours the societies of European origin. Structuring a precise play of oppositions allows Canada to give itself a higher rating on the scales. Chapter 2 looks at the transnational circulation of educational knowledge and examines the construction of alterity in language and ideology. Chapter 3 dissects the rhetorical function of body otherness. The division of the human species into races is analyzed. Chapter 4 deals with Indigenous otherness as a pivotal point in developing the Canadian identity in the nineteenth-century school. The prevalence of representations of the Indian perfectly illustrates the rhetorical process of cultural and body otherness analyzed in Chapters 2 and 3.

In 1899, Nora Casey, a student in the *3e année du cours moyen* (fifth or sixth year of primary school) at the Académie Sainte-Agnès in Montreal, was asked to complete this English grammar exercise: "Grammar. Change the singular to the plural: (a) A black man is called a negro. (b) This Indian tribe has a fierce chief. (c) A volcano is a burning mountain."[13] In the same time period, the teaching journal *L'Enseignement primaire* published a logical analysis exercise addressing the *proposition absolue*, or independent clause:

> On appelle Proposition absolue toute proposition qui forme un sens complet par elle-même, c'est-à-dire sans le secours d'aucune autre proposition:
>
> La France est une nation puissante.
>
> Les Arabes demeurent sous des tentes.
>
> Le dévouement de Léonidas sauva la Grèce.
>
> Voilà trois propositions absolues.[14]
>
> (An independent clause is any clause that conveys a complete thought by itself, that is, without the addition of another clause:
>
> France is a powerful nation.
>
> Arabs live under tents.
>
> The devotion of Leonidas saved Greece.
>
> Those are three independent clauses.)

The alterity that shows up in these rather ordinary language exercises is all the more effective because it is disguised in statements whose explicit educational aims do not concern it, in this case, grammar. If such grammar lessons were to be possible, the Other must have long been shaped by the educational discourse. At the same time, these trivial exercises both repeated and reinforced the otherness of Arab Muslim communities (Chapter 2), racialized individuals (Chapter 3), and First Nations (Chapter 4). The process of constructing alterity was therefore circular. Those three figures of the Other—the Arab, Black, and Indian—are precisely those whom the nineteenth-century educational discourse essentialized. While presenting a general analysis of the representations of alterity in school, Chapters 2, 3, and 4 examine the construction of these particular figures in detail.

Originating in the social, racial, and colonial hierarchies that ensured various forms of dominance and their reinforcement, the Others in the educational discourse were part of a dynamic of knowledge/power. But how were these representations used? What pedagogical ends did alterity serve? Which of a child's faculties did it develop? What kind of emotional order did it set up in the classroom? In short, not only did the construction of otherness contribute to maintaining global domination, it was also essential to the success of the educational enterprise itself. The last chapters approach these issues from two very particular angles: images of the Other in Chapter 5 and the emotions related to the missionary mobilization of students in Chapter 6.

Inspired by an anti-racist approach to education,[15] I hope with this book to help identify and deconstruct nationalist narratives. As mentioned by Hieu Van Ngo, anti-racist education "calls for structural analyses of power and oppression, particularly historical and contemporary relations of domination and subordination among ethnoracial groups, cultural appropriation, institutional power and discretionary use by people in

authority."[16] My analyses of the alterity rhetoric that generates racialization could serve as examples for today's anti-racist educators who
are seeking tools for understanding the contemporary forms these
racializing representations take.

Since I began my research in 2013, various events have recalled the
very live legacy of the story I am telling in this book. Recent examples
are the Quebec government's obstinate refusal in fall 2020 to call the
racism experienced by different groups "systemic," and the "discovery"
in summer 2021 of unmarked graves on the grounds of several former
residential schools in Canada. My study illustrates the historical existence of systemic racism in Quebec's educational community. Moreover,
it provides some keys to understanding the stubbornness on the part of
the government, as well as a portion of the population, in rejecting the
terms "systemic" and also "genocide." The racism in Quebec's schools
defined the majority of French-Canadian ancestry as White, allowed
its members to construct themselves as individuals, and fed them a
nationalist narrative of survival, featuring the nation as a surviving
victim. Recognizing systemic racism and the genocide of the Indigenous
peoples sounds to some like a judgement that finds them guilty by
reason of their White identity and, in doing so, explodes the nationalist
epic of victimhood that papers over their vision of the world. Why is
this? That is the question this book answers.

1.

The Theories of
Otherness

Otherness has many dimensions—the welcome stranger and the individual whose difference justifies extermination are not in the same register. The other human, the one in an ethical relationship, is the Finite Other, the "being." Whether they take the form of our fellow person, our neighbour, or our enemy, the Finite Other is essentially another, that is, their humanity and individuality are recognized. This dimension of otherness is more commonly linked to identity, owing to the emotional freight it carries and the relationship of proximity in which it takes part.

The Absolute Other represents a second dimension of otherness. It is in the register of metaphysics, transcendence, and grand representations. Theologians have often written of God as wholly Other. History and the Past are also figures of absolute otherness. In the end absolute otherness takes the form of a radically different totality, which underpins the quest for metaphysical meaning. In Western thinking, the Orient and the figures of the Savage and the Barbarian are among the most significant expressions of this dimension of alterity.

The figures of the absolute Other are many. However, they do not all operate on the same level. In the nineteenth century, the types of otherness personified by those who were marginal, criminal, or homosexual belonged to what I call "internal otherness." Communities define themselves by silencing what does not correspond, even within their symbolic borders, to the idea that they have of themselves. The internal Others are the figures the society has pushed away to its margins in order not to have to see much of them. This first level of absolute otherness is characterized by the anxiety and threat provoked by those "outside the norms," since these groups disrupt social ties and the collective self-representation.

To what level of otherness does the stranger belong? The historiography of nation building has paid much attention to this figure, contributing, in a way, to what the thinker Sara Ahmed calls "stranger fetishism." Although they may come from outside, the stranger does not acquire the status of Other until they integrate into society, thus no longer acting from outside. Ahmed explains that the stranger is not simply "they who are not from here" but they whose body says that they are not from here.[1] They are therefore distanced through the encounter and not simply by co-presence. The status of stranger does not precede the encounter with the "we" of "here," where they do not come from. In this sense, they intervene on the same level of absolute otherness as criminal and marginal figures: that is, they acquire meaning only when inside the society.

The nineteenth-century educational discourse did not teach children to recognize these characters—strangers, criminals, and so on—as radical alterities. The collective identity with which they were presented did not acquire its shape in a confrontation with Others who were nearby and disturbing. It was developed through learning about a second level of absolute differentiation, that of external otherness. While the first is disturbing, the second is indispensable, since it serves to unify the community. The savage, barbarian, slave, racialized person: such are the figures of external otherness—naturalized, dehumanized, universalized. Because their humanity has been neutralized, they are no longer disturbing. They in fact take on the opposite function—they are what reassures the Self and makes it feel safe in its quest for identity.

The two levels of absolute otherness sometimes come together in diachrony. In this way, certain external Others of the nineteenth century have gradually become internal strangers, in part owing to migrating populations. The ontological construction of an external otherness has influenced the social connection established with these immigrants. The analysis of otherness construction that I am proposing will improve our understanding of many contemporary situations. In order to grasp how recognition of the stranger operates, we must look at the history of learning the marks of differentiation, such as which bodies are Other to White eyes and which Others have been—and still are—refused the ability to belong.

Defining alterity, attempting to grasp its nature and essence, and analyzing its function—this is the aim of my book. Does an Other exist in the gaze or the face? The answer to this question will make it possible to locate the gap between the otherness of ethical relation and the difference at the centre of social relationships. In order to be recognized, social otherness must be learned. The Other must be objectified and grasped by the consciousness. What purpose does their representation serve, and for whom? What forms does the narrative of difference take? And what does the work of writing teach us about the rejection of alterity manifested in textual dehumanization? While it is posed in the context of a particular historical study, the question of alterity cannot shirk from pursuing a philosophical, political, and sociological understanding of its contours and its effects.

The Gaze and the Knowledge: Ethics and Otherness

Jean-Paul Sartre and Emmanuel Levinas each dedicated a portion of their philosophical reflections to studying the question of otherness. In *Being and Nothingness*, Sartre devoted an entire section of his phenomenological ontology to relating to the Other. In his view, the Other should be considered to be a principle of relation to the Self. It reveals itself first as an object, "that is, as a system of representations out of reach, as a concrete and knowable object."[2] Then how to posit one's existence as a subject, how to establish an intersubjective relation? Sartre introduces the gaze, the real key to interpreting the relationship to the Other. To paraphrase him, other people first appear to me as objects: it is the I-subject that *sees* another "man-object."[3] But suddenly, this "man-object" turns and *sees* the I-subject. And then there is a shift in perspective: I become *object* in the gaze of the other become *subject*. The gaze of another person coming to rest on the Self certifies the existence of this other man as subject.[4] Not only does the gaze produce him as a subject, but from then on, it blocks his objectification.[5] Sartre presents the Other as an objectifying gaze. Thus, the encounter with other people sets up the battle of the gazes, the "consciousnesses in conflict"—who will be the gaze's object, and who will be its subject? As Bernard Munono Muyembe writes, "this is the world of petrifying otherness that Sartre calls Hell."[6]

Emmanuel Levinas, on his side, posits ethics as the basis for relation to the Other. In a summary of Levinas's philosophy of alterity, Muyembe presents his key concepts: "The thinking of Emmanuel Levinas is commonly associated with a certain ethical reflection on the face of the other and the requirements of sociality that are derived. And there can be no doubt that we must consider Levinas to be the thinker about alterity who reminds the modern conscience of the irreducibility of the other's position in the form of an ethical duty."[7] For Levinas, the ontological question of being already contains the Other's presence-absence. Being, as for-the-other, has a primary relation to other people: it is the non-indifference of responsibility.[8] The relationship to the Other—obvious in ethics—is not reciprocity or fusion in a synthesis. The non-indifference evident in responsibility toward the other being is the basis of a radical, insuperable otherness. This responsibility precedes freedom of the Self. It is an order that compels the Self, but that the

Self obeys even before it has been uttered. Levinas writes, "Sociality is the alterity of the face, of the for-the-other that calls out to me, a voice that rises within me before all verbal expression, in the mortality of the *I*, from the depths of my weakness. That voice is an order. I have the order to answer for the life of the other person. I do not have the right to leave him alone to his death."[9]

Ethics, considered by Levinas to be goodness, are established in the emanation of the Other's face: "The presence [of Others] consists in coming unto us, *making an entry*. This can be stated in this way: the phenomenon which is the apparition of the other is also a face. Again, to show this entry at every moment into the immanence and historicity of the phenomenon, we can say: the epiphany of a face is alive. Its life consists in undoing the form in which every entity, when it enters into immanence, that is, when it exposes itself as a theme, is already dissimulated."[10]

For Levinas, the intersubjective relationship is manifested in a very specific way. It is not a fusion, since the other cannot be possessed. Absorbing the Other into the Self would be a failure of relationship. Levinas does not conceive of it as consciousness, since objectifying the Other makes him disappear.[11] As an ethical relationship, knowing is also impossible owing to the absence of communication it implies.[12]

The conceptions of Sartre and Levinas regarding relation to the Other differ in many respects. The former explains the battle of the gazes—who will be the gazer (subject) and who the gazed at (object)? The latter lays the foundation of the ethical relationship regarding *dévisagement* or staring, "which means 'looking at someone,' but more precisely in the sense of eavesdropping on the face, as it were."[13] Sartre's gaze and Levinas's face nonetheless coincide on one important point: the primacy given to sight in relating to other people.

The history of representations can seem far removed from the ontological reflections on relations to the Other proposed by Sartre and Levinas. At the same time, an interdisciplinarity of reflection on otherness is vital to understanding the importance of *seeing* as the basis of

knowledge of the Other that was transmitted in school. A large proportion of the representations analyzed in this book harbour an intrinsic
violence that is also violence in a state of becoming. Transmission by the
school of the (non-)relation to the Other therefore took part in ethical
relations only under false pretences. The student's encounter with the
Other never involved the Other but was limited to his own image. In
turn, the Other never questioned the student's gaze. In this regard, how
Sartre and Levinas conceive of this relationship clarifies several aspects
of my study and leads me to a final question: Can and should relations
with the Other move beyond the primacy of seeing?

The context from which the school's representation of the Other
emerged was not that of ethical relations. The Other *appeared* to the
students as an object of knowledge. In this sense, learning otherness,
which of course operates in part through a visual prism, coincides with
the objectification by the gaze described by Sartre. He develops this
idea in his book *Anti-Semite and Jew*. In particular, he discusses how
the Jew is objectified by the gaze of others, because he appears to be
always-already Jewish in others' eyes and cannot reject this identity.
He is object, because he is constrained by the identity others assign to
him.[14] In the school representations, the Other was a photograph of
himself, an object, part of the Self's exterior. He was not a "being" whose
individuality was recognized. The Other became an external object that
was integrated through the possession of knowledge. Basically, we could
say that otherness happens because of knowledge. On this point, Sara
Ahmed writes: "This chapter has already posed an alternative question,
'who knows?' It is this question that brings the ethnographic desire
to know more about strangers into contact with the post-colonial
concern with the politics of representing others. [. . .] In other words,
we need to move our attention from the production of otherness to the
(re)production of strangerness."[15] It is because he is *known* that the Other
can be judged to be different. His difference is recognizable because
already familiar. Knowledge reifies, and from that point on it permits
the formation of figure types—the Indian, the Barbarian, the Black.

The gaze played a critical role in defining alterity as it developed in the nineteenth century:

> A return to the use of visual metaphors to describe knowledge is one of the essential elements of the discourse on modern reasoning. [. . .] The knowing subject watches, observes, from above and outside, the object of knowledge. In the visual metaphor, the subject is in direct contact with the reality, without being involved. By comparison, the sense of touch involves the person who is touching as much as what is touched; we cannot touch without ourselves being touched. Seeing, on the other hand, is distant and thought to be unidirectional; the observer is pure—he embodies an agency that is always more attentive—while the observed object is a passive "be-seen."[16]

In this passage, theoretician Iris Marion Young duly underlines the detachment—literally, the distance—that exists between the gazing-knowing subject and the human object being studied by modern reasoning. Contrary to ways of apprehending other people that may bring other senses into play, such as touch, seeing makes it possible to acquire a knowledge of the Other that does not involve relationship and does not require confirmation of one's state as subject. Sociologist Stuart Hall believes that the biological discourse about race still haunts us, owing to the importance given to visible attributes in modern-day racism.[17]

Recognizing the Other can be understood in two ways, and that is why I draw a distinction between recognition and *re*cognition. The former relates to the reciprocity of an intersubjective relationship, as in Sartre's view: "The value of the Other's recognition of me depends on the value of my recognition of the Other."[18] It is a matter of mutuality, of giving that is also receiving, as discussed by Paul Ricoeur in *Soi-même comme un autre* (Oneself like another). In this essay, Ricoeur takes up

Levinas's idea that the Self receives an order from the Other to take responsibility.[19] He adds that in order to reach the level of ethics, and thus escape the morality of the norm, this order should be combined with giving that is expressed in a benevolent spontaneity.[20] The recognition of others in an ethical relation is not that of learning difference. As Madeleine Ouellette-Michalska so eloquently writes, "In a reciprocal relationship, we would differ *between ourselves* and not *from* this other person who constantly serves as a point of reference."[21]

The second meaning, that of *recognition*, refers directly to the process by which the knowledge is acquired. This form of identifying otherness proceeds from being taught about difference and exclusion. There should be a form of knowledge for *recognition*: "We know the savage less than we recognize him," writes Ouellette-Michalska.[22] In *Strange Encounters*, Sara Ahmed closely examines the question of recognizing the stranger. For her, the stranger is not just any body who is not from here. Only certain bodies are recognized by the community as being strange: "How do you recognise a stranger? To ask such a question, is to challenge the assumption that the stranger is the one we simply fail to recognise, that the stranger is simply *any-body* whom we do not know. It is to suggest that the stranger is *some-body* whom we have *already recognised* in the very moment in which they are 'seen' or 'faced' as a stranger. The figure of the stranger is far from simply being strange; it is a figure that is painfully familiar in that very strange(r) ness."[23] For Ahmed, the identification of a genuine stranger, an *alien stranger*, makes it possible to establish what is *beyond* humanity. Coming face to face with the Other offers the community we belong to—the "Us"—an opportunity to share a fantasy, that of believing that we are the authentic humans.[24]

Learning's role is central to the issue of the *recognition* of otherness. Acquiring social representations of difference occurs in different places and times throughout a person's life: the family, the Church, the workplace, and the street are all places in which representations of Others are transmitted. But the school plays a separate role in this process. It is not only one of the first sites of "literacy" regarding otherness but is in addition one of the only ones that can claim the authority of the State, the Church, especially in Quebec, and science. The value of focusing attention on educational institutions in examining the construction of alterity is all the more justified.

Uses and Functions of Alterity

Systems for representing difference respond first of all to a need to establish hierarchy.[25] In fact, rarely is a construction of alterity not part of a hierarchy. The politics of differentiation are located at the heart of the logics of power.[26] The determination to organize human groups into hierarchies aims as much to put Others in their place as to instill a vision of the world in the group of belonging. Jan Neverdeen Pieterse writes, "Images of otherness as the furthest boundary of normality exert a disciplinary influence, as reverse reflections, warning signals."[27] For example, describing savagery makes it possible to paint the portrait of a civilization.[28] The representation of otherness thus offers the elites the possibility of establishing modes of social regulation and normalizing references.[29] Using the Other also ensures cohesion and neutralizes social protest by projecting the insubordination onto a guilty party who is outside the community.[30]

In her study of representation of the Indian in Euro-American literature, writer Madeleine Quellette-Michalska masterfully sums up the power and effects of the otherness narrative:

> [The Indian] is fascinating for the markers that
> identify him as purely external: the regalia, jewellery and
> adornments become elements of fantasy, like the actual
> body. The Indians cease to be Indigenous people subject to
> a social relation that degrades and denies them. Out of this
> disappearance of the human being comes the reassuring
> beauty of the sign. These body-objects, subject to the code's

dictatorship, are insurance against social insubordination. Torn out of their socio-cultural environment and stripped of any significant difference, they bear witness to a Western ego that projects its fantasies and needs onto them. There is a dual effect. By dressing up the primitive savagery, we protect ourselves against our own savagery. The urges become ritualized in a process of writing that will render the fleshy body less awful, starting with one's own.[31]

The diversity of alterity images produced by a society sheds light on the internal contradictions it is grappling with. Others are simultaneously objects of desire and revulsion. Their identity is appropriated for performative and transgressive uses even as their real existence is denied. They are at once what the society does not want to recognize in itself—the barbarian, the demon, the animal—and also what it seeks to regain—the lost paradise and primitive freedom.

The storytelling of alterity creates systems of discourse because, as Stuart Hall writes, "the interplay between the representation of racial difference, the writing of power and the production of knowledge is crucial to the way in which they are generated, and the way in which they function."[32] Previously, I mentioned the importance of seeing in the *recognition* of alterity. A second essential component in developing a logic of differentiation is language. We must look at the role of narration, that is, the discursive construction of difference, in order to gain a complete understanding of the process of identity building.[33] Drawing on the concept of the identity narrative developed by Paul Ricoeur,[34] I call the storytelling of difference, as analyzed in this book, the *narrative alterity*. The contours of alterity appear through the recurrence of certain tactics of opposition and the emphasis on certain particular figures that have been constructed narratively in the semantic field of difference. The constant reproduction and repeated use of these figures render them familiar. By becoming natural and being *re*cognizable, these figures are all the more radically different. When constructing the Other is complete, it is because essentialization has been achieved.

The various Others were not developed and used in independent stories, with representations of Indigenous people here and Black people there. The rhetorical construction of difference mobilized multiple figures within the same school metanarrative, and this discursive inter-relationship increased the narrative depth of each of the characters. The importance of this global perspective is immense, as it enables a holistic understanding of the social use of differentiation.

When the relation to the Other is reduced to his representation as a figure known through observation, a relation of imaginary and material domination is established. This relation with the objectified Other almost always remains partial. The phenomenon of genocide is probably the most radical and most complete form of rejecting otherness. The scientific approach to the Other has an effect that is no less dehumanizing. As Tzvetan Todorov insists, regarding the conquest of America, dehumanization is not necessarily based on a total refusal of otherness:

> Cortez had a relatively good understanding of the world that had revealed itself to his eyes, certainly better than Moctezuma's understanding of Spanish realities. And yet this superior understanding did not deter the conquistadors from destroying Mexican civilization and society, just the opposite; we have the impression that it is this understanding that made the destruction possible. It implies a terrifying train of thought, in which understanding leads to taking and taking to destroying, a sequence whose inevitability we long to challenge. [. . .] The paradox of the understanding-that-kills would easily be resolved if we could simultaneously see, in the understanders, a completely negative value judgement regarding the other, if achieving understanding were accompanied by an axiological rejection. [. . .] And yet, on

> reading the conquistadors' accounts, we see that this is not
> the case and that, on some levels at least, the Aztecs won
> the Spaniards' admiration.[35]

Thus, even when the representation includes positive aspects, the dehumanizing effect of the overall image remains.

The colonial archives provide examples of the textual dehumanization process. However, few academics have studied—or even simply noted—their degrading content and their role in the phenomenon of genocide. On this front, Emma LaRocque, a writer of Cree and Métis origin, reminds us that the Canadian documents tracing this dehumanization are neither exceptional nor hidden. In her view, the issue resides in the gaze of the researchers: "But when the records are re-examined with [a] corrective lens, what comes into focus is an overwhelming presence of Eurocentric and hate material in our archives, histories, literatures, school textbooks, and contemporary popular cultural productions."[36] LaRocque would like to take a positive approach to the archives, but the colonial texts are offensive. And who can read hateful texts with generosity? she asks. The academics' silence on this score has structuring effects, contributing to the sidelining of Indigenous people in Canada's academic community. In this regard, a better understanding of the discursive processes of exclusion is urgently needed.

Dehumanization and the other strategies for differentiation are simply rejections of alterity. With her interest in how the Indigenous peoples of America are represented, Ouellette-Michalska describes how the denial of the Indian's existence operates: "The rejection effectively kills the Other through the exaggerated naturalism that obliges them to act the part of a curiosity, a cast-off, a negation of the culture that arouses contempt or inflames the evangelical passion. The seduction's goal is to assimilate by primitivism or exotism. Primitivism places the Other outside of time, far from the physical and social proximity that would challenge it; exotism freezes their contours in the reassuring parody of a postcard."[37]

According to Hans-Jürgen Lüsebrink, negating the Other is one of the three forms of building otherness, along with knowledge and fascination.[38] In this regard, he explains that Sigmund Freud and the ethnopsychologist Mario Erdheim "demonstrated the anthropolitical interrelationship between even radical forms of exclusion, such as xenophobia, and forms of attraction and fascination, such as exotism, because they have in common similar strategies of psychological avoidance [. . .] diverted from any serious attempt to understand or know the Other."[39] The negation of alterity is an ontological refusal of the existence of other people in their difference, which translates, in the genocidal phenomenon, into the annihilation of the Other. At the root of the rejection of alterity lies a fragile identity. Thus, in order to neutralize the danger posed by the Other to our identity, we refuse their right to be what they are. With Paul Ricoeur, we ask ourselves, "Must our identity be fragile to the point of not being able to bear, not to allow, that Others should have different ways from ours to live their life, understand each other, and make their identity part of the fabric of living together?"[40]

Another manifestation of rejecting alterity is the will to assimilate and the desire for homogenization, which have a direct link to a logic of identity from the Age of Enlightenment that consists in reducing the individual to the universal.[41] In his book *Anti-Semite and Jew*, Sartre associates the anti-Semite with the democrat in their common desire to see Jewish otherness abolished. The former desires his extermination, pure and simple, while the latter would like to "destroy him as a Jew and leave nothing in him but the man, the abstract and universal subject of the rights of man and the rights of the citizen."[42] Starting with the same observation, Iris Marion Young deconstructs the Euro-American vision of universality, which, in her view, is no more and no less than cultural imperialism. This power structure is paradoxical since, on the one hand, it renders the Other invisible because of their position outside the norms, but on the other, it identifies them as being different: "Culturally imperialist groups project their own values, experience, and perspective as normative and universal. Victims of cultural imperialism are thereby rendered invisible as subjects, as persons with their own perspective and group-specific experience and interests. At the same time they are marked out, frozen into being marked as Other, deviant in relation to the dominant norm."[43] The rejection of alterity that is manifested in this desire for homogenization is central to several historical phenomena, among them the Euro-American Christian societies' "civilizing mission" of the nineteenth and twentieth centuries.

The Other, Time, and Death: Return to the Self

The definition, classification, and knowledge of Others occur in a discursive universe in which identity relates to the universal and not to difference. Otherness takes shape in a narrative in which the Self is the norm, and the norm, in this context, requires no definition. The knowledge of the Other is not accompanied by a knowledge of the Self presented as such. However, studying the psychological and narrative parameters and mechanisms of defining alterity makes it possible to discern certain characteristics associated with identity. To do so, one must *read the objectifying gaze*. What arguments underlie belonging to "us"? What relationality does the racism in school representations support? How has manipulating its Others served the quest for meaning in Euro-American thinking? Examining the relation of the representation of otherness to history, time, and individuation provides a key to interpreting the construction of alterity.

In developing my research, I started with the hypothesis that the various Euro-American populations would be represented as culturally dissimilar in the Canadian educational discourse. The American, English, or German would thus be, for Canadians, figures of the Other that, while less radical than the figure of the Indian, would be no less necessary to developing the national identity. And yet that is not the case. These peoples appeared in the school narrative as part of the storytelling of history. They existed through the "great men" they had produced, who were models to emulate and tools for the edification of the Self, the student individual. The inclusion of a people in the history confirmed a relationship of identity. As actors in the same history—the History—the various Euro-American nations were not figures of alterity.

In the educational discourse, the Western nations were historical owing to the individualized presentation of their members; that is, the German, French, or American characters had a proper name and were not archetypes of their people. For example, students learned about Prussia through the narrative of the life of Frederick the Great, or about the United States by reading anecdotes from Benjamin Franklin's life. The individual figures of women, even in the narrative of Euro-American history, remained the exception. The invisibilization of women attests to the importance of access to representation in the battle of identities. Those who could make their voices heard were able to promote their individuality. Individuation thus allows White men to escape the process of essentialization. An absence of collective essentialization and the historical, individualized presence were the criteria that made it possible to affirm that the various Euro-American peoples were not Others in the Canadian school discourse of the nineteenth century; they were all members of the same big family, civilized, White, Christian, and historical. If they were at times enemies, that did not make them fundamentally different.

Western civilization and the Christian world of meaning were built on a universal vision of their history and their religion.[44] How then to represent those who lived outside the universal? Added to the processes of differentiation already presented was the expulsion of Others beyond time, the time of progressive history.[45] "That history should have a direction and that we, Westerners, feel that we are the bearers of time's arrow, is doubtless the most powerful and least questioned feature of our conception of the world," writes Thierry Hentsch.[46] In this world vision, the one transmitted by the Canadian school in the nineteenth century, time belonged to Euro-American societies. Not only were they the only ones to be part of a progressive, contemporary timespan, in the present tense, but they also endeavoured to control the time of the Other.

On 27 January 1868, Hectorine Langevin, twelve years old, a pupil of the Ursulines in Quebec City, wrote a letter to her friend Amélie. In what is obviously a school exercise, Hectorine explains to Amélie the relevance of education and the usefulness of the various sciences she is studying. At the same time, she provides an ideal illustration of the respective places of the Self and the Other at school (my emphasis in italics):

Ma bien chère Amélie,

[. . .] Tu me demandes l'utilité des sciences que nous apprenons [. . .]. Parcourons les différentes branches qui composent nos études pour voir en quoi elles nous rendent meilleures. L'histoire en nous présentant *la vie des personnages les plus illustres* nous encourage à *imiter leurs vertus.* La Géographie *nous montre les différents peuples,* leurs coutumes, leur religion, leurs mœurs et nous engage à louer et admirer Dieu qui a fait tout l'univers. [. . .]

Ton amie dévouée Hectorine Langevin[47]

(My very dear Amélie,

[. . .] You ask of what use are the sciences we are learning [. . .]. Let's take a tour of the various branches that make up our studies to see in what ways they make us better. History, by presenting the *lives of figures who are highly regarded* encourages us to *imitate their virtues.* Geography *shows us the different peoples,* their customs, religion, morals and encourages us to praise and admire God who made the entire universe. [. . .]

Your devoted friend Hectorine Langevin)

What Hectorine's words confirm for us is that in a Canadian school in the nineteenth century, history was the story of the Self and geography was the science of the Others. The "highly regarded figures" were Euro-American individuals who left traces in the historical writing. In her own way, Hectorine also expresses the timeless nature (God made them), visual perception (geography *shows* us), and collectivization of Others, those "different peoples."

The question of time inevitably leads to the relationship that Western thinking maintains with death. A complex relationship, if ever there was one. On the one hand, man's death, on the individual level, is inevitable and undisputed. In the school narrative, the death facing the schoolchildren was the death of Euro-American or Christian *individuals*. The death of great figures, a death on the battlefield or in the home of a poor man, was a human death. Occasionally, the missionary stories would deal with the death of a newly converted pagan. It was then a matter of a Christian whose otherness had been diminished by conversion. On the other hand, the modern ideal of progressive history took eternity as the outer limit of civilization.[48] How is the symbolism of death reflected in the relationship to alterity? The Other was both a symbol of immortality, being timeless, and a figure of death, being frozen out of progress, that is, out of life. Regarding the "discovery" of the New World by Europeans, Ouellette-Michalska writes: "From now on, [nature, of which the savage is a part] will signify less of a law than an original reality that is lost, repressed, and which we will consider it a duty if not a pleasure to regain. Nature is therefore suspended between a timeless past and an ideal future, which combine their efforts to liberate the vital strength of a being on the march toward progress."[49] Being on the margins of Time, the Other is at once *already dead* and *immortal*.

The Codes of Difference

Objectification, the primacy of the visual, developing figures as types, the absence of individuation, and placement outside of historical time—these features characterize the rhetorical and narrative construction of radical alterity. Through what codes of difference are they manifested? My study will work with various registers of alterity to identify the representations of Others in the educational institution. The concepts of race and gender resided in the alterity of the body, while religion, stages of civilization, and political systems were associated with cultural alterity. Between these two poles lay class and nation, which acquired meaning as both corporality and culture.

Despite the potential difficulty associated with taking these various alterities into account, I wanted to distance myself from a historiography that too often focuses on only one of these concepts. Inspired by the anthology *Les codes de la différence,* edited by Riva Kastoryano, I have taken a broad, diversified perspective on the issue of alterity's function in society by pairing up many of the codes. This theoretical base allows for a more effective translation of the heterogeneity of identity building by contraposing various figures of the Other. Not only does this approach offer a new way of looking at the external influences on nation building, it also "de-natures" the known oppositions.

Race and gender are not "universal" already existing markers of differentiation. They exist owing to the rhetorical construction of alterity.[50] The *visible* difference of race or sex becomes *legible* only when the dominant discourse endows it with meaning and value. It is the analysis of this discursive construction that interests me. In the nineteenth century, the gaze that defined race and gender as physical markers of differentiation was that of the masculine Euro-American middle class, as Sara Ahmed puts it: "Within feminist theory, 'bodies' certainly have become a privileged focus of attention. Partly, this attention can be explained by the feminist recognition that women's marginalisation from philosophical discourses and the public sphere has been produced through the association between masculinity and reason and femininity and the body."[51] As liberal modernity progressively constructed men as free and equal, it became necessary to revise the forms of exclusion. The body, directly accessible, became the depository of individual stigmatization. On this subject, Todorov writes: "Every society has its stratifications, made up of heterogeneous groups occupying places that are unequally valued in the social hierarchy. But these places, in modern societies, are not immutable—the peanut vendor can become president. Practically, the only differences that are ineradicable are physical, those attributed to 'race' and those of sex. Having social differences super-imposed on physical differences for a sufficiently long time then gives rise to those attitudes that rest on social and physical syncretism, that is, racism and sexism."[52] How does alterity become *legible* on bodies? How do we assign to *certain* bodies a meaning or value? How, out of the significance assigned to different bodies, do we establish a hierarchy? One of this book's objectives is to answer these questions about how otherness is learned.

The function of race goes beyond identifying physical difference. What we must understand is the racializing gaze: How does one become racist? How is racist thinking articulated? Examining these questions inevitably leads into political territory. In this regard, I second the opinion of historian Jean-Frédéric Schaub, who advocates for greater understanding, in particular in the francophone world, of the politi-cal history of race.[53]

Alterity based on gender does not appear, in my study, as a type of figure. And yet the issue pervades the entire study. While the idea of "woman" definitely corresponds to an Other figure, in particular owing to an absence of individuality and being relegated to a few particular roles, it does not constitute an autonomous figure of external alterity. Sexual differentiation, like that of race, operates throughout school life. In this connection, most representations of White women, rarely addressed in this book, are related to construction processes for differ-ence and dehumanization. Thus, if children learned that they belonged to the civilized White world, they also received instruction on partic-ipating in the world of patriarchal capitalism. The historical, fictional, and contemporary representations of White women in educational materials were limited to a few key figures, rarely individualized—the

little girl, the nun, sometimes the heroine, and always the mother. When
I managed to get hold of school assignments composed by young girls,
I made an extra effort to name the students and discover their age with
the help of a census, to give them greater humanity. I wanted to make
heard the voices of those whose writing is even today considered to
be anecdotal. This feminist perspective is paired with an intersectional
approach, since the voice of these young White students was in most
cases used to translate the racist system that they, as much as the White
men, supported and reproduced.

The intersection between gender and race makes it possible to
constitute the White woman, principally the middle-class woman, as an
historical *subject*, as explained by Gayatri Spivak. As Catherine Hall says,
"The imperialist project, Spivak insists, was at the heart of this white
woman's subjecthood. It is family and empire which are proposed here
as the constitutive agents in the construction of the female bourgeois
subject, and it is the discourses of race which cast the Western female
as an agent of history, while the 'native' woman is excluded. [. . .] No
binary, whether of class, race, or gender, is adequate to these multiple
constructions of difference."[54] In this book, the gender difference is
therefore revealed in a subtler, more indirect way—it operates once
racial or cultural difference has been established.

Alongside the otherness that could be read on the individual
body, a cultural alterity associated with specific societies was also being
constructed. In order to position themselves to advantage in the world
order—and eventually to control it—the Euro-American nations held
up civilization (singular), Christianity, and commerce as universal aspi-
rations, engines of history and progress that every society must strive
toward. But in order for this "civilizing" logic to work, it was necessary
to postulate the existence of primitive stages, savagery and barbarism.[55]
As Chantal Delsol puts it, "The awareness of political alterity, just one
expression among many of cultural alterity, has historically provoked
all kinds of reactions, from surprise to hatred. The barbarianization
of the other often rests on suppositions linked to politics—they are

the slaves of their kings, we are free under our laws, said the Greeks, implying the existence of two forms of humanity that are almost ontologically distinct."[56] Societies were judged for their mode of social and political organization, and precise characteristics were assigned to the different stages of civilization, among them types of government and religious systems.

As foundational markers of alterity, the body and culture are often evoked in tandem. This rhetorical process is based on developing statements of causality in which the body determines the culture or the reverse. In his analysis of racialist thinking, Todorov provides an example of this type of causal manipulation:

> Note here a striking feature of the rhetoric in Buffon's scientific discourse: before *telling* us that a continuity exists between the physical and the moral, he *suggests* it indirectly. The major figure of monistic determinism, as practised by Buffon, is exactly this kind of *coordination*; through the power of a comma, a conjunction, a listing, the author suggests without stating; the reader can absorb with far less mistrust what is "assumed" than what is "posited." By pledging to deal in the same pages with physical *and* cultural differences, Buffon acts as if the correlation between the two had been established; when he comes to stating it as a thesis, his reader can only acquiesce.[57]

In many ways, my book illustrates the juxtaposition of body otherness based on race and the cultural inferiority associated with the stage of civilization.

Representing social class as a difference pertained to both the body and the culture. The division of labour between "manual" jobs and "intellectual" professions immediately associated the labourer with his body, which was his principal tool of work. The social discourse would also establish links between the working class and certain cultural practices: for example, drunkenness. Class had little presence in the school's representation of the society of belonging, but like gender, it appeared in the rhetoric of differentiation only once the Other had been racially or culturally described. The educational discourse put the children on a footing of equality; that is to say that the staging of poor or working-class communities could not be likened to a representation of alterity. These communities functioned in the narrative as did sketches set in royal or aristocratic Euro-American circles.

The nation, as constructed in the nineteenth century by historical storytelling, constitutes another important parameter in the definition of alterity. However, a question arises: Did the importance granted to history in nation building result from a genuine hegemony of the discipline in the collective's symbol system at that time, or has the attention it has received from historians created this impression? Whatever the case, it is certain that the fascination with historiography, especially in Quebec, has had a fundamental impact on the shaping of historical discourse on conceptions of Western societies. By focusing too squarely on the role of the discipline of history in nationalism, historians have minimized the function of non-Western alterity in forming national identities in the nineteenth century. While the historians of imperialism have not failed to connect the rise of nationalism to the imperial reality, the historians of nation building have been slow to examine these connections.

Taking account of the imperial and colonial context of which Canada was a part in the nineteenth century would surely help in understanding how Canadian national identities were formed. As Bruce A. Harvey maintains about the United States, "The geographical gaze when directed at non-European nations and races contrastively produced the body of the nation itself, which otherwise could not quite 'see' itself, or only rhetorically so in, for example, July 4th speeches and other self-laudatory occasions."[58] While representation of the different Western countries undoubtedly influenced the form and content of the national narrative, it seems that radical, that is, non-Euro-American, alterity acted directly on the very establishment of the idea of the nation. In other words, did the Canadian communities identify themselves as nations owing to and through their contacts with France, the United States, and the United Kingdom? Or was it not rather the confrontation with so-called uncivilized—and thus ahistorical and non-national— peoples that caused a need in Canada to call itself national so as to be able to say "civilized"? In this respect, I agree with Sara Ahmed's argument that the "colonial project was not *external* to the constitution of the modernity of European nations: rather, the identity of these nations became predicated on their relationship to the colonised others."[59]

Learning Otherness: Difference, Representation, and Education

The interaction between the representation of difference, the transmission of stereotypes, and educational institutions has been of interest to academic researchers for several decades. The critical analysis of textbooks in European societies saw a rapid expansion immediately after the First World War. Many intellectuals, under the aegis of the League of Nations, became interested at that time in xenophobia and the hatred transmitted through educational discourse.[60] Around the same period, the first pedagogical reforms motivated by the idea of social justice were launched.[61] Since the 1960s, numerous research projects have shown that bias is still present in the representation of racial, cultural, sexual, and gender diversity in educational materials. As Peter Pericles Trifonas remarks in the introduction to the collective work *Pedagogies of Difference*, the majority of these studies were oriented "toward the ethical purpose of actualizing equitable curricular contexts for teaching and learning that are responsive to individuals and groups within a society or culture regardless of race, class, gender or sexuality."[62]

In Canada and Quebec, several research projects on stereotypes transmitted through textbooks have been conducted in recent decades. As early as the 1960s and 1970s, certain critics were denouncing the presence of racist content in teaching materials.[63] More recently, scholarly attention has been directed to the image of the "stranger" and Muslim cultures and Islam in didactic content in Quebec.[64] Considering the large number of studies produced by scholars in education,[65] research on its history is relatively scarce.[66] Most of the studies dealing with connections between education and the transmission of stereotypes do not take a historical perspective. However, the teaching and learning of alterity, mainly through racist ideology and the colonial imagination, coincided with the development of public education in the nineteenth century in most Euro-American societies. I therefore agree with Eugene F. Provenzo Jr.'s observation from 2010: "While educational theorists such as Michael Apple and others have discussed in great detail how schools function to make and remake a dominant culture—and of the hegemonic functions they serve—virtually all of their work has focused on contemporary education. Little attention has been given to historical studies of hegemony and education."[67]

Some academics simply accept it as "normal" that the educational discourse in the nineteenth century should have contributed to the dehumanization of certain groups.[68] This trivializing, often implicit in the racism contained in the educational discourse of the nineteenth century, does not help us to understand its functioning and its influence on the development of Euro-American national identities. By ignoring this history, we are also cutting ourselves off from part of what explains the discriminatory and xenophobic social practices of the nineteenth, twentieth, and twenty-first centuries.

Fortunately, since the 1990s, historical research has started to lift the curtain on the influence of imperialism and colonialism on Western systems of education.[69] Although an exhaustive study of the pedagogic use of alterity in the nineteenth century has yet to appear,[70] many collective works and articles dealing with the curricula and specific colonial contexts have demonstrated the importance of imperialist content in the Euro-American schools of the time. Historians of the British Empire were the first to show an interest in the influence of imperialism on educational institutions, in the metropolis as well as in the colony.[71] As early as 1988, James Anthony Mangan underscored the issue of this problematic: "The roots of current attitudes to 'race' and colour lie deep in the imperial past."[72] As to the French Empire, more recent studies have focused on the dissemination of a colonial ideology and justification of the "civilizing mission" by schools, from the Third Republic until the mid-nineteenth century.[73] In 2009, in a special issue of the journal *Paedagogica Historica*, the angle of approach to this theme was reversed. The authors of the various articles addressed education as a factor of social change in colonized and colonizing societies. Thus, instead of imperialism's influence over the educational world, it was the role of education in the colonial order that became the focus of analysis.[74] This perspective made it possible to avoid the interpretation that imperialism was disseminated from the metropolis out to the periphery. Without completely addressing it head-on, this historiography interweaving imperialism and education repeatedly pointed to the role played by the school in teaching alterity in the nineteenth and twentieth centuries.

The colonial and imperial imagery intended for children has also been the subject of many historical studies. An interest in the children's place in imperial realities was seen as early as 1990 in studies of the images of the Indian or Black person in Euro-American culture, and it has grown over the past several years. How were Euro-American children from different social classes convinced of the relevance of Europe's "civilizing mission"? Was the intention to fire them with a passion for the Empire and its indigenous populations? What role did a distant alterity play in the storytelling of colonial adventures written for them? Many studies that answer these questions deal in particular with children's literature.[75] However, to participate in the rapidly growing field of the history of emotions, historians are now looking at the ways in which imperial and missionary realities influenced the emotional regimes of childhood in the West.[76] Without claiming that all was colonial, these studies mainly demonstrate that the multiple discourses addressed to children "intersected with the colonial,"[77] as Bowersox puts it, and that this theme was adopted for a variety of purposes, in particular to inspire nationalism or religious practice.

According to the scholarly literature that addresses intersections between children, education, and colonialism, the principal point of contact between youth in Euro-American societies and a distant, exotic otherness was the geographical imagination.[78] Through travel accounts and geography textbooks, children explored the world and its inhabitants without leaving their classroom or bedroom. The knowledge of geography that was transmitted in the wake of imperial conquests made an important contribution to the categorization and definition of otherness. As John Wilinsky remarks, "Geography, as a discourse of difference, was about learning to attribute that difference to a people within their landscape."[79] As elsewhere in the West, children in Quebec learned to categorize the planet's inhabitants through geography. Although the geographical discourse was not the only vector for learning difference at school, my study confirms its primacy in this process.

In exploring the issue of the construction of alterity through the educational discourse in Quebec in the nineteenth century, I want first to outline the colonial and imperial context that was shaping the national identity. Contrary to the received idea of Quebec as becoming "open to the world" thanks to Expo '67, my research shows that the educational discourse of the nineteenth century had already resolutely redirected the focus outside the country. Exploring the function of alterity in pedagogy also allows us to address the undeniable role of childhood in the history of racism in Canada.

2.

Other Societies: Imperialist Knowledge and Orientalist Representations

As a student at the Saint-Nom de Marie Convent in Hochelaga in the 1860s, a young New Yorker named Agnes Hallock was asked to make a detailed record of her program of study in a register.[1] On page 227, when presenting her geography studies, Agnes quoted John George Hodgins in describing the Earth's two hemispheres. Part of the eastern hemisphere, Europe had a special place in the world order. As Agnes wrote, "The European parts of this hemisphere have long been the seat of Christian civilization and of commerce; the influence of both of which is now rapidly spreading to every part of the habitable Globe."[2] Several years later, in the "Miscellany" section of its issue for May/June 1879, the *Journal of Education* listed a new French-language publication entitled *Les peuples étranges* (Strange peoples). Among other things, the book provided "some curious information" about Chinese medicine. Following a brief presentation of remedies used in the "Celestial Empire," its writers added: "In China, ar [*sic*] in all Eastern countries, the physicians are made an object of raillery in stories."[3]

These two excerpts exemplify the representation of the world conveyed through Canadian schools in the nineteenth century. Simultaneously, they provide a definition of "We" and evidence of the interest in alterity nurtured by the schools. Although she was an American student at a convent in Montreal run by a French-Canadian Catholic religious order, Agnes nonetheless used a geography text written by an Ontario Protestant born in Ireland and proudly British. The idea conveyed by Hodgins and picked up by Agnes that Europe was not only the cradle of their common race but also the bedrock of Christianity and commerce, the era's two civilizing forces, defined the contours of a transnational "We." Before being Protestants or Catholics, francophones or anglophones, Americans or Canadians, the students were civilized, Christian, White, and of European descent, as the school constantly reminded them. The cultural transnationality endorsed by the excerpts confirms that the pedagogical knowledge knew no national boundaries. In this regard, it is significant that between the two publications produced by the Department of Public Instruction of the province of Quebec, it is the English-language version that summed up the "information" to be found in the French-language book *Les peuples étranges.*

In writing that Europe was rapidly extending its civilization throughout the entire world, Agnes reminds us of the imperial context in which Canada was evolving. The young woman's assignment also refers to the existence of non-Christian and non-civilized populations, in short, the *peuples étranges,* who, in the essentialist view of the *Journal of Education*'s writers, were Orientals. The imperial adventures and the Orientalist representations presented by the schools were constituents of a narrative mechanism, that of constructing alterity. These rhetorical resources found a home in the teaching provided by Quebec's schools.

The "We" of Education

In the nineteenth century, pedagogical knowledge and the educational discourse of the European and North American countries were transnational. Canada perhaps provided one of the most telling examples. While schooling was being organized for the masses and the public discourse often dwelt on the importance of education, the teachers were exchanging their knowledge in newly established professional networks. The historiography has studied in detail how the school became one of the critical pillars of nation building in Europe and America in the nineteenth century. What this wealth of literature occasionally mentions, and what must be emphasized, is that although they contributed intensely to creating a nation, the schools were not, despite that, a "national" product. The different countries shared their experiences and methods, and a wealth of disciplinary and pedagogical knowledge circulated freely.

In the case of Quebec, this knowledge transfer can easily be seen in the various educational publications, whether school textbooks or periodicals intended for teachers. The Québécois teacher who would read the *Journal de l'instruction publique, Journal of Education, L'enseignement primaire,* or *The Educational Record of the Province of Quebec* had access to translations or reprints of articles that had appeared in journals from the United States, France, Scotland, England, Ireland, and Australia. At the same time, Quebec journals were read by actors in the teaching field in the anglophone and francophone worlds, and their pages were sometimes reproduced in specialized foreign periodicals. The articles borrowed from various journals dealt with all subjects. They reported the progress of public education in various regions of the world and covered methods used elsewhere for teaching all of the disciplines. For example, the *Journal of Education* picked up articles from the *Rhode Island Schoolmaster* on teaching the natural sciences. The author, identified by the initials H.M., wrote: "Geography may be made doubly interesting, if among its dry questions some brief description be given of the customs, manners, language, or general characteristics of the people who inhabit the countries and cities whose crooked names are so formidable to the beginner."[4] To make their teaching more interesting, as a note from the *Rhode Island Schoolmaster* suggested, the teachers could also draw directly on the international information relayed by the pedagogical journals. School Inspector Hubbard did not fail to comment, in his 1861 report, that "outre les renseignements utiles et amusants [que les journaux péda-gogiques] renferme[nt], [ils] ne peu[vent] que rendre plus facile la tâche de celui qui est chargé d'enseigner" (besides the useful and amusing pieces of information [that the teaching journals] contain, [they] can only make the task easier for the person responsible for teaching).[5] Imperial events were also regularly discussed, and various exploratory expeditions took up a large portion of geography bulletins. For the most part, this information was copied from European publications.

In school textbooks, transnational borrowings were sometimes explicit and mentioned in the preface or pointed out in footnotes, as in geography textbooks. For example, after having justified the publica-tion of his *Géographie moderne* with an absence of "géographie adaptée aux besoins des élèves canadiens-français" (geography adapted to the needs of French-Canadian schoolchildren), François-Xavier Toussaint explained that he had "amplement puisé à plusieurs sources [. . .]. Les géographies françaises surtout ont été mises largement à contribution" (liberally drawn on many sources [. . .]. French geographies in particular have been largely called upon).[6] Several decades earlier, Father Jean Holmes had retranscribed entire passages of the writings of the Franco-Danish geographer Malte-Brun in his *Nouvel abrégé de géographie moderne*.[7] In 1880, the publisher John Lovell was less explicit. He simply confirmed that the author of his advanced geography had consulted "the latest and most reliable authorities."[8] In other disciplines, the use of foreign writers' work was equally obvious. "Reading textbooks" provide numerous examples. A reading book was made up of a succession of short texts and poems that were anonymously written or taken from the works of famous writers. Canadian textbooks reprinted material by writers from many countries. French authors predominated in French-language textbooks; English-language books drew for the most part on the American and English literary corpus. A large number of foreign textbooks were also directly adopted for use by Canadian schoolchildren.

The knowledge taught and the ideologies transmitted through the school were therefore not, strictly speaking, Canadian. Far from being an exception, the Canadian school system was in that respect similar to those of other Western countries. Moreover, countries as varied as Finland, Hungary, and the United States drew their educational knowledge from the same sources as Canada did. There was therefore in the European countries and their White colonies a common knowledge that created a collective "Western" identity. This commonly held knowledge was particularly evident in geography when it came to describing the populations of the four corners of the globe. As the Frères des écoles chrétiennes recalled it, "For, had an author traversed all the oceans [. . .]; had he lived, for years, amongst all the nations of the world, and carefully studied their characters, manners and customs—all practically impossible,—he could not still assure himself of being exactly correct in every particular."[9] Thus, in Finland, as in Great Britain, Germany, or Canada, children were taught about Africa thanks to the accounts of the explorers David Livingstone and Henry Stanley. By studying the same image of far-off peoples, the Canadian, English, German, and Finnish students took in a similar concept of the Self. While the schools were being mobilized to establish the national identity, they helped at the same time to create a cultural space that in the end would be called "Western."

The real nationalism in Quebec's educational content—to the saturation point—did not come about until the turn of the twentieth century. This observation results from a close reading of nearly 100 textbooks from Quebec and Canada published from 1833 to 1914 and of many school archives from the same period. Of course, debates about the Canadianization of teaching took place much earlier. In mid-century, the newly formed Conseil de l'Instruction publique had already asked publishers to Canadianize the content of foreign textbooks printed in Canada, but in practice it was a matter of adding a little

Canadian content and not of erasing foreign influences. The apparent independence achieved by Quebec textbooks in the last quarter of the century did not inhibit writers in drawing on European and American sources. The demand for "Québécois" textbooks also sometimes came from teachers, as shown in a discussion on this topic at a meeting of the province's Protestant teachers in Granby in 1874.[10]

Beginning in the 1860s, reading textbooks, or "readers," were, along with Canadian history books, the principal and primary vectors for the patriotic feeling that teachers sought to inspire in young people. In 1860, in the preface to his reader, John Douglas Borthwick wrote: "Our youth have hitherto been taught far too little of their native land, and whilst School Books from other countries have been widely used, the pupils have been left in total or at least partial ignorance of the History and Geography, Geology and Botany, Natural History and Productions, Climate and Scenery of those Provinces which truly constitute the 'brightest gem in the diadem of England.'"[11] French-language readers included a growing number of excerpts from the works of Canadian writers, and most of these texts celebrated the homeland or recalled its history. However, it was only on the eve of the First World War that patriotic teaching was truly omnipresent in the everyday school life of Quebec children.

The incidence of an increasing and undeniably vigorous nationalism in textbooks, starting in the last decades of the nineteenth century, should nonetheless be weighed against the continuing presence of transnational borrowings. *The New Illustrated Geography* published by the Frères des écoles chrétiennes in 1877 is evidently a textbook intended for the Canadian population of Irish origin.[12] The section devoted to Ireland is unusually long and the text is unequivocal: Ireland is lauded, its trials are described, the people's character is inflated, and England is not well regarded. On reading this passage, we would tend to think that the textbook was truly "Canadian," in the sense that the Frères des écoles chrétiennes wrote it specially for the Irish population they were teaching. And yet it was not. Further reading finds long excerpts from an American textbook of the same period by Samuel Augustus Mitchell, copied word for word.[13] The section on Africa and part of that on Asia were taken directly from Mitchell's book, even if the writers did not mention it in the preface or anywhere else in their text. Mitchell published some of the most popular geography textbooks in the United States in the mid-nineteenth century. They were reprinted many times after they were first released in the 1840s. Moreover, I have noted that some of the prints in Mitchell's book were reproduced not only by the Frères des écoles chrétiennes but also by the Sœurs de la congrégation de Notre-Dame in 1897![14] Even in the case of publications that at first seemed to be completely Canadian, the representation of the world presented to children remained transnational.

The case in Quebec's Anglo-Protestant schools was slightly different. As Canadian patriotism also assumed an increasingly important place in those schools at the dawn of the new century, it was accompanied by a renewed enthusiasm for imperialism. "Had we gone too far in Canadianizing [textbooks?]," wonders researcher Paul Aubin; "In 1899, the Protestant committee truly wanted a Canadian geography published by Renouf in Montreal, but on condition that we enlarge the section dedicated to the British Isles."[15] Let us not forget that the turn of the century saw the Boer War, Queen Victoria's Jubilee in 1897, and the pinnacle of Canada's importance in the British Empire. In 1897, a committee was formed at Montreal High School to decide how to celebrate the Queen's Diamond Jubilee. Among other things, the members recommended "that teachers of all grades give special attention to instructing their classes on such subjects as—The principal events [of] Her Majesty's Reign, The extant [sic] of the Empire, The Growth of its Commerce, The Arny [sic] and Navy and especially The Moral and other benefits of British Rule."[16] The teachers were encouraged to instruct their students about the British Empire's "civilizing mission." The school celebration of Empire Day was instituted the following year; in the years preceding the First World War, it became the most important annual school celebration in Canadian Anglo-Protestant schools. In 1900, on the occasion of this special day, Montreal High School students received a visit from the Reverend Dr. Barclay. "His eloquent and enthusiastic description of the proud position and vast resources of our country, and his sympathetic reference to the Mother Empire, and to our sister Republic made a lasting impression upon the thousand young hearts who formed his audience,"[17] wrote Rector Rexford in his annual report. Six years later, the students heard an "inspiring" speech by Rev. John Mackay on "True Imperialism."[18] These Montreal students thus regularly received instruction about the current state of the British Empire. The window on the outside world and the interest in alterity offered by the Canadian schools would gradually diminish in the decades preceding 1914. In an increasingly nationalist world vision, the era's imperial realities still had a place, and curiosity persisted about the Empire's various populations.

At the end of the 1870s, a speech on public education in France and the United States delivered by A. Martin at a meeting of teachers from the district of the École normale Jacques-Cartier in Montreal began with these words:

> Toute nation, comme toute société ou administration
> qui attache quelque importance au rang qu'elle occupe
> dans le monde et à la mission qui lui a été confiée par la
> Providence, doit nécessairement tendre vers le progrès.
> [. . .] L'enseignement ne peut rester stationnaire; il faut
> qu'il progresse ou déchoie, et son premier principe de
> progrès est l'observation. Observer attentivement les
> progrès faits de toutes parts pour élever et généraliser
> l'enseignement primaire, profiter de l'expérience des
> peuples en cette matière, étudier leurs institutions scolaires
> et les comparer avec les résultats obtenus, telle doit être la
> sollicitude constante de ceux qui ont à cœur le progrès de
> l'éducation populaire.[19]

(Every nation, like every society or administration that
attaches some importance to the rank it occupies in the
world and the mission entrusted to it by Providence, must
necessarily tend toward progress. [. . .] Teaching cannot
be stationary; it must move forward or lose ground, and
its first principle of progress is observation. To observe
with attention the progress made on all sides in elevating
and generalizing primary teaching, taking advantage
of the peoples' experience in this regard, studying their
educational institutions and comparing them with the
results obtained, this is what should be the constant
concern of those who hold the progress of public education
close to their hearts.)

In his speech, Martin clearly expressed two ideas. First, the transnational circulation of teaching experiences was essential to developing
a system of public primary education, and, second, the possibility of
carving out an honourable place among civilized nations relies on
public education. Education was conceived of in tautological terms—a
civilized nation is one where public education is well established, and
an educated nation is one where civilization prospers. In this regard,
teaching journals repeatedly noted attempts at education on the part
of certain colonized populations. For example, in 1857, the *Journal de
l'instruction publique* wrote: "Le gouvernement français s'occupe d'établir
en Algérie un collège ou [*sic*] le français et l'arabe seront enseignés. C'est
une des mesures les plus habiles qui pouvaient être prises pour activer la
civilisation et la colonisation de cette partie de l'Afrique."[20] (In Algeria,
the French government is establishing a college where both French
and Arabic will be taught. It is one of the most astute measures that
could have been taken to actuate the civilization and colonization of
this part of Africa.) In Canada, this debate concerned immigrants and
Indigenous groups. In its annual report for 1864, the Colonial Church

and School Society for the Diocese of Montreal wrote: "But there are many settlements where the School is composed in great part of children of lately arrived emigrants, seeking a living in the backwoods [. . .]. Now it is very important that these children should not be allowed to grow up like young savages."[21] Education was therefore both a tool of civilization and evidence of it. Again in 1911, a geography book for elementary grades published by Lovell of Montreal reaffirmed this idea by asking: "How do nations become civilized?" The children would have to answer, "By means of education and good government."[22] During the second half of the nineteenth century, the association between civilization and education was constantly asserted.

The world to which Canada belonged was the civilized one. And to describe civilized societies, the authors of school geography texts set out multiple criteria: urbanity, education, commerce, and Christian religion. Obviously, Europe remained the main point of comparison. Wasn't it remarkable, as the Frères des écoles chrétiennes noted, "for its civilisation, commerce, industry and its magnificent cities, which contain numberless works of art and science," in addition to which it possessed "a great number of institutions which disseminate education among the people"?[23] We thus learn that "l'éducation au Canada ne le cède en rien à celle des autres pays du monde; un grand nombre d'établissements soit religieux, soit laïques répandent l'instruction dans tout le pays avec un zèle digne de louanges" (in education Canada can hold its own among the countries of the world; a large number of establishments, whether religious or secular, take teaching throughout the country with a zeal worthy of high praise).[24] André-Napoléon Montpetit and Léopold Devisme articulated the same idea when they wrote, "Notre système d'éducation, légèrement modifié ne nous laissons [sic] rien à envier aux systèmes du même genre, chez les nations les mieux policées de l'Europe."[25] (Our educational system, slightly modified, leaves nothing to be desired when compared to systems of the same type within the most civilized nations in Europe.) At the same time, an absence of public education was a criterion for exclusion. According to Montpetit and

Devisme, it was the nature and state of its public education that tipped Turkey out of Europe and into otherness. While the writers pointed out the structural and institutional characteristics of the educational systems in other European countries, they dwelt on the content of Turkish education. In Turkey, they wrote, "l'instruction est peu répandue [. . .]. Elle se borne en général aux premiers éléments de la langue, à la lecture du Koran et à quelques notions d'histoire et de géographie" (primary education is not very widespread [. . .]. It is generally limited to the basic elements of language, reading the Koran and a few rudiments of history and geography).[26] Education therefore had an important place in the idealization of civilized countries as transmitted by the school; conversely, its absence in other regions of the world confirmed the unfortunate state in which those countries existed. As well, the danger of belonging to this second group was sometimes spelled out. In the introduction to a reader published by the Frères des écoles chrétiennes was the following warning from Bishop Langevin: "D'ailleurs, dans le temps où nous vivons, l'instruction est si généralement répandue, qu'un peuple qui la néglige ne peut éviter d'être dans un état d'humiliante infériorité. Pour nous particulièrement, Canadiens, qui sommes environnés de gens possédant tous un certain degré d'instruction, il est indispensable de la répandre parmi nous, si nous voulons marcher de pair avec eux."[27] (Moreover, in these times of ours education is so generally widespread that a people neglecting it cannot avoid being in a humiliating state of inferiority. For us, in particular, French Canadians, surrounded as we are by people who all possess a certain degree of schooling, it is indispensable to spread it among us, if we want to move forward in step with them.)

As large gatherings for members of what was called the civilized world, universal exhibitions played an important part in the transnational circulation of knowledge and techniques in the second half of the nineteenth century. Beginning with London's event in 1862, a space was dedicated to the exhibition of objects associated with education.[28] But it was in Vienna in 1873 that for the first time an entire section was devoted to education, teaching, and training. In the years following, from one event to the next, education would gradually assume a little more importance in the exhibition's overall organization. Taking note of the attention Canada received in Philadelphia, and the attention Quebec did not, Gédéon Ouimet, the superintendent of public education, sent a circular message to educational institutions in June 1877 in which he wrote: "La nature de mes fonctions me permet d'embrasser dans son ensemble notre système d'instruction publique: eh bien! J'ose affirmer que si, grâce à une bonne volonté active, nous parvenions à réunir toutes nos forces, nous pourrions, même dans une exposition internationale, soutenir toute concurrence."[29] (The nature of my functions enables me to take in our entire system of public education: Well! I dare say that if, thanks to active good will, we manage to combine our strengths, we could, even at an international exhibition, get the better of any competition.) Ouimet hoped that Quebec's schools would be represented at the fair in Paris the following year. Several years later, in 1892, in an initial circular to educational institutions with the Chicago exhibition in view, the superintendent recalled the successes achieved in Paris in 1878 and in London in 1886, and the importance of "figurer de manière convenable à ce déploiement des forces vives de toutes les nations, au point de vue de la science, de l'industrie, du commerce et de l'agriculture" (making a showing appropriate to this display of the active strengths of all nations in the realms of science, industry, commerce and agriculture).[30] The instructions issued for the Paris exhibition of 1900 repeated the same motivations, and now added to previous successes was that at Chicago's event in 1893. Participation of the Quebec schools was motivated by the desire to prove to the world that French Canada had a place, and a place of note, among the civilized nations.

The same issues were debated in the Anglo-Protestant community. For example, for the writers of the *Educational Record of the Province of Quebec*, the Anglo-Protestant schools' participation in the colonial exhibition in London in 1886 was a question of national and colonial honour. It was a matter of showing the metropolitans the state of industrial and intellectual life in the colony, and thus of encouraging emigration. The writers believed that the exhibition was an opportunity to establish Canada's position in the imperial order. "It's a great occasion," they wrote, "to put Canada in her place as the premier colony of the British Empire and to establish her proper position before the world."[31] The Canadian schools' participation in these exhibitions was therefore closely linked to the issue of a claim to civilization, leading to a controversy on the subject that received spirited coverage in the Dominion's English-language press.

The controversy's history began in 1879 with the publication of an editorial in the inaugural issue of a new teaching journal out of Toronto, the *Educational Monthly and School Chronicle*. The editorial denied Quebec any part in the honours bestowed on Canada in Paris the previous year; according to its author, the accolades should have been granted only to Ontario and the Maritime Provinces.[32] The response from Montreal's English-language newspapers was immediate. The *Journal of Education*'s writers waxed ironic about the ability of their Toronto counterparts to read French, since had they been able to, they would have clearly seen that the list of awards published by the French government featured the Province of Quebec at least as much, if not more. They also reminded readers that the Maritime Provinces had not even organized an educational exhibit in Paris. For its part, the *Montreal Gazette* believed that all of the credit should be given to the Province of Quebec. Was it not, the journalist noted, four French Canadians who received the honour in Paris of the title of Officers of Public Education? He also recalled the steps taken by Pierre-Joseph-Olivier Chauveau to ensure that the Canadian educational system would be included in a German encyclopedia. As the journalist wrote: "Thus it comes that 'Canada' occupies no less than sixty-seven pages in the great Encyclopedia [. ...], being, in this respect, on a footing with all the great countries of civilization. And for this honour the Dominion is indebted to the Province of Quebec."[33] This interprovincial controversy effectively illustrates the importance of these major world events, where the interest was in earning a place of respect as a civilized nation. To reach this goal, as a colony Canada was required to step up its efforts and its visibility.

Imperialism and Constructing the Others

> Colomb prit ensuite possession de l'île pour la Couronne de Castille et de Léon. Cependant les insulaires ne s'étaient pas éloignés; ils regardaient en silence toutes ces cérémonies auxquelles ils ne comprenaient rien; mais ils semblaient être dominés par le respect en voyant tant de choses extraordinaires [. . .]. Les Espagnols étaient surpris aussi des nouveautés qui frappaient leurs regards: une nature inconnue s'offrait à leurs yeux, et elle était magnifique. Les plantes, les arbres différents de ceux de l'Europe attestaient, par leur belle végétation, la fertilité de la terre. Les habitants étaient nus; leurs cheveux noirs, longs et droits, flottaient sur leurs épaules, leur teint était couleur de cuivre foncé, et leur physionomie paraissait douce et timide; leurs corps et leurs visages étaient peints de couleurs éclatantes.[34]

> (Columbus then took possession of the island for the Crown of Castile and León. In the meantime, the islanders had not withdrawn; in silence they watched all these ceremonies, of which they understood nothing; but they seemed to be dominated by a sense of respect on seeing so many extraordinary things [. . .]. The Spaniards were also surprised at the striking things that met their gaze: an unfamiliar nature offered itself to their sight, and it was magnificent. The plants and trees, different from those in Europe, spoke to the earth's fertility with beautiful vegetation. The inhabitants were naked; their long, straight

black hair floated around their shoulders. Their skin was
the colour of dark copper and their physiognomy looked
gentle and shy; their bodies and faces were painted with
vivid colours.)

In this reading for elementary school students, the "discovery" of
America was an example of the encounter between Europe and the
rest of the world. In addition to being an essential anecdote in the
school universe of the nineteenth century, the story of Columbus's first
relation to the Indigenous peoples of America represented the concept
of alterity that was necessary to the European imperial enterprises of
the same era. Before the European who is taking possession of the
territory appears the figure of the naïve native. He does not understand
the European universe of meaning but already feels dominated. As for
the European, he first sees the natural world for his domination and
then the strangeness of the Indigenous body, which demands description. Childlike, dominated, with his "gentle, shy physiognomy," this
Indigenous person is no match for Christian civilization. He has two
possible options: to be civilized or die. That is what the student was
taught. Some peoples, half-civilized and barbaric, would be called to
join civilization; others, like the Indigenous peoples of the Americas
and Australia, would disappear.

In the nineteenth century, the construction of alterity carried out
in school was intimately linked to Europe's imperial adventures and the
knowledge they created. By classifying, categorizing, and dividing the
world appropriated by the colonial powers, the scientific enterprises of
the eighteenth and nineteenth centuries exemplified the relationship
between knowledge and power. Through them a new concept of alterity
was born. Primary schools recycled and simplified this knowledge and
thus gave children a discourse that divided the world into categories
that were accessible, being within everyone's reach.

The Other appeared in the imperial school story in three ways. He
first revealed himself in the narrative of the European conquests. School

initiated children into the exploits of European explorers and spoke of conquered or "discovered" peoples. From that point on, the discourse established a hierarchy of people that was endlessly reiterated. Informed by contemporary learned debates, the curriculum also took part in the scientific interpretation of difference. The world categorization thus acquired meaning thanks to scientific luminaries. In the end, simply evoking the European conquests was not always enough to justify them. Then brought into consideration was the issue of the "civilizing mission" that would serve not only to reaffirm the difference between "them" and "us" but also to make European domination in the four corners of the world morally acceptable.

Civilization, European expansion, and commerce are thus intimately connected, and the school textbooks do not fail to teach that to the children. In the geography text they published in 1891, the Sœurs de la congrégation de Notre-Dame explained to their pupils the nature of the differences between a colony of exploitation and a colony for settlement. When asked, "Pourquoi la Malaisie, l'Inde, la Cochinchine et le Tonkin ne sont-ils que des colonies d'exploitation?" (Why are Malaysia, India, Cochinchina and Tonkin only colonies to be exploited?), the young girls were expected to reply, "Parce que leur climat est dangereux pour les Européens; ils se contentent de s'enrichir des précieux produits de ces contrées." (Because their climate is dangerous to Europeans; they are content to enrich themselves with the regions' precious products.) And "Que s'en suit-il?" (What is the result?) "Qu'un très grand nombre d'indigènes travaillent pour le compte d'un très petit nombre de colons européens," they learned. (That a very large number of natives work for the benefit of a very small number of European colonists.) A certain criticism of the hierarchy set up by imperialism seems to be present in the formulations the nuns offered ("enrich themselves," "work for the benefit"), but reading the textbook in its entirety invalidates this anachronistic perception. Several pages earlier, the nuns explained that before the Europeans arrived, Australia was inhabited by "quelques tribus de sauvages, placés au dernier échelon des races humaines" (a few tribes of savages, on the very last rung of the human races). When asked, "Que sont devenus ces sauvages?" (What became of these savages?), they answer—incorrectly—that "Ils sont entièrement disparus" (They have completely disappeared).[35] Another clue that the nuns did not really criticize the employment of this "very large number of natives" for the profit of "a few colonists" is to be found in their presentation of another type of colony, the penal colony, about which they write: "Quel est le principal élément de la colonisation en Nouvelle-Calédonie? Ce sont les déportés qu'on envoie à Nouméa. Ce genre de colonisation est-il une grande source de prospérité? Non. Une colonie ne peut prospérer que par le travail libre."[36] (What is the principal component of colonization in New Caledonia? It is the deportees that we send to Nouméa. Is this type of colonization a great source of prosperity? No. A colony can only prosper through free labour.) Did the nuns of the Congrégation de Notre-Dame who wrote this textbook think that the "natives" who worked for the "colonists" in the exploitation colonies were free? It is what this argument implies. Otherwise, the authors of the various Canadian textbooks never created ambiguity regarding the importance of imperialism, to which Canada had a connection. Imperialism was good; it brought prosperity to the advanced nations and civilization to the nations they invaded.

The important role of imperialism in building alterity in schools is also to be found in the influence of travel writing on the curriculum. The first geography textbooks included many ethnographic anecdotes drawn from travel accounts. These "fun facts" were not the only items borrowed from the travellers' writings. The textbooks were regularly updated to include the most recent exploits and the advances of civilization and commerce, such as exploring Africa and building the Suez Canal. The population statistics were changed for each new edition, and authors directed the students' attention to the most recent acquisitions of the great British and French empires. In her book *Imperial Eyes*, Marie Louise Pratt states that the travel accounts, which were very popular in the eighteenth and nineteenth centuries, helped to create an awareness of and interest in the imperial aspect in metropolitan Europe.[37] To pursue her argument, I would add that the travel writing the school textbooks were drawing on helped to engender this imperialist sentiment not only in the metropolis but also on the periphery of the European world, as in Quebec. The use of travel writing helped to fashion an image of the world order in which Canadian students had a well-defined place.

The educational journals also played a part in shaping the interest in "other" lands, empires, and tales of exploration. Europe's world domination, whether through exploration or conquest, was virtually inevitable. In the pages of the *Journal d'instruction publique*, China's interior and the central Asian countries were spaces "à conquérir pour nos explorateurs" and "dont les portes s'ouvriront pour nous" (to be conquered for our explorers [and] whose doors will be opened to us).[38] And yet, the triumphant quality of imperialism sometimes gave way to a more disturbing colonial reality, and it was then important to reaffirm the differences and hierarchies. In July 1857, the *Journal of Education* referred to the mutiny of Indian soldiers. In their monthly review, the editors wrote: "While France is engaged as usual, in warring against the Kabyles, England has three great contests to carry on in Persia, in China and in India. The mutiny in the native army renders the latter more onerous and dangerous than the two others."[39] History proved them right, and a few months later the journal devoted almost an entire issue to the events in India. It also reprinted an article from the *Edinburgh Review*, published in translation the letters of French-Canadian Officer Edmond Joly[40] that had initially appeared in the newspaper *Le Canadien*, and included the insert of a large map of India. With the pedagogical nature of their publication in mind, the editors explained: "We think it of great importance that teachers should be well informed on the great events of the day, inasmuch as facts from contemporaneous history may be usefully availed of for the illustration of history and geography."[41] The mutiny was the opportunity to reaffirm the "grammar of difference,"[42] to paraphrase Catherine Hall, and remind readers that one must not trust the natives too readily. An imitation of civilization was in the end more dangerous than obvious barbarity. The description of the sepoys, which goes on for many pages, combines clichés, the most racist possible terms, and a contemptuous essentialism: "But this tincture of military discipline, this disguise of civilization, was altogether superficial; the natural Asiatic remained quite unchanged; even his manner of life was scarcely altered; his character was still overshadowed by low animal propensities, by the bestial superstitions of the worst form of heathenism, by the impenetrable cunning of a feeble race. [. . .] But these savage propensities lay concealed beneath an exterior which had, in ordinary times, much of the simplicity and the sportiveness of chilhood [sic]."[43]

After having read this "able article," teachers were invited to follow the young Joly's adventures in India through his letters to his parents. Eager to avenge the death of his companions, he travelled alone, on foot, from Burdwan to Benares at the end of August. Incidentally to the story of his adventures and his states of mind, Joly's letters feature a mosaic of alterity and the responsibilities of the civilized man: "Toutes les femmes et [tous les] enfants ont été massacr[és] à Cawnpour, où on les avait laissés pour plus grande sûreté. Ces scélérats sont pires que les Chinois, Caffres, ou Indiens de l'Amérique, gare à ces canailles si je les trouve au bout de mon revolver!," he wrote on 13 August. (All the women and [all the] children were massacred at Cawnpore, where they had been left for greater safety. These villains are worse than the Chinese, Kaffirs, or Indians of America, beware to the scoundrels if I find them at the end of my revolver!) How to avenge these atrocities? Some of his colleagues intended to treat the guilty the same way. Joly did not agree: "Montrons-nous civilisés, épargnons les femmes et les enfants, mais soyons sans pitié pour ceux qui auront les armes à la main, ou qui auront trempés [sic] dans ces atrocités [. . .], mais pas de torture."[44] (Let us show ourselves to be civilized, spare the women and children, but be without pity for those who carry weapons, or who have had a hand in these atrocities [. . .], but no torture.)

The event was still on the agenda several years later. In 1883, Miss Jane Luttress of the Royal Arthur School in Montreal published an article in the *Educational Record of the Province of Quebec*. Her topic was the various ways in which a liking for literature could be culti-vated in the young. She suggested the Indian Mutiny as a subject that could arouse their interest, with a moral sense much greater than that of the "scurrilous" literature that in her view only too often attracted their interest.[45] Throughout the nineteenth century, Canadian students were taught about the colonial reality of their time and learned the fundamental difference between the natives who were to be subjugated and the Europeans who explored and dominated the world. It was from these exploratory expeditions that contemporary scholars drew the information necessary to the increasingly varied classification of the human species.

In September 1891, the magazine *L'Enseignement primaire* suggested to teachers a dictation entitled "La fin d'une race" (The end of a race). Citing the disappearance of the people it called the "Redskins," the article by the Marquis de Nadaillac explained that "la civilisation [. . .] écrase ceux qui ne peuvent se l'assimiler" (civilization [. . .] crushes those who cannot assimilate it). The destruction of "cette race intéressante au point de vue anthropologique et ethnographique n'est plus qu'une question de temps" (this race, which is of interest from an anthropological and ethnographic viewpoint, is only a matter of time).[46] This discourse on the "vanishing race," a form of social Darwinism from the nineteenth century, insinuated that the different human races do not exist in the same social time and are not contemporaries. While history studied the European nations, the study of the so-called savage societies was rather associated with anthropology and ethnography. These sciences, which were becoming more strongly established in the nineteenth century, infiltrated the educational discourse and influenced how the different peoples on Earth were to be seen by children. A long piece in *The Fifth Book of Reading Lessons for the Use of Schools in the British-American Provinces* introduced students to the various historical sciences, such as philology and ethnology. From the outset, the author disqualified "savage" and "half-civilized" societies from study because "in reality, [they] have nothing fit to be called history, since the life they lead, from year to year, and from generation to generation, is as uniform and monotonous as that of an animal or a plant."[47]

These two school exercises perfectly illustrate what anthropologist Johannes Fabian stated: "The absence of the Other from our Time has been his mode of presence in our discourse—as an object and victim."[48] In his study of otherness and temporality in the history of anthropology, Fabian looks at how this science of Others was erected on a foundation of denying the coevalness of the observer (the anthropologist) and the observed. He shows how time became central to the development of Western sciences in the nineteenth century and how these last were intrinsically connected to colonial projects. Science paved the way for colonialism and then justified it. How can two bodies, one European and one Native, occupy the same land at the same time? To get around this existential dilemma, science banished the Native to another temporality, to the primitive's time or the Oriental's immutability. Science made it possible to relegate the conquered society to another time, both in humanity's infancy and in the absence of a historical future, since the race's extinction was imminent.

The alterity constructed by science is manifested in many ways. In presenting the science of ethnology, the reader excerpt mentioned earlier lists a series of questions that this "discourse about nations" attempts to answer. Many of these questions invite students to reflect on the colonial project in which they take part: "Before we, or our ancestors, came to this continent, it was inhabited by Indian tribes. But what people did they displace? Where did they come from? [. . .] How many are the varieties of mankind? Had climate anything to do with change of colour? To what family do we belong? Have any families perished altogether?"[49] Reading this passage would lead the student to the following rationale: "My ancestors displaced the Indians, but they themselves had taken the place of other peoples, they themselves did not originate on this continent, and other peoples died before they did. European colonialism is justified; it is only an episode, among others, in human history." The student's conscience was spared.

Questions in the reader also refer to the scientific discourse regarding human races: Into how many races is the great human family divided? What is responsible for these differences? How does climate figure in these explanations? Relentlessly repeating to the children that they were members of a superior race, civilization, and religion was not enough. It also had to be explained to them why this is. The school did so by relying on the various ephemeral scientific theories of the time, among them the climate theory. Beginning in 1833, Father Holmes stated that Europe's climate "favorise le développement de toutes les facultés de l'homme" (favours the development of all of man's faculties).[50] A few years later, a description of the Canadian climate by a Montreal physician found a place in the national reader. Dr. Hingston provided students with a long scientific explanation of the climate's effects on humans. With a sincere patriotic flourish, he concluded: "The maritime and continental features, harmoniously blended in our Canadian climate, are favourable to the highest development of a hardy, long-lived, intelligent people. May that people be a Canadian people—not loving the land of their European forefathers less—but loving Canada more."[51] In the subsequent decades, the Frères des écoles chrétiennes, Sœurs de la congrégation de Notre-Dame, and writer John Calkin presented a climate theory in their respective geography textbooks. In addition to rendering men indolent, weak, stupid, and inactive, the environment of torrid and glacial regions influenced skin colour as well as physical and mental development.[52] At the same time, the environmental cause was used to explain the Europeans' superiority. Calkin wrote: "It is only in the temperate regions, however, that man's powers of body and mind appear in all their strength; and it is here only that we find the civilized and powerful nations."[53] These excerpts show how science had penetrated the educational discourse and how, in doing so, it supported the racial hierarchy with the statement of a conclusive truth.

The young people were finally able to apply this hierarchy themselves. In an article in *High School Magazine* put out by students at Montreal High School in 1912, one of them wrote a brief text under the title "The Languages of Our Globe." The student had taken a count of existing languages and dialects around the world. After having mentioned locations with an impressive number of dialects, such as Brazil, Mexico, Borneo, and Australia, he went on, "It is said that generally the number of dialects decreases with the intellectual culture of the population."[54] It is easy to find the connection between the two statements: the student suggests that the Indigenous peoples who contribute to the very high number of dialects in the countries mentioned are intellectually weak. Insidiously, the hierarchy is established.

Another feature of the Canadian school in the nineteenth century was the omnipresence of religion, which appeared to be a normal part of the educational discourse and curriculum. Being aware of the events of their time, the schools kept the children informed about the propagation of the Christian faith across the globe. By the very act of referring to the "civilizing mission" of the European peoples, the educational discourse constructed otherness, which was from then on tainted with an inferiority, if not a dangerous obscurantism, which the Christian nations must remedy. Civilization, the one way to "Salvation" and "Progress," was inextricably linked to Christianity. Also, ministry was a necessary part of civilizing Others. This is exactly what the school textbooks were teaching the children.

The "civilizing mission" first appears as a justification for colonialism. It was necessary to find a valid moral motive for the colonial enterprises since students and teachers were often aware of expansion's inconsistencies and abuses. Propagating Christian civilization was thus the premier pretext for a European presence on all continents. In 1891, the Sœurs de la congrégation de Notre-Dame wrote that, as the eldest daughter of the Catholic Church, "[la France] a, pour une large part, contribuée [*sic*] au progrès et à la civilisation des peuples de toutes les contrées du monde. [. . .] C'est aussi de son sein que partent

les généreux missionnaires qui vont au prix des plus grands sacrifices
porter la lumière de l'Évangile aux nations encore plongées dans les
ténèbres de l'idolâtrie." ([France] has contributed in large part to the
progress and civilization of peoples in all regions of the world. [. . .]
It is also from its bosom that the generous missionaries go, at the cost
of the greatest of sacrifices, to bring the Gospel's light to nations still
engulfed in the darkness of idolatry.) Further on in the book, they
propose Christian missionary work as the only way to *humanize* the
population of Central Africa.[55]

The discursive stereotype or ideological superstructure that was the
civilizing mission functioned through associating indigeneity with childhood. For one thing, the correlation was necessary to place the Other
in an inferior and dependent position. Hartog reminds us that with the
discovery of the Savage came the question of justifying domination. The
European philosophers of the modern era quickly made the shift from
the Savage-Slave to the Savage-Child, who experienced a "potential"
evolution that the colonizers were responsible for activating.[56] Fabian
expresses the same idea, while more directly alluding to its implications:
"Even worse, are we to forget that talk about the childlike nature of the
primitive has never been just a neutral classificatory act, but a powerful
rhetorical figure and motive, informing colonial practice in every aspect
from religious indoctrination to labor laws and the granting of basic
political rights? [. . .] Aside from the evolutionist figure of the savage
there has been no conception more obviously implicated in political and
cultural oppression than that of the childlike native."[57]

In the missionary discourse of the Europeans and Americans,
the representation of the childlike native, or simply the native child,
referred to the need to redeem him through baptism. Every Christian
was therefore responsible, before God, for converting the idolators. This
argument worked well with Canadian students, who were regularly
informed of missionary activities across the planet. By the century's end,
the textbooks even mentioned Canadian missionaries who were helping
to save the world through their work in Indochina and the Pacific

Islands. A letter written by students at the Pensionnat de Notre-Dame in Montreal in 1851 raised this issue of Christian responsibility. In a missive addressed to the Archbishop of Chalcedon, president of the Holy Childhood Association, the girls express their hope of seeing the situation of Chinese children made less difficult by their alms: "Nous serions d'autant plus heureuses," they wrote, "que nous aurions là un moyen facile d'acquitter envers Dieu la dette de notre reconnaissance. [. . .] un de nos souhaits les plus ardents est de voir prospérer [l'Œuvre de la Sainte-Enfance], afin que par son moyen il soit donné aux enfants des autres pays de jouir comme nous du bienfait inestimable d'une éducation chrétienne."[58] (We would be even happier if in this way we could easily repay our debt of gratitude to God. [. . .] one of our most cherished wishes is to see [the Holy Childhood Association] prosper, so that through its means children of other countries can enjoy, like us, the invaluable blessing of a Christian education.) Fifty years later, along similar lines, Reverend Rexford reminded Protestant teachers in Quebec of "the glorious effects of the Mission Schools changing barbarism to civilization" in Yukon and Alaska.[59]

The "civilizing mission" that accompanied and justified imperialism also contributed to the differentiation between Us and Them in the educational discourse. And yet, the peculiarity of constructing alterity through the rhetorical process of Christian missions was that it constructed the Other as a child and created compassion that otherwise had little presence in the discourse.

The General Economy of Difference

[Le maître] — Jean-Charles, n'avez-vous jamais vu des sauvages? (C'est ainsi que nos gens appellent les Indiens.)

J.-Charles — Oh oui, Monsieur, il en est venu deux chez nous l'année dernière, et j'en ai eu tellement peur que j'ai failli m'évanouir.

[Le maître] — Vous avez eu tort, mon enfant, car les
sauvages d'aujourd'hui ne font de mal à personne. Pourquoi
avez-vous eu tant peur des deux que vous avez vus?

J.-Charles — Parce qu'ils avaient la peau jaune, les cheveux
longs, et un costume étrange.[60]

([The schoolmaster] — Jean-Charles, have you never seen
any savages? (This is what our people called the Indians.)

J.-Charles — Oh yes, sir, two of them came to our house
last year, and I was so scared that I almost fainted.

[The schoolmaster] — You were wrong, my child, because
today the savages don't hurt anyone. Why were you so
scared of the two you saw?

J.-Charles — Because they had yellow skin, long hair, and
strange clothes.)

This Canadian history lesson also taught children that formerly around
their school there was "qu'une vaste et épaisse forêt habitée par des
peuples et des animaux sauvages et féroces [. . .] [et que] ces pauvres
gens, qui ignoraient l'art de cultiver la terre et qui n'avaient pour outils
que des haches de pierre (le fer et l'acier leur étant inconnus), vivaient
dans la plus grande misère" (only a vast, dense forest inhabited by fierce,
savage peoples and animals [. . .] [and that] these poor people, who
did not know how to farm the land and for tools had only stone axes
[iron and steel being unknown to them], lived in great misery).[61] It
provides an example of how otherness was discursively constructed
by educational institutions in the nineteenth century. This lesson from
the journal *L'Enseignment primaire* in 1895 is basically a lightly revised
version of a school inspector's account of a dialogue he had heard in
School No. 1 of the Parish of Saint-J— in 1882. In the inspector's
account, the "Savages" are called "Indians," the name of the child being

questioned is Antoinette, and the teacher did not ask her why she was scared. In retrieving this first-person account to use it as a sample lesson, the journal's writers added certain details that increased the Indian's otherness and made the anecdote's actors more universal by changing them into male characters.[62]

In this pedagogical exercise, the Savages (or Indians) are essentialized and their existence is more or less considered to be in the past. These discursive methods, combined with use of the familiar vocabulary of difference ("strange," "fierce") and an opposition between civilization and savagery, construct the Indians as an Other people. In this sense, the Indians are ranked with the Chinese, Arabs, and Hottentots. As they are presented to the student, these peoples do not really exist; they are rather a product of the Western imagination. Hartog states: "The others, *they*, are present in the story as a third person, that is, a non-person. Nothing surprising in that: introduced by the narrator into his narrative as the subject of the utterance, but in no way of its uttering, they perform for [the children]."[63]

On page 162 of his *Nouvel abrégé de géographie moderne* (1833), Father Holmes produced a breach in his textbook's narrativity. In so doing, he introduced a *topos* that would be copied by all writers of geography textbooks up until the eve of the First World War. Page 162 offered the reader a general description of the geography of Asia. However, the description's content is very different from what Holmes had previously written about Europe and America. With this passage, he recognizes and restates Asia's radical otherness.

> Malheureusement cette terre fortunée qu'habite une
> moitié de la race humaine, est plongée depuis bien des
> siècles dans une ignorance profonde des vrais principes
> religieux, moraux, et politiques. Le polythéisme sous ses
> diverses formes est la croyance la plus commune; les mœurs
> sont dissolues, les lois civiles en petit nombre et souvent
> absurdes, bizarres, ou cruelles; la forme imparfaite des

gouvernemens est le monarchique [*sic*] absolu, ou plutôt le
despotique [*sic*], qui ne connaît d'autre frein que la force—
excepté les peuples nomades du centre et de l'occident,
qui suivent une espèce de régime féodal assez semblable à
celui de l'Europe au moyen âge. On peut dire des nations
asiatiques, surtout des habitans de la Chine et de l'Inde,
que l'immutabilité est devenue leur caractère. Ils n'avancent
ni ne reculent en civilisation.[64]

(Sadly, this bountiful land inhabited by half the human
race has been plunged for many centuries in a profound
ignorance of true religious, moral, and political principles.
The most common belief is in polytheism in all its various
forms; behaviour is dissolute, civil laws are few in number
and often absurd, bizarre, or cruel; the imperfect form of
government is the absolute, or rather despotic, monarchy,
which knows no constraint but force—except for the
nomadic peoples of the centre and the West, who follow
a type of feudal system resembling that of Europe in
the Middle Ages. It could be said of the Asiatic nations,
especially the inhabitants of China and India, that
immutability has become their character. They neither
advance nor retreat in terms of civilization.)

Writing about the dissolute behaviour, absurd or bizarre laws, and
unchanging nature of Asian peoples branded them with alterity. The
uniform, regular design of geography textbooks, to the point of catechet-
ical organization, creates the initial impression that each country and
region would be presented using the same categories. But a close reading
reveals that it was according to their alterity (and to reaffirm it) that
the societies in Asia, Africa, and Oceania were described. The authors
often took pains to give a detailed description of each people's physical
type—ears, nose, height—in addition to paying special attention to

bizarre clothing, different ways of living, and despotic governments. In repeating these stereotypes, the geography textbook produced, reinforced, and perpetuated them. A primary characteristic of a rhetoric of alterity can be seen in the simple fact that certain peoples were described while others were not.

In his book *Time and the Other*, Fabian elaborates on the concept of allochrony, which he also calls the "denial of coevalness." About the colonizing nations of the nineteenth century, he writes: "[They] needed Space to occupy. More profoundly and problematically, they required Time to accommodate the schemes of a one-way history: progress, development, modernity (and their negative mirror images: stagnation, underdevelopment, tradition)."[65] This world vision, which was necessary to colonialism and came in part out of a nascent anthropology, is very visible in the educational material for children. Like Father Holmes, Toussaint wrote that Asia was the cradle of civilization, "mais elle-même est restée stationnaire" (but has itself remained stationary), and while he appreciated the region's industrious activity, "la civilisation n'y fait pas de progrès, elle reste ce qu'elle était il y a plusieurs siècles" (civilization has not advanced there, it remains as it was many centuries ago).[66] Similarly, in the early 1890s a student at the Académie Visitation in Montreal copied Holmes's text from 1833 in an assignment on Asian Turkey. She wrote: "La Turquie d'Asie est un sol fertile en grands souvenirs; mais ces souvenirs même [sic] n'existent point pour les habitants actuels abrutis par l'ignorance et l'esclavage."[67] (The soil of Asian Turkey is fertile with memories of greatness; but these memories themselves do not exist for today's inhabitants, who have been stupefied by ignorance and slavery.) These inhabitants were located outside time and had no awareness of the land's history. And so "un pasteur arabe vient avec indifférence appuyer sa tente aux colonnes brisées de Palmyre" (an Arab shepherd heedlessly supports his tent on the broken columns of Palmyra), wrote the young Montrealer. The Other, set apart from civilization, commerce, and Christianity, was relegated to a place outside historical time. Worse yet, they could even have been expelled if, after having taken part in the movement of history, they fell back into a state of ignorance and slavery, as was the case for the peoples of western Asia.[68]

In addition to a dissimilar description and being expelled from time, alterity was also constructed through the ethnographic attention given to certain populations. National history textbooks almost all contained an ethnographic section on the customs of those they called the "Indians" or "Savages" of America at the time of "discovery." In the geography books, it can be seen that this often essentialist ethnographic attention was paid to almost all non-European peoples. The natives of Chile were generous, courageous, and proud, but pillagers, belligerent, vindictive, and drunkards. The Abyssinians were barbaric and indecent, while the Japanese were slow to forgive an offence. Some national dress by itself constituted a form of alterity, as did cannibalism. The authors of these textbooks never failed to point out the former or current cannibalistic practices of various peoples. If some were "cannibals by inclination," others were so in a more "civilized" way, eating only criminals or "prisoners of war too severely wounded." The reported anthropophagy of certain peoples is surprising, because they were also known for "a great ability to become civilized." Even when cannibalism was no longer practised, the writers mentioned it, taking the opportunity to discredit the people in question, as Holmes did with the Chinese.[69]

Another type of behaviour that acted as a marker of alterity in certain societies was the treatment of women. On this topic I must first explain that, without exception, the geography textbooks were silent on the subject of half the human race. This exclusion of women from the representation of the world promoted in the geography textbooks was in keeping with the masculine representation of travel and adventure that developed over the nineteenth century. In the presentation of European and American countries, women were depicted in illustrations only as middle class in big cities or farm workers in southern countries.

Aside from these situations, on the rare occasions when women were mentioned, it was to point out that certain Asian or African peoples treated them like slaves. As early as 1833, Holmes wrote that in China, "le sexe est tenu dans une espèce d'esclavage; le paysan chinois attelle, en même temps, dit-on, à sa charrue sa femme et son âne" (the sex is kept in a sort of slavery; they say that the Chinese farmer will harness both his wife and his donkey to his plough at the same time). Many decades later, at the dawn of the twentieth century, J.N. Miller[70] wrote about Asia that "les femmes ne sont guère mieux traitées que des esclaves" (the women are treated not much better than slaves).[71] Allusion to the slavery of women, a real marker of alterity, was also used by the writers of Canadian history textbooks to discredit the country's first inhabitants. In the section on those he called the Savages, Toussaint wrote: "Les femmes, regardées comme des esclaves, étaient traitées avec mépris et chargées des travaux les plus pénibles."[72] (The women, looked on as slaves, were treated with contempt and assigned the most difficult tasks.) As Lisa L. Zagumny and Lydia Mihelic Pulsipher remark about American textbooks, while the authors described the inferiorization of women in certain "barbaric" cultures, nothing was said about their inferiorization in European or American culture.[73] At a time when the word "freedom" was so important, the state of slavery in which certain female Others seemed to exist should have been mentioned. In these didactic works from which women were almost absent, the few mentions they received put the status of the civilized woman in perspective: she was free . . . within the private realm!

In the nineteenth century, composition was one of the subjects students were obliged to take. The Frères des écoles chrétiennes cautioned their pupils to use a suitable style: "Tenez compte des lieux où se passent les événements. [. . .] Ne faites pas parler le barde de l'Écosse comme le bonze de l'Inde, ni le sauvage du Labrador, comme le bourgeois de Paris."[74] (Keep the places where the events take place in mind. [. . .] Do not make the bard from Scotland speak like the bonze from India, nor the savage from Labrador like the bourgeois from Paris.) Using the rhetorical device of comparison, the statement reveals the radical difference between the Labrador savage and the Parisian bourgeois. This process is exemplified by Hartog in his book *Le miroir d'Hérodote.* He explains that comparison is used by Hérodote as a process for translating the Other.[75] In the textbooks, comparison served to tilt a group into otherness when the people with whom they are compared have already been constructed as Other. This discursive process also served to establish a hierarchy of others, of whom some were prouder and others less uncouth, while still others were morally superior. As a result, stereotypes and imagination were the principal tools available to children who had never before heard of a bonze from India or a savage from Labrador, or even a Scottish bard or a Parisian bourgeois.

A last procedure in the rhetoric of alterity consisted in essentializing, in a literary piece, an entire population through the example of a single individual. This literary practice was not unknown in the narrative modes of travel accounts and anthropological writing. As Pratt explains it: "The initial ethnographic gesture is the one that homogenizes the people to be subjected, that is, produced as subjects, into a collective *they,* which distills down even further into an iconic *he* (= the standard adult male specimen). This abstracted *he/they* is the subject of verbs in a timeless present tense. These characterize anything 'he' is or does not as a particular event in time but as an instance of a pregiven custom or trait (as a particular plant is an instance of its genus and species)."[76]

The textbooks students used for reading exercises provided various exotic anecdotes featuring characters who could be Arab, Chinese, Japanese, Indian, and Black. In these texts, alterity showed up in the absence of a first name or trade among these characters, in contrast to the Euro-Americans. This narrative or literary alterity functions by depersonalizing the Other. The Black person is called the Negro. The narration is set up with an absence of individuation of the characters, and essentialization confirms the radical otherness of various peoples. "L'Abénaki," "Mgr Cheverus et le Nègre," "Les Sauvages," "Kléber et le petit Arabe," "La petite Métisse"—through the phrasing of his titles, Father J.-Roch Magnan provided wonderful examples of this objectifying literary otherness.[77] Reading a story with a title like "L'Anglais" would have been impossible. By contrast, the title "L'Abénaki" evoked a generic Abenaki whose alterity was already recognized. The exoticism of the title also gave the statement a compelling poetic force.

The difference constructed by the educational discourse can also be seen in a study of the lexical field associated with it. A composition exercise from a textbook of the Clercs de Saint-Viateur introduced students to one of the most common terms used to describe the Other. The lesson reads as follows:

> SAUVAGE, FAROUCHE. Un objet est sauvage par défaut de culture. Un animal est farouche par vice d'humeur. Le sauvage serait farouche, s'il avait dans le caractère et dans les mœurs de la rudesse, de la brutalité, de la dureté. Apprivoisez l'animal sauvage, il deviendra domestique; domptez l'animal farouche, il paraîtra soumis.

> APPLICATION. L'écureuil est un animal sauvage. La panthère est. . . . Les Gaulois étaient un peuple . . . ne respirant que la guerre et le carnage. Les peuplades . . . des îles Sandwich sont d'un naturel doux et pacifique; les naturels de la Nouvelle-Zélande sont, au contraire, . . . et sanguinaires. Les herbes . . . croissent dans les terrains incultes.[78]

> (SAVAGE, FIERCE. An object is savage owing to a lack of culture. An animal is fierce because it lacks feeling. The savage would be fierce if his character and behaviour were harsh, brutal, or hard. Tame the savage animal, and it will become domesticated; tame a fierce animal, and it will appear submissive.

> APPLICATION. The squirrel is a savage animal. The panther is. . . . The Gauls were a . . . people breathing only war and carnage. The . . . tribes of the Sandwich Islands have a gentle, peace-loving nature; the natives of New Zealand

are, by contrast, . . . and bloodthirsty . . . grasses grow on
uncultivated land.)

Calling a people "savage" or "barbaric" positioned them as the symmet-
rical reverse of the society to which the student belonged. And yet the
"savages," if they are at times "fierce" or, much more often, "ferocious,"
can also be "gentle and peace-loving." This lexicon was reserved for
the Others. The Belgians or Swiss were not "gentle"; the Hottentots,
Tahitians, Brazilians, or Hurons were. In one of Toussaint's textbooks,
the Laplanders, Lao, Ainu, Abyssinians, Kru, and Hottentots were all
"gentle" people.[79] Astonishingly, the members of a given society could
even both be gentle and seem ferocious; thus, in one of the Frères des
écoles chrétiennes' textbooks, "the inhabitants of the Friendly Islands
are mild and affable although ferocious in appearance."[80]

"Gentle," "ferocious," "bloodthirsty," "indolent," "effeminate," "of
quite developed intelligence"—these were just a few ways of describing
the Others. The vocabulary of alterity included several words related
to exoticism that refer back to the reader's assumed normativeness.
Thus the words "strange," "bizarre," or "extraordinary" often recurred
in the writing of the textbooks' authors.[81] The word most commonly
used to describe the strangeness of the Other was still "curious," along
with its derivative, "curiosities." The Laplanders thus appeared to be "a
curious people" living in "curious little huts."[82] The Pygmies were "les
populations les plus curieuses de l'Afrique" (the most curious populations in Africa).[83] China boasted many curiosities. Asia was truly
fascinating for its mysteries and foreignness, and the words to describe
it did not exist. How to make its radically Other nature understandable by children? The use of alterity's lexical field then assumed its
full meaning: "The people dress in strange fashions; they have curious
manners, and speak languages that we do not understand," as J.N. Miller
summed it up in 1905.[84]

During the school year 1896–97, Anny Pilon, a fifth-grade student
at Saint-Joseph in the county of Deux-Montagnes, consigned her

various "daily assignments" to a notebook that miraculously survived her.[85] In-between a mapping exercise on Europe and a dictation on "the song of our soul," Anny completed a lexicology assignment. Her task was to "find three suitable attributes" for several words such as "mouth," "water," and "surface." For the word "people," Anny wrote: "Les peuples sont civilisés, barbares ou sauvages" (peoples are civilized, barbaric or savage). Condensed in the innocuous response of this young fifth-grade student is the essence of the symbolic and ideological universe in which the representations of the Self and the Other were at play in Quebec's schools in the nineteenth century.

Without the Savages or Barbarians, school would not have been able to remind children that they belonged to the civilized world. Use of these categories was essential to the school's inculcation of a civilized person's identity, and, whatever the context, they made it possible to set up the boundaries of identity and civilization. The terms "savage" and "barbaric" effectively assumed a different meaning in the educational discourse. First of all, they pointed out one of the stages of civilization that the children learned about in studying political geography. According to the Frères des écoles chrétiennes, peoples were savage, barbaric, half-civilized, or civilized. In the writings of Montpetit and Devisme or of Hodgins, they were savage, half-civilized, or civilized. Along with the other causal factors cited in the geographical discourse to justify a society's political status—for instance, the climate theory—this stage-based vision of the development of various human societies was inherited from Enlightenment philosophy. The same school of thinking also engendered the division of the world offered by John Calkin to anglophone students: "The various conditions of human society may be reduced to three principal classes, represented by the hunter, the shepherd and the agriculturist."[86] While the terminology used here did not imply a moral judgement as directly as the terms "savage" and "barbaric" did, the hierarchy remained strong, and Canadian society was always found in the last phase of the process, at the summit of social evolution.

This categorization of the world was not limited to Canadian text-books but was also present in those from south of the border. It replicated the stages of progress in political treatises from the Enlightenment—but the textbooks obscured their complexity, offering simplified definitions of the various stages. For the Frères des écoles chrétiennes, "savage" peoples "vivent errants, sans lois fixes, sans gouvernement régulier, et dont tout le soin se borne au besoin du moment" (lead a life of wander-ing, without definite laws or regular government, caring only about the needs of the moment).[87] Moreover, they are "generally blood-thirsty and revengeful; some eat the flesh of the enemies they take in war."[88] At the opposite extreme were the civilized peoples, characterized by their politeness and honesty, their gentle, sociable manners, and the cultivation of literature, science, arts, agriculture, and commerce. This representation of the "savage" peoples was atemporal. In the Canadian history textbook produced by the Frères des écoles chrétiennes, after having introduced the contemporary status of a Canada inhabited by "un peuple intelligent, qui forme une société de plusieurs millions d'in-dividus [. . .], régie par des lois sages, profess[ant] la religion chrétienne et cultiv[ant] avec succès les arts et les sciences" (an intelligent populace making up a society of several million [. . .], governed by wise laws, practising the Christian religion and successfully cultivating the arts and sciences), they went on to say: "Le Canada, ainsi que l'Amérique dont il fait partie, n'a pas toujours possédé ces précieux avantages. Il y a trois siècles, notre territoire n'était qu'une immense solitude, habitée çà et là par une race d'hommes demi-nus, vivant à l'état sauvage."[89] (Canada, like America, of which it is a part, has not always had these precious advantages. Three centuries ago, our land was nothing but an immense solitude, inhabited here and there by a race of half-naked men, living in the savage state.)

When they did not directly mention the different stages of civi-lization, the textbooks' authors nonetheless alluded to the hierarchy associated with them. J.N. Miller thus reminded the reader that "aucun peuple de l'Asie n'est aussi civilisé que les nations européennes ou leurs descendants dans les autres parties du monde" (no population in Asia is as civilized as the European nations and their descendants in other parts of the world).[90] He also brought up the civilized-savage coupling in a questionnaire from the English-language version of his textbook. He asks the students: "Are the people of America savage or civilized? From what grand division was civilization brought to America? What savage race owned America before the Europeans took possession of it? Were the Europeans themselves ever in a savage condition? In what part of Europe did the people first become civilized? [. . .] Tell five things which are done in the Dominion to-day which the Indians have not yet learned to do. Do uncivilized people build large cities and fine buildings?"[91] Whether through "scientific" notions of political geography or more insidiously through exercise questions, the difference between the civilized peoples of European origin and the Others was taught with the help of well-defined categories.

In the nomenclature described by the Frères des écoles chrétiennes in their textbooks, the "barbaric" peoples, for their part, were described as "généralement cruels, inhumains, ne cultivant ni littérature, ni arts, ni sciences" (generally cruel, inhumane, cultivating neither literature, nor arts, nor sciences). Contrary to the term "savage," which refers mainly to a people's "primitivity" or the natural state, the word "barbaric" involves several levels of meaning. In addition to being a stage of civilization, barbarism is the result of barbaric behaviour on the part of a person or a people. The "barbarian" is the ultimate Other. An ancient representation, they do not themselves exist, but constitute "polymorphous beings, because subjective. They do not exist for themselves, but for others,"[92] as Bruno Dumézil writes. And yet, contrary to the representation of barbarians developed by the ancients, which did not necessarily entail a pejorative judgement, the barbarians described to a Canadian student in the nineteenth century were constantly put in a moral relation to the norm. They were at once inferior, contemptible, and inhumane. In geography textbooks, the use of the qualifier "barbaric" usually referred to cruel customs, slavery, cannibalism, and human sacrifice. Outside this discipline, the "barbarian" appeared to the pupil as a narrative image most often associated with the Iroquois, or more generally with Indigenous peoples. Of course, the story of the martyrdom of the Jesuit priests in the era of New France, which had a large presence in the school curriculum, made the figure of the Iroquois still more barbaric: "Jamais de votre sang vous ne fûtes avares / Vous êtes accourus, et les peuples barbares / Connurent bientôt leurs vainqueurs! / [. . .] Combien ont expiré dans leurs courses lointaines / En évangélisant des tribus inhumaines!" (Never with your blood were you miserly / You came running, and the barbaric peoples / Soon came to know their conquerors! / [. . .] How many expired on their distant journeys / Evangelizing inhumane tribes!). This is Adolphe Basile Routhier's poem about the priests that pupils of the Frères des écoles chrétiennes were required to commit to memory.[93] The figure of the barbaric Iroquois was essential to constructing the French-Canadian national history. By itself, that confirms the central role of the barbarian in identity construction.

The coupling of "civilized" and "barbarian" was not an invention of nineteenth-century Europe. What was new in this nth resurgence of the barbarians was the didactic, scientific, and grass-roots nature of the narrative universe into which they were inserted. In this case, the Barbarian was not a fictional character created by Victor Hugo or the historical being who fuelled the reflections of French historians in the same era. The Barbarian was rather the "metaphorical" barbarian, the one who was often confused with the Savage, the Cannibal, the Nomad, and all the discursive forms of otherness summoned up in the children's minds and instilled there by the school.

The Appearance of a Liberal Double Standard

Freedom and domination were two key themes in the political history of the nineteenth century, and the educational culture was not excluded from these ideological discussions. In the conception of the world that they transmitted to their pupils, the schools defined these notions and played with them. There then appeared, in their representations, two opposing visions of freedom and domination. On the one hand, the liberty was that of both liberalism and the more or less savage nomad; on the other, the European powers and indigenous governments exerted a domination that was, to some, enlightened and, to others, despotic. A double standard is thus exposed: all freedoms are not desirable, all domination is not bad. The civilized peoples are always exempt; the freedom and domination exercised by the Others are those to be proscribed.

In his book *The Pauper's Freedom*, Jean-Marie Fecteau examines how "the immensely appealing ideal of freedom running through the nineteenth century" manifested itself. Far from considering liberalism in its middle-class manifestation alone, he studies the "societal reflexes or basic representations underlying the idea of freedom."[94] According to Fecteau, this new mode of social organization became consecrated only in mid-century. At that time, liberalism "is a veritable mode of existence that wraps the individual within a specific *ethic* of personhood. It lays out a framework for behaviour that constrains and channels agency even down to its ethical dimension."[95] The school transmitted this liberal ideology to the children in the latter half of the nineteenth century. In educational materials, the representation of Euro-American societies was based on attention to the individual, his responsibility and his will to action. In this realm of thought, freedom was one of the pillars of civilization, and its manifestation in a type of political regime such as democracy made it possible for civilized nations to prosper. Conversely, the decadence or poverty of certain countries was attributed to their "less fortunate political regime."[96]

The liberal ideal was thus based first and foremost on political freedom. England was recognized by certain writers for "her great political freedom"[97] and it was explained that over there "it is really the people who rule, and no nation has more freedom or a better government."[98] Besides, an attachment to freedom was at the core of the American character.[99] This attachment was not without its dangers. The school then became invested in training future citizens in the appropriate exercise of freedom. As Zagumny and Pulsipher put it: "Many Americans feared that too much or uncontrolled freedom might lead to decadence, so they sought balance through education that emphasized virtue and proper behavior. Citizens were to internalize control over their behavior in order to exercise their freedom properly."[100]

Two other criteria were also applied to teach the children about the conditions necessary for a mass exercise of freedom: the existence of public opinion, and religious tolerance. These attributes, which were to be found notably in England and the Netherlands, were also present in certain despotic societies, thus becoming the sign of their possible entry into civilization. In this regard, Montpetit and Devisme noted that "depuis un certain nombre d'années, le gouvernement de la Perse tend à se modifier dans le sens de la politique européenne. [. . .] Une opinion publique se forme petit à petit et la liberté envahit le despotisme."[101] (For a number of years now, the Persian government has been tending toward change in the direction of European politics. [. . .] Public opinion is gradually gaining ground and freedom is taking over from despotism.) For its part, Tunisia, already more civilized and better able to cultivate its land than the other North African states, "has a constitution by which liberty of speech and religion is guaranteed to the people,"[102] as Frères des écoles chrétiennes noted.

The "bonne liberté" (good freedom) was also mentioned in commentary on the struggle for independence of certain peoples, notably the Greeks and French Canadians. Thus, following the insurrection of 1821 to which "the French contributed much, [. . .] Greece has recovered its freedom." The writer, Toussaint, went so far as to recognize the value of freedom won "en résistant aux détachements envoyés contre eux" (in resisting the detachments sent against them) by the "nègres marrons" (maroon Negroes) of Dutch Guyana. "Heureux soit ce peuple énergique et intelligent."[103] (May these energetic, intelligent people be happy.) But rare were the racialized people who had the possibility of liberating themselves from the yoke, European or not, under which they lived. In the 1830s, for example, Jean Holmes maintained that the "nègres qui [. . .] sont devenus les seuls maîtres [d'Hayti ne savent] pas profiter de la liberté dont ils jouissent" (Negroes who [. . .] have become the sole masters [of Haiti do not know] how to turn the freedom they enjoy to their advantage).[104]

However, Canada remained the most exemplary case of this just and legitimate quest for freedom. The teachings of the national history were eloquent on this score. While the narrative of the history of New France dealt with the often conflicted relationships with Indian tribes, the sections on English domination, starting in 1760, were built around ideas of freedom, despotism, and justice. French-Canadian children were taught how their "pères ont su défendre dans la lutte de la tribune [leur] langue, [leur] liberté et [leur] religion" (fathers were able to defend, in the public forum, their language, liberty, and religion).[105] In discussing the mission of Canada's people, who had known two great dangers, *"l'Indien féroce"* (the ferocious Indian) and the English conquest, the Sœurs de la congrégation de Notre-Dame wrote that "l'Angleterre [dut] céder devant la fermeté du Canadien catholique réclamant de justes droits" (England had to give way before the resolve of the Canadian Catholic demanding fair rights).[106] But it was Toussaint who, once again, best expressed the importance of this freedom to the Canadian people:

> Aujourd'hui, les Canadiens Français sont maîtres de leur destinée, quoique sous la tutelle britannique. Et, cependant qu'il y a à peine trente ans que leurs ennemis mettaient encore en question si les fils de la France avaient droit aux libertés civiles, et que ces derniers étaient obligés de combattre de toutes leurs forces pour conserver les libertés qu'ils avaient, et acquérir celles qui leur manquaient [référence aux Rébellions]. Ils jouissent maintenant de la plénitude de toutes les libertés.
>
> Aussi, chez eux, la civilisation accueille tous les progrès moraux et matériels. Les sciences, les lettres, les arts

s'agrandissent, s'élèvent, se perfectionnent: tout concourt à
faire des Canadiens Français un peuple digne du présent, et
digne de ses grandes destinées futures.

Il ne s'agit plus de guerroyer contre un ennemi envahisseur,
ou de s'opposer à une souveraineté qui veut imposer des lois
arbitraires. Maintenant, c'est la joute des talents entre les
membres de la famille canadienne, joute pacifique, mais la
plus grandiose qui fût jamais.[107]

(Today, the French Canadians are the masters of their
destiny, although under British guardianship. And yet it
was only some thirty years ago that their enemies again
challenged the right to civil liberties of the sons of France,
and that they were obliged to fight with all their strength
to preserve the liberties they had won and gain those they
had not [reference to the Rebellions]. They can now enjoy
the fullness of all the freedoms.

Also, for them, civilization welcomes all the moral and
material forms of progress. The sciences, letters, and arts
are growing, raising up and developing: everything is
coming together to make the French Canadians a people
worthy of the present and worthy of their great destiny in
the future.

It is no longer a matter of waging war on an invading
enemy or opposing a sovereignty seeking to impose
arbitrary laws. Now, it is a contest of talents between
members of the Canadian family, a peaceful contest, but
the greatest that ever was.)

Toussaint's text could very well be included in the mid-century discourse
of triumphant liberalism as analyzed in Fecteau's book. Since the text

was intended for children, the ideology had been reduced to its simplest expression, which made it that much stronger.

The theme of a political freedom acquired at great cost by Canadians has often been treated by francophone writers. How was it covered in the English-language textbooks? A Canadian reader took up the themes of freedom and democracy to explain Canada's astounding growth during the 1840s: "But giving full effect to the influence of these causes [free trade and emigration] which without doubt were the main-spring of Canadian prosperity, it seems, at the same time, not unreasonable to conclude that much also is to be ascribed to the establishment, in 1841, of a form of government essentially democratic, and therefore suited to the circumstances of the country, and calculated to soften down, and at length extinguish, its unhappy rivalry of races."[108] Whether thanks to the magnanimity of the British administration or to the proud battles of the Canadians, beginning in mid-century children were taught about the eminently liberal character of their society. This idea was still present at the turn of the century, as evidenced by the writing of J.N. Miller in 1901: "Le Canada est un des pays les plus libres du monde"(Canada is one of the freest countries in the world).[109] Liberal, democratic freedom therefore represented the "true" freedom, that of progress, commerce, and the future.

Alongside this liberal ideology, also appearing in the educational corpus were the sometimes dangerous freedoms of the Savage and the Nomad. At first, the nomadic way of life of certain societies exerted a fascination, sometimes mixed with admiration, on the textbooks' authors. As François-Xavier Garneau wrote about Canada's Natives in the era of New France, "Un peuple qui n'était point fixé au sol, devait jouir de la plus grande liberté. En effet, chacun vivait dans une indépendance presqu'absolue."[110] (A people that was not rooted in the earth must have enjoyed the greatest degree of freedom. Indeed, each one lived in an almost absolute independence.) The same was true of the Laplanders, who escaped all governmental control. The Patagonians also aroused the textbook writers' curiosity: "Vivant en liberté sur un sol aride et ingrat [ceux-ci ne] montrent [pourtant que] peu de goût pour la civilisation."[111] ("Living in freedom on poor, arid soil," they "[nonetheless] display little appetite for civilization.")

The nomad's freedom had a special, almost romantic aura. In fact, in some ways it recalled the lives of adventurers and explorers, real or fictional characters who were enormously popular in the nineteenth century. The nomadic life, whether that of the "Savage" or the "Adventurer," was also associated with masculinity. A sedentary existence speaks to a people's industrial skills, but it does not offer the model of an independent man who is physically accustomed to life in the great outdoors. In a reading about Champlain's expeditions, children learned that the Hurons of the past, while more industrious than other peoples on the continent, "were more effeminate and had less of the proud independence of savage life."[112] However, it is Toussaint's pen that gives us the masculine savage man in his most resplendent guise:

> Les Gauchos sont d'origine espagnole, et ont embrassé les habitudes de la vie sauvage. [. . .] Infatiguables [*sic*], presque toujours à cheval, occupés de la chasse et de la garde des bœufs et des chevaux, ils vivent continuellement en plein air, et ne construisent de petites huttes que pour abriter leurs femmes et leurs enfants. Ils ont peu de besoin et préfèrent leur vie dure et active, mais indépendante, aux douceurs et aux jouissances de l'état social. Les voyageurs sont toujours reçus par eux avec bienveillance, politesse et désintéressement.[113]

> (The Gauchos are of Spanish origin and have embraced the habits of the savage life. [. . .] Tireless, almost always on horseback, engaged in hunting and herding cattle and horses, they live constantly outdoors, building small huts only to shelter their wives and children. They have little need for shelter and prefer a life that is hard and active but

independent to the pleasures and joys of the social state. To
travellers they are always kind, polite and generous.)

This description of the Gauchos is not devoid of racial logic. Gauchos of
Spanish origin are White, but they have voluntarily adopted the savage
way of life. In this example of masculinity, we find the savage freedom
that accounts for the Gaucho's physical virility combined in a way with
the liberal freedom that allows him to act voluntarily, while also making
him an attentive husband and father.

Undoubtedly, the freedom associated with nomadism heightened
the virile qualities of a people—that is, of the male portion of the
population—but it was also a source of danger. In this regard, the
nomadic freedom as practised by the tribes of the Asian or African
desert mostly symbolized wandering, insubordination, and banditry.
The Arabs, Bedouin, and Berbers were most often cited as examples.
"Adonnés au brigandage" (addicted to banditry), these wandering
nomads "habitant sous la tente" (living in tents) were fierce looters.
Moreover, "these lawless people" had long terrorized Mediterranean
sailors.[114] The danger embodied in the desert tribes' freedom obviously
related to the colonial experience—because they were difficult to subdue,
the tribes were dangerous.

The opposite of freedom is domination, of which one form was
Oriental despotism. As a key theme in the West's representation of the
Orient, despotism was antithetical to the democratic and republican
ideas under discussion in Europe and the United States in the nineteenth century. Like the term "barbaric," references to the despotism of
Asian and African governments were always imbued with a pejorative
moral judgement. Students learned that certain European countries
were absolute monarchies, but it was only while studying Asia that
they were informed about despotism. The despot is a *tyrannical* absolute monarch. John Calkin is one of the few writers who explained
exactly what despotism is: "The countries of Asia are generally badly
governed. The laws are not made by representatives chosen by the people,

as in our own country. The chief ruler, who is often a selfish, ignorant tyrant, makes such laws as please himself. Then he oppresses his people with taxes, and spends the money on his own pleasures rather than in improving the country."[115]

Most often, the only information provided about the types of government in Asia or Africa was that they were "despotic." The term alone was sufficient. In the geography assignment she was given in 1883, Montrealer Oriana Lévac, aged fifteen, was interested mostly in describing elements of the physical geography of these continents. At the very end of the assignment, one line addresses the types of government, which are in Asia "tous monarchiques et abolus" (all monarchist and absolute); specifically, "presque tous les souverains sont despotes" (almost all the sovereigns are despots). Regarding Africa, she wrote that the governments are "presque tous des monarchies absolues, le plus souvent très despotiques" (almost all absolute monarchies, most often very despotic).[116] It is impossible to know what the difference is between governments that are "despotic" and "very despotic," which are also to be found in Toussaint's textbook. For Séraphine Marchand, aged thirteen, a student at the Académie Saint-Joseph in Montreal at the end of the nineteenth century, "les peuples [de l'Asie] sont opprimés par leurs gouvernements, qui sont presque tous despotiques" (the peoples [of Asia] are oppressed by their governments, which are almost all despotic).[117] These assignments reflect multiple descriptions of Asia and Africa contained in the school materials.

Despotism was also associated with the opulence of the Orient's palaces and the cruelty of its monarchs. In the *Fourth Reading Book* of the Royal Canadian Series, a reading describing the then very recent battle of Tel-el-Kébir provided an opportunity to mention Oriental barbarism. If not for the humanity of the English who interceded with the Khedive, the prisoners taken in battle[118] "would probably have been put to death."[119] However, the writer explains, making no moral judgement, it was the English who wanted to put a stop to the rebel Urabi's uprising because they feared for their financial interests in Egypt. This reading provides a good illustration of the double standard: A massacre, if perpetrated to protect commerce, that engine of civilization, was not inhumane. By contrast, the death penalty, when imposed by an African sovereign, was barbaric.

We occasionally come across mentions of English despotism in America, which are to be found in French-language textbooks. The episode of the Acadian deportation or the hangings of the Patriots provoked such commentaries on colonial despotism. Garneau judged it to be an even greater injustice than Oriental despotism: "Le peuple libre qui se met à tyranniser est cent fois plus injuste que le despote absolu, car sa violence se porte pour ainsi dire par chaque individu du peuple opprimant sur chaque individu du peuple opprimé toujours face à face avec lui."[120] (A free people who engage in tyranny are one hundred times more unjust than an absolute despot, since their violence is directed as it were by every individual member of the people doing the oppressing against every individual member of the people being oppressed, always face to face with him.) The freedom gained by a certain people, notably the French Canadians, presents certain imperial powers as illegitimate, because barbaric. In the Canadian case, it is a matter of recognizing—in the past—the fallibility of English civilization and the illegitimacy of its conquest of a White populace. In a text that is still very topical, Thierry Hentsch wrote in 2006 that when the Self discovers the Other who resides in them, they find themselves confronting the nature of their identity: "Taken to the scale of a civilization, in this instance Western civilization, it is a radical incomprehension that surges forward before, for example, the juxtaposition of Nazi extermination camps and Bach's music."[121]

Once in a while, the educational discourse would truly become engaged in pursuing recognition of the barbarian in the Self. For example, certain history books denounced Jacques Cartier's actions during his travels in America: "Il eut cependant tort en s'attribuant le droit d'enlever deux naturels dans le but de les montrer au roi: on ne doit jamais abuser de la force."[122] (However, he erred in assuming the right to abduct two naturals with the intention of showing them to the king: we must never abuse our strength.) But denouncing the conquest of racialized peoples remains a rarity, and when it is mentioned, it is only in denying the Other any ability to take action against the conquest.

Hentsch goes on to write that "we are not deeply civilized enough to admit and confront the existence in us of the barbarian." In the school's display of imperialism's realities and topicality in the nineteenth century, Canadian society exhibited the double standard that is so hard to avoid. As we have seen, domination, when exerted by the Other, is despotic, barbaric.

The Other, as Hentsch has it, "then has to perform the *fonction occulte* of bearing for us, in our place and for our benefit, what we cannot bear to discover in ourselves. *Without our knowing it*, the barbaric Other protects us from our own barbarism. Which can from then on be exerted with impunity against the Other, from the time when it is only a momentary response—attenuated, moderated, civilized—to their response, which is on principle essential, fundamental, radical."[123]

Hentsch's ideas about today's society are mirrored in the history of the nineteenth century. Except for a few unavoidable glitches, Europe's colonial and imperial domination was presented as enlightened, and its legitimacy was based on the racial hierarchy and the civilizing mission. The non-European peoples would all eventually submit to the genius of civilization, like Canada's Indigenous peoples during the time of New France—"dominés par le génie de la civilisation, [ils] craignaient et respectaient partout la puissance française" (dominated by the genius of civilization, [they] everywhere feared and respected French power), and the Persians of the nineteenth century—"La Perse doit prévoir l'époque où le génie européen lui-même commandera à Téhéran" (Persia must foresee a time when European genius will itself rule in Tehran).[124] Racial differentiation was clearly visible. In an English-language textbook, it was written that the Mi'kmaq of Nova Scotia "finally submitted to the whites" in 1761.[125] Using similar terms to describe the conquest of the French Canadians was unthinkable. In this case, as written up by the anglophones, it was rather a battle between two masculine heroes, Montcalm and Wolfe.

The representation of the conquest of New France as a male battle refers to the sexual character of the construction of alterity. Post-colonial studies have effectively shown how the colonial imagination often identified otherness with femininity. Not only does the theme of the peoples' submission to the Europeans reinforce the masculine representation of the West confronting the rest of the world—which is, as a result, feminized—but the storytelling employs a discourse that recalls reports of sexual domination. Summing up the history of India, the Frères des écoles chrétiennes used language that evokes a rape: "La douceur [du] caractère [des peuples des Indes] jointe à un physique peu vigoureux, les ont exposés de tout temps à la domination des étrangers, attirés d'ailleurs par la beauté du climat, etc."[126] (The gentle nature [of the Indian peoples], combined with a physique that is not vigorous, has always exposed them to domination by foreigners who are drawn by the beauty of the climate, etc.) This feminized representation is to be found in many passages that all mentioned, in their way, the enlightened, even benevolent nature of British domination. In its administration of a growing portion of Indian territory, England made the "Native princes" into "d'humbles pensionnaires du gouvernement" (the government's humble boarders). Montpetit and Devisme suggested that while it had the power to govern all of its Indian subjects, "l'Angleterre laisse [cependant] aux populations leurs lois, leur religion et leurs chefs locaux" (England [nonetheless] leaves the populace their laws, religion, and local chiefs).[127] In the early twentieth century, when scientific racism became much more evident in the textbooks, J.N. Miller used it to discuss Great Britain's various possessions. While the settlement colonies were granted autonomy, like young men reaching the age of majority, the colonies populated by the "dark races" were governed by English civil servants. But "as they see that their condition is greatly improved under the British flag, they are loyal and contented." According to Miller, like women, "the Indian people are not fitted for free government like Canadians and Australians."[128]

The representations of freedom and domination transmitted to children in school revealed the power relations on which colonial administrations were founded in the nineteenth century. To be maintained, the hierarchies had to be not only reaffirmed but also complex and nuanced. The benefit was in clearly differentiating the dominated societies, and their subordinate classes and genders, from the dominant White men.

Educational Orientalism

The Orient/Occident opposition is probably the most frequent manifestation of the narrative construction of socio-cultural alterity in Euro-American discourses and representations. It often shows up in Canada's educational corpus, whether in an examination of Oriental despotism, nomadic freedom, or Asian immutability. The Orient is a central image in Europe's definition of its identity, and more broadly that of Western culture, and it appears in the educational discourse as a foundational alterity. The study of the Orientalist discourse at work in educational institutions in the nineteenth century has not yet attracted the attention of the academic community. And yet, can not the taste for "the Orient" of European and American societies in the nineteenth century be explained, at least in part, by the importance of images and discourses transmitted in school?

The school is in fact a preferred domain in which to capture the image of the Orient that was current in Quebec at that time. The Orientalist discourse was present throughout a student's educational career, whether it was that of romantics, geographers, or archaeologists, whether in textbooks, homework, or the student's social activities. Authors included many Orientalist excerpts, themes, and illustrations in their textbooks. And since numerous school textbooks published in Quebec were often adapted copies of French books, the same excerpts concerning the Arab world could be found in them.

From first grade, children were introduced to the Oriental world, contemporary or sacred, principally through the oral teaching of sacred history. In primers or reading guides, teaching the letters "k" and "y" often made use of the word "Kabyle." As for the term "Arab," it served as an example in various spelling lessons. While using an Oriental vocabulary to learn to read and write speaks to the importance of Orientalism, the presence of the "essentials" of the Orientalist corpus in reading textbooks remains the most obvious sign of its hegemony over the imaginary. Excerpts from accounts of travel in the East by François-René Chateaubriand and Alphonse Lamartine, two classics of the genre that also were listed in the *Index of Forbidden Books*, were frequently reproduced in reading textbooks. Other passages, for example, "Le simoun. Récit d'un voyageur" (The simoon. A traveller's tale) or "Frères dans la mort" (Brothers in death), were included without attribution. These travel accounts and an interest in the Mediterranean Orient showed up much more frequently in French-language reading texts. Not surprisingly, the content of English-language textbooks featured more colonial "adventures" in India.

Orientalism, as defined by Edward Said, is not limited to romantic literature. Very broadly, it consists of a colonial and intellectual enterprise of knowledge power over the Orient, and schools embraced this *style de pensée* (style of thought) in its entirety. Aside from the frequent use of travel writing, educational materials also drew upon scholarly Orientalism. The Orient was a territory to be known, and this desire for knowledge shows up in descriptions of the land, industries, resources, Oriental populations, and their clothing. At the same time, this knowledge relied on scientific advances in the fields of ethnography and archaeology and on the expansion of commerce.

Up against this contemporary Orient, despotic and decadent or mysterious and elusive, there existed, anachronistically, an original, sacred Orient with a close link to Christianity. For example, the geography textbooks often contained a chapter on the geography of the Bible, a section that featured a map of Palestine at the time of Christ. Like the travellers in the Orient, the editors of atlases saw no contradiction in the co-existence in their books of the Orient of the Other (contemporary) and the Orient of the Self (sacred). The importance of this identity relationship to the Oriental (Biblical) territory could be parsed in several ways. In addition to their classes of sacred history, many boys from the *collèges* and girls from the convents forged a closer relation to the territory through theatre performances. Excerpts from such plays as *Esther* and *Athalie* were often staged in educational institutions.[129] However imaginary it might have been, students also experienced travelling in the Orient.

To the study of school textbooks we must add the examination of some rare homework assignments by schoolchildren that have come down to us. These archival materials provide a more lifelike account of the children's experience. The discourse on the Orient plays on the same contradictions and mines the same imaginaries and ideologies as the travel accounts and school textbooks. Shortly before the Paris Exhibition of 1900, Marie-Louise Larcher, a student in Class 1 of the Cours Moyen at the convent of the Congrégation de Notre-Dame in Ottawa, wrote a class dictation entitled "Les ruines de Palmyre" (The ruins of Palmyra).[130] The dictation text is an excerpt from the work of Constantin Volney,[131] and is examined by Marie-Louise. "Ce travail est très intéressant. La dictée est analysée de toutes manières" (This work is very interesting. The dictation has been analyzed in every way), the teacher wrote in the margin, a judgement that reading the archive in fact confirms. In the section headed "Developing some passages in the text," Marie-Louise reflects on the excerpt "[Ces lieux solitaires, cette soirée paisible, cette scène majestueuse] imprimèrent à mon esprit un recueillement religieux" ([These lonely places, this peaceful evening, this majestic scene] imprinted on my spirit a religious meditation):

> Dans le recueillement religieux, l'homme se pose le
> problème de sa destinée: d'où vient-il? où va-t-il? Qu'est-ce
> que la gloire, la fortune, la renommée? Fragilité et néant.

On est prêt à s'écrier comme Bélisaire: "Vanités des vanités, tout n'est que vanité." Telles sont, parmi les mille pensées qui naissent en lui, celles qu'il cueille ou choisit; de là le recueillement. Plus loin, l'auteur nous montre les hautes pensées qui naissent à son esprit "à l'aspect d'une grande cité désertes [*sic*]," celles qui résultent de "la *mémoire des temps* passés" et de "la comparaison de l'état présent."

(In his religious meditation, the man addresses the problem of his destiny: where does he come from? where is he going? What is glory, fortune, fame? Frailty and nothingness. One is ready to cry out like Bélisaire: "Vanities of vanities, all is vanity." Such are, among the thousand thoughts that rise up in him, those that he picks and chooses; hence the meditation. Further on, the writer shows us the lofty thoughts that arise in his mind "looking like a great deserted city," thoughts that come from "the memory of times past" and "comparison with the present state.")

The mythic Orient serves as a backdrop for Volney's reflections and those of Marie-Louise. Something they have in common is the fact that they have seen Palmyra only in their imagination. Hentsch writes about Volney: "The site of his meditations was Palmyra—fabulous ruin *par excellence*. The ruins were fabulous, too, in the literal sense of the word. Volney himself had never visited the place, and knew of it only through his readings. The site was both real and imagined—in the image of the mythical Orient."[132]

At about this time, Mila Vanasse, a student in the same class at the Sorel convent, was asked to write a geographical composition about Africa. This assignment allowed her to express her thoughts about Egypt, imperialism, and world fairs. These discourses, as well as the clarity with which she expresses them, are incisive:

L'Égypte est une des plus intéressantes contrées du globe par ses rapports avec l'histoire sacrée et les ruines de ses monuments qui attestent qu'elle a joui d'une civilisation avancée dès les premiers âges du monde. Aujourd'hui désorganisée au dedans et au dehors, elle n'a pour défenseurs que les intérêts anglais.

Pour moi, si j'avais le privilège d'aller visiter l'exposition internationale de Paris, je me rendrais en Égypte pour voir ce coin de terre africaine qui a eu le bonheur de posséder la sainte famille durant sept ans. Je contemplerais aussi avec une vive admiration les pyramides colossales de ce pays. Mais d'elles, comme de toutes les beautés parisiennes, je ne puis me faire une idée qu'à l'aide de ma faible imagination impuissante à satisfaire l'insatiable curiosité de mon esprit.[133]

(Egypt is one of the most interesting regions of the globe for its connections to sacred history and the ruins of its monuments, evidence that it enjoyed an advanced civilization from the world's earliest times. Today disorganized within and without, it has only English interests to come to its defence.

For myself, if I had the privilege of visiting the international exhibition in Paris, I would make my way to Egypt to see this corner of African lands that had the boon of sheltering the holy family for seven years. I would also contemplate with vivid admiration the country's colossal pyramids. But of them, like all the beauties of Paris, I can only form an idea with the help of my feeble imagination, powerless to satisfy my mind's insatiable curiosity.)

The assignments completed by Mila and Marie-Louise attest to the fact that, for them, the Orient was not a trivial territory. Its strong tie to sacred history, as well as the possibility of making it a mirror of modernity, progress, the future—in other words, identity—can be read in their reflection.

In addition to appearing in the texts, Orientalism also showed up in the various cultural events organized by the educational institutions. Some teachers developed dramatic and musical shows that featured the works of European Orientalists, such as Félicien David's ode-symphony *Le désert*. David's piece had met with enormous success in Europe since it was performed in Paris in 1844, and it had similar success in Canada in the nineteenth century. This is confirmed by, among other things, an allusion to it in the obituary of Brother Flamian of the Frères des écoles chrétiennes: "Le Désert de Félicien David, exécuté sous sa direction (1869) dans la salle Saint-Patrice—détruite peu après par un incendie—révéla son talent d'artiste: au dire de M. Barbarin, dont le témoignage était difficile à récuser, ce fut la meilleure à Montréal."[134] (Félicien David's *Le désert*, performed under his direction [1869] in the Saint-Patrice auditorium—destroyed shortly thereafter by fire— revealed his talent as an artist: in the words of M. Barbarin, whose report was hard to gainsay, it was the best in Montreal.) In 1861, the *Journal de l'instruction publique* mentioned that "les amateurs de cette ville [Montréal?] ont exécuté, au profit de l'Asile des Orphelins [. . .] *le Désert*, de Félicien David" (the amateurs of the city [Montreal?] performed, for the benefit of the Asile des Orphelins, Félicien David's *Le désert*).[135] In January 1875, the work was again performed in Montreal, this time "par le Chœur et l'orchestre du Gesù avec le précieux concours des élèves du collège" (by the Choir and orchestra of the Gesù with the invaluable collaboration of the students from the Collège) Sainte-Marie de Montréal. The archives reveal that "ce chef-d'œuvre [est] donné, pour la première fois, en costume. Une scène égyptienne nouvelle—avec décorations et accessoires spéciaux—a été commandée pour la circonstance."[136] (This masterpiece is, for the first time, being performed in costume. A new Egyptian set—with special decorations and props—has been ordered for the occasion.)

Twenty years later, on the afternoon of 30 April 1895, the ode was once again heard in the city by a select audience at Mont-Saint-Louis, a *collège*, or secondary school for boys, run by the Frères des écoles chrétiennes.[137] This dramatic and musical event was presided over by the Archbishop of Saint-Boniface, Mgr A. Langevin, and was completely Oriental—David's *Le désert* resounded between acts of the drama *L'enfant prodigue* (The prodigal son). What did Mgr Langevin think of the performance by the students of the "Chant du muezzin" (Muezzin's song)? We can suppose that he appreciated the event's Oriental theme since, when he returned to the same institution in 1901, the students again presented a program with an Oriental theme. These two shows exemplify the schools' Orientalist universe: they combine the Sacred Orient and the Imperial or Romantic Orient. They also mark the presence of this theme in nineteenth-century student theatre—for boys and girls. The Orient was often reproduced in the main auditorium of certain convents and *collèges*. Several French-Canadian children disguised themselves, for a few hours, as Orientals. *La malédiction* (The curse), *Fort comme un Turc* (Strong as a Turk), *Séance historique (Un épisode de la vie de Saladin)* (History play [An episode from the life of Saladin]), *Une page d'histoire de France (Guerre d'Algérie)* (A page from French history [The war in Algeria]), and *Dimitri* were some of the plays that staged the history of East meeting West.

Studying the exploitation of the Orientalist theme in school reveals and sharpens the figure of the Arab as a foundational figure of the Other. Notably, it is through language instruction—for example, in dictations and readings—that we can see the image of the Arab emerging. The Arab's relations with his horse and the desert, along with his legendary cunning, are some of the *topoï* that created the narrative universe in which this figure took on meaning.

The connection between the Arab and his horse was a recurring theme in educational literature. In a composition textbook, the Frères maristes asked students to complete the following sentence: "Le cheval de l'arabe est son meilleur . . ." (The Arab's horse is his best . . .).[138] In an exercise on synonyms for "horse—steed—nag," the journal *L'Enseignement primaire* wrote: "L'Arabe est souvent plus attaché à son fidèle coursier qu'à sa propre famille."[139] (The Arab is often more attached to his faithful steed than to his own family.) The friendship described in these quotations was dramatized in a legend recounted by Lamartine in his *Voyage en Orient* and repeated several times in the teaching materials. The French-Canadian students who had not read, or written, the story "L'Arabe et son cheval" (The Arab and his horse) must have been few in number, since as well as having appeared in numerous reading textbooks, the legend was proposed as a dictation subject in pedagogical journals or as the framework for writing in composition textbooks.

In this legend, an Arab nomad, taken prisoner by the Turks, finds his faithful friend in the middle of the night:

> Il reconnut sa voix, et ne pouvant résister au désir d'aller parler encore une fois au compagnon de sa vie, il se traîna péniblement sur la terre, à l'aide de ses mains et ses genoux, et parvint jusqu'à son coursier. "Pauvre ami [. . .] qu'au moins, si je suis esclave, tu restes libre! Tiens, va, retourne à la tente que tu connais, va dire à ma femme qu'Abou-el-Marsch ne reviendra plus, et passe la tête entre les rideaux de la tente pour lécher la main de mes petits enfants."[140]

> (He recognized his voice, and being unable to resist the desire to go and speak one more time to his life's companion, he dragged himself painfully across the ground, using his hands and knees, and drew up close to his steed. "My poor friend [. . .] at least, if I am a slave, you remain free! Here, go, return to the tent you know, go and tell my wife that Abou-el-Marsch will return no more, and put

your head between the tent's curtains to lick the hands of
my little children.")

As he speaks, the Arab sets the horse free, who then takes him by
the belt and carries him all the way to his tent in the desert before
dying of exhaustion. The association of the Other with animality,
whether through a relationship of fusion, as in this instance, or through
comparison between the human and the animal, is a familiar feature
of the rhetoric of alterity. What the legend also refers to is the very
special rapport that unites the Arab with the environment in which he
lives, the desert. It is very often in the desert that the Arab of readings
and dictations glides about. And so lessons were developed to render
"L'Arabe affamé" (The starving Arab) in the plural, or "Les Arabes
nomades" (Nomadic Arabs) in dictation. In its description of "l'Arabe
pur sang" (The thoroughbred Arab), the following dictation conveys
a perfect communion between the desert environment and the Arab's
physical constitution:

> Le grand air, la poussière, le soleil tannent la peau et lui
> donnent cette belle teinte bronzée qui se marie si bien
> au dessin énergique du visage. C'est surtout parmi les
> nomades que ce type se retrouve dans toute sa beauté:
> on voit réellement un magnifique spécimen de l'espèce
> quand un homme de grande tente apparaît drapé dans ses
> bournous.[141]

> (The fresh air, the dust and the sun tan his skin and give
> him the beautiful bronze tint that matches the energetic
> modelling of his face so well. It is mainly among the
> nomads that this type is to be found in all its beauty—we
> can really see a magnificent specimen of the species when a
> man from a noble clan appears, draped in his burnous.)

The Arab lives free in a natural environment that is sometimes hostile but with which he is in harmony.

The effeminate Oriental is a well-known manifestation of the Orientalist discourse. And yet, as it was conveyed by the educational institutions, the Arab's representation granted him attributes that are rather masculine, not so different from those we recognize in the European adventurer. Again and again, the readings, dictations, and geographical descriptions regarding Arabs provided an opportunity to mention their courage and describe their skill in handling horses and rifles. The Arabs are clever and cunning in hunting ostriches. Moreover, they are courageous in battle, as Guy de Maupassant remarks in an excerpt used by the nuns of the Congrégation de Notre-Dame for dictation exercises in their classrooms.[142] One such dictation on "La Fantasia" describes the Gunpowder Games organized by the Arabs in someone's honour. "Il faut que celui à qui les Arabes rendent cet honneur paraisse y prendre plaisir; sinon, il passe pour ne pas aimer la poudre, les émotions qu'elle donne, et cela est pris en mauvaise part."[143] (The person thus honoured by the Arabs must appear to be pleased; if not, it is assumed that he does not like the gunpowder and the emotions it arouses, and that is viewed with resentment.) The Arabs are thus skilful in handling—and discharging!—a rifle, and this agility is yet another reflection of their masculinity, even their idea of masculinity.

The large number of school texts depicting the Arab give rise to an archetype. The Arab enlisted by educational culture is a wise, loyal, virile man. This image agreed with the pedagogical intention behind the schools' utilization of the Orient, which was to elevate the students' morality through the example of the Other. The educational materials of the nineteenth century abounded with tales, legends, and moral reflections to teach children various kinds of virtues, both individual and social. In addition to European tales, the textbooks presented different moral vignettes in which the action takes place in the Orient. The origins of these stories were rarely identified. Were they authentic products of Arabic mythological culture? Through whose mediation did they become part of francophone and anglophone cultures? The study of these textbooks leaves these questions unresolved. What is more interesting to know, for my purposes, is how these legends exploited the theme of Oriental wisdom, with the Orient then appearing as a moral model.

The Oriental stories presented different characters: the just Algerian qadi, the little patriotic Arab boy, the offended dervish, the loyal servant, the pious mullah, the generous brother, and so on. Including this "Arab" or "Oriental" wisdom in the pedagogical literature spoke to a closeness between Arab and European cultures. It also illustrated a strong, distinct, respectable identity that was recognized in peoples of the Mediterranean Orient, the Arabs and Persians. These stories drew up a list of values considered important by Orientals: hospitality, generosity, modesty, wise justice, patriotism, mercy. These values were not opposed to those upheld in Canadian culture, and this is exactly why the writers included Oriental tales in the school textbooks. But this community of values did nothing to reduce the distance between the West and the East. Indeed, recognizing the richness of Oriental civilization could not nullify the fact that these excerpts reinforced the fundamentally "other" nature of the Orient. Taking as an example the fable "The Sagacious Cadi," we can see that while it reiterates several Orientalist clichés, the story of Sheik Bou-Akas and the astute qadi provides an interesting lesson in the fair administration of justice. The story was first published in the English-language magazine *Household Words* and then reprinted in American and Canadian reading textbooks, both Catholic and Protestant, throughout the latter half of the nineteenth century. The lesson in justice it depicts takes place in a setting that is completely Oriental: the sheik reigns despotically over twelve tribes and rides a docile Arabian horse, the woman is presented as the man's possession, and many Oriental customs are described.

As a figure of the foundational Other in the Euro-American imaginary, the Orient appeared in multiple forms in Canada's school discourse. It accompanied students in their dictations, the stories they were told, images they were shown, geography lessons they received, theatre scenes they were asked to perform, and compositions they wrote. As a powerful lever for the narrative identity of European cultures,[144] Orientalism penetrated all facets of the educational discourse in the nineteenth century. The multiplicity of the allusions and the various meanings they conveyed faithfully reflect the construction of alterity in school.

In a century in which education was essential to being able to call oneself "civilized," learning about the political, social, and racial hierarchies was necessary to position oneself on those scales. Because learning about the inferiority of the Other was central to colonial control, the school disseminated an ideology that played with double standards and the attributes of masculinity and femininity. Linguistic and ideological practices were elaborated so as to define "alterity" rhetorically. And yet one piece of the picture was missing, and not the least of them. While the Others were distinguished by their different social conventions and attributes, they appeared first through the exhibition of their body, from the moment it differed from the body of the person watching them.

3.

The Other-Body, or Alterity Inscribed in the Flesh

In the geography newsletter it published in October 1892, the magazine *L'Enseignement primaire* described the Arabs of Arabia as beings that were "énergiques, spirituels, ardents et rêveurs à la fois" (at once energetic, spiritual, passionate and dreamers). A few weeks later, the teaching journal took its readers to Dahomey. To describe that African country's inhabitants, the author used other qualifiers: "Les nègres qui forment la population du Dahomey sont de petite taille, mais robustes, bien découplés, infatigables marcheurs et d'une agilité surprenante."[1] (The Negroes who make up Dahomey's population are short in stature but strong, well-proportioned, tireless walkers, and surprisingly agile.) While the Arabs appear to be men of the spirit, the Blacks of Dahomey are only bodies—robust, tireless, agile bodies. Over the nineteenth century, the conception, meaning, and rationalization of the human body evolved considerably. The body, whether of women, workers, children, or Indigenous people, was studied, exhibited, and disciplined by European

society's academics, artists, and public administrators. The sight of someone's body was vested with the capacity to judge that person's identity. By
the colour of the skin and the ornamentation or clothing that covered
it, the body made it possible to perceive and name the otherness.

The racialized body held an important place in the rhetorical
construction of alterity in the school. Heavily influenced by evolving
scientific theories about race, the school curriculum made sure to
introduce children to "knowledges" based on reducing human beings
to their body. As David Le Breton puts it so well, "The body of a
stranger becomes the strange body. The presence of the Other is reduced
to morphological clues that define it racially. They are their body and
their anatomy is their destiny because, owing to its conformation, it
simultaneously encloses a particular morality, a type of beauty and
an intelligence that are a direct function of indicators that have been
expertly measured."[2] While the schoolchild's body must be disciplined
and bridled for the sake of rational thinking, the racialized body is fully
described and shown to the children. The Other's representation and
the Self's experience are thus linked together, participating in a power
relation based on the domination of bodies.

"Avez-vous déjà vu des nègres?" (Have you ever seen any Negroes?),
teacher J.N. Miller asked his young readers in 1901.[3] Inserted into a
geography textbook, this sentence signals both a major pedagogical
change and the impact of sight, the fact of "seeing," in gaining awareness
of Other-bodies. Throughout the nineteenth century, the presentation
of the various races in school was very simple, often limited to a brief
listing. By directly addressing the children and varying the general attributes of each race, Miller was trying out a new didactic teaching strategy
for geography. The value granted to sight is particularly important in
Western culture. The domination, segregation, and even the genocide of
entire peoples by European societies relied on the visuality of difference
inscribed in the bodies of those to be dominated. Le Breton maintains
that the importance of sight in these racist ideologies was taken to an
extreme during the Holocaust: "The yellow star worn where passersby

could see it pushed the logic to its limit; since obvious corporal signs were not available to the racist to single out members of the population, a clearly visible external marker served the purpose."[4]

As for the children, the educational institution trained them in the ability to recognize the Other by sight alone. From detailed descriptions of bodies to changes in the racial typology, the rule of sight and the system of racial thinking permeated all educational materials. Whether beautiful or hideous, the body of the Other is polysemic, and an examination of the racial conceptions being transmitted clearly shows that. Teaching this taxonomy also set up a hierarchy of the races and an essentialization of human groups that are deeply connected to Canada's colonial and genocidal political project.

Strange Bodies and Visuality

Photography, city streetlights, the illustrated press, eyewear—many of the West's technological innovations in the nineteenth century were part of the history of seeing. The faculties of observation and perception therefore became favoured. The development of sight's ascendancy and how that played out in inspecting bodies set up a range of power relations. One of them manifested itself in the exhibition and study of "human races." In his book *Time and the Other*, anthropologist Johannes Fabian analyzes anthropology's complex relation to visuality. Based on observation, "early ethnological practices established seldom articulated but firm convictions that presentations of knowledge through visual and spatial images [...] are particularly well suited to the description of primitive cultures which, as everyone knows, are supremely 'synchronic' objects for visual-esthetic perception."[5] Together with the development of these ethnological practices, the growing number of exhibitions of all types in the latter half of the nineteenth century promoted the "visual" study of Others' bodies.

Racialized bodies were exhibited, studied, measured, photographed, circulated, and made alien through performance at these popular events.

Far from being impervious to this particular context, the school reproduced these visual representations of exoticism while ensuring their persistence. Moreover, the appearance of images of Other bodies in educational materials coincided with the era of large exhibitions and other ethnological fairs. Integrated into the textbooks, human diversity as taught through the monstration of Other bodies, an already reductive experience, was simplified and stereotyped to an even greater degree. The visual stereotypes were created through reproduction and longevity, and the school thus contributed greatly to the unchanging morphology in visual representations of "human types."

The school participated in the methodical monstration of the Other's body and the related knowledge regime. In the case of exhibitions, the monstration was motivated by commercial considerations, since exhibiting the "savages" attracted the public. In the educational institution, it was a pedagogical view that justified using the presentation of the racialized body, since alterity would stimulate the students' interest. Beginning in the nineteenth century, observation was considered to be a child's natural faculty, and along with its role in teaching, observation was discussed with increasing frequency. In its issue of September 1857, the *Journal of Education* reprinted an article from the English periodical *Papers for the Schoolmaster* on teaching grammar, with observation among young children as its subject: "The faculty of *observation* is the earliest in the order of development, and such subjects of instruction as excite and direct the power of observation should be the first to which the attention of children should be introduced. On this account, *object lessons on natural history* may be given to infants even before the power of reading is attained. On this account also *geography* should be taught before *arithmetic* and *grammar*."[6]

Primary school relied heavily on the children's capacity for observation and perception, and studying Other bodies held pride of place among the school subjects that appealed directly to sight. In a reading entitled "Une tribu des Îles de Mingan" (A tribe from the Mingan archipelago), the importance given to seeing the Other-body is evident:

Mais ce qui nous frappa surtout à première vue, ce fut un campement de 500 sauvages, venus de 100 à 300 lieues de distance, pour assister à la mission. [. . .] Ces feux de bivouac allumés çà et là et autour desquels se tenaient pittoresquement groupés des sauvages de tout âge, avec leurs figures cuivrées et leurs costumes variés [. . .] le tout formait un tableau d'une originalité toute locale, qu'il ne nous sera peut-être jamais donné de contempler encore.[7]

(But what struck us most at first sight was an encampment of 500 savages who had come from 100 to 300 leagues away, to attend the mission. [. . .] The campfires alight here and there, around which groups of savages of all ages were picturesquely arranged, with their bronzed faces and varied costumes [. . .] it all made up a picture of an originality completely of the place, which we will perhaps never have the chance to contemplate again.)

We should also keep in mind the lesson in national history published in *L'Enseignement primaire* in which the teacher asked, "Jean-Charles, n'avez vous jamais vu des sauvages?" (Jean-Charles, have you never seen any savages?) or the sentence from Miller's geography: "Avez-vous déjà vu des nègres?" which, in the English-language version of his text-book, became "Have you ever seen any negroes? Chinamen? Indians?" Similarly, a composition textbook asked the children to build on the following premise: "Claudius parle à son ami de la foire de X. . . . Il a vu des saltimbanques, des lions, des tigres, un nègre, etc."[8] (Claudius is talking to his friend about the fair at X. . . . He saw acrobats, lions, tigers, a Negro, etc.) Whether the children answered in the affirmative to these questions or they had in fact seen these Afro-descendants at the fair was in the end of no importance. In the exercise described, what counted for the student was the power to "imagine" these scenes, be it a family picnic or meeting a Black person. In that regard, owing to the knowledge they had received at school, students were ready to form a mental picture of these "characters," Black, Chinese, or Indigenous. Seeing the Other meant first seeing their body as different. Just as a depiction of their way of life would indicate the presence of an Other people, the body's description would signal otherness. On this point, it is to be noted that the White man's body was almost never described. Only occasionally in the history textbooks did physical details accompany the presentation of a prominent individual. In this way the disciplinary division previously mentioned was again confirmed—history belongs to the White race; ethnography, to the other races. Aside from a few very popular "savage" peoples, what most fascinated the textbook authors was the physical appearance of the inhabitants of Oceania. Beginning in the 1830s, Father Jean Holmes offered precise, detailed information about their bodies. While the region's Malays had an "olive or swarthy" complexion, the Oceanic Negroes "se distinguent par une couleur noire ou brune noirâtre, par l'angle facial très obtus, le nez épaté, les lèvres épaisses, les cheveux crépus sans être laineux, et par une longueur démesurée des bras, des jambes et des cuisses, qui sont en même temps excessivement grêles" (are distinguished by a black or brownish-black colour, very blunt facial angles, flat noses, thick lips, hair that is kinky without being woolly, and the disproportionate length of their arms, legs and thighs, which are at the same time extremely spindly).[9] Further along, the reader would learn that "au sud de Palembang vivent des nègres qui ont la tête extraordinairement grosse, avec une taille, des jambes et des bras de pygmées" (south of Palembang live Negroes who have extraordinarily big heads, with the height, legs and arms of pygmies).

Until the 1880s, most school geographies included a reference to the physical appearance of the inhabitants of Oceania. In 1877, the Frères des écoles chrétiennes wrote: "The Malays are robust; they are low in stature, and have small, black eyes, short noses, long, black hair, and square chins. The Papuan race, or negroes of Oceania, are distinguished by large lips or woolly hair; they are of diminutive size, seldom exceeding five feet."[10] Several years later, George John Hodgins also described the "aboriginals" of Australia by emphasizing their small stature, thin, puny bodies, skin the colour of copper or soot, flat noses, protruding lips, prominent brow ridge, and curly hair.[11] This fascination with the peoples of Oceania related directly to the popularity of the Europeans' exploration accounts of the eighteenth and nineteenth centuries. Students were very familiar with the voyages of Jules Dumont d'Urville, Louis-Antoine de Bougainville, and James Cook, whose routes they traced on geographical maps.

John Calkin bridged two ways of presenting the Indigenous peoples of Oceania by combining the physical description in the textbooks of the mid-nineteenth century with the idea of a dying race propagated by writers who published at the turn of the next century. After having specified that Australia's "degraded savages" were Black but did not have the flat noses, thick lips, or woolly hair of the African Negroes, he added, "The race is rapidly dying out."[12] Calkin's statements provide a good illustration of how the representation of these peoples in the educational materials had evolved. The fascination for the Other-body of the Oceanic peoples loses its power at the turn of the twentieth century. Although anthropology maintained an interest in these so-called savage populations, Canadian geography textbooks ceased to pay them any particular attention. The few remarks about them still to be found by the turn of the century were more concerned with the ideology of the civilizing mission and the race's extinction than a fascination with difference. And so in 1901, J.N. Miller wrote: "La population indigène de l'Australie, sorte de nègres misérables, est réfractaire à la civilisation et disparaît rapidement."[13] (Australia's indigenous population, a miserable sort of Negroes, is resistant to civilization and rapidly disappearing.) A few years earlier, the Sœurs de la congrégation de Notre-Dame stated that these Australian tribes "placé[e]s au dernier échelon des races humaines [. . .] sont entièrement disparu[e]s" (placed on the very last rung of the human races [. . .] have completely disappeared).[14] The fact that the textbook authors were writing that they were almost extinct provides one reason for the loss of fascination. It can also be explained by a reduction by then in the unknown and in the mysterious elements that had for so long been associated with the faraway regions of Oceania.

Even if the schoolchildren's textbooks or assignments also made occasional reference to the physical attributes of the Chinese, Hindus, or young girls from the Egyptian countryside, references to the Indigenous populations of North America were the most often accompanied by comments about their bodies. In the colourful style that enlivened his textbook, Toussaint wrote the following about the Saguenay region of Quebec: "Jetez-vous dans un léger canot d'écorce, dirigé par deux robustes Montagnais, et parcourez rapidement dans toute sa longueur les eaux limpides du lac St. Jean."[15] (Throw yourself into a light birchbark canoe, piloted by two robust Montagnais, and move rapidly across the entire expanse of Lac St. Jean's limpid waters.) For their part, after having mentioned America's White and Black populations in no greater detail, the Frères des écoles chrétiennes offered a precise portrait of the Indian tribes: they are "beardless, of a copper-color, and have black, straight, and coarse hair."[16] In a more romantic style, the pupils of the Sœurs de la congrégation de Notre-Dame read this description of the Iroquois taken from a text by Father Brasseur de Bourbourg: "Ils étaient grands, d'une taille avantageuse; les traits de leur visage étaient réguliers; ils avaient le nez aquilin, et rarement on en vit qui fussent affligés de quelque difformité. Leur regard était farouche, leur port rustique."[17] (They were tall, of an imposing height; their facial features were regular; they had aquiline noses, and rarely did we see any who were afflicted with a deformity. Their gaze was fierce, their bearing rough.)

An excerpt from Montesquieu's *Lettres persanes* appearing in a popular Québécois reading textbook explains the critical role of physical appearance in recognizing the stranger:

Je souriais quelquefois des gens qui n'étaient presque jamais sortis de leur chambre, et qui disaient entre eux: Il faut avouer qu'il a l'air bien Persan. [. . .] Cela me fit résoudre à quitter l'habit persan, et à en endosser un à l'européenne:

pour voir s'il resterait encore dans ma physionomie quelque
chose d'admirable. Cet essai me fit connaître ce que je
valais réellement. Libre de tous les ornements étrangers,
je me vis apprécié au plus juste. J'eus sujet de me plaindre
de mon tailleur, qui m'avait fait perdre en un instant
l'attention et l'estime publiques, car j'entrai tout à coup
dans un néant affreux. [. . .] Montesquieu.[18]

(I sometimes smiled at people who had almost never left
their room, and who said to each other: I have to admit
that he really does look Persian. [. . .] That decided me
to stop wearing Persian clothing, and to dress like a
European: to see whether anything admirable would be left
in my physiognomy. This attempt let me know what I was
really worth. Freed from all those foreign ornaments, I saw
that I was very justly assessed. I had reason to complain of
my tailor, who in an instant had cost me public attention
and esteem, because I suddenly found myself in a dreadful
void. [. . .] Montesquieu.)

Before illustrations and photographs were included in school textbooks,
the supposed physical attributes of certain peoples were described in
great detail. Moreover, recognition of a society's alterity also operated
through its cultural practices regarding clothing and adornments.
Tattoos and other aesthetic modifications, nudity, and so-called strange
dress codes were mentioned to excite the reader's fascination.

Taking his readers to Asia, Miller explains that the inhabitants of
the region "dress in strange fashions."[19] In the educational materials,
the apparent difference in Orientals resides mainly in their clothing.
Already in the mid-nineteenth century, a teacher from Quebec's Eastern
Townships wrote this detail about the Turks in his notebook: "Men &
women dress alike."[20] This type of ethnographic detail, to which must
be added the Turks' polygamy and consumption of opium, was not to

be found in descriptions from British India, Australia, or Europe in the
same notebook. Two images contained in textbooks from the end of
the century also recalled stereotypes associated with the Turks' sarto-
rial appearance. The description accompanying one of them (Figure 1)
reads: "There is a funny looking man, who looks like a Turk in-deed!"
and once again refers to seeing in the recognition of the Other. The
text accompanying the second (Figure 2) is more precise, describing
the Turks' way of dressing in detail: "Both men and women wear long
flowing dresses, with a belt around the waist. The men wind a long scarf,
called a turban, about their heads; and the women wear a thick white
veil over their faces when they go out,"[21] wrote Calkin. The dress codes
of other Oriental peoples, such as the Persians and Arabs, were also
occasionally highlighted in the materials.

In 1857, one month after its English-language counterpart had
printed an article on the Revolt of the Sepoys, the *Journal de l'instruction
publique* followed suit. Picking up an excerpt from the book by Eugène
de Valbezen entitled *Les Anglais et l'Inde*, the *Journal*'s writers took aim
at the Sepoys' apparent civilization: "L'Angleterre avait à peine réussi à
civiliser extérieurement ces hommes, qui, au fonds [*sic*], n'avaient guères
[*sic*] changé." (England had only just succeeded in externally civilizing
these men, who at bottom had scarcely changed.) Following that introduction, the excerpt from De Valbezen's book gives a detailed picture
of the Sepoys' bodies: "En somme, la tenue extérieure du cipaye laisse
bien peu de chose à désirer: mais il lui manque, on le devine au premier
coup d'oeil, le sentiment de dignité de l'habit qu'il porte." (To sum up,
the Sepoy's external dress leaves very little to be desired: but as can
be guessed at first sight, he lacks the feeling of dignity of the military
dress he wears.) The clothing is a poor disguise; "at first sight," the
Sepoy's attitude betrays him. Otherwise, taken on a tour of an infantry
company's camp by the writer, the reader found the Sepoy "revêtu [du]
costume indien dans toute sa simplicité" (clad in Indian dress in all its
simplicity). Then, describing the soldiers' physical aspect, De Valbezen
mentions the "savages'" semi-nudity, their fantastic hair arrangements,

LESSON VII.

_____

rk *and* rp, *final, with digrams in* a, e, i, o, u.

New words. | la rk   ba rk   fo rk   ca rp

Figure 1. Untitled, Anonymous, *First Reader: Part II*, W.J. Gage, 1884, 23.

scarring, and jewellery.[22] This description provides a good example of practices for dressing and adorning the body that, in the educational discourse, are included to signal contempt or fascination, and sometimes both at once, for a distant or "primitive" people.

Among the people called "savages," whose partial or total nudity was mentioned as a (non)clothing of the body, aesthetic modifications, such as tattoos, inserts, or hairdressing, seemed to be worthy of note. The people to whom such aesthetic corporal practices were attributed were the same as those whose body was described in detail, the Pacific Islanders and North America's Indigenous populations. The descriptions of these cultural practices were sometimes supplemented with ethnographic illustrations, such as "Head-dresses of the Natives of New Guinea" or "A Tatooed [*sic*] New-Zealand [*sic*] Chief."[23] The textbook

Figure 2. "A Turk," Calkin,
*Calkin's New Introductory
Geography*, 1898, 62.

by Father Holmes is the most forthcoming on this subject. Until late in the century, the oldest of the boys and girls in *collèges* and convents learned, among other things, that the Papuans would "ramassent les cheveux sur leur tête en touffes qui ont jusqu'à 3 pieds de tour" (gather their hair on their head in clumps that measure as much as 3 feet around), the Indigenous peoples of New South Wales "se colorant la figure en blanc ou en rouge" (coloured their face white or red), the inhabitants of Espiritu Santo in the Vanuatu Archipelago inserted a wooden dowel four to six inches long into the end of their nose, and in the Sandwich Islands, "les femmes se tatouent le bout de la langue" (women tattoo the tip of their tongue).[24] In books by Hodgins and by the Frères des écoles chrétiennes, it was mainly the Maori's tattoos that caught their attention.

Alluding to traditions of dress and adornment signals an alterity unveiled by observation of the body. Other peoples were treated to an interest that went beyond these simple allusions and was generated by a mythification that was also constructed on the idea of a different body.

A Voyage to the Ends of the Earth, Encounters at the Limits of Humanity

European philosophical reflection on human diversity was strongly shaken, beginning in the sixteenth century, by the rise of ocean voyages of exploration. The peoples encountered at the ends of the Earth, such as the Hottentots (Khoikhoi), the Patagonians (Tehuelches), Laplanders (Sámi), or the Eskimos (Inuit), would influence the European definition of humanity for many centuries. In the nineteenth century, as Jacqueline Duvernay-Bolens states, this "mythology of extremes that travels across the centuries and societies, and that could be considered a shared universal,"[25] gradually comes to be questioned. Studying the educational corpus of this period makes it possible to assess what remained constant and what evolved in the dissemination of this "mythology of extremes." While these "strange" people still exerted a considerable fascination in the first half of the century, they would gradually be abandoned in favour of a racial taxonomy.

Mythical peoples whose representation would become almost mundane in the eighteenth century, the Patagonians and Hottentots inhabited southern extremities of the continents the Europeans had to go around in order to reach Asia. In a metaphor of their geographical position, François-Xavier Fauvelle-Aymar writes, these peoples "offered the greatest variation relative to the norm, that of the medial peoples, namely Europeans."[26] In an analysis of the dissemination of European discourses regarding the Khoikhoi in the seventeenth century, Fauvelle-Aymar adds: "Conforming to this 'spatialization of knowledge,' the description of the [Hottentots] was for its part organized into a genuine 'full-length portrait' that took in all aspects of physique, clothing and adornment. It is a narration that progressively takes on moral considerations and 'ethnological' elements no longer involving the body as a vector to model clothing and adornments for an audience, but as an actor who eats, makes things, and talks."[27]

Father Holmes, who wrote his textbook in the first half of the nineteenth century, is the only Canadian author of geography texts truly to take part in this tradition. After having mentioned the enormous difference between the Kaffirs and the Hottentots, a *topos* that was repeated in other textbooks, Holmes went into lengthy detail on the latter's body. Altogether, the description is not contemptuous and at one point even seems positive: Holmes described them as being "droits, bien faits, et d'une grande taille" (straight, well-built, and tall). Like many writers who came after him, he then dwelt on a "branch" of the Hottentot race "qu'on nomme Boshimiens ou Saabs" (that we call Boshimians or Saabs). This time around, fascination cedes to disgust, and there is no lack of detail in depicting the life of populations who have been "réduite[s] à un état de dégradation au-dessous duquel on ne conçoit guère que la nature humaine puisse descendre" (reduced to a state of degradation below which we can scarcely conceive that human nature could sink).[28] With "les plus difformes et les plus barbares des

Hottentots" (the most deformed and most barbaric of the Hottentots), about whom "on dit que la vue du sang et l'odeur des cadavres leur procurent des sensations agréables" (it is said that the sight of blood and the smell of dead bodies give them pleasurable sensations), the limits of humanity have been reached.

The long, 350-word description that Holmes offered in his text-book comes from the "common fonds of automatic references, identical images, ready-made expressions and analogies,"[29] according to Fauvelle-Aymar, engendered by the accounts of seventeenth- and eighteenth-century voyages. From that moment on, the figure of the Hottentot was trivialized and alternately took on the features of the good savage and the (almost) inhuman monster. This binary representation could even be found in the educational discourse. While most writers presented the Hottentots as "*sales*" (dirty), "*hideux*" (hideous), "filthy," or "degraded," Toussaint used the figure of the good savage instead. While they might be lazy and dirty, Toussaint wrote, he praised the Hottentots' cool heads and thoughtful bearing, as distinct from the other "nations noires ou basanées" (Black or swarthy nations), in addition to specifying that they were "doux, humains et susceptibles d'un grand attachement pour leur semblables" (gentle, humane, and capable of great attachment to their kind).[30] The Hottentots' descriptions had a presence in the literature until the last decades of the nineteenth century. But after 1891, the Sœurs de la congrégation de Notre-Dame made only one allusion, which speaks more to the nineteenth century's racial taxonomies than to the mythical figure of the previous centuries.[31] Finally, the textbooks published in the first decade of the twentieth century no longer mentioned them.

Like the Hottentot, the "giant" Patagonian was a mythical figure that for a long time fuelled the scientific debates about human diversity. Duvernay-Bolens states: "Compared to the accounts of voyages, the learned arguments in different fields of knowledge controlled by geographers, theologians and naturalists only added up to variations on the Patagonian corpus that can be contained in a clearly defined chronological bracket extending from the 16th to the beginning of the

19th century."[32] It was a sign of the power the myth had acquired that it would take an entire century for the giant Patagonian to disappear from the educational discourse. The first geography textbook written and printed in Quebec was released in 1804. The very succinct text contains not a single ethnographic detail. The only people mentioned in the abstract were the Patagonians, Eskimos, and "plusieurs peuples Sauvages" (several Savage peoples)[33] in Louisiana. Thus the Patagonian saga made its discreet entry into Canadian school textbooks. Thirty years later, a detailed report flowed from the pen of Father Holmes, and a long ethnographic account was devoted to describing this fascinating population, including details on height, facial features, character, clothes, hairdressing, weapons, and even women. While nothing in his description of the Hottentots and Boshimians suggested why he should spend so much time on those people, the Patagonians were a different case. Father Holmes in fact wrote: "Les premiers voyageurs avaient représenté les Patagons comme des géans; mais d'aprés des rapports plus fidèles, il paraît certain que leur hauteur commune n'est que de 6 à 7 pieds."[34] (The first voyagers had represented the Patagonians as giants; but according to more faithful reports, it seems certain that their usual height was only 6 to 7 feet.) The myth is simultaneously recognized and refuted.

"Les Patagons sont d'une taille très élevée, quoiqu'on l'ait exagérée dans les premières descriptions qu'on en a données" (The Patagonians are very tall, although this was exaggerated in the first descriptions we were given of them); "Ils sont de taille assez élevée, mais non pas gigantesque comme on l'a cru longtemps" (They are rather tall but not gigantic, as has long been believed); "Les habitants sont des Indiens Pantagons [sic], ou Téhueltches et Peuliches, remarquables par leur force, leur grande taille, que l'on a toutefois exagérée" (The inhabitants are Pantagonian [sic] Indians, or Tehueltches and Peuliches, remarkable for their strength and their great height, which has nevertheless been exaggerated); "though not giants, as was said of old, they are yet tall of stature": within a single decade (1868 to 1877), the writers of four textbooks considered it necessary to remind readers of the myth's inaccuracy.

Figure 3. "Patagonians," *Lovell's Advanced Geography*, 1880, 73.

Had the Patagonians' role in reflections on human nature then come to
an end? Not yet. The importance of the ethnographic details concerning
them and the familiar tone in which they were described signified that
still, in the 1870s, they embodied a radical and essential form of alterity.
As Jacqueline Duvernay-Bolens writes, "By lending their tall silhouette
to servicing beliefs that since the Greeks and throughout the entire
Middle Ages had circulated about the peoples of the Antipodes, [the
Patagonians] had contributed, in the spirit of the navigators, to moving
the borders of alterity."[35]

In the textbook he published with Lovell in 1867, Hodgins did
not inform his readers about the Patagonians and they did not appear
in the illustrations. Surprisingly, in the textbook he wrote in 1880, this
figure made a brief reappearance. While the text still did not mention
them, the section on South America was embellished with an engraving entitled "Patagonians" (Figure 3). Following this final ripple, the
mythic Patagonian was seen no more. At the turn of the twentieth

century, the inhabitants of Patagonia were simply, for Calkin, "uncivilized Indians."[36] Ignoring the myth, the Sœurs de la congrégation de
Notre-Dame went one step further. The response they required of their
pupils to the question "Que savez-vous de cette contrée [Patagonie]?"
(What do you know about this region [Patagonia]?) contradicts all
the ethnographic descriptions put forward by previous writers. There
were no more Patagonians, only "des Indiens peu connus" (little-known
Indians) inhabiting this "région froide, encore non cultivée" (cold region,
still not cultivated).[37] At the beginning of the twentieth century, the
bodies and curious customs of the Hottentots and Patagonians were
no longer objects of fascination.

The northern part of America contained "vastes contrées [peuplées]
par une foule de nations sauvages presque toutes idolâtres, parmi
lesquelles les Esquimaux sont les plus remarquables" (vast regions
[peopled] by a multitude of savage nations, almost all idolatrous, among
whom the Eskimos are the most remarkable).[38] Curiosity about the
Eskimos, a "remarkable" or "singular" people, increased steadily during
the nineteenth century. The European and American expeditions looking
for the Northwest Passage, such as those of Franklin, Ross, Parry, and
Rae, were no strangers to this fascination. Moreover, the pedagogical
journals, school textbooks, and cartography exercises carried out by the
students attest to this interest in Arctic exploration.

Father Holmes's textbook allows us to gauge the importance of the
Eskimos in the exhibition of human diversity. As for the Hottentots and
the Patagonians, it was their body and way of life that placed them at
the outer limits of humanity. The Eskimo was conceived of in relation
to a human norm represented by the Euro-American body and society.
"Les Esquimaux sont d'une stature au-dessous de la médiocre" (Eskimo
stature is below the mediocre),[39] wrote Holmes, to begin his ethnographic description. In other textbooks, it was a matter of their clothing
and dwellings but most of all their short stature and uncleanliness.
Montpetit and Devisme even established a hierarchy of the people called
Eskimos. Those of the boreal archipelago were "de la même famille,

mais moins intelligents et aussi moins robustes que ceux du Groenland"
(of the same family, but less intelligent and also less robust than those
in Greenland). An interesting fact that Devisme and Montpetit were
the only ones to raise was that "ils considèrent comme une injure la
dénomination d'Esquimaux qui signifie mangeurs de poisson cru" (they
consider being called Eskimos an insult, because it signifies eaters of
raw fish).[40] This single allusion briefly alleviated the ethnocentricity of
the educational discourse.

In contrast to other mythical peoples, the Eskimos were of special
importance owing to Canada's geographical position and its expansion
across the continent throughout the nineteenth century. In addition to
receiving consistent attention in the geography textbooks, these populations found a place in the English-language reading textbooks, thus
contributing to the imperial and continental imaginary constructed by
the educational corpus in the mid-nineteenth century. At this time, the
conquest of the Arctic was a topical subject, as demonstrated in two
reading textbooks from the 1860s.[41] The number of texts concerning
the northern lands and populations or taken from accounts of Arctic
expeditions is out of proportion with the rest of the educational corpus
for the nineteenth century.

"Remarquable par sa petite taille, son visage large, sa peau brune
et huileuse, sa voix aigre et désagréable" (Remarkable for his short
stature, large face, brown, oily skin, and disagreeably rasping voice),[42]
as Toussaint wrote, the Laplander is another inhabitant of extreme
regions. While he did not excite as much interest as the Hottentot,
Patagonian, or Eskimo, he was described in similar terms. The attention
he received from textbook authors, as well as the many illustrations of
his way of life, show that he also fulfilled a special role in the report on
human diversity. Africa's Pygmies, owing to their diminutive height,
were also among the "curious" populations that excited the academic
and commercial worlds of Europe and America. The *Journal of Education*
mentions the passion for Pygmies in an article published in the summer
of 1874. The article, which dealt with the arrival and exhibition of "real

Pygmies" in Naples, explained, "They are under three feet and a half in height, and are supposed to be age fifteen and nine respectively. [. . .] Schweinfurth promises to disinter and convey to Europe the remains of an Akka pigmy, who died while accompanying him on his return from Central Africa."[43] The two peoples, who are directly compared in a reading in a textbook by Montpetit, received this attention only because of their small stature and their existence at the outer reaches of the world known to Europeans.

Hottentots, Patagonians, Laplanders, Pygmies, Eskimos. Encountered at the Earth's outer limits by European explorers, these people whose body differed from the Western representation of the human fuelled the imagination about "other places" for a long time. However, in the course of the nineteenth century, societies at the outer limits of humanity gradually lost their mythic aura. Driven by new debates on human origins and diversity, the taxonomies changed and the vocabulary of "race" took up more and more space. But before its hegemony became inevitable, the two concepts of human nature co-existed for a time, in an 1867 textbook: "What a vast variety of human life must exhibit itself to [the historian], what a strange assemblage of men of all colours, and forms, and characters, must fall within the sphere of his observation! [. . .] And now, who shall enumerate them all? White men and black, red Indians and yellow Chinamen, fierce Malays and peaceful Sandwich Islanders, Esquimaux and Patagonians, are but a few among the many families into which the great human race is divided."[44]

The Human Races

The term "race" was central to European reflection on human nature during the nineteenth century. Although the word has many meanings even now, it mainly signifies a division of the human genus according to skin colour. In the Canadian school curriculum, the "ideas about human races" figured in the geographical knowledge that primary students were expected to master. Race, like the degree of civilization, was first a notion of political geography. "The human family presents a great variety in respect to color, features, stature, &c."[45]—race is difference inscribed in the body, as stated in this textbook from 1877. From the 1830s until the turn of the twentieth century, the racial taxonomies presented in geography textbooks echoed the theoretical debates in the Euro-American learned community. It was no longer the humanity of the Patagonians that was under discussion but the very essence of humans: Should the human genus be divided into three, five, or twelve races? Do all men belong to a single species? Is man descended from a monkey? "In this new frame of reference, race functions as a substitute for the mythical representations of alterity."[46] The description of racialized bodies, as well as their visual representation, reached its zenith in the 1870s and 1880s. Without fading away, the concept of race was then made to serve an imperialist and hierarchical ideology, which was derived from hegemonic scientific racism at the turn of the twentieth century.

In most of the nineteenth-century geography textbooks, the world's population was divided into three or five races, all associated with the skin colour and geographical origin of their representatives. In Father Holmes's textbook, as in those of Toussaint and the Sœurs de la congrégation de Notre-Dame, mankind belonged to "trois races principales: la *blanche* ou race *causasique* [*sic*] ; la *jaune* [. . .] ; la troisième race est la *nègre*" (three principal races: the *white* or *caucasic* [*sic*] race; the *yellow* [. . .]; the third race is the *Negro*).[47] In many English-language textbooks and in those written by the Frères des écoles chrétiennes, "on partage ordinairement le genre humain en cinq races distinctes" (we usually divide the human species into five distinct races).[48] To the preceding three were added the olive, brown, or Malay race, and the red, copper, or American race. This system, identified as Blumenbach's,[49] lasted until the twentieth century. At that time, scientific racism was much more present. In the textbook they published in 1910, the Frères maristes wrote, "On constate entre [les hommes] des différences notables de couleurs, de traits, d'intelligence, etc." (We have observed notable differences among men in colour, features, intelligence, etc.). A few lines later, they assign "une intelligence apathique et une civilisation arrièrée" (an apathetic intelligence and a backward civilization)[50] to the Black race. Even if the previous textbooks imposed a hierarchical order on the races, intelligence had never figured among the criteria justifying it.

Added to these two systems of classification was the ethnological thesis regarding Noah's sons. In the mid-nineteenth century, Hodgins outlined the multiplicity of theories concerning human variety:

> Man—descended from Adam and Eve, who were originally placed in Eden (in some part of Asia)—is now found in every region of the Globe. He has been enabled to adapt himself to almost every variety of soil and climate; which have in turn reacted upon his physical constitution, so as to produce the different varieties which now exist. Some naturalists have arranged mankind into five classes, according to the form of the skull, vis. the Mongolian, the Negro or Ethiopic, the Caucasian or Indo-European, the Malayan, and the American. Modern ethnologists arrange them into three classes, after the three sons of Noah, vis. Shem's or the Mongolian (yellow), Ham's or the Negro (black), and Japheth's or the Caucasian (white). Another mode of classifying mankind is by the affinity of languages.[51]

Hodgins's exposition attests to his great erudition—he succeeded in explaining the theories of naturalists, ethnologists, and linguists in a few lines. At the same time, he clearly expressed the imprecision of the racial taxonomy of the 1860s. It is also important to remember the monogenist presupposition. All of the geography textbooks I analyzed based their conception of human variety on the original idea that all humans descend from Adam. While the polygenist theses that posited the existence of many human species had been discussed in certain Montreal teaching institutions,[52] the educational material directed at children in primary and secondary grades did not address this hypothesis. These texts, and to a certain extent the schools in general, were not obliged to explain the system of racial classification; the textbooks were obliged to transmit knowledge. Accordingly, race was presented as an objective construct. At first glance, we can literally *see* the ideological content that was transmitted to students. Until the last decade of the century, the illustrations representing the various human races all followed the same pattern. The White race is in the middle of the image, overshadowing the other four (Figures 4 to 7). The hierarchy also becomes evident on reading the text illustrated by these iconographic representations.

In most of the enumerations, the Black race is named last, and sometimes the terms of its presentation are different from those for the other races. Thus, in a textbook they published in 1876, the Frères des écoles chrétiennes wrote that Europe was populated by Japheth's descendants and Asia by Shem's. The words "White race" or "Yellow race" were not used. In discussing Africa, they reported: "Africa is the residence of the Black Race. It was peopled by the children of Cham, the second son of Noe."[53] Africa is then the only region for which the race was expressly named, and the Africans were not Cham's "descendants" but rather his "children." A subtle lexical difference exposes both reducing African populations to their bodies and relegating them to childhood, a familiar rhetorical structure of abasement. In a French-language textbook published in the same year by the same religious community, the enumeration of the races ends with a mention of the Black race that explains "ceux qui appartiennent à cette race sont appelés nègres" (those who belong to this race are called Negroes).[54] The information provided by the Frères des écoles chrétiennes was considered to be necessary and useful to the students' knowledge. This kind of detail, which had no meaning for the other races, reiterates the biological essentialism of Black individuals. While the Chinese are first recognized as members of a particular empire, the "Negroes" have nothing particular about them but belonging to a particular race.

Beginning in the last decade of the nineteenth century, a pedagogical change was produced in the presentation of the human races. While the dry, succinct enumeration of the races persisted in certain books, other writers now directly addressed the students as follows: "How does the color of negroes differ from that of white men? How does their hair differ?" "Quelle idée vous faite-vous de la Chine et des Chinois?" (What sense do you get of China and the Chinese?) "Où habitent les nègres?" (Where do the Negroes live?)[55] In addition to exemplifying the change in pedagogy, these questions demonstrate that at the end of the nineteenth century, a pedagogue could expect that the Canadian student would already possess some knowledge of the peoples of the Earth when starting to learn geography. Intellectual abilities are also sometimes directly associated with physical difference. In previous decades, allusions to the innate intelligence of certain races were to be found in the body of the book's text, in the description of certain countries, but never in the general presentation of the races. For example, in one of their textbooks, the Frères des écoles chrétiennes wrote: "Contrairement aux deux républiques précédentes [le Pérou et la Bolivie], le Chili a une population formée principalement de blancs, aussi est-il plus progressif, plus éclairé et plus stable que les autres états espagnols."[56] (Contrary to the two previous republics [Peru and Bolivia], Chile has a population made up mainly of White people, and it is also more progressive, more enlightened and more stable than the other Spanish states.) The pinnacle of scientific racism and social Darwinism was reached in the textbooks published by the Frères maristes at the end of the 1900s:

La race *blanche* a la peau blanche, le visage ovale, les
cheveux ondulés, une intelligence très développée; sa
civilisation est la plus progressive.

La race *jaune* a la peau jaunâtre, le visage plat et triangulaire, les cheveux rudes, la barbe rare; cette race, restée longtemps dans une demi-barbarie, fait des efforts pour se mettre au niveau des peuples les plus civilisés du monde.

La race *noire* ou nègre a la peau plus ou moins noire, les mâchoires proéminentes, les lèvres épaisses, les cheveux crépus; sa civilisation est la plus arriérée.

La race *rouge* a la peau rougeâtre ou cuivré [*sic*], le front fuyant, la taille grande; elle est presque identifiée avec la race blanche qui la domine.[57]

(The *white* race has white skin, an oval face, wavy hair, a highly developed intelligence; its civilization is the most progressive.

The *yellow* race has yellowish skin, a flat, triangular face, coarse, unruly hair, little facial hair; this race, which remained semi-barbaric for a long time, is making efforts to reach the level of the most civilized peoples in the world.

The *black* or Negro race has more or less black skin, prominent jaws, thick lips, frizzy hair; its civilization is the most backward.

The *red* race has reddish or copper-coloured skin, a receding forehead, tall stature; it is almost identified with the white race, which dominates it.)

The text was not the only thing to change; the visual representations of the human races were also updated. From being presented in a diagrammatic display, they became separate, contextualized images, sometimes arranged horizontally.

Fig. 25.—SPECIMENS OF THE FIVE CLASSES OF MANKIND.

Figure 4. "Specimens of the Five Classes of Mankind," Hodgins, *Lovell's General Geography*, 1867, 11.

1. Blanche ou Caucasienne.   2. Jaune ou Mongole.   3. Cuivrée ou Américai:
4. Olivâtre ou Malaise.   5. Noire ou Ethiopienne.

Figure 5. Untitled, Frères des écoles chrétiennes, *Nouvelle géographie illustrée*, 1875, 10.

RACES : 1, race blanche ; — 2, race jaune ; — 3, race brune ; — 4, race rouge ; — 5, race noire.

Figure 6. Untitled, Frères des écoles chrétiennes, *Géographie illustrée. Cours moyen*, 1876, 8.

The *Nouvelle géographie illustrée* (1875) produced by the Frères des écoles chrétiennes provides an example of the multiplicity of mankind's classifications in the nineteenth century. After having established the common origin of all men, the text describes the distinctive characteristics of the five human races. Each is identified by two terms: White/Caucasian, Yellow/Mongol, Copper/American, Olive/Malay, and Black/Ethiopian.[58] This followed Johann Blumenbach's system. The apparent simplicity of this classification becomes hazy beginning on page 15, when the Europeans are identified as being both Japheth's descendants and representatives of the White, Yellow, and Brown races. What was this mysterious Brown race that did not appear in the introductory

SPECIMENS OF THE FIVE CLASSES OF MANKIND.

Figure 7. "The Geographical Distribution of Man," *Lovell's Advanced Geography*, 1880, 13.

exposition? The description of Africa further complicated the issue. The cradle of Cham's line, Africa, is peopled by Whites in the north, by "noirs ou nègres, dans l'Afrique centrale et méridionale" (Blacks or Negroes in central and southern Africa), and by . . . Browns![59] In addition, these last were heathens, barbaric, and ignorant, like the Black populations. This Brown race's identity was finally unveiled in the "table of general ethnography" that concluded the textbook (Figure 8).

The ethnographic table's ideological impact is enormous. In addition to disseminating the racist ideology by which the White race is superior to the others, it brought together some of the classification systems that were in fashion at the time. In this table, the sizeable races—White, Yellow, Brown (!), and Black—are divided into branches and then into families and peoples. The French, and the French Canadians, therefore belong to the Latin family of the European branch of the White race. The hierarchy is obvious. The White race, while not the most populous, with 425 million people versus 430 for the Yellow race, has pride of place at the top of the table, as do the European branch and the Teutonic family. The Black race sits at the bottom of the page, even if it includes many more representatives than the Brown and Red races coming before it. In the last row, on its own, are to be found the "hybrids of all races" who were living mainly in America. The way these "hybrids" are positioned betrays the fear of degeneracy associated at that time with racial mixing. Further, the "evolutionist" ideology can be seen in the multiple subdivisions of each race. The White race has three branches and thirteen families. The other races include between two and four branches and no families. The White race's subdivisions thus take up almost half the table. The racist ideology that at first glance seems subtle is, in fact, very powerful.

The three textbooks published by Lovell in the second half of the century also provide a rich case study. At least two of them were written by John George Hodgins (1867 and 1880). The various classifications Hodgins set forth in the 1867 textbook show that he was well-informed about the scholarly theories. To the system of five human races determined by the shape of the skull, Hodgins added the "ethnological" division according to Noah's sons as well as the linguistic classification. Several years later, in Lovell's intermediate textbook, he described the physical differences between men: "[the] stature, the shape of the body, the proportion and shape of the limbs, the color and texture of the hair, the color of the eyes and skin, and the size and shape of the skull"[60] were all elements that varied among the races. Surprisingly, the races

678.—TABLEAU D'ETHNOGRAPHIE GENERALE.

RACE BLANCHE '425 millions d'individus).	Rameau Européen (330 millions d'individus).	FAMILLE *teutonne* (115 m.).	Germains, (Allemands, Hollandais, Flamands). Scandinaves, (Danois, Suédois, Norwégiens). Anglais, Yankies, Ecossais.
		— *latine* (110 m.)	Français (Canadiens). Espagnols et Portugais Italiens et Roumains.
		— *grecque* (5 m.).	Grecs et Albanais
		— *slave* (86 m.).	Russes, Cosaques, Polonais. Bulgares, Serbos. Tchéques (Bohêmes), Moraves.
		— *erso-kymrique ou celtique* (12 m.).	Kymris (Gallois, Bas-Bretons). Erses (Irlandais, Highlanders).
	R. Araméen (55 m.)	— *basque :* Basques — *berbère :* Maures, Kabyles, Touaregs, Coptes et Fellahs. — *sémile .* Arabes, Juifs, Syriens. — *persane :* Tadjiks, Afghans, Bélouchis, Arméniens. — *géorgienne et circassienne.*	
	R. Scythique (40 m.)	— *magyare :* Hongrois. — *turque :* Osmanlis, Turcomans, Kirghiz, Ousbecks. — *finnoise :* de Russie et Sibérie.	
R. JAUNE (430 m.)	R. Hyperboréen.	Lapons, Samoyèdes, Iénesséens, Kamtschadales. Esquimaux, Aléoutes, Groënlandais.	
	R. Mongol.	Jakoutes, Mongols et Kalmouks. Mantchoux et Tongous.	
	R. Sinique (420 m.)	Thibélains, Coréens, Chinois et Japonais.	
R. BRUNE (22 m).	R. Ethiopien (10 m.).	Barabras, Abyssins, Gallas, Fellatas, Ovas.	
	R. Hindou (190 m.)	Indis, Mahralles, Bengalis, Malabars.	
	R. Indochinois (20 m.).	Birmans, Siamois, Annamites, Cambodgiens.	
	R Malais (30 m.).	Malais, Battas, Javanais, Dayaks, Tagales. Polynésiens : Néo-Zélandais, Tongas, Taïtiens, Havaïens, Kanacks. Micronésiens.	
R ROUGE (10 m)	R Méridional.	Andiens, Quichuas, Araucaniens, Pampéens, Patagons, Guaranis.	
	R. Septentr.	Astèques ou anciens Mexicains, Chérokois, Natchez. Hurons, Iroquois, Sioux, Apaches, Peaux-Rouges.	
R NOIRE (70 m).	R Africain.	Nègres, Guinéens, Yolofs, Cafres, Hottentots.	
	R. Océanien.	Andamènes, Papous, Fidjiens, Australiens.	

HYBRIDES de toutes races (15 m.), surtout en Amérique : métis, mulâtres, zambos.

Figure 8. "Table of General Ethnography," Frères des écoles chrétiennes, *Nouvelle géographie illustrée*, 1875, 89.

were not directly identified. The Earth's inhabitants were instead split up among races with frizzy or woolly hair and races with smooth hair.

In the advanced textbook published in 1880, which was intended to replace that of 1867, Hodgins again displayed the currency and breadth of his scholarship. Human variety is still due to man's adaptation to the Earth's different climates. And yet, the division he presented picked up on the little-known theory of English biologist Thomas Henry Huxley. In this evolutionist classification, the Whites are divided between *Fair Whites/Xanthochroic* and *Dark Whites/Malanchroic*. The students learned that the *Xanthochroic* were to be found in northern Europe and Great Britain, while the *Malanchroic* lived around the Mediterranean. Hodgins modified Huxley's theory slightly and simplified it a lot. Equally fascinating to examine is the illustration that accompanies this classification (Figure 7), as well as the quotation from the Bible that surmounts it "God . . . hath made of one blood all nations of men to dwell on all the face of the earth," which reaffirms the descendance from Adam of all men. The image illustrating the races combines the old classification of *Caucasian, Mongolian, American, Malay,* and *African* with the new one of *Xanthochroic, Australoid, Mongoloid, Malanochroic,* and *Negroid*. The representations of the African and Mongol races are consistent; that is, the old classification and the new refer to the same geographical areas. For the rest, one image illustrates two diverging concepts: the *Malanchroic* man, from the Mediterranean, is also the *Malay* from Southeast Asia; and the *Australoid* is also the *American*. And in the middle of these men, whose continent of origin and race are less than clear, is the *Xanthochroic/Caucasian*, occupying the place of honour.

The development of public education took place just as the idea of a nation was being articulated in the latter half of the nineteenth century. That the two should mutually energize each other is not surprising. But how did the issue of race play into this relationship? Following the abolition of slavery in the United States and with Canada's conquest of the North American West, the legitimacy of ownership of the land by inhabitants of European origin was increasingly grounded in a racial ideology. While America was sometimes called "pays des Peaux-Rouges" (land of the Redskins),[61] the ideology transmitted in school in fact insisted on the idea that North America was a White territory. The White race always came first in the enumeration of the various races present on the continent. "The greater number of the inhabitants of North America are white people,"[62] wrote John Calkin. Other writers mention that America's place of eminence in the world order is due to the size of its White population. Thus, America started to exist historically only with colonization by Whites, as Calkin said in his study of Nova Scotia: "Three hundred years ago Nova Scotia was wholly a dense forest, inhabited by Indians and wild animals. The first settlement of white people in Nova Scotia was formed by the French, at Annapolis, in the year 1605."[63]

It was in this context that J.N. Miller wrote two elementary geography textbooks, in 1901 (French-language version) and 1905 (English-language version). For him, as well, the American continent existed first in racial terms: "Le premier blanc qui mit pied à terre sur ces îles fut Christophe Colomb. Jusqu'au temps de Colomb, peu de personnes croyaient que la terre est ronde et personne ne connaissait le continent américain."[64] (The first White man to set foot on land in these islands was Christopher Columbus. Until Columbus's time, few people believed that the earth was round and no one knew about the American continent.) Miller's two textbooks are almost identical. The English-language version contains a translation of the French-language text that was published four years earlier. And yet the differences that do exist between them deal specifically with racial ideologies, and analyzing the two allows an understanding of the meaning and importance of race at the turn of the twentieth century between Canada's two major population groups. The idea of race, which was more diffuse among the francophones, was accompanied by a discourse on French blood and rapprochement with the "Redskin" race. For the anglophones, the place held by race was central, and the difference between the White ("Anglo-Saxon") and the rest was very clear. It was accompanied by the idea of a moral and intellectual superiority that granted the Whites, and most especially British Whites, the right to govern the world.

In Miller's textbook, the general presentation of human races appeared in the introduction, as was the case for all the textbooks. However, Miller effected an important pedagogical change by going beyond simple enumeration and addressing the children directly. He also issued an ideological discourse that was much more obvious than those to be found in the textbooks published in previous decades. It was not a matter of exposing human diversity but of clearly affirming what was a commonly accepted hierarchization. The White race, "infatigable et intelligente, a peuplé l'Amérique de ses colons et s'est rendue maîtresse de presque tout le reste du monde" (tireless and intelligent, has peopled America with its colonists and made itself the master of almost all the rest of the world).[65] This no longer had to be described in physical terms, and even the iconography was no longer needed. The other races were handled differently. In presenting the Black race, Miller drew a parallel between the apparent civilization of the Black American populations and their lasting cohabitation with the White race. Moreover, two illustrations helped to reinforce the difference between the American populations that had received the benefit of White influence and the African populations.

The exposition of human races ended with describing the "Redskins," whose existence occurred mostly in the past. "Peu nombreux aujo-urd'hui" (few in number today), they were Christians and had become the responsibility of the Canadian government, which "paye leurs écoles et leurs missionnaires et leur accorde d'autres avantages" (pays for their schools and missionaries and grants them other advantages). As was done for the Black American populations, a parallel was drawn between the "Redskins'" relative civilization, their conversion to Christianity, and the influence of the White race. Where this rapprochement is surprising is in the following physical description: "Les Peaux-Rouges se rapprochent de la race blanche par leur visage régulier, leurs cheveux soyeux et les belles proportions de leurs corps."[66] (The Redskins come close to the White race for their regular facial features, silky hair, and well-proportioned bodies.) How is this association between the two races to be explained? And how is its absence in the English-language version to be understood? Should this difference be attributed to a distinct French-Canadian view of race? This is suggested by a study of the textbook the Frères maristes published a few years later, since, for them, the Red race "est presque identifièe avec la race blanche qui la domine" (is almost identified with the White race that dominates it).[67]

What does this racial proximity between Indians and Whites signify? In the anxiety over survival that permeated the national discourse at the end of the nineteenth century and the beginning of the twentieth, the truly dangerous racial mixing is that with the English. In her analysis of the role race plays in Québécois literature, Corrie Scott has shown that this very fear of mixing with the "Anglo-Saxon" race is a dominant theme in Lionel Groulx's famous essay "L'appel de la race" (The call of the race) (1922): "In a context of assimilation, the consolation of racial homogeneity may indicate above all a spirit of anxiety seeking a secure shelter in the racial uniformity that seems to be the only thing capable of ensuring a certain continuity of identity."[68] Moreover, some of the patriotic readings assigned to French-Canadian students underscore the idea that the Canadian race descended from "le plus pur sang de France" (France's purest blood). The Canadian race is "la plus forte race qui se soit implantée sur le continent américain" (the strongest race to have settled on the American continent) and "le sang le plus noble qui ait jamais coulé dans les veines de l'humanité circule dans ses veines: le sang français" (the most noble blood ever to have coursed through humanity's veins circulates in its veins: French blood).[69]

How to explain why, in this context, a racial affinity with the "Redskins" should be seen as positive? The contemporary discourse about the Indians almost always confirmed the idea of a dying race. The prospect of absorbing the Indian "element" into the French-Canadian race was therefore understandable, all the more because many enviable qualities were recognized in that race. This affirmation of racial affinity also partook of the desire to indigenize French-Canadian communities. By affirming the extinction of the "Redskin" race while simultaneously establishing the existence of a certain hybridization with it, the French Canadians were consolidating their national claim. If there were no more Indians, who would be the first nation? Finally, the racial affinity underscored by the textbook authors suggests the "*désir métis*" (desire to be Métis), as Scott calls it, or simply integrating the "Métis" character who had existed since the last decades of the nineteenth century in Canadian literature.

The racial ideology in the English-language version of Miller's textbook, for its part, was permeated with adherence to and support for the British Empire. It was more essentialist in alluding to the characteristics of the various races and frequently reiterated the idea that the world belonged to "White men." The general description of the races differed from that presented in the French-language version. Addressing himself to the children, Miller asked: "How is the color of negroes different from that of white men? How is their hair different?" Further, the idea of an insurmountable difference between the White and Black races was regularly alluded to.[70] It seemed that the White race was defined above all through constant comparison with the Black race, as expressed in these two questions from the book's final section, "Correlations and Comparisons": "What race has spread over the whole world as conquerors? What race was spread over the Western Continent to serve as slaves?"[71]

Europe's White race had conquered the world and now governed it—this was what the schoolchildren learned on reading Miller's textbook. As for the Indians, those peoples the "White men" discovered and named on arriving in Canada, they were now far fewer in number. No reference was made to the reserves or to the "advantages" they had received from the Canadian government, in contrast to the contents of the French-language version of Miller's textbook. Moreover, the link between the physical beauty of the Indians and the Whites did not appear in Miller's English-language version. His representation of the

Red race is much less positive. For instance, he asked the pupils: "Are the people of America savage or civilized? From what grand division was civilization brought to America? What savage race owned America before the Europeans took possession of it? [. . .] Tell five things which are done in the Dominion to-day which the Indians have not yet learned to do. Do uncivilized people build large cities and fine buildings?"[72]

The English-language version of Miller's textbook was in the end an apology for the British Empire couched in racial terms. The idea that Canada was the White man's country and that it must remain so was very strong. For example, in contrast to the French-language text, it alluded to the "Yellow peril" in writing that "our laws do not permit Chinese laborers to enter the Dominion without paying a heavy poll tax."[73] The analysis shows that these two textbooks sketch the evolution of racial theories developed from the nineteenth century to the beginning of the twentieth. Around 1850 the theories were still rudimentary, but by the early 1900s they had crystallized into an increasingly binary vision of the racial issue in Canada. Some put the emphasis on defining the French-Canadian race as the perfect type of White American, while others promoted belonging to the "Anglo-Saxon" race, masters of a vast empire. Since they were both predicated on the presupposition of the White race's absolute superiority, these visions, without being completely incompatible, were correlatives of the national constructions that were operating at that time in Canada.

Racialized Bodies and Sexuality

In the rhetorical construction of alterity produced by schools in the nineteenth century, the Other's racialized body was at some times an object of desire; at others, the source of disgust. Which peoples are beautiful and "shapely"? Are these desirable bodies masculine or feminine? Does this sexual desire come up as often in French- and English-language writing, in textbooks written by men and women?

These are some of the questions around which the school's tentative response probably concealed a much more explicit social discourse.

In the colonial context of the nineteenth century, the theories of race were tied up with culture and sexuality. The descriptions of racialized bodies offered in school were part of this history. Of all the details in travel accounts and anthropological treatises, the textbook writers chose to select allusions to the beauty or ugliness of the Other-body. In this regard, many African and Oceanian peoples were treated as "well-made" and "beautiful." Their features were pleasing, their height imposing, and their body strong. Associated with these aesthetic qualities are certain intellectual and moral attributes. "Aptes à une certaine civilization" (Capable of a certain degree of civilization) or "ouvrant facilement leur esprit aux idées de la civilisation" (easily opening their minds to ideas of civilization), these populations stood out among the region's savage tribes for their intelligence and industry.[74]

A description of one group's beauty was sometimes followed by that of another group's hideousness and repugnancy. While beauty was a sign of intelligence or civilization, ugliness spelled a degraded, savage state. As Robert Young notes, "The repulsion that writers commonly express when describing other races, particularly Africans, is, however, often accompanied at other points, with an equal emphasis, sometimes apparently inadvertent, on the beauty, attractiveness or desirability of the racial other."[75] The beautiful, robust Kaffirs are near neighbours of the degraded, deformed Hottentots. The "filthy," "squalid," and "small" Samoyeds, Ostyaks, and Koryaks live next to the "better featured" and "more skilled" Chukchi.[76] Opposed to the Polynesians, with their tall stature and intelligence, are the Papuans, "noirs, moins beaux et ordinairement sauvages" (Black, less beautiful, and usually savage).[77] Ironically, in overturning the old representations of Australia's Black populations, the Frères maristes reiterate the opposition of beauty to repugnancy:

Les Polynésiens ou Canaques diffèrent des Malais proprement dits par la taille et par la couleur de la peau; ils sont grands, bien faits, et leur visage est généralement beau, quand le type n'a pas été altéré par son mélange avec la race noire.

2. La race noire (famille australienne) habite la Mélanésie. Elle est inférieure à la race malaise; mais les récits des premiers voyageurs ont beaucoup exagéré l'abrutissement moral et la laideur physique des individus qui la composent.[78]

(The Polynesians or Kanaks differ from the actual Malays for their height and the colour of their skin; they are tall, well-built, and their face is generally handsome, when the type has not been altered through mixing with the Black race.

2. The Black race (Australian family) lives in Melanesia. It is inferior to the Malay race; but the moral degradation and physical ugliness of the individuals constituting the population were much exaggerated in the accounts of the first voyagers.)

Most often, the beauty or ugliness is attributed to the peoples of Africa and Oceania, confirming that these peoples exist first, in the discourse, through their bodies.

The racial ideology transmitted in school saw the various races as deviations from the norm represented by the White race, which was, in the illustrations, often represented by a man of European appearance. What did it become in the texts? Which people were the "type de la race blanche" (typical of the White race)? Two candidates vied for the title. On the one hand, from 1833 to 1870, many writers mentioned the remarkable beauty of the Caucasian populations in Georgia and Circassia. While the textbook published by the Société d'éducation de Québec in 1841 stated that the women of these regions "passent pour les plus belles de l'Asie" (are regarded as the most beautiful in Asia),[79] Holmes is more specific:

> Les Circassiens et les Géorgiens se distinguent de tous les peuples de l'Asie et peut-être du monde par la beauté du sang. Les traits de leur visage sont remplis d'expression; ils ont la peau d'une extrême blancheur; leurs cheveux sont châtains ou noirs ou bien d'une couleur rousse. Les hommes sont d'une taille d'Hercule; ils ont le pied petit et le poignet fort; leur démarche annonce le courage et une noble fierté. Les femmes ont soin de relever par une parure élégante, modeste, et propre, les charmes que la nature leur a prodigués.[80]

> (The Circassians and Georgians stand out among all the peoples of Asia and perhaps the world for the beauty of their stock. Their facial features are full of expression; their skin is extremely white; their hair is chestnut or black or of a reddish colour. The men stand as tall as Hercules; they have small feet and strong fists; their step bespeaks courage and a noble pride. The women take care to heighten the charms nature has lavished on them with adornments that are elegant, modest and clean.)

For his part, Toussaint considered these peoples "remarquables par les belles proportions de leurs traits, par l'élégance de leur taille" (remarkable for the beautiful proportions of their features and the elegance of their shape), and in 1868 declared them the "type de la race blanche" (the type of the White race).[81] Yet another people attracted praise from the textbook writers—the Arabs. And this time, beauty was only attributed to the male body. The dictation published in *L'Enseignement primaire* in 1885 and titled "Les Arabes nomades" (The nomadic Arabs) describes "l'Arabe pur sang" (the thoroughbred Arab) in unambiguous terms: "belle teinte bronzée," "toute sa beauté," and "magnifique spécimen de l'espèce" (beautiful tanned colouring, all his beauty, a magnificent specimen of the species).[82] Like a number of French-language textbook authors, Montpetit and Devisme expressed a similar idea when they wrote that it is in Arabia that "l'on trouve des prototypes de la beauté mâle" (we find prototypes of male beauty).[83] The Frères des écoles chrétiennes went still further in writing that they are "l'un des types les mieux caractérisés [de la race blanche]" (one of the clearest types [of the White race]).[84] Orientalism as an expression of European fantasies was probably not unfamiliar in this projection of the racial beauty of Whites onto Oriental peoples. But why should this attention be directed to the man's body?

For a long time, post-colonial historiography has been dissecting White man's desire in the imperial context of the eighteenth and nineteenth centuries.[85] Ann Laura Stoler has reframed Foucault's writings on sexuality in terms of imperialism and the issue of race. Robert Young's book *Colonial Desire* analyzes the meaning of race, hybridity, and desire in Western theories and the culture of the colonial era. For his part, Christopher Lane has studied the representation of homosexuality in British colonial literature. In his analysis, he refuses to consider homosexual desire and virility as having been opposed representations historically: "Instead, we must emphasize the turbulent incongruencies *between* homosexual desires and masculine identities precisely because no single signifier is adequate to their representations."[86] These analyses shed a first ray of light on the desire suggested by the representations examined above. But why was the physical beauty of the male body mentioned so often while the female body was completely invisible? The two references to the beauty of women in the Caucasus are exceptions, and they date from 1833 and 1841, respectively—that is, at the beginning of the period under study. Furthermore, why does this aesthetic relation to the body occur only in male writing? The number of textbooks written by women is certainly not large enough to permit stating a strong thesis on this subject. However, the fact remains that the textbooks of the Sœurs de la congrégation de Notre-Dame did not pay the same aesthetic attention to the bodies of described populations as did the textbooks written by men. And the only allusions to sexuality they did contain did not inflame desire: Mohammedanism had a "sensualist and demoralizing" influence on the populations of western Asia, and the Hindus were said to be "effeminate."[87]

The allusions' subtlety makes it difficult to find a definite answer to these questions. It is probable that many factors explain the presence of these sexual representations in the educational materials. First, the representation of a strong, handsome masculine body harks back to the importance of gymnastics and Muscular Christianity, both increasingly present in concepts of masculinity at the end of the nineteenth century. In addition, at that time, a fear was expressed in many so-called civilized societies that, pushed to the extreme, civilization would pervert men by making them effeminate. Could the Indigenous or colonized people have been a model to emulate? Did the man who had to have civilization brought to him in return set the standard for the White man's relation to his body? Another hypothesis touches on male homoerotic desire. In her book, Stoler writes: "Colonialism itself has been construed as the sublimated sexual outlet of virile and homoerotic energies in the West."[88] Despite the discourse on the dangers of homosexuality, the sensuality inherent in the representations of the Other-bodies perhaps also served to channel homosexual desire. When this desire was vested in the body of a distant, inaccessible Other, the homoerotic remained on the level of allegory. Similarly, by exorcising masculine desire on the colonized man, the dangerous racial hybridity could be avoided. In the educational materials, the people of South America did not excite a fascination like that stimulated by the peoples of the Orient, Africa, or Oceania; the particular character of their countries resided in the political regime rather than in the clothing or bodies of the inhabitants. In fact, while absolute monarchy or Oriental despotism characterized the Old World, anarchy was breaking out south of the United States. But what, or who, caused these political troubles and the delay in joining civilization? The political anarchy was in part explained by the large number of "half-breed" people in the population; in fact, it was not surprising that the question of mixed races should be broached while South America was the subject of study. As Young comments, "South America was always cited as the prime example of the degenerative results of racial hybridization." Some writers even directly blamed the state of South America's politics, with its frequent revolutions, "on their degenerate racial mixing."[89]

Holmes and Hodgins offered their readers definitions of the terms "Métis/Mestizos," "Zambos," and "Mulâtres/Mulattos" as referring to individuals "né[e]s de parents dont l'un est blanc et l'autre sauvage" (born of parents of whom one is White and the other savage), "l'un est sauvage et l'autre nègre" (one is savage and the other Negro)," or of European and African parents.[90] Subsequent textbooks also mentioned populations with "mixed blood." In Calkin's book, South America's White population was recognized as being less enterprising and advanced in its civilization than the Canadians and Americans; it was considered possible that the recognized hybridity of the region accounted for this backwardness. Indeed, immediately after mentioning the inferiority of South American Whites, Calkin mentioned the racially Black population and, most importantly, the "mixed races," which were most numerous in these countries. While the link between the Whites' lack of enterprise and racial mixing was not clearly established, it was understood.

The issue of hybridity referred back to the concern for preserving the race's purity, an anxiety that gained power in the latter decades of the century. A text by Dr. Clyde, "Characteristics of the New World," which certain Canadian anglophone students were required to read, clearly expresses the importance given to racial purity in English-language writings. After having written that the Spaniards and Portuguese had freely mixed their blood with that of native and Black populations, Clyde adds: "The French have mingled their blood more sparingly than the Spaniards and Portuguese with the non-European races in America, and the British more sparingly still. The British race alone has been able, not only to maintain but rapidly to multiply, its numbers in the New

World. It is also the only race there which, instead of merely following in the wake of European civilisation, keeps pace with it, and even contributes to its development."[91] It is because it stayed pure that the British race was also prolific and enterprising. It is relevant to point out that the descendants of the French in America were also judged to be more "mixed" than the colonists of British origin. Recognizing this blending could have contributed to a racialization of the French Canadians by their anglophone fellow citizens. At the end of the century, this fear of hybridity and radicalization of racial thinking were more present in English-language writing.

Black Bodies

[The category of "Negro"] has been fashioned within a framework of innumerable discursive and non-discursive practices [. . .]. In each of these practices, the tension between same and other, similar and different is problematized in a specific, localized way. In Western modernity, however, a constant characterizes them: the category of "negro" stands out in scholarly and laymen's problematizations that have been inscribed in a privileged manner in the register of the body's *physicality.*[92]

The human diversity that fuelled these philosophical and scientific reflections by European scholars for several centuries was based first of all on seeing a difference that was assessed against a norm located in western Europe. It was the body's appearance that made it possible to establish the racial classifications discussed earlier. But, in preparation of their textbooks, writers had to determine which body was the true Other-body. Which human race was conceived of as being in a relation of duality with the White race? Put another way, the question was to know which group, which Other figure, existed first and always when evoking the body.

African Representations with the Shy Incursion of a Narrating Character
In a copybook from the end of the nineteenth century, Berthe Girard, a pupil at the Mont Sainte-Marie convent, transcribed her sister's compositions. In one of them, the reader follows the narrator on a trip that takes her from "Québec à S. Francisco [avec] retour à N.Y. par [La] N. Orléans." In the course of her journey the narrator crosses the Utah desert, which prompted her to write: "Le sable que le vent nous fait avaler bon gré mal gré et les moustiques qui font rage [*sic*] (il est vrai qu'elles [*sic*] rencontrent assez rarement la chair tendre des septentrionaux et la peau lisse et dure des nègres ne leur est qu'une maigre pâture). Elles n'en constituent pas moins un grave inconvénient."[93] (The sand we are forced to swallow by the wind, whether we want to or not, and the mosquitoes that are maddening [it is true that they seldom encounter the tender flesh of northerners, and the Negroes' smooth, hard skin leaves them little to feed on]. They are no less serious an inconvenience.) This playful account expressed the essence of the opposition between the Whites, or northern *Septentrionaux,* and the Blacks. While the alterity of the Orientals was primarily cultural or religious, that of the Blacks was corporal. The representation of Black populations, more often called "Negroes" as in this composition, was complex. Images abounded, and the stereotypes of the Black populations of Africa and America differed. Where this was concerned, the school corpus called on the entire range of popular Western representations of Afro-descendant groups.

"[L'Afrique] est remarquable par ses immenses déserts, par la chaleur excessive de son climat et par la couleur noire d'une grande partie de ses habitants, dont la plupart sont encore dans l'état de barbarie."[94] ([Africa] is remarkable for its immense deserts, the excessive heat of its climate, and the black colour of a large proportion of its inhabitants, most of whom are still in a state of barbarity.) With these words the Frères des écoles chrétiennes presented the "géographie générale de l'Afrique" (general geography of Africa) in a textbook published in 1875. By mentioning their skin colour, the authors made the Africans' bodies what was so "remarkable" about the continent. This sentence also attests to the association between race and the degree of civilization. Using "most of whom" following the comma suggests a correlation between the inhabitants' skin colour and the state of barbarity in which they lived. In addition, as in the accounts of explorers from the same era, the Africans were part of the landscape. They showed up as set decoration. They were one detail among many in Africa's physical geography. The authors of these textbooks sometimes took the time to describe in detail the physiognomy of these populations: the "nègres, au teint tout à fait noir, au front déprimé, aux joues proéminentes, au nez large et épaté, aux cheveux laineux" (Negroes, of a completely black colour, with a low forehead, protruding cheeks, a large, flat nose and woolly hair),[95] wrote Toussaint, for example. However, they also often mentioned the beauty of certain African tribes. This was never gratuitous. For example, the Abyssinians had a "taille bien prise, les cheveux longs, et les traits du visage assez semblables à ceux des Européens" (slender waist, long hair, and facial features that are quite similar to those of the Europeans), although they were not exactly black, but rather of a "teinte particulière, que les uns comparent à l'encre pâle, les autres au bronzé" (particular colouring, which some compare to pale ink, others to a tan).[96] Similarly, the Kaffirs, "dont la couleur est d'un gris d'ardoise," are "plus intelligents et mieux faits que les nègres" (whose colour is slate grey, are more intelligent and better built than the Negroes). In comparison, the Yolofs, who "passent pour les plus noirs des nègres" (are regarded as the blackest of the Negroes), were also the shapeliest.[97] Not only were they "beaux et bien faits" (beautiful and well-built), like the Foulahs and Mandingos, but "de plus assez intelligents" (also quite intelligent).[98] Allusions to the beauty of some African populations were almost always articulated in opposition to the type of "ordinary Negro"; they were "more" or "better," while others simply did not belong to the race per se.

The writings of the Frères des écoles chrétiennes included the
most contemptuous description of the Black race of any in the nineteenth-century textbooks:

> Le Nègre, l'un des trois types primordiaux de l'espèce
> humaine, se distingue par ses formes robustes, ses cheveux
> laineux, ses lèvres épaisses, son teint noir, etc. Moins
> intelligent et moins actif que les autres races, le Nègre
> est resté généralement sauvage, ignorant, superstitieux,
> adorateur des fétiches; il se laisse dominer par des chefs
> absolus et féroces, qui le traitent comme bête de somme, le
> sacrifient à leurs plaisirs ou le vendent à vil prix.[99]

> (The Negro, one of the three primordial types of the
> human species, is distinguished by his robust shape, woolly
> hair, thick lips, black colouring, etc. Less intelligent and
> less active than the other races, the Negro has remained
> generally savage, ignorant, and superstitious, adoring
> fetishes; he allows himself to be dominated by fierce
> absolute chiefs who treat him like a beast of burden,
> sacrifice him to their pleasure or sell him for a pittance.)

In a few lines, this description brings together the various themes related
to the representation of Black people in the educational corpus: the
body, animality, inferiority, and slavery.

In comparing the Black man to a "beast of burden," the Frères des
écoles chrétiennes made use of a familiar concept of the time suggesting that a special connection existed between Blacks and animals. In
the scholarly theories, they were sometimes represented as the missing
link between man and animal. To this point, Jan Nederveen Pieterse
writes: "In addition to representations of Africans *as* animals there are
representations of Africans *and* animals, brought together in a single
picture."[100] Even if the school did not present Black individuals literally
as being animals, with one exception that I will come back to, animality

and dark-skinned characters were frequently associated in the images and the texts. This recurring association lumped Africans together with animals and created confusion about their humanity and animality.

Copying a section of a textbook by American Samuel Augustus Mitchell, the Frères des écoles chrétiennes included the following about West Africa: "Here, the gorilla, the largest of the apo species, abounds. The Fans and other inland tribes are cannibals. Human flesh is bought and sold in the markets."[101] The text, passing without transition from the gorilla to the cannibals, clearly expressed the ambiguous association mentioned above. Other excerpts were still more explicit. For example, Father Holmes compared the sovereigns' palace in Nigritia to "bâtimens où un riche cultivateur européen loge ses chevaux et ses bestiaux (buildings in which a rich European farmer would house his horses and cattle), as well as writing that the inhabitants of Benguela "s'habillent de peaux d'animaux et de serpens, percées d'un trou pour y passer la tête" (dress in the skins of animals and snakes, with a hole cut out for the head).[102] For his part, Toussaint wrote in the journal *L'Enseignement primaire* that the despots of Central and Equatorial Africa "disposent de la vie de leurs sujets comme nous disposons de [celle] d'un animal domestique" (treat their subjects' lives the way we would treat a domestic animal's).[103]

The connection between Black Africans and animality can also be seen in the illustrations. Repeatedly, engravings representing such wild animals as a gorilla, giraffe, or elephant would feature one or more Black individuals (Figures 9 and 10). In the case of the elephant, neither the text of the reading nor the accompanying engraving's caption explains the presence of Black people. Students were nonetheless required to say what they "perceived" in the illustration. What they perceived would inevitably be Black men chasing the elephant in a tropical forest. In most cases, the powerful symbolism linking Black populations to animality refers to wild, not domesticated, animals. Other peoples are associated with animals, but it is in a relation of domesticity, as in the case of the Arabs and their camels and horses.

Éléphants.

Figure 9. "Elephants," J.-Roch Magnan, *Cours français de lectures graduées*, 1902, 280.

A final aspect of the representation of African people concerns the supposed savagery of the populations in sub-Saharan Africa. Ultimately, this characteristic allegedly manifested itself in cannibalism. Holmes reported that some peoples "livraient leurs prisonniers invalides aux bouchers" (delivered their disabled prisoners to the butchers) and that the latter also benefited from the voluntary offers of inhabitants who were "dégoûtés de la vie ou égarés par un faux point d'honneur" (sick of living or misled by a false point of honour).[104]

Cannibals were to be found in Equatorial Africa, as reported in *L'Enseignement primaire* in Toussaint's article previously mentioned. Using a comically ironic tone, the author explains that "s'ils font la chasse aux étrangers, c'est sans haine et uniquement pour se procurer une viande très estimée de ces barbares; comme dans le Nord-Ouest, nos indiens poursuivent le buffle pour se nourrir de sa chair" (if they hunt strangers, it is without hatred and only to obtain a kind of meat that is highly prized by these barbarians; just as in the Northwest, our Indians chase the buffalo to feed on its flesh).[105] A few months later, the magazine clarified that there were perhaps errors regarding the population numbers for Africa in Toussaint's new geography textbook: "On devine qu'il est plus difficile de faire des recensements parmi ces mangeurs de chair humaine que dans la province de Québec."[106] (One can guess that it is harder to take the census among these eaters of human flesh than it is in the province of Quebec.) This kind of humorous touch was the forerunner of cannibal jokes that would be very popular from the end of the nineteenth century into the middle of the twentieth. In both citations, the African cannibal's alterity was produced through comparison. In the first case, the analogy between the cannibalistic hunter and the Indian not only establishes the alterity of the cannibal but reiterates that of the Indian, who nonetheless appears to be a much less radical Other. In the second case, it is a rhetorical device of simple comparison, opposing the African populations to the population of Quebec, where the reliability of the census suggests a high degree of civilization.

The Black Africans first appeared in the educational texts as an element of the African landscape, and in this perspective, their body was an important aspect of the description being given. Elsewhere, the fictional texts used in school allowed the children to go on their own voyages and "meet" characters from different cultures. Stories featuring Black characters were far less numerous than Oriental tales. The Black character, most often called "Negro," who was almost never given individual characteristics, showed up in two types of narratives: the stories of slaves and moral "storiettes." In these narratives, the Black characters always had the leading role. As Eliane Itti remarks regarding French textbooks: "While the physical and intellectual qualities are appreciated in various ways, those of the heart, by contrast, are celebrated over and over again in readers and books on morals: [. . .] they praise the one who is hospitable, or grateful, or devoted to the point of self-sacrifice."[107]

The slaves who figured in the various stories for schoolchildren were all models of self-denial, and themes of admirable devotion and

Le Gorille

Figure 10. "The Gorilla," Frères des écoles chrétiennes, *Nouvelle géographie illustrée*, 1875, 21.

reconciliation with their masters were frequently featured. At times, self-denial went as far as self-sacrifice, as in "The Two Negroes." In this story, shipwreck survivors trapped in a small boat must sacrifice passengers in order to avoid a second wreck. The captain at first wants to sacrifice the two Blacks in the group, but he changes his mind, fearing another kind of danger if the two slaves resist. Next in line are the slaves' mistress and her child. Hearing this, and over the woman's protests, the two slaves then throw themselves into the sea to save her.[108] Certain stories did not present such harmonious relations between the master and the slave. Others had a strong abolitionist flavour, as in the case of the poem "L'esclave noir" (The black slave) that young Tétreau recopied in the notebook of his friend Rodolphe Lemieux in 1880.[109] In this account, the "unhappy Negro" declares his humanity and equality to the "pale-faced man" who is exploiting him. Whether these fictions depicted Black characters as devoted, loyal slaves or as rebels attempting to escape the White man's mistreatment, they presented a figure of the Black man that had a certain narrative depth. But in all cases, the status of slave remained the only element of their identity to be learned.

In 1891, the magazine *L'Enseignement primaire* proposed a dictation in which the students would write the following sentence: "Les nègres ont une âme comme les blancs" (Negroes have a soul, like White people). This sentence, coming after "Saül était jaloux de David" (Saul was jealous of David) and before "La troisième fois" (The third time), shows that once again in 1891, it was appropriate to explain to pupils that Blacks were humans the same as Whites were.[110] Moreover, various excerpts used Black characters to illustrate moral or religious lessons. Despite his continually reiterated inferiority, the Black person appeared in these stories as a model of wisdom or Christian goodness. As in the stories of Muslim piety, the Other was then used as a moral example.

Slavery

Many times in their pedagogical writings, the Sœurs de la congrégation de Notre-Dame used a lexicon that clearly presented Black people as objects or resources. After having asked their pupils where White people "live," and in what country Yellow people "live," the sisters asked, "Où se trouvent les noirs?" (Where are the Blacks to be found?) In another textbook, they made a direct reference to Blacks on two occasions, asking "Où habitent les nègres?" (Where do Negroes live?) and "Combien compte-t-on de nègres?" (How many Negroes are there?), while referring in the same paragraphs to "representatives" of the White and Yellow races or the "individuals belonging" to these races.[111] The semantic shift was all the more powerful for being subtle. As in the association with animality, the vocabulary used by the Sœurs to talk about Black populations was not innocent. It clearly referred to the fact that those populations had for a long time been thought of as a resource, as part of the Atlantic slave trade. Had Sister Saint-Fabien not written in her notes for the community's teachers that Blacks were "introduced" to America?[112] Why did she not write that they were "introduced" as slaves? It was because the recognition of the Atlantic slave trade completely disappeared from educational materials after the first decades of the nineteenth century.

Regarding the reality of the slavery practised by Euro-American populations for centuries, the silence in the educational corpus is not surprising. As Pieterse remarks, slavery was for a long time the hidden face of European culture: "Invisibility was one way in which slavery was kept psychologically at bay."[113] Paradoxically, it was abolitionist imagery that provided copious illustrations of the reality of slavery. The few mentions of Euro-American slavery in the educational discourse occurred in the first decades of the nineteenth century, when abolitionist trends were still popular and slavery was still legal in the United States. In August 1838, the newspaper *Le Canadien* described in detail the public exercises given by students at the Séminaire de Québec. One of the fifth-year students performed an English-language speech on

"Un discours de Lord Brougham sur la traite des nègres" (a speech by Lord Brougham on the slave trade).[114] This speech of Brougham's was very likely the address he had given in February of the same year in the House of Lords, in which he demanded the immediate emancipation of the Black slaves and an end to the slave trade. At that same time, Holmes did not hesitate to associate the cruel customs of coastal populations in Africa "à leur commerce avec les Européens" (with their trade with the Europeans). It was in order to obtain slaves that these African peoples were always at war.[115] In addition, Holmes and the Quebec City district educational society were the only ones to allude directly to the enslaved population of the United States.[116] Hodgins, whose textbook was published in the 1860s, mentioned the American Black population but without referring to its members' initial status as slaves; the association with slavery was to be seen only in the vocabulary he used. In his description of the southern states, he wrote that they were "noted for their products of cotton, tobacco, and sugar; and for their large Negro population."[117]

Published shortly after the end of the American Civil War, the textbook by Toussaint perfectly illustrates the sudden invisibility of slavery in North America. There was no mention of any Black population in his study of the United States, although he reports on the war that ended in 1866 in which "les sécessionistes [ont] combattu comme des héros" (the secessionists [. . .] fought like heroes).[118] Until the end of the century, the history of slavery in the European countries and North America became the elephant in the room. Finally, at the turn of the twentieth century, Calkin and the Sœurs de la congrégation de Notre-Dame very quickly addressed slavery in order to explain the presence of the Black populations in America, while the reality of slavery in Canada was not discussed in the textbooks, either.

As Pieterse writes regarding Western popular culture, "the myth of the Dark Continent put forth by explorers, exculpated the West of the slave trade, which was redefined as a manifestation of African primitivism; and it shifted attention to the Arabic slave trade."[119] This new representation is perfectly visible in Canada's educational corpus. Decrying the "sale of human beings" practised by the peoples of Africa (and "even" some Europeans), Toussaint explained that "les lois des nations éclairées le prohibent aujourd'hui sévèrement" (the laws of enlightened nations now severely prohibit it).[120] While the Frères des écoles chrétiennes and the Sœurs de la congrégation de Notre-Dame mentioned the practice of slavery by North African Arabs, it was Miller who identified the Arabs most explicitly as being responsible for the slave trade: "Tous les peuples civilisés de l'Europe et de l'Amérique condamnent l'esclavage et l'ont aboli dans les pays qui leur apparti-ennent. La traite des noirs est faite surtout par les Arabes; elle existe encore, mais elle a bien diminué."[121] (All the civilized peoples in Europe and America condemn slavery and have abolished it in the countries that belong to them. The trade of Black people is mostly carried on by the Arabs; it still exists but has diminished considerably.) In the English-language edition of his textbook, Miller remained silent about the history of slavery in the United States, but he mentioned that history in the West Indies and Brazil.

Not only did the textbooks pass over the involvement of European and North American peoples in the Atlantic slave trade, they associated them with the more positively regarded initiatives taken by emanci-pated slaves to establish colonies in Liberia and Sierra Leone. Toussaint presented Sierra Leone as a colony set up by the English and "destinée particulièrement à la civilisation des Nègres qu'on a enlevés aux navires négriers pour les attacher à la culture libre du sol et leur donner les premiers éléments de l'instruction. [. . .] Malheureusement le climat de cette colonie est devenu pernicieux pour les Européens."[122] ([The colony was] destined especially for the civilization of Negroes who had been taken away from the slavers' ships to attach them to the free cultivation of the soil and give them the initial elements of education. [. . .] Unfortunately, the colony's climate became pernicious to the Europeans.) Toussaint's vocabulary is revelatory. In his terms, the Blacks were "taken away" to be "attached" to the "free" cultivation of the soil.

This "civilizing" enterprise finally operated on the same principle as slavery: the Black individuals were not agents of their own destiny. And yet, Toussaint refused to credit the Europeans with the success of the emancipated colonies. He explained that "unfortunately" the climate forced them to leave.

In 1902, in an exercise of intelligence and invention for students in the middle levels, the magazine *L'Enseignement primaire* asked the children to find the verb to be used to complete the following comparison: ". . . comme un nègre."[123] The expected response was "work." The triteness and legitimacy revealed in the expression used in this language exercise were consistent with an association of America's Black population with work that persisted throughout the nineteenth century. In an assignment prepared two years earlier for the Exposition de Paris dealing with the geography of the West Indies, a pupil of the Sœurs de la congrégation de Notre-Dame wrote: "The productions, which are abundant include sugar, coffee, cotton, corn [. . .]. The soil is cultivated by negroes."[124]

Some geography textbooks thus directly associated Black people with cultivating the land in the West Indies and Brazil. However, this relation was mostly presented in instructive lectures about cotton. In a text addressed to children in the elementary years, young Eva asks her mother about the origin of cotton. Impressed by everything being produced thanks to the cotton tree, Eva exclaims: "Mais en vérité, cet arbre est un trésor! Il doit falloir des quantités d'ouvriers pour récolter tout ce coton." (But this tree is truly a treasure! It must take large numbers of workers to harvest all that cotton.) To which her mother replies, "Ce sont des nègres qui travaillent la plupart [*sic*] des plantations de cotonniers."[125] (It is Negroes who work most [*sic*] of the cotton plantations.). If young Eva was concerned about the number of workers required to farm the cotton, her mother's answer seemed meant to reassure her: it was not workers picking cotton, but "Negroes," *naturally*. The Black person farming cotton was not working at a trade; the mere fact of mentioning his body ("Negro") was enough. This is explicit in the dictation entitled "Nos Habits" (Our clothes): "Pour t'habiller, le cultivateur cultive le lin et le chanvre, le nègre récolte le coton, le fermier élève et tond ses moutons." (To clothe you, the farmer grows flax and hemp, the Negro harvests cotton, the rancher raises and shears his sheep.) Also mentioned are the worker, weaver, tailor, tanner, cobbler, and milliner.[126] Father Magnan expressed it in his own way when he wrote: "Ce sont des hommes tout noirs, les nègres, qui cultivent, en général, le cotonier. [...] Les nègres recueillent ce duvet qui est le coton. D'autres hommes l'apportent à la filature."[127] (It is men who are black all over, the Negroes, who generally grow the cotton trees. [...] The Negroes harvest the down that is cotton. Other men take it to the mill.)

At the end of his cotton lesson, Magnan asks the children: "Comment appelez-vous ceux qui le cultivent généralement?" (What do you call those who generally grow it?) On the one hand, there are the White workers or planters; on the other, the Blacks, whose individualization is limited to the blackness of their body. All these lessons about cotton taught the students that the difficult work of harvesting cotton could be done only by Blacks, whose bodies were believed to be stronger than those of Whites. In explaining why the island of Haiti was less prosperous than it had been before slavery was abolished ("les nègres libres sont généralement paresseux" [free Negroes are generally lazy]), Toussaint wrote: "Les planteurs, à cause de l'extrême chaleur de ce climat, ont absolument besoin du bras des noirs pour exploiter leurs riches plantations."[128] (Because of the climate's extreme heat, the planters absolutely need the strong arms of the Blacks in order to run their rich plantations.) A race that was associated with nature in Africa became an essential part of "cultivating" the soil in America, as shown in all the engravings and etchings illustrating it.

"I have seen a picture of a cotton-field," said John. "There were some negroes picking the cotton."[129] The image John mentions to his father heads up the reading about cotton from which this speech has been taken. In the foreground three Black people—a woman, a man, and a child—are picking cotton. Two inserted vignettes show White women spinning and weaving the cotton. This illustration is not exceptional—almost all of the illustrations representing Black people in America place them in a context of farm work. When they are not harvesting cotton, they appear in illustrations about sugar cane, coffee, rice, or diamonds (Figures 11 to 16).

A particular feature of images of Black workers is the frequent presence of women and, in some cases, children. In contrast to the texts, in which women were invisible, Black women occupied a prominent place in these illustrations. This representation placed them in a relation of obvious alterity to the White women in America who appeared in such illustrations, since the latter were staged as urban middle-class women or mothers of families. Restricting Black women to farm work, in a "sphere" that was neither truly public (urban) nor truly private (family), excluded them from an existence outside the plantations. In the end, the abolition of slavery has changed nothing, these images seemed to say.

The association of Black populations with commodities produced in America was a recurrent stereotype in images presented to schoolchildren. This representation confirms an essentialization of Black communities that was driven by the educational discourse. As accessories or set elements in American farm culture, Blacks themselves came to be represented as a product. This is evident in the illustration titled "West India Products," which features two Black men (Figure 17).

The representation of people with dark skin put forward in the Canadian educational discourse exemplifies the rhetorical construction of alterity through the body. In the process, the Black populations are dehumanized. The racial hierarchy that renders them inferior and the individual identity that is constantly denied them are among the numerous manifestations of this dehumanization. Rather than invalidating it, the sentence "Negroes have a soul like White people" confirms it. Despite the realities associated with slavery and its abolition, which in any case were passed over in silence, Black people were presented to Canadian schoolchildren, in both texts and images, as resources in America and as cannibalistic savages in Africa whose humanity is combined with a certain animality. By reifying these populations, about

whom it was said that they could be *found* in Africa and were *introduced* to America, it was the Sœurs de la congrégation de Notre-Dame who took dehumanization to the furthest degree.

In the educational discourse of the nineteenth century, the human diversity that is *visible* in the body progressively goes from a fascination for the strange peoples the Europeans encountered all around the globe to creating a hierarchy of the peoples of the Earth according to a racial taxonomy that grew less and less ambiguous. The various tattooed Maoris, giant Patagonians, dirty Eskimos, and gentle Hottentots were gradually forgotten in favour of Yellow, Black, or Red people to be converted and civilized.

In 1899, the teachers' magazine *L'Enseignement primaire* offered its readers a dictation entitled "Le marché d'Halifax" (The Halifax market), taken from a book by French-Canadian author Narcisse-Henri-Édouard Faucher de Saint-Maurice. The significance of its representations justifies presenting the entire piece:

> Je ne pouvais quitter Halifax sans visiter son marché.
> De ma vie je n'oublierai le spectacle de ce jour-là. Ici, les
> vendeurs forment trois groupes bien distincts: les indiens,
> les nègres, les blancs.
>
> Les indiens appartiennent tous à ces puissantes tribus qui
> jadis, sous les ordres du baron de Saint-Castin, tinrent si
> longtemps les Anglais en échec. Accroupis sur leurs talons,
> ils attendent silencieusement que l'acheteur se présente et
> marchande les peaux repassées, les mocassins, les raquettes,
> les paniers, les petits objets de fantaisies qui composent le
> fonds de leur commerce. Quelques-uns d'entre eux parlent

Figure 11. "Sugar Cane," Frères des écoles chrétiennes, *Nouvelle géographie illustrée*, 1875, 45.

Figure 12. "Harvesting Coffee," Frères des écoles chrétiennes, *Géographie illustrée. Cours moyen*, 1876, 25.

RICE PLANTING.

DIAMOND MINES.

COTTON.

"FATHER, I should like to know all about cotton, and how it is made into cloth," said John.

"Very well,

Figure 13. "Rice Planting," *Lovell's Advanced Geography*, 1880, 55.

Figure 14. "Diamond Mines," *Lovell's Advanced Geography*, 1880, 72.

Figure 15. "Cotton," Anonymous, *Second Reader*, 1884, 96.

Récolte du coton.

WEST INDIA PRODUCTS.

encore le français et s'en montrent très fiers; la plupart sont catholiques.

La gaieté bruyante du second groupe fait contraste avec l'immobilité du premier. Partout ce ne sont que lazzis, éclats de rire, démonstrations de joie enfantine. Nègres, négresses, négrillons, jadis tous princes et princesses du sang en leur pays, sont là, entassés pêle-mêle, criant à tue-tête leurs fruits et leurs denrées! Le marché d'Halifax est unique sous ce rapport, et je ne crois pas qu'il existe au monde un endroit où l'on puisse rencontrer autant de nez camus, de dents blanches, d'yeux noirs et ardents, de lèvres épaisses de trois pouces, de bottes éculées, d'habits noirs râpés, d'uniformes et de livrées flétris, de cravates blanches, rouges ou bleues longues d'un pied, de robes jaunes surmontées d'un fichu vert, de cachemires en loques, de pantalon à jour et de chapeaux de castor fantastiques. . . .

Faucher de Saint-Maurice. (La Gaspésie.)[130]

(I couldn't leave Halifax without visiting its market. Never in my life will I forget the spectacle that day. Here, the vendors formed three very distinct groups: the Indians, the Negroes, and the Whites.

The Indians all belonged to the powerful tribes that, in bygone days, on the orders of the Baron de Saint-Castin, held off the English for so long. Hunkered down on their heels, they waited in silence for a buyer to present himself and haggle over the pressed skins, moccasins,

Figure 16. "Harvesting Cotton," Sœurs de la congrégation de Notre-Dame, *Géographie . . . Cours moyen et cours supérieur*, 1897, 225.

Figure 17. "West India Products," *Lovell's Advanced Geography*, 1880, 61.

snowshoes, baskets, and small decorative objects that make up their stock in trade. Some of them still speak French and showed themselves to be very proud of it; most are Catholics.

The noisy gaiety of the second group contrasted with the stillness of the first. All about, nothing was to be heard but gibes, bursts of laughter, demonstrations of childlike joy. Negroes, Negresses, *négrillons*, all former princes and princesses of the blood in their country, were there, crowded together pell-mell, hawking their fruits and foodstuffs at the tops of their voices! Halifax's market is unique in this respect, and I don't believe that there is a place in the world where you can find so many snub noses, white teeth, bright black eyes, lips three inches thick, round-heeled boots, threadbare black coats, faded uniforms and livery, white, red and blue ties a foot long, yellow dresses topped with a green scarf, ragged sweaters, fashionable trousers and fantastic beaver hats. . . .

Faucher de Saint-Maurice. [The Gaspé.])

The description of the "Negroes, Negresses, *négrillons*" makes reference to their "childlike joy" and uses a series of adjectives to dismiss their body, clothing, and attitude. As Boëtsch and Villain-Gandossi write: "At this point we must emphasize that the experience attributed to the body is not located only in the register of physical appearance, but in a series of poses that simultaneously take in morphology, clothing, language and gestures, forming an aggregate in which each element reinforces the others and which ends up—within the framework of the stereotype—being the sign of the whole."[131] The representations transmitted in this dictation text could not be better analyzed.

The rhetorical construction of alterity through a differentiation of the body is not limited to a single description of an Other physique. While some peoples exist only through their body, others are *recognized* by their customs and dress. The cultural alterity of the Orientals corresponds to the corporal alterity of the Blacks. Merging these two pieces of alterity rhetoric leads to the construction of a third figure, one that, in the Canadian context, is still more fundamental than the first two: the Indian.

4.

The Indian: Domination, Erasure, and Appropriation

In 1912, in a speech delivered on the occasion of the Convention des institutrices de Montréal, a gathering of female primary school teachers, Father Élie-J. Auclair recalled that it was not required in the program of the Conseil de l'Instruction publique to teach the history of Canada to young schoolchildren, but "qu'on ne risque rien à leur conter des histoires vraies, au lieu des contes de croquemitaine" (we run no risk in telling them true stories, instead of tales about the bogeyman). What was the first example of those "true stories" suggested by Auclair? Indian ethnography, of course!

> Je trouve comme thème de lecture et de copie, une petite
> note sur les *Sauvages du Canada*, de forme très simple
> et très nette. Je la lis posément aux enfants: "À l'arrivée
> de Jacques Cartier au Canada, notre pays était couvert
> d'immenses forêts. Les habitants, appelés indiens ou
> sauvages, étaient des hommes grands, bien faits, robustes.
> Ils avaient le teint cuivré, les cheveux noirs et plats. Ils

portaient des habits de peaux de bêtes. Ils voyageaient
en canots d'écorce. Ils aimaient les jeux et les combats, et
partageaient presque tout leur temps entre la chasse et la
guerre." Eh! bien, voilà tout ce qu'il faut pour intéresser les
enfants pendant une heure et plus.[1]

(As a subject for reading and copying, I've found a little
note on the *Savages of Canada* in a very clear and very
simple form. I read it calmly to the children: "On Jacques
Cartier's arrival in Canada, our country was covered with
immense forests. The inhabitants, called indians or savages,
were tall men, well-built, robust. They had coppery skin
and smooth black hair. They wore clothing made of animal
skins. They travelled in birchbark canoes. They liked games
and fighting, and divided nearly all their time between
hunting and making war." Well, that is all it takes to keep
the children interested for an hour and more.)

By recommending interesting children in the "savages" rather than in
the bogeymen of European legends, Auclair put forward a dual movement in the rationalization and nationalization of Canadian school
culture. The culmination of almost a century's existence for the "school"
Indian, Father Auclair's offering introduced the central themes in the
representation of an alterity that was fundamental to Canadian identity:
ethnographic interest, national history, authenticity, and an appropriation of Indigeneity. Moreover, to be able to use the fictional Indian
in this way, the necessary corollary was to presume the real Indian's
inevitable disappearance. By placing them in a different temporality,
it became justifiable to appropriate the Indigenous people's identity
in order to preserve their memory. How does such an alterity, built on
the negation of its own existence, take shape? How to historicize this
rhetorical construction while maintaining a critical interpretation and
without minimizing its violent colonial nature? Such are the challenges

of analyzing Canadian representations of Indigenous people in the educational corpus of the nineteenth century.

The Indian, First of the Others

The figure of the "imaginary Indian"[2] held pride of place in the parade of characters offered to children. The representation of America's Indigenous peoples constituted the principal figure of alterity in the educational discourse. In addition to the much more frequent occurrence of the figure in the corpus, the ways in which this alterity differed from the Oriental and Black versions can be seen in the material and pedagogical teaching aids in which it was presented. Unlike the Others constructed mainly in geography textbooks, the "ethnographic" Indian was presented for the students' knowledge in language and history courses. In order to legitimize the colonists' claims to their land and their dispossession by the colonial state, it was necessary to erase these populations from geographical studies of the American territory. At the time, this erasure supported the thesis of the dying race, while the fictional Indian was nonetheless very present in the classroom, beginning in the early grades.

On 2 November 1898, young Albertine Simard, a first-year pupil of the Sœurs de la congrégation de Notre-Dame in Baie-Saint-Paul, was writing an assignment in Canadian history.[3] After having answered, "Oui, il y trouva beaucoup d'Indigènes" (Yes, he found many Natives there), to the question "[Cartier] trouva-t-il du monde à cet endroit?" (Did [Cartier] find anyone at that place?), Albertine was required to explain "qu'est-ce qu'un Indigène" (what a Native is). The answer was simple: a Native was "un sauvage de l'Amérique" (a savage from America). In her first months of schooling Albertine was introduced to this figure, which, owing to its frequent presence in the educational material, would quickly become familiar: that of the Savage from America.

But what did we know about this Savage? In what way was he Other? Alterity's rhetorical methods converged in many texts reprinted in the language textbooks and in school compositions; for example, "Les Sauvages" and "Tribus sauvages du Canada au temps de Champlain" (Savage tribes in Champlain's time).[4] Almost without fail, mentions of the Indians were always accompanied by essentializing modifiers. "Fierce and bloodthirsty," "stately and intelligent," "nation belliqueuse" (bellicose nation), or "pauvres enfants des bois" (poor children of the forest), the people called "Savages" were rarely mentioned without reference to an attribute of their character or their customs. The same applied to their body. The numerous ethnographically inclined texts did not fail to describe in detail their physical build, clothing, tattoos, and ornaments. For example, in the section titled "Aborigènes du Canada—Moeurs des Indiens" (Canada's Aboriginals—Customs of the Indians) in a "Notebook" of Canadian history assembled by the Villa Maria convent students in 1899–1900, Pulchérie Brosseau wrote:

> Bien que malpropres, ils étaient fiers et portaient des pendants aux oreilles et aux narines, des bracelets de peaux de couleuvre, des colliers de rassade et autres ornements brodés de poil de porc-épic. Ils s'arrangeaient les cheveux de la manière la plus bizarre et se peignaient le visage de vermillon ou de noir de chaudron. Le tatouage était la principale parure. Pour se tatouer, les sauvages se perçaient la peau au moyen d'épines ou de pierres très aiguës. Après cette opération douloureuse, ils frottaient ces piqûres encore toutes sanglantes avec du charbon pilé ou de la poudre.[5]

> (Although dirty, they were proud and wore pendants from their ears and nostrils, bracelets of snakeskin, wampum collars, and other ornaments embroidered with porcupine quills. They arranged their hair in the most bizarre fashion and painted their face with vermilion or soot from cooking pots. Tattoos were the principal adornment. To tattoo

themselves, the savages pierced their skin with thorns or
very sharp stones. Following this painful operation, they
rubbed the still bleeding wounds with crushed coal or
powder.)

The figure of the Savage was defined in keeping with the discursive techniques used to construct alterity: special qualifiers, attention paid to the body, and an opposition of civilization/barbarity or civilized/primitive. The Indigenous nations were, moreover, very often essentialized by the generalizations that applied to all of North America's First Peoples. On reading a text by Dr. Clyde, the students learned that "the aboriginal inhabitants of the New World present [. . .] a remarkable uniformity of type." As well, they lack "any distinctive national character."[6] Historian F.-X. Garneau wrote that "tous les Sauvages [de la Floride au Canada] se ressemblaient" (all the Savages [from Florida to Canada] looked alike).[7] For Toussaint, "tous les Indiens étaient d'une haute stature et bien proportionnés" (all the Indians were tall in stature and well-proportioned). Do these generalizations respond to a pedagogical imperative? This is suggested by what Toussaint next asked the students: "Faites-nous connaître *en peu de mots* les caractères et les moeurs des Sauvages."[8] (Let us know *in a few words* about the characters and customs of the Savages.) True to the scientific culture that engendered it, the ethnographic knowledge offered to children was often reduced to a simplification that reified the Indigenous peoples in an unchanging, fossilized image. On occasion, certain writers recognized the variety within the Indigenous nations, but it was to facilitate the establishment of a hierarchy among them, valorizing a particular nation to the detriment of another.

Published in 1900 and intended for schoolchildren in the first and second year, *Mon premier livre* (My first book) was the first school textbook to have been distributed for free across the entire province of Quebec by the Conseil de l'Instruction publique. A page dedicated to the history of Canada provides a perfect example of this simplification:

"Le Canada, à cette époque reculée, était peuplé de sauvages qui ignoraient le nom du bon Dieu. C'étaient des barbares qui vivaient dans les
ténèbres du paganisme. Ils ne pardonnaient jamais à leurs ennemis. Les
sauvages vivaient de chasse et de pêche et se couvraient à demi de peaux
de bêtes."[9] (Canada, in those remote times, was populated by savages
who did not know the name of the true God. They were barbarians who
dwelt in the darkness of heathenism. They never forgave their enemies.
The savages lived by hunting and fishing and half-clothed themselves
in animal skins.) While it is appropriate to contextualize these texts,
not only in relation to the era's ideologies but also in terms of the
pedagogical imperatives to which they are responding, we must not
minimize the contempt and hatred they harbour. For far too long, the
academic community has been manipulating and analyzing archives that
contributed directly to the racism directed at Indigenous peoples and to
their dehumanization without remarking on it. In Emma LaRocque's
words, the fact "that few scholars have noticed the connection between
hate literature and violence against indigenous peoples is a testament
to the powers of prejudice and propaganda."[10] In particular, LaRocque
interrogates our responsibility in recognizing the violent consequences
of the textual dehumanization of Indigenous nations. The excerpt cited
from *Mon premier livre*, like most of the archival materials I quote from,
contributed to the dehumanization of Canada's First Nations.

Did ethnography sometimes avoid falling into contempt and demonization? In 1902, in his *Cours français de lectures graduées* (French course
of graded readings), Father Magnan wrote:

Les sauvages de l'Amérique du Nord étaient des hommes
d'une constitution robuste, d'une force physique peu
commune; leurs sens, comme ceux de l'homme primitif,
étaient d'une admirable perfection; l'acuité de leur vue,
la finesse de leur ouïe et de leur odorat les rendaient
redoutables. Aucune surprise n'était possible avec eux. [. . .]
La vertu dominante de ces sauvages, c'était la force d'âme,

le courage, l'insensibilité. Ils supportaient sans se plaindre
la chaleur, le froid, la fatigue, la souffrance, et passaient
facilement plusieurs jours sans prendre de nourriture. Les
enfants étaient élevés à cette rude discipline, et les femmes
elles-mêmes partageaient ce stoïcisme.[11]

(The savages of North America were men with a strong
constitution, with unusual physical strength; their
senses, like those of primitive man, were of an admirable
perfection; the acuity of their vision, the keenness of their
hearing and sense of smell made them formidable. It was
not possible to take them by surprise. [. . .] The dominant
virtue of these savages was their strength of spirit, courage,
and insensitivity to pain. Without complaining they
endured heat, cold, weariness, suffering, and easily went
for many days without food. The children were raised up
in this rough discipline, and even the women shared the
stoicism.)

This depiction, which could be called "laudatory," relies on several familiar discursive processes. Its subject appears to be the "noble savage," a
figure made popular by Jean-Jacques Rousseau in the eighteenth century.
The idea that the Indians would have a highly developed instinct and a
singular acuity of the senses could moreover be found in other educational texts. These texts also suggested that the Indians lived very close to
nature, an association that reinforces the civilized/primitive dichotomy.

Nonetheless, Magnan's text could never be seen as a positive
description of the Indigenous nations. After having praised their
"strength of spirit" and their "courage," he went on to say: "Mais ces
quelques vertus naturelles étaient largement compensées par des vices
odieux ou ridicules." (But these few natural virtues were greatly offset
by odious or ridiculous vices.) And then introduced were their "pride,"
their "spirit of hatred and revenge," and their "ferocity." Playing on the

Indians' qualities and flaws in the same portrait, Magnan used what LaRocque calls the exceptionalization technique, "in which 'positive' features of Natives are set up, only to smash them down. This does not negate the positive qualities or 'Indian virtues' that missionaries (and other archival sources) recorded, but it does remind us that not all words are as they appear. [. . .] There was nothing that 'Indians' could be or do that would meet with approval because the judgements, contradictory as they were, were cemented within colonial dogma, not objective accounting of behaviour or ethnography."[12] Magnan's text in fact contributed to this colonial dogma, as his conclusion went even further: "À la parole du missionnaire et sous la bienfaisante influence de l'Évangile, ces farouches enfants des bois déposèrent graduellement leur primitive férocité et baissèrent le front devant les forces supérieures de la civilisation."[13] (At the missionary's word and under the benevolent influence of the Gospel, these wild children of the forest gradually put aside their primitive ferocity and bowed their heads before the superior forces of civilization.) Despite attributing a few valorizing qualities to the Indigenous nations, Father Magnan ultimately imposed the rule of exceptionalization on them. The positive description did not abolish the world view to which he subscribed and which was made up in part of the civilization/savagery dichotomy. Like many of his contemporaries, Magnan considered his culture to be superior.

The only text written by an Indigenous person to be found in the educational corpus was an ethnographic description. In his piece "Indian Fasting,"[14] Francis Assikinack[15] described the fasting practices of the Odahwah. While this rare inclusion of an Indigenous voice in the educational materials must of course be remarked on, it is relevant to note the intertextual context in which this utterance took place. Unlike other readings in the same textbook, Assikinack's is followed by a biographical note:

The writer of the above is Francis Assikinack, a fullblooded Indian, and the son of one of the Chiefs of the Odahwahs or Ottawas, as they are more generally designated—now settled in the Manitoulin Island in Lake Huron. In A.D. 1840, he was sent, at the age of 16, to the Upper Canada College, Toronto. At that time he was totally ignorant of the English language, and after having been three months in the Institution, he got one of the other boys to interpret for him, and solicit permission to return home, as he thought he could never learn the English language. The request was not complied with, and he remained so long in the Institution, not only to acquire such a command of English as is seen in his papers, read before the Canadian Institute, Toronto, but also to obtain a familiar knowledge of Latin and Greek.[16]

This note uses the technique of exceptionalization. The civilized Indigenous person is presented as extraordinary, so that his individualization will function to prevent his valorized characteristics from being extended to other members of his community. In addition, it is understood in the text that Assikinack could acquire White culture only through a protracted immersion in a civilized environment. The fact that attempts were made to prevent him from returning to his home points to the idea that it takes time to civilize the Indian, and that returning to the community of origin would compromise the entire process. The way in which Assikinack's example was ideologically recycled foreshadowed the motivations stated by the Canadian government to establish the system of residential schools twenty years later.[17]

To fully understand the semantic and ideological analysis of the Indian's representation in school textbooks, a contextual analysis must be added. What was the internal composition of the textbooks into which these ethnographic texts were inserted? In other words, what was the context of utterance and of staging the figure of the Indian in these works? Let's start with Canada's history textbooks. Most books in this discipline included an ethnographic description of Canada's "Indigenous

nations." The exposition of the physical, cultural, and religious characteristics of the Indians was sometimes found at the beginning of the
book, right next to the physical description of Canada, or else in the
introduction. Other writers preferred to make a real breach in their
narrative to introduce children to the "principales peuplades sauvages"
(principal savage tribes) living in Canada at the time of the "discoveries."
In the textbooks of Henry Hopper Miles and the Frères des écoles
chrétiennes, this presentation appeared between the history of Cartier's
voyages and Champlain's activities. Adrien Leblond de Brumath chose
to insert his description between accounts of the voyages of Christopher
Columbus and Jacques Cartier.[18]

In his book *Les Authochtones dans le Québec post-confédéral*
(Indigenous peoples in post-Confederation Quebec), Claude Gélinas
observes that the presence of Indigenous people in colonial texts was
frequently associated with the description of the physical geography:
"From the outset, what is striking in the historical representation of the
Indigenous people by Quebec's post-confederation intellectuals is that
they are almost completely confined to a precise period, that of pre-his-
tory."[19] Since history textbooks were also written by Quebec's intellectual
élite, it is not surprising to see that Gélinas's conclusions also apply
to those didactic works. In Canadian history textbooks, however, the
Indigenous peoples were not confined to "prehistory"—their existence
was in fact located outside history. The pedagogical justifications given
by certain writers to explain the narrative breach created by presenting
the Indigenous nations clearly illustrates this situation. Hodgins, the
only writer to insert his description between the "French domination"
and the "English domination," made this anhistorical feature explicit in
a note to teachers: "As the following chapter, on the Indian Tribes, does
not form any Consecutive part of the History of Canada, the Teacher
can omit it in whole or in part at his discretion, when going over the
History for the first time in the ordinary course, or when teaching it
to the younger pupils."[20] On their side, in their textbook's introduction,
after having presented the state of "today's Canada," the Frères des

écoles chrétiennes noted the state of "primitive Canada": "Le Canada, ainsi que l'Amérique dont il fait partie, n'a pas toujours possédé ces précieux avantages. Il y a trois siècles, notre territoire n'était qu'une immense solitude, habitée çà et là par une race d'hommes demi-nus, vivant à l'état sauvage." (Canada, like America, of which it is a part, has not always had these precious advantages. Three centuries ago, our land was nothing but an immense solitude, inhabited here and there by a race of half-naked men, living in the savage state.) The study of history was intended to enable children to understand "cette transformation graduelle qu'a subie [le] pays" (the gradual transformation the country has undergone).[21] A knowledge of ethnography was essential to grasping the significance of this transformation, which bordered on the wondrous.

The anhistorical status and essentialization of the Indigenous nations reinforced the historical, progressive nature of the Canadian nation. According to Miles, Canada's history would have been simply incomprehensible without such knowledge: "We have here spoken of the savages, or Indians, because no one can pursue the history of Canada without some knowledge of them." This knowledge, which as we have seen was very general and simplified, could certainly be more complex, Miles believed, but it would be inappropriate and tedious to make it so in the context of a Canadian history course, he clarified.[22]

While present in the history textbooks, the Indigenous people were still not considered to be historical peoples. The context of utterance for ethnographic excerpts about the "Indians" was nonetheless different in the reading textbooks. These books, which were used in language courses, contained a variety of texts that went from pious poetry to general science by way of the pastoral tale and geographical notes. In them, ethnographic lessons on the Indians, such as "Les Sauvages de l'Amérique," "La finesse des Indiens" (The Indians' subtlety), or "The Canadian Indians," did not at first glance seem to have a special place in the content being taught; that is, they seemed to be one reading among others. However, a close study of these textbooks makes it possible to determine that the figure of the Indian was often one of the first figures of alterity to be presented to children during their time at school.

A study of many Canadian readers published in the 1860s and 1880s casts an interesting light on the evolving role played by the Indian in the "Canadian" identity. *The British-American Reader* (1860) by John Douglas Borthwick and *The Fifth Book of Reading Lessons* (1867) published by Campbell of Toronto both owed their "British American" character in large part to the importance given to Indigenous subjects. In the case of *The Fifth Book*, the large number of texts about "Eskimos" (Inuit) also contributed to this American specificity.

Borthwick explains his motivation in his preface: "Our youth have hitherto been taught far too little of their native land, and whilst School Books from other countries have been widely used, the pupils have been left in total or at least partial ignorance of the History and Geography, Geology and Botany, Natural History and Productions, Climate and Scenery of those Provinces which truly constitute the 'brightest gem in the diadem of England.'"[23] These textbooks were published a few years before Confederation; did their authors feel an urgency to create a feeling of belonging to the Canadian land and a national cultural imaginary? If that is the case, the imaginary's content was rapidly changing.

In the 1880s, two series of Canadian readers were published in Ontario, the Royal Readers series by Campbell and another series by Gage. The textbooks, which had a very obvious patriotic, imperialist scope, included surprisingly few allusions to Indigenous people in Canada, except in a few passages harking back to the distant past. The publishers had therefore taken up the practice of erasure that, we must remember, was part of the context of conquering the West and instituting genocidal policies. The readings concerning Canada exploited the imaginary of colonizing a virgin land. The patriotic content to be transmitted to young anglophone Canadians thus changed considerably from the 1860s to the 1880s. The first readers painted a picturesque image of the Canadian land in which the Indians were one of the principal elements. By contrast, the textbooks published in the 1880s reflected, through the erasure they were performing, the context of dispossession of the Indigenous nations in the West and the associated movement of colonization. It was the way of life of the White colonists that was then highlighted and, ultimately, magnified.

Thanks to the importance given by the school to transmitting ethnographic "knowledge" about Indians in the various educational materials, the children would acquire a feeling of authority over these subjects.[24] Despite the small amount of power they wielded at that age, they *knew* what the Indians were and came away with a feeling of control that most often lasted into adulthood. Among all of the "facts" about the First Peoples that were taught to children, one was eminently political.

While the stories about the Indians of the past were intended to entertain, those about the contemporary state of what was depicted as their nearly extinct descendants should have moved their audience with the myth of the dying race.

Throughout the period under study, 1830 to 1915, the geography textbook, when it did not include specific historical sections, was the textbook that conveyed the "current state of the world." In their prefaces, the authors often boasted of being at the cutting edge of the latest advances in scientific knowledge. And yet ethnographic descriptions of othered peoples, for their part, were only rarely changed from one edition to the next, the most flagrant case being that of Father Holmes's textbook. This fact also largely attests to the attribution of a fixed, anhistoric character to these populations. As a science of the contemporary land, geography erased Canada's Indigenous populations. To legitimize dispossessing them of their lands, the school taught children that in any case they were no more than a shadow cast on Canada's contemporary territory. In presenting the population of Manitoba, Calkin expressed the idea that his country was that of the White man. While the past had been peopled with Indians, the future was reserved for settlers: "The inhabitants in 1870 were principally Indians and halfbreeds; but since that date many settlers have come in from the other Provinces and from

Europe."[25] That fact may have been true, but it is the vehemence with which it was expressed that is significant.

In 1882, in a geography composition on Canada's power, Marie-Louise Brunet recites its inhabitants' origins: "Canadiens-Français, habitant particulièrement le Province de Québec, Anglais, Irlandais, Écossais, quelques milliers de Nègres et de Sauvages" (French Canadians, living particularly in Quebec, English, Irish, Scottish, a few thousand Negroes and Savages).[26] This enumeration is typical. While the textbooks do not all mention the presence of people of African descent in Canada, most of them, like Marie-Louise, put the Indigenous populations aside, especially in describing the eastern provinces. The phrasing the young girl uses, "a few thousand," signals an alterity through the simple fact that, unlike the other peoples mentioned, these two are quantified. The quantification used by Marie-Louise also stipulates the erasure of the Indigenous population. Some textbook authors went much further. Not only did they place the Indigenous people and African descendants at the end of their list, but they separated them from the White population through the use of precise terms: "Plus d'un million d'habitants sont Canadiens-Français; les autres sont Anglais, Irlandais, Écossais, outre 13,000 Indiens, reste des anciens indigènes de ce pays."[27] (More than a million inhabitants are French Canadians; the others are English, Irish, Scottish, aside from over 13,000 Indians, the remainder of the ancient indigenous peoples of this country.) Thus distanced from the Whites, the contemporary Indigenous people are only, as the authors put it, "the remainder" or "the debris" of ancient Indigenous peoples.[28] "Leur nombre décroît chaque jour" (Their number is rapidly decreasing); "La plupart ont disparu" (Most of them have disappeared); "peu nombreux aujourd'hui" (few in number today)—when they had not been completely eradicated from the account of the current state of America, the Indigenous peoples were described as dying.

By the beginning of the twentieth century, the erasure was complete. In 1915, a teaching guide produced by the Congrégation de Notre-Dame addressed the city of Montreal's cosmopolitanism. However, the First Peoples were not part of it:

> Notre ville de Montréal est de toutes les villes du Canada, celle qui a le plus d'habitants. Ils ne sont pas tous des Canadiens-Français. Vous avez entendu parler l'anglais dans les rues, même vous avez des compagnes qui ne parlent que l'anglais. Les Français ont commencé notre belle ville et en ont été les premiers habitants. Les Anglais sont venus plus tard. À présent, bien que les Canadiens-Français soient les plus nombreux, il y a beaucoup d'Anglais. Dans notre ville nous rencontrons aussi des Juifs, des Syriens, des Italiens, des Polonais, des Belges, des Russes, des Nègres.[29]

> (Of all the cities in Canada, our city of Montreal has the most inhabitants. They are not all French Canadians. You have heard English spoken in the street, you even have friends who speak only English. The French started our beautiful city and were the first inhabitants. The English came later. Right now, although the French Canadians are the most numerous, there are a lot of English people. In our city we also encounter Jews, Syrians, Italians, Poles, Belgians, Russians, Negroes.)

The geography texts mentioned the disappearance of the Indians, but they did not explain it. What could a child make of it, since the Indian was nonetheless a well-known imaginary character?

In the introduction to his Canadian history textbook, as the Frères des écoles chrétiennes did in the texts they produced, James Frith Jeffers compared the current state of Canada at that time to that of America at the time of the European "discoveries." "You seldom see an Indian now," he wrote, "and most of the people of America have light complexions like the people of Europe."[30] How did these changes come about? In proposing to answer these questions, did Jeffers provide an explanation for the unenviable fate of the Indians? He said, "If you look around you thoughtfully, you will learn the very cause that led to the settlement of America. You will see that the people do not spend their time in hunting and fishing, as the Indians did, but in tilling the ground, in buying and selling, and sending their grain and merchandize to other lands, for which they bring back goods not produced in this country. It was this desire to trade which led the white man across the Atlantic."[31] The explanation is rather unclear. All we can conclude is that the Indians no longer dominated America because they did not have the spirit of commerce and agriculture. In a way, they are responsible for their own disappearance.

"But how soon not a trace / Of the red-man's race / Shall be found in the landscape fair."[32] Like this poem by Mrs. Moodie, the school textbooks often spoke to the disappearance of America's Indigenous people in the form of an elegy, without offering any further explanation regarding the causes of this sad fate. It was because, as J.-C. Taché recalled in "Le géant des Méchins" (The giant of the Méchins), it was a question of their destiny: "Alors si, comme tout semble le présager, ces belles races primitives du Canada sont destinées à disparaître des rangs de la famille humaine, elles iront finir et se perdre dans le sein de Dieu. Pauvres, mais heureuses nations!"[33] (So then if, as everything seems to foretell, the beautiful primitive races of Canada are doomed to vanish from the ranks of the human family, they will end by losing themselves in the bosom of God. Poor, but happy nations!) Can the fate of a people really be understood? The myth of the dying race belonged to the rhetoric of fatalism, and explaining it was optional. Most often, the school material would encourage the students to imagine the past existence of the "Savages" and be more compassionate about their disappearance. A text from the *Second Reading Book* in the series published by Campbell suggests this nostalgic attitude to the children. In an excerpt entitled "Our Trip to the Country," the children could read: "Long ago the Indians camped, and perhaps fought, on the broad meadow. We thought of all the brawl and bloodshed they had made. Now no quieter spot could be sought."[34] Erased from the contemporary territory by a genocidal intention that was halfway camouflaged by the effects of language, the Indians were relegated to a romantic or nostalgic past. These excerpts are so much historical evidence of the knowledge that Canadians, both francophones and anglophones, had about the Indigenous genocide in the nineteenth century and their very real participation in it.

Two school texts, one dating from 1860 and the other from 1891, offer a rare analytical version of the myth of the dying race. The excerpt, entitled "Character and Decay of the North American Indians," is a perfect example of what Patrick Brantlinger calls the "proleptic elegy."[35] The "unfortunate" fate of the Indians should elicit the sympathy of the White man, inasmuch as he is in part responsible for their disappearance. The text nonetheless reminds us of the impossibility of really under-standing the situation of the Indians with the tools of reason: "Reason as we may, it is impossible not to read, in such a fate, much that we know not how to interpret."[36] Even if it does not completely solve the riddle, the second text is slightly more explicit. In the dictation "La fin d'une race" (The end of a race), published in the magazine *L'Enseignement primaire* and signed the "Marquis de Nadaillac," the extinction of the "Redskins" is attributed to their inability to become civilized.[37] Even if they mention the illnesses and the violence, these texts still empha-size the Indians' "self-genocide." As Brantlinger observes, "The fantasy of auto-genocide or racial suicide is an extreme version of blaming the victim, which throughout the last three centuries has helped to rationalize or occlude the genocidal aspects of European conquest and colonization."[38] By transmitting this idea of a mysterious disappearance and possible self-genocide to the children, the school ensured the naïve complicity of a good part of Quebec's population in the imperial and colonial enterprises of North America.

The National History and Colonial Violence

Was the history of Canada taught in French-Canadian schools in the nineteenth century the very model of a national history, as many people thought,[39] or could it rather be seen as a colonial history? In observing how the figure of the Indian was built up as a radical Other, I maintain that before being a nationalist history, the Canadian history of the nineteenth century as taught in school is a prime example of a colonialist history and is directly influenced by the context of imperialism and the cult of heroes. It is undeniable that the history being taught was a national history, in the sense that its goal was to strengthen the national sentiment of the French-Canadian population, but the problem of alterity demands an interpretative shift, which has not received enough attention in the historiography. Furthermore, the importance of the national history in the school curriculum should be re-evaluated. It is true that it was taught beginning in the mid-nineteenth century in many schools, but it is an exaggeration to talk about the "*triomphe de l'histoire*" (triumph of history)[40] in that period. The omnipresence of "national" themes in the school curriculum did not really appear until the last years of the nineteenth century. In the early twentieth century, many actors were complaining of shortcomings in the "national" or "patriotic" education of French-Canadian students.

By observing the colonial aspects in the narrative of Canadian history, I want to "recolonize" Québécois history, to borrow a concept introduced by Brian Gettler.[41] It is a question of recognizing the indispensable presence of the Indigenous people in the national story that was developed 150 years ago.[42] In order to commit fully to the process of decolonization, (re)cognizing the colonial—and not "colonized"—aspect of the French-Canadian historical narrative is also indispensable. As LaRocque put it: "Again, and perhaps this is a rhetorical question, how could intelligent Canadians have missed so much racism in their research and writings? It is not as if it were obscure. To go into the many historically rooted reasons for all this tolerance of suspect literature is to go right back to the point of the struggle: that colonial constructs are for the purpose of conquest, not knowledge, and that they serve to blind and condition subsequent generations to see through 'stereotypic eyes.'"[43] Indeed, having been involved in the nation building, how was the Québécois historiography allowed to ignore to this point the imperial, colonial, and racist dynamics at the very roots of the idea of the nation? It is a colonial agnosia that we must overcome.

In a more or less explicit extension of Benedict Anderson's works, but also of those assembled by Pierre Nora, the study of identity construction and the national imagination has occupied an important place in Quebec's academic—and public—space for many decades. Many intellectuals have taken an interest in the study of nation building with the aim of clarifying contemporary debates. Gérard Bouchard, Fernand Dumont, Yvan Lamonde, Jocelyn Létourneau, and Louis Rousseau are among those who have attempted to outline the contours and content of the French-Canadian "nation" as it was constructed in the nineteenth and twentieth centuries. Many aspects of their writings stand out: the importance of the grand narrative and the élites' discourse, the antagonism of the inner Englishman, influence of the great powers, and religious construction of the nation. Taken together, these elements of the Québécois national identity lead to the last: ambivalence or equivocity. Being unable to retrace, in Québécois history, the construction of an identity that is strong, simple, adopted, and specific, some intellectuals applied themselves to clearing away the contradictions, inertia, and failures of French-Canadian thinking. Bouchard talks about ineffectual, equivocal thought; Dumont states that the society has focused on its conservative culture; Lamond addresses ambivalence.

In his book *La mémoire, l'histoire, l'oubli* (Memory, history, forgetting), Paul Ricoeur talks about the wounds of collective memory. He believes that they are often the object of too much memory (*mémoire-répétition* [memory-repetition]) or too little memory (*fuite loin de cette mémoire* [fleeing far from this memory]).[44] While certain aspects of the Québécois national construction have been the object of a *mémoire-répétition*, the place of Indigenous peoples in the narrative has been studied "too little." By attending mainly to the internal mechanisms of the national construction and its connections with foreign powers such as France, Great Britain, and the United States, the historiography has ignored the importance of the gaze directed at the Other in the collective's cultural and discursive construction.

For a long time, Québécois historiography has insisted on the role of the "English" in Quebec's national construction. The interpretation takes on different meanings depending on the academics questioned. In some narratives, the English person appears as the quintessential Other for the French-Canadian nation. Other writers have instead recognized the absence of antagonistic representation or promoted a pacified vision of these identity representations. What significance do these issues assume in the analysis of the schooling discourse? What is the narrative alterity in teaching the history of Canada? In their introduction, the authors of the book *L'histoire nationale à l'école québécoise* (The national history in Quebec schools) ask an interesting question that deserves to be considered in greater depth: "Isn't it part of teaching the national history to shape the perceptions and behaviours of the next generations with its biases?"[45] If there was a bias in the history that had repercussions for the perceptions and behaviours of many generations of French Canadians, it was the dehumanizing representation of the First Nations that this teaching disseminated. By avoiding addressing this thorny issue, despite what their introduction suggests, the book's authors perpetuate the historical erasure of these peoples.

Why isn't the "Anglais" the real Other in the French-Canadian history of Canada? To go back to the rhetorical criteria of alterity construction, have the English qualified in the same way as the Indigenous people? In recounting the episode of the Acadian deportation, Toussaint wrote: "Joignant la perfidie à la cruauté, les Anglais firent main basse sur la population Acadienne, incendièrent les habitations, entassèrent les Acadiens sur leurs navires et les dispersèrent sur les côtes de la Nouvelle-Angleterre, sans pain et sans protection."[46] (Adding treachery to cruelty, the English laid hold of the Acadian populace, burned down the houses, crowded the Acadians together on their ships and scattered them along the coast of New England, without food or shelter.) If the Iroquois were almost always "ferocious," "haughty," and "barbaric," the English were, for their part, given to treachery and cruelty. Or rather, they themselves were not treacherous or cruel; the text does not qualify them, but it qualifies their actions. This is a fundamental, essential difference in the construction of alterity. The English were not *essentially* treacherous and cruel, but they acted with treachery and cruelty.

What about the anglophone side? Who was presented as the "Other"? Altogether, the school materials were rooted in Canada's long-term memory and offered anglophone students a narrative with a positive presentation of the French-Canadian heroes from the era of New France. Certainly, the feuds with France and then with the United States are mentioned, but the enemy was not represented as Other. For example, in the narrative of the heroic episode of the War of 1812, the American enemy was not demonized or even qualified. In fact, attention was paid almost exclusively to the Canadian heroes, the identity that at that time took up all the space.

A question arises: Could the "national" construction have been based on the demonization of a White rival of European origin? The French example, as David A. Bell has analyzed it, is enlightening on many levels. Bell addresses the exclusion of the English from European identity in French writings and the demonization that is its corollary. He shows how the French rhetoric had to "barbarize" or "ensavage" the English to make them into an alterity figure that could be useful in national construction.[47] The identity constructed by Canadians, francophones as well as anglophones, did not have to metamorphose a rival European into an "American Savage." It could build its own from a colonial history that rests directly on Indian savagery. The same is true of the United States, as Brantlinger notes: "*The Last of the Mohicans* represents the emergence of the modern United States out of the colonial past as the process of defeating those of its enemies who were prior to Britain, namely, the French and their Indian allies. But the French are never much of a factor; at the center, instead, are the Indians and their fate, which is already inherent in their racial identity as savages."[48]

In 1909, a report by an ecclesiastic visitor from the Commission des écoles catholiques de Montréal (CECM) stressed the importance of teaching history and geography from a national, patriotic point of view. To facilitate this kind of teaching, the publisher who produced wall-hung pictures illustrating the principal historical facts would be doing a real work of patriotism, he wrote. Of the "five principal facts" that Father Perrier considered should be displayed ("the arrival of Cartier, the Founding of Montreal, the Massacre of Lachine, the Heroism of Dollard, the Martyrdom of P. Brébeuf"),[49] four would be inconceivable without an Indigenous presence. The Indigenous people represented therefore almost never existed for their own sake. As well, they were rarely individualized. Their presence in the text did not ensure that they would make a real contribution to the narrative as historical agents. And yet, without them, there is no Cartier, Champlain, Dollard, de Verchères, Brébeuf, Jogues, and so on. None of these heroic figures could exist without the narrative alterity provided by the Indigenous peoples' representation.

Canada's educational history, by basing itself on encountering and for a long time battling the "natives," the civilizing mission among the "savages," and the cult of heroes, adopted the narrative aspects of nine-teenth-century imperialism. Moreover, it is appropriate to point out the history's gendered nature. With few exceptions, women, White as well as Indigenous, are absent. Aside from a few references to such figures as Marguerite Bourgeoys, Hélène de Champlain, and other women who marked the colony's early history, and which are to be found mostly in the school materials produced by the Sœurs de la congrégation de Notre-Dame, Madeleine de Verchères was in fact Canada's only heroine. As noted by Colin M. Coates and Cecilia Morgan, the tangle of gender, race, and imperialism in the narrative of Madeleine de Verchères's heroism is meaningful.[50]

In mentioning the episode from the life of de Verchères analyzed by Coates and Morgan and giving it a commemorative slant, the educational texts often highlighted this heroine's exceptional quality. In an excerpt from his second reading book entitled "Courage de deux Canadiennes" (Courage of two Canadian women), Montpetit wrote, "Les femmes, dans leur faiblesse, trouvent souvent en elles un courage, une résignation, une patience dont serait fier le sexe dominant, le sexe de la force et de la guerre."[51] (Women, in their weakness, often find within themselves a courage, resignation, and patience of which the dominant sex, the sex of strength and war, would be proud.) Even if he inflated the young girl's heroism, Montpetit essentialized women. The important role that they could play was itself part of their weakness, a foregone conclusion. Father Ferland created the same gendered distinction in his interpretation of the colonial history, as can be seen in the excerpt "Les temps héroïques de la Nouvelle-France" (The heroic times of New France). This "lutte entre la civilisation chrétienne et le naturalisme sauvage des aborigènes" (battle between Christian civilization and the natives' savage naturalism) features "weak, delicate women" and "bold explorers": "Cette période en effet présente des traits nombreux de dévouement religieux, de courage, de foi, de persévérance. Le même esprit animait les simples laïcs et les religieux, des femmes faibles et délicates, aussi bien que les soldats et les hardis explorateurs qui s'aventuraient au milieu des tribus sauvages."[52] (This period in effect displays the numerous features of religious devotion, courage, faith, perseverance. The same spirit moved simple laymen, members of the religious orders, and weak, delicate women as much as the soldiers and bold explorers who ventured among the savage tribes.)

The narrative of Canada's history is therefore aligned with a gendered perspective. What about its teaching? Were the accounts of heroic battles waged by these "bold explorers" intended equally for boys and girls? The school materials were generally conceived for use by the two sexes, and what I analyzed did not offer different versions of the national history depending on the sex of the reader. In 1893, Napoléon

Brisebois, a pedagogue, specified that history instruction should be the same for boys and girls. And yet, rather than abolishing the gender division, the argument he uses strengthens and actualizes it:

> Il serait à souhaiter, dit-il, que nos femmes en général s'adonnassent plutôt à la lecture de l'histoire qu'à celle du roman ou du feuilleton, lecture plutôt propre à ramollir l'intelligence qu'à la nourrir.
>
> Aussi quelle est dans la famille, la personne la plus particulièrement préposée à l'éducation des enfants, sinon la femme?
>
> Comment pourra-t-elle inculquer dans l'âme de ses enfants l'amour de Dieu et de la patrie, si elle ignore l'histoire? Comment pourra-t-elle au moment du danger leur dire: allez et faites comme ont fait nos pères. Comme eux ne souffrez jamais l'insulte. Comme eux soyez fiers, vaillants, courageux et vertueux et sachez sans crainte et sans faiblesse défendre ce que vous avez de plus cher, le foyer, la patrie.[53]
>
> (It is to be hoped, he said, that our women should in general take up reading history rather than novels or serials, reading that is more likely to weaken the intelligence than to nurture it.
>
> Also, in the family, who is the person most especially likely to be in charge of the children's education, if not the woman?
>
> How could she instill in her children's soul a love of God and the homeland, if she is ignorant about history? How could she, in a time of danger, tell them: go and do what our fathers did. Like them, never endure an insult. Like

them be proud, brave, courageous and righteous and know
how to defend without fear or weakness what is most dear
to you, the home, the homeland.)

The women's place in the patriotic effort was to help disseminate the
history. To do this, it was critical that they themselves be educated. As
future defenders of the homeland, like the schoolboys, schoolgirls were
the primary custodians of the historical memory.

Another aspect of colonialism inherent in the school's history of
Canada is a sustained and recurrent effort in the texts to affirm the
legitimate claim of the French to the American territory. As Gélinas
notes, the "imaginary" representation of the Indigenous people then at
play "was aiming for other ideological objectives directly related to the
legitimacy of territorial ownership and the proposed development of
the French Canadian nation."[54] This quest for legitimacy was enacted on
several fronts: military, moral, and genealogical. The argument relied first
of all on repeating the litany of battles waged by the French and their
victories. The confrontation absolved the French of having dispossessed
the Indigenous peoples of their lands and contributed to their supposed
disappearance. As Garneau wrote: "Les fiers Iroquois qui semblaient
marcher à la domination de toutes les contrées baignées par les eaux du
Saint-Laurent et de l'Atlantique, furent arrêtés ici par les Français pour
la première fois. Ils soutinrent la lutte contre les blancs pendant près de
deux siècles, jusqu'à ce qu'ils se fussent effacés comme les forêts qui leur
servaient de refuge."[55] (The proud Iroquois, who seemed to be marching
toward domination of all the regions bathed by the waters of the St.
Lawrence and the Atlantic, were stopped here by the French for the
first time. They continued to battle the Whites for nearly two centuries,
until they were erased like the forests that served as their refuge.) This
context also took in multiple scenes of the Indigenous peoples' subjection, forced or not, mentioned in the history. Their submission, similar
to that contained in the imperialist accounts of the conquest of Africa,
presented groups of Indigenous people admiring the French, submitting

to them, or fearing them. It can be seen as clearly in the texts as in the iconography, Garneau wrote: "Le terrible fléau qui décimait les Sauvages, les effrayait and les rendait aussi soumis qu'on le voulait."[56] (The terrible scourge that decimated the Savages, frightened them and made them as submissive as we wanted.)

The colonial legitimacy was also based on moral imperatives, as in the civilizing mission. In a textbook by the Frères des écoles chrétiennes, for example, the students could read: "Quand, l'histoire en main, on voit que ce million d'âmes n'est que l'épanouissement régulier des quelques familles françaises qui sont venues s'établir ici il y a à peine deux cent cinquante ans, pour évangéliser les peuplades sauvages et infidèles de ces contrées, il faut bien en convenir et dire: 'Digitus Dei est hic: Le doigt de Dieu est-là.'"[57] (When, history in hand, we see that these million souls are only the regular progeny of those few French families who came to settle here barely 250 years ago, to evangelize the savage, heathen tribes of these regions, we can only agree and say: 'Digitus Dei est hic: The finger of God is here.") The evangelization of the Indigenous peoples thus justified taking possession of Canadian land. The civilizing mission sometimes led to their subjection, as in this dictation by schoolgirl Emma Comtois: "Et cet homme, ce Champlain, voulut créer un temple et il voulut Cristianiser [sic] le Sauvage. [. . .] En 1615, a [sic] sa voix trois Pères Récollets arrivaient au Canada. L'Iroquois et le Huron cœurs captivés s'ouvraient avec grandes pensées a toutes les espérances du chrétien [sic]."[58] (And this man, this Champlain, wanted to create a temple and he wanted to Christianize the Savage. [. . .] In 1615, at his call three Récollet Fathers arrived in Canada. The captivated Iroquois and Huron hearts opened themselves with great thoughts to all the hopes of the Christian.)

The myth of wild virgin soil is another of the rhetorical processes employed. In her dictation, young Emma also writes: "Rien qu'une nature richement ornée par les mains du Créateur que ce rocher sur lequel ce farouche Sauvage a [sic] l'exemple de l'aigle avait érigé sa demeure."[59] (Nothing but nature richly adorned by the Creator's hands was this

boulder on which the fierce Savage following the eagle's example had
built his dwelling.) The ideology instilled in the children is patent: it
is agriculture, the intensive exploitation of the soil, and commerce that
qualified ownership. The conversation titled "Notre pays" (Our land),
placed at the end of a graduated syllabary produced by the Sœurs de la
congrégation de Notre-Dame, concisely conveys this dichotomy:

> *Madame D.* Quand les aïeux de vos grands-parents
> arrivèrent en Canada, le pays était-il comme il est
> aujourd'hui ?
>
> *L.* Oh, non Madame! Il était couvert de grandes forêts. Il
> n'y avait ni champs, ni jardins, ni maisons. . . . Les aïeux de
> nos grands parents n'y trouvèrent que des cabanes, groupées
> çà et là . . . et habitées par des sauvages.
>
> *Mme D.* Savez-vous ce qu'étaient ces sauvages?
>
> *L.* Des hommes qui ne connaissaient pas le bon Dieu …
> qui n'étaient pas civilisés, et qui vivaient de pêche et de
> chasse.[60]
>
> (*Madame D.* When the ancestors of your grandparents
> arrived in Canada, was the country the same as it is today?
>
> *L.* Oh, no, Madame! It was covered with great forests.
> There were no fields, nor gardens, nor houses. . . . Our
> grandparents' ancestors found only huts, grouped here and
> there . . . and inhabited by savages.
>
> *Madame D.* Do you know what these savages were?
>
> *L.* Men who did not know God . . . who were not civilized,
> and who lived by fishing and hunting.)

It was by staging a lazy Indian, in keeping with the archetype of the
Native who disdains work and neglects to cultivate the land, that the

legitimacy of claiming the contemporary territory was established. The Canadian won the right to the land by the sweat of his brow. Finally, at the pinnacle of all these justifications sits the argument of "spilt blood." This could not be more explicitly put than in an exercise from the *Cours théorique et pratique* by the Frères des écoles chrétiennes: "Arrosée de nos sueurs et de notre sang, nous avons droit à la possession de la terre du Canada."[61] (Watered with our sweat and blood, we have the right to possess the land of Canada.) The legitimacy of occupying the land haunts the teaching of history. But on what does it rest? On violence: the savage violence of the barbarians, the civilizing violence of the colonists.

Mon premier livre, a textbook for children aged six and seven, includes several pages of Canadian history. In the excerpt about Champlain, they could read: "Champlain eut à lutter contre les Iroquois, les sauvages les plus redoutables de l'Amérique." (Champlain had to fight against the Iroquois, the most formidable savages in America.) A few pages on, it dealt with De Maisonneuve: "À cette époque, la colonie naissante était constamment exposée aux dépradations des Iroquois." (At this time, the nascent colony was constantly exposed to the depradations of the Iroquois.) Like the great majority of texts that dealt with the Indigenous populations in the era of New France, these excerpts represented the Indian in a situation of violence or as Gélinas puts it: "In fact, it was often the only pretext for talking about them."[62] When the Indians were not attacking the French, they were at war with one another. Violence is central to the colonial story. Imputed to both the Indigenous peoples and the French, it is nonetheless presented in accordance with two different narrativities and calls up a specific ideological framework.

We can start with the violence perpetrated by the Indigenous people. First of all, its description's extent (long expositions) and frequency (constant reminders of cruelty) characterized it. In 1909, at the Saint-Jean convent of the Congrégation de Notre-Dame, a teacher asked the students: "Quels furent les religieux martyrisés par les Iroquois en 1648 et 1649? Racontez le martyre de chacun d'eux."[63] (Who were the priests martyred by the Iroquois in 1648 and 1649? Recount each one's martyrdom.) The pupil whose assignment came down to us meticulously described the tortures inflicted on the Jesuit martyrs. Considering the school curriculum, which frequently depicted the Indians' violence, it is not surprising to see such a raw text penned by a young girl. Several years before, in the margins of a composition about "L'Héroïne de Verchères," another of the congregation's pupils had reproduced an equally violent drawing of a scalp—a hand holding a bloody knot of hair.[64] The primary symbol of Indigenous violence, the practice of scalping, had nothing to do with the account of Madeleine de Verchères's heroism. As evidence of the scalp's power to recall the Indians' cruelty, the same engraving of the scalp had been glued just a few pages before, alongside the description of the Lachine massacre (Figure 18).

> Les Iroquois leur firent endurer des tortures épouvantables, allant jusqu'à leur attacher autour du cou des plaques de fer rouge. Ces barbares s'appliquèrent surtout à torturer le Père de Brébeuf. Ils lui coupèrent les lèvres, lui enfoncèrent un charbon ardent dans la bouche, et pour comble de cruauté, ils le scalpèrent, puis lui versèrent de l'eau bouillante sur la tête.[65]

> (The Iroquois made them endure dreadful tortures, going so far as to attach red-hot iron plates around their neck. These barbarians tortured Father de Brébeuf most of all. They cut off his lips, forced a hot coal into his mouth and, as the greatest cruelty, scalped him and then poured boiling water over his head.)

As shown by this reading from *Mon premier livre*, the strongest examples of how central the description of Indigenous violence is can be found mainly in readings about the Jesuit martyrs and the Lachine massacre. It is very important to mention that accounts of violence by "Indians" were an exception throughout the entire educational corpus; this was the only kind of violence to be described in so much lurid detail. Moreover, the analyzed corpus backs up the thesis maintained by Daniel Francis that the image of the "ferocious Indian" is stronger and recurs more frequently in francophone than in anglophone school textbooks. The sensationalism of the Indians' "savagery" was nonetheless frequently exploited by English-Canadian fiction writers of the same era.

What distinguishes the violence of the French relative to that of the Indians is, first of all, the nature and form of its exposition. The long descriptions of the Savages' tortures corresponded to brief allusions to actions taken by the French. There were really two kinds of violence inserted into the narrative, each with its own ideological import. On the one hand, the Indigenous cruelty fell outside the moral system recognized by Canadian society. From the moment that it became amoral, it was therefore excluded from the debate over legitimacy versus illegitimacy. Besides, the Indian "ravages" were rarely justified in the text, if not for recurring references to the "spirit of revenge." Located outside the moral system, the "ferocity" of these "savage hordes" resembled that of the animal or the demon: the alterity is absolute. Like predators, the "barbarian" Iroquois leave "des traces sanglantes [de leur] passage" and are "de plus en plus altérés du sang des Français" (bloody tracks behind them [and are] more and more altered by the blood of the Frenchmen).[66]

Next to this savage and even animal violence stands the colonial violence, which exists within a civilized reality. When they were considered to be legitimate, the violent actions of the French did not have to be justified. They were located inside a moral system that absolved them so obviously that the pedagogues were not obliged to attribute a motivation. In describing the geography "from Lévis to Huntington," Toussaint indicates, "C'est sur ses bords [de la rivière Richelieu], ou sur ceux du grand lac qui lui sert de couronne, que se fit entendre la première détonation de l'arme à feu et que le Sauvage reçut le premier plomb meurtrier de l'Européen qui venait lui ravir ses terres de chasse."[67] (It was on the banks [of the Richelieu River], or of the large lake that crowns

Scalp.

Figure 18. "Scalp," Miles, *The Child's History of Canada*, 2nd ed., 1876, 73.

it, that the first blast of a firearm was heard and the Savage caught the first deadly shot of lead from the European who had come to rob him of his hunting grounds.) In the *Cours théorique et pratique* by the Frères des écoles chrétiennes, the students were asked to "distinguer dans [la phrase suivante] l'imitation par le son, de l'imitation par le mouvement [. . .]: 'Champlain décharge son arquebuse, les balles partent, sifflent, volent et s'enfoncent dans le front de l'Iroquois'" (in [the following sentence], distinguish imitation through sound from imitation through movement [. . .]: 'Champlain discharges his musket, the bullets are launched, whistle, fly and bury themselves in the Iroquois's forehead').[68]

The excerpt, entitled "Daulac" in Pierre Lagacé's textbook, clearly signals the implicit legitimacy of colonial violence. In this text, which constructs Daulac (Dollard) and his companions as heroes, Lagacé wrote: "Les Français [firent des Iroquois] un horrible carnage, sans pouvoir cependant les empêcher de s'avancer jusqu'au pied de la palissade qu'ils attaquèrent à coups de hache. [. . .] Les Iroquois furent frappés de terreur en comparant le nombre de leurs morts à celui de leurs victimes. Après avoir assouvi leur vengeance sur les prisonniers français, ils retournèrent dans leurs villages, n'osant aller attaquer un pays peuplé de tels héros."[69] (The French made a horrible carnage [of the Iroquois], without nonetheless being able to stop them from advancing to the foot of the palisade, which they attacked with axes. [. . .] The Iroquois were struck with terror when comparing the number of their dead to that of their victims. After having slaked their desire for revenge on the French prisoners, they returned to their villages, not daring to attack a country peopled by such heroes.) Colonial violence is unconditionally part of the idea of the civilizing mission, as clearly explained by LaRocque:

> The idea of an abstract civilization inevitably winning
> over savagery neatly served the White North American
> usurper. Everything the White man did was legitimized by
> "civilization" and everything Indians did was "explained"
> by their supposed savagery. This was ideology at its brutal

best, and clearly fits the profile of what Memmi calls the "Nero complex." As Pearce has established, Americans developed a doctrine of savagery as a moral antithesis to progress. In the United States it became a morality script in which the cowboys finished what Columbus, the conquistadores, or the Puritans began. Cowboys—and before them Puritans, the frontiersmen, and the cavalry—moving west and killing "Indians" could then be equated with moral and human progress.[70]

It is precisely this ideology, which provides a framework for Canada's expansion into the West in the same era, that pervades the narrative of Daulac's "exploit." The hero and his companions kill hundreds of Iroquois to "save" the colony.

Faced with having to account for a rather despotic and murderous act by Monsieur de Tracy, Garneau found a way to pass the whole thing off as part of the battle between civilization and barbarity: "Il fallait en agir ainsi, sans doute, pour en imposer à ces Barbares,"[71] he wrote. (They no doubt had to act that way, in order to prevail over those Barbarians.) In his justification, Garneau nonetheless hesitated, which makes it possible to suppose that certain acts, even if they were committed in the name of civilization, were immoral. This was the case in two particular episodes, the abduction of Donnacona by Cartier and Champlain's involvement in conflicts with Indigenous people. Thus, in the 1860s, members of the Société Laval at the Petit Séminaire de Québec debated these questions: "Champlain a-t-il bien ou mal fait de faire la guerre aux Iroquois, au risque d'attirer sur la colonie des ennemis acharnés? [. . .] Champlain était-il autorisé à tirer sur les Iroquois? N'a-t-il pas fait un meurtre en tuant un Iroquois?"[72] (Did Champlain act for good or ill in waging war on the Iroquois, at the risk of making bitter enemies for the colony? [. . .] Was Champlain authorized to fire on the Iroquois? Did he not commit murder by killing an Iroquois?) These acts were judged and sometimes condemned according to a moral system. For its part, being outside any morality, the Indian violence has no place on the horizon of good and evil.

In June 1914, at the conference of the Association des instituteurs in the École Normale de Laval district, Education Specialist Dorion was militating for better patriotic teaching in the primary schools "afin que nos enfants (les hommes de demain) soient à la hauteur de la mission de notre race sur cette terre que nos missionnaires ont sanctifiée, que nos pères ont ouverte à la civilisation et au progrès" (so that our children, the men of tomorrow, are ready to take on the mission of our race on this Earth that our missionaries have sanctified, that our fathers have opened up to civilization and progress).[73] The epic of the French-Canadian race began with the heroic times of New France, and this history, intended to inspire our youth, was marked by violence. Without the violence of the "bad Indian," no more heroes or martyrs. And without heroes, no nation.

Indian Histories and the Cult of Heroes

In June 1915, the pedagogy magazine *L'Enseignement primaire* published a methodological article by school inspector H. Nansot entitled "La rédaction à la petite école" (Composition in the primary school).[74] Nansot suggested that teachers urge their pupils to produce a "composition on an image" (Figure 19). The illustration that serves as a model for this pedagogical exercise shows a young boy dressed up as an Indian regretting having scalped his sister's doll. Inspector Nansot invited the teachers to prepare the assignment with a verbal exchange that would lead the children to comment on the image. To illustrate his proposal, he included a fictional conversation between a schoolmaster and his pupils:

> *Master* — [. . .] Voyons, Paul, qu'est-ce que vous voyez dans cette image?
>
> *Paul* — Monsieur, je vois un petit Sauvage et une petite fille; une poupée, un chien et des chars.

Figure 19. Untitled, *L'Enseignement primaire*, 36th year, no. 10, [June 1915], 597. The image was reprinted from the American magazine *Life* and first appeared on its cover with the title "Another Indian Outrage" (11 March 1915).

M. — [. . .] Allons, réfléchissez un peu, pensez-vous réellement que vous voyez un vrai petit Sauvage?

Paul — Non, M.: c'est un petit garçon qui joue au sauvage; il a une coiffure de plumes comme en ont les Sauvages et une hache à la main.

M. — Bien! Y a-t-il encore quelque chose qui lui donne l'air d'un Sauvage?

Paul — Oui, M., il se tient la pointe des pieds en dedans.

M. — Oui, en effet, les Sauvages marchent ainsi; mais d'où leur vient cette habitude? Joseph pourrait-il nous le dire?

Joseph — Cela vient de ce qu'ils marchent beaucoup en raquettes pendant l'hiver. Pour bien marcher en raquettes, il faut envoyer la queue de la raquette en dehors et, pour cela, ramener les pointes des pieds en dedans.

(*Master* — [. . .] Come, Paul, what do you see in this image?

Paul — Sir, I see a little Savage and a little girl; a doll, a dog and some train cars.

M. — [. . .] Go on, think a little, do you truly believe that you're seeing a real little Savage?

Paul — No, Sir, it's a little boy who's playing Indian; he has a headdress of feathers like the Savages have and a hatchet in his hand.

M. — Good! Is there anything else that makes him look like a Savage?

Paul — Yes, Sir, he keeps his toes pointed in.

M. — Yes, that's right, the Savages walk like this; but how do they get this habit? Can Joseph tell us?

Joseph — That comes from walking a lot using snowshoes in the winter. To walk properly using snowshoes, you have to keep the snowshoes' tails on the outside, and to do that, bring your toes closer together.)

Recognizable at first sight by his "plumage" and his hatchet, the Savage also has a particular posture. To "play" Indian properly, the boy has to keep his toes pointing in. The explanation that Joseph gives for this detail shows a good "knowledge" of the way of life of these people called "Savages." Well-versed in the ethnography of Indians, the students of that time would indeed have been prepared to pick up subtle details from the image that serve to characterize and thus create a difference. The exchange continues:

M. — Croyez-vous que le petit garçon se tient toujours comme on le voit ici?

Joseph — Peut-être bien; mais peut-être aussi qu'il le fait seulement pour bien jouer au sauvage.

[. . .]

Lucien — M., il a trop bien joué son rôle de sauvage; on le voit par l'état de la pauvre poupée.

M. — Expliquez-vous davantage.

Lucien — M., la poupée est attachée par les pieds et par les mains; le petit Sauvage lui a ôté la chevelure à coup de hache. On voit les beaux cheveux étendus à terre, et le chien, qui a pris l'air féroce comme son maître, à [*sic*] l'air de les garder.

[. . .]

M. — [. . .] Lequel de vous, à présent, pourrait me dire si le petit Sauvage a agi avec malice? pour faire du mal? . . . Vous Joseph?

Joseph — Je crois que non, M., le petit garçon a entendu dire tout ce que les vrais Sauvages faisaient et il a cru que pour bien jouer au Sauvage il fallait faire des actes de cruauté. Mais il ne pensait pas à briser la poupée de sa petite sœur pour lui faire de la peine.

(*M.* — Do you believe that the little boy always stands the way we see him here?

Joseph — Maybe; but maybe he's also only doing it to play Indian properly.

[. . .]

Lucien — Sir, he has played the role of the Savage too well; we can see that from the state of the poor doll.

M. — Explain yourself.

Lucien — Sir, the doll has her feet and hands tied; the little Savage has taken off her hair with the hatchet. We can see the beautiful hair lying on the ground, and the dog, who has taken on a fierce look like his master, looks like he's guarding it.

[. . .]

M. — [. . .] Which of you can now tell me whether the little Savage acted with malice? to do some harm? . . . You, Joseph?

Joseph — I don't think so, Sir; the little boy heard all about what real Savages did and he believed that to play Indian well he had to perform acts of cruelty. But he wasn't thinking about breaking his little sister's doll to make her sad.)

A detailed examination of this article is revealing. In this three-page text, the word "sauvage" recurs twenty-two times. The author also deploys the lexical field related, in educational texts of the time, to the figure of the Indian: "barbarian" three times, "cruelty" and "cruel" four times, "ferocious" twice, and "hair" twice. In addition to mere vocabulary, the article also reproduces the voluntarily confused temporality of Indian history. The text points out at the beginning that Savages *have* headdresses and carry hatchets. Does Nansot recognize a contemporary existence for Indigenous people? Nothing is less certain. Does Joseph not then remember that the "little boy heard all about what real Savages *did*?"[75] And so the existence of the "real" Savages was conjugated in the past tense, and what the children knew came from their national socialization, as was well summed up in the next example of composition Inspector Nansot wrote:

Il a coiffé son bonnet sauvage fait de plumes aux couleurs voyantes, il s'est armé de la hache de guerre, marche les pieds en dedans sans faire de bruit, et feint dans son bon petit cœur les sentiments de cruauté des barbares Iroquois dont il a entendu raconter l'histoire. La poupée de Laurette sa sœur s'est rencontrée sur son chemin, ennemi facile à surprendre. Le vilain sauvage lui a, dans le temps de le dire, lié les pieds et les mains et, avec une joie féroce, l'a cruellement dépouillée de sa chevelure en lui taillant la tête à coups de hache [. . .].

(He put on his savage's bonnet made of brightly coloured feathers, he armed himself with his war axe, walks toes in without making any noise, and in his good little heart feigns the feelings of cruelty of the barbaric Iroquois whose story he has heard. His sister Laurette's doll lay across his path, an enemy easy to capture. In the time it took to say it, the naughty savage tied her hands and feet and, with a ferocious joy, cruelly skinned her hair by cutting into her head with blows of the hatchet [. . .].)

The generic Savage in question in the fictional conversation between the schoolmaster and the students becomes, in the proposed model for composition, the "barbaric Iroquois" whom the national history had built as an archetype. The fact that the child "plays" the Iroquois is a good illustration of this picturesque figure's narrative importance in the school's story. The performance of Indigeneity by White children confirms the very real incarnation of this history in the students' everyday life. The emotions that the boy must feel are critical to "playing the savage properly." He must feign "in his good little heart the feelings of cruelty" to successfully complete his disguise. The Indian's personification by the Canadian child represents the end product of what today's discourse would call "cultural appropriation." This appropriation made it impossible, for the Indigenous peoples of the time, to produce their own image in the eyes of White people. It is a total annihilation of the voice of the Other within White culture that has allowed this appropriation of the figure of the Indian, an appropriation that lies at the very foundation of the Canadian identity.

The representation of Canada's Indigenous populations was omnipresent in educational materials. It constituted the quintessential Other. The image of the Savage transmitted in this article from 1915 is an example of the figure constructed by the Canadian school in the preceding decades. It also signals the image's evolution over time. Between the middle of the nineteenth century and the first years of the next, knowledge about the Indigenous peoples of America transmitted in school looked more and more like a caricature. The engraving of the boy "playing" Indian is also the result of the growing popularity of this figure in Western culture at the end of the nineteenth century, as shown in the "Indian stories" that abounded in the school culture.[76]

Beginning in the nineteenth century, educators recognized the entertainment potential for children of the fictional figure of the Indian. In fact, they repeatedly underscored the rewards of using Indian stories to arouse their students' curiosity and hold their attention. In the January 1891 issue of *L'Enseignement primaire*, Magnan advised primary school teachers on how to capture the interest of very young children in school. He recommended relying on short oral presentations that, for example, the older students could deliver to their classmates while the school-master took care of another group of children:

> Comme ils seront émerveillés, ces pauvres enfants, au récit intéressant de la création du monde, de ce qu'était [*sic*] nos premiers parents, du péché originel, du meurtre d'Abel par Caïn, du déluge, de la tour de Babel, etc.! comme leur jeune imagination s'éveillera en apprenant qu'autrefois notre pays n'était peuplé que par de farouches Indiens, à la chevelure hérissée de plumes, à la ceinture garnie des peaux de tête enlevées aux ennemis![77]

> (How amazed they will be, these poor children, by the interesting story of the creation of the world, by who our first parents were, original sin, the murder of Abel by Cain, the flood, the Tower of Babel, etc.! how quickly their young imaginations will awaken on learning that long ago our country was only populated by fierce Indians, their hair bristling with feathers and their belts garnished with scalps taken from their enemies!)

A few years later, in a speech on teaching geography delivered to the Association des instituteurs de Québec, a teacher suggested introducing young children to the subject with emotionally stirring stories:

des Esquimaux pourchassant le phoque et l'ours blanc
sur les glaces polaires; des caravannes [*sic*] entraînées par
les chameaux sur les sables arides du désert; des navires
démâtés par la tempête en plein océan; l'éruption soudaine
d'un volcan, ensevelissant des villages superbes; les
mœurs barbares de nos indigènes; la découverte du grand
Mississipi [*sic*], etc.[78]

(Eskimos pursuing the walrus and the white bear across
the polar ice; caravannes [*sic*] pulled by camels across the
desert's arid sands; ships losing their masts to a storm
on the open ocean; a volcano's sudden eruption, burying
superb villages; the barbaric customs of our natives; the
discovery of the mighty Mississipi [*sic*], etc.)

These lists prove two things. First, that the history of Canada told to the little ones interested them thanks to stories about the "fierce Indians"; and then, that the ethnography of the natives was an integral part of natural history, like a volcanic eruption.

The same concerns about education were still on the agenda at the beginning of the twentieth century. In 1908, Professor Thomas Blais spoke to participants in a pedagogical congress in St. Hyacinthe about teaching the national history in primary school. Like other educators before him, he advised the teachers to inject lively, picturesque details into their narration, especially when it was addressed to the very young. Among these "picturesque details" was of course the "cruelty of the savages": "Ils se feront une idée de la grandeur du dévouement de Dollard et de ses compagnons, de l'héroïsme de Mlle de Verchères, quand on leur aura fait connaître la barbare cruauté des sauvages. Alors aussi ils ressentiront toute l'horreur du massacre de Lachine."[79] (They will gain an idea of the greatness of Dollard's dedication and that of his companions, the heroism of Miss de Verchères, when we have let them know about the barbaric cruelty of the savages. Then they will also feel all the horror of the Lachine massacre.)

Stories about Indians were also used in the children's moral training. Through their careful selection, the stories could provide examples of "the defence of the home against the savage,"[80] as the journal *Educational Record of the Province of Quebec* stated in 1893. In all of these compositions, stories, and dictations, the character of the Indian would take on, in turn, the roles of Barbarian, Drunk Indian, Childlike Savage, the wise, paternal figure, and the generous or hard-working Savage. This variety in the rhetorical uses of the figure of the Indian (or the Savage) still never produced a truly positive representation of the First Peoples. While some dictations and readings exist that offer a favourable image of the Indian, they often functioned as a reaffirmation of the civilization/savagery dichotomy. They promoted the exceptional character of the illustrious Indian or good Savage, whose function was to criticize civilized society. As we saw regarding the Arab and Black characters, staging an Indian as the Other in a moral historiette served to civilize the Canadian child rather than to reduce the distance from the Self.

The representations of Native populations also contributed to identity construction, as the cult of colonial heroes attests. In spring 1908, the Montreal daily newspaper *La Patrie* launched a contest for its young readers: "Quel est votre héros favori? Expliquer votre prédilection. Racontez la plus belle action de ce personnage historique."[81] (Who is your favourite hero? Explain your preference. Tell the story of the greatest action taken by this historical figure.) The rules specified that the children "devront choisir leur héros dans *l'Histoire du Canada*. C'est une condition essentielle du Concours" (should choose their hero from the *History of Canada*. This is an essential condition of the Contest). Several weeks later, the newspaper published the fifteen best texts they received. Among the winners' favourite heroes were Champlain (four times), Dollard (three), Montcalm (two), Madeleine de Verchères (First Prize), Amador de Latour, Lévis, Frontenac, and Beaujeu.[82] *La Patrie*'s contest, both an architect and a result of the cult of national or colonial heroes, offers a rare glimpse into how the educational and social discourses were received by the children.

A review of the prize-winning compositions reveals the importance of the international context to which the cult of heroes contributed. First, the construction of the "heroes" had developed in large part within the framework of the opposition between civilization and barbarity, where the Indigenous actors played a critical role. Tenth-prize winner Elba chose Dollard as her hero. She wrote:

> En vain la Nouvelle-France suppliait-elle la Mère patrie de lui envoyer des secours, en vain le petit nombre de Français qui était pour ainsi dire perdu dans ces immenses forêts, sacrifiaient leur vie pour le triomphe de la France, tout semblait contribuer à la perte de cette belle colonie. Les vivres et les munitions manquaient, le nombre des braves diminuait de jour en jour, mais les Iroquois semblaient plus nombreux et plus féroces que jamais. [. . .] Après avoir soutenu le combat durant 17 jours tous tombèrent sous le fer de ces barbares 100 fois plus nombreux qu'eux, et ce fut Dollard qui rendit son âme le dernier. Quelle belle mort, que la mort de ce héros, mais plus encore était [*sic*] la couronne et la récompense qui l'attendaient là-haut. . . .
>
> Les Iroquois honteux d'avoir essuyé une pareille résistance, s'enfuirent dans les bois, et, cessèrent d'inquiéter les blancs.
>
> Après avoir reçu la nouvelle de leur glorieuse mort par un Huron échappé à ce carnage, la population leur rendit gloire, car, si elle jouissait de sa liberté, c'était dû encore une fois au dévouement de Dollard. Après ce sublime dévouement qui ne l'aimerait pas???[83]
>
> (In vain did New France beg the Mother Country to send help, in vain did the small number of Frenchmen who were virtually lost in those immense forests, sacrifice their life

for the triumph of France, everything seemed to contribute
to the loss of this beautiful colony. Food and munitions had
run out, the number of brave men diminished from day to
day, but the Iroquois seemed more numerous and fiercer
than ever. [. . .] After having endured the fighting for 17
days they all fell before the iron of those barbarians 100
times more numerous than they were, and Dollard was the
last to render up his soul. What a beautiful death, the death
of that hero, but even more beautiful was [*sic*] the crown
and the reward that awaited him above. . . .

The Iroquois, ashamed at having met such resistance, fled
into the woods, and, stopped worrying the Whites.

After having received the news of their glorious death from
a Huron who escaped the carnage, the populace glorified
them, since, if they could enjoy their freedom, it was once
again due to Dollard's dedication. After this sublime
dedication who wouldn't love him???)

Elba's childlike exaggeration in praising Dollard's heroism harmonizes
with the romantic tone of her story—the number of adversaries and the
event's duration were substantially overestimated.

Dollard was not the only "hero" to win fame in a confrontation
with the "savages." Having fixed on Champlain, Gabrielle Pelletier also
set his exploits in a situation of colonial violence. "Quelle gloire plus
grande que celle de Champlain? À peine fixé à Québec, il dirige trois
expéditions contre les Iroquois. Deux fois, il est vainqueur de ces terri-
bles sauvages."[84] (What greater glory than Champlain's? Having hardly
settled in at Quebec, he led three expeditions against the Iroquois.
Twice he vanquished those terrible savages.) Finally, wounded in a third
encounter with "*l'infâme Indien*" (the vile Indian), as another child called
him, Champlain "profite de cette mésaventure pour connaître la province
d'Ontario" (takes advantage of this misadventure to get to know the

province of Ontario). Thus, in addition to being the civilized military man who allowed civilization to triumph over savagery, Champlain was an explorer. He was, in a way, the prototype of the imperial hero.

The winner of the contest's first prize, Jeanne Lapierre,[85] alias "Violette de la Montagne," chose Madeleine de Verchères. Convinced that she had made a subversive choice, Jeanne allowed for some distance on the cult of heroes: "Je laisse à des plus savants que moi les grand héros qui ont versé leur sang pour la défense du pays, qui se sont immortalisés par des actes de bravoure et dont les noms retentissent sans cesse dans l'histoire."[86] (I leave to people more knowledgeable than I am the great heroes who shed their blood to defend the country, who made themselves immortal with acts of bravery and whose names resound without ceasing in history.) To justify her choice, she outlines the usual characteristics of heroes: "Cette jeune héroïne n'a pas découvert un monde; elle n'a pas non plus sauvé son pays, mais elle a accompli des actes de courage que je ne saurais vanter." (This young heroine did not discover a world; nor did she save her country, but she performed acts of courage that I cannot begin to praise.) Recalling the actions attributed to heroic figures, Jeanne clearly conveys the interweaving of imperialism and nationalism that resided at the heart of the cult of colonial heroes.

In his master's thesis, Maxime Raymond-Dufour maintains that building Canadian heroes for schools had nothing to do with the paradigm of *survival*. Rather, it derived from a historiographic process that led to the centrality of the "great man" model in historical narration that was common to many nations at that time.[87] This argument only partially exposes the circumstances that, beginning in the mid-nineteenth century, contributed to the success of the heroization enterprise. Added to an internal transformation of the history discipline itself cited by Raymond-Dufour are the importance of imperialist propaganda and the mythification of "imperial" heroes. At the same time that the "great" figures in New France's history were being refurbished, the populations of the imperial powers, one of them being Canada, made certain actors in colonial expansion into "heroes."

The fate of Canada's school heroes thus became involved with the larger movements of expansion into the West in America and the conquest of Africa. These contemporary events opposing Whites and Natives provided the opportunity to reactualize French America's "imperial" past. The *Cours théorique et pratique* by the Frères des écoles chrétiennes provides an example of this reconciliation across time. The following two sentences, separated by less than two pages, illustrate exercises in lexicology: 'Les guerres de l'Algérie ont fait des héros. [. . .] Dollard était un lion pendant le combat."[88] (The wars in Algeria made heroes. [. . .] Dollard was a lion during the fighting.) Benjamin Sulte established a similar parallel in a text reprinted by the Sœurs de la congrégation de Notre-Dame in one of their textbooks. It compared Champlain and La Vérendrye to the African explorers: "De 1608 à 1750, bien des noms brillent dans l'histoire des découvertes. C'est au point que nos ancêtres apparaissent comme autant de Livingstones et de Stanleys sur la carte de l'Amérique du Nord."[89] (From 1608 to 1750, many names shone in the history of discoveries. It is to the point that our ancestors appear to be so many Livingstones and Stanleys on the map of North America.) Sulte very clearly included Champlain and La Vérendrye in the pantheon of European discoverers, among those who had "rangé sous l'étendard de la civilisation un nouveau coin de terre que la barbarie ne recouvrerait pas" (placed under the banner of civilization a new corner of the Earth that barbarity would not cover), when he presented Livingstone and Stanley as their "more fortunate imitators." In his mind, the comparison was mostly flattering to the African explorers, whose adventures drew them along in the wake of the older French discoverers of America. In asking their students to "expliquer cette comparaison de nos ancêtres avec les Livingstones et les Stanleys" (explain this comparison of our ancestors to the Livingstones and Stanleys), the sisters were promoting a "triumphant" version of Canadian history. They inserted these ancestors into the course of the heroic epic of Christian civilization in the world, an epic that seemed to reach its height at the end of the nineteenth century. They thus strengthened the students' feeling of belonging to the already long and always active history of the Europeans' civilizing mission.

Father Lagacé published two textbooks on reading aloud in 1875. Intending to fill a gap he perceived in Canadian reading, that of *"bien parler"* (speaking well), Lagacé did not want to transmit knowledge to the children; he simply intended to exercise them in reading well. It is therefore important to think of these manuals as tools and artifacts of reading that is oral and thus emotive. The third part of the textbook, intended specifically for students attending boarding and normal schools, was devoted to "expression": "Avant tout, pour bien lire à haute voix, il faut bien penser," he wrote, "il faut se pénétrer intimement des idées, des sentiments de l'auteur, en imprégner fortement son âme, et ensuite la laisser parler."[90] (First of all, to read well aloud, one must allow oneself to be intimately penetrated by the author's ideas and feelings, strongly imbue one's soul with them, and then let it speak.) Despite what Lagacé might have said in maintaining that the substance of the texts he selected was of no importance and that they served only as reading exercises, the choice of topics appropriate for teaching young people to let their soul speak was not left up to chance. Invited to read, with expression, texts about Daulac (Dollard) and the martyrs Jogues and Lalemant, the students were required to render with intensity the tragedy that permeated these episodes. It would be difficult to overestimate the power of emotion that interpreting such texts could provoke in adolescent orators. Reading aloud these accounts of the bloodiest episodes in colonial history no doubt imparted a performative quality that would likely lead to a more profound appropriation of New France's heroic figures than would a silent reading.

> Les os de nos frères blanchissent la terre, ils crient contre nous; il faut les satisfaire. Peignez-vous de couleurs lugubres, saisissez vos armes qui portent la terreur, que nos chants de guerre et nos cris de vengeance réjouissent les ombres des morts, et fassent trembler les ennemis. Allons

faire des prisonniers et combattre tant que l'eau coulera
dans les rivières, que l'herbe croîtra dans les champs, que
le soleil et la lune resteront fixés au firmament. Lieux que
le soleil inonde de sa lumière, et que la nuit blanchit de
son pâle flambeau; lieux où se balance la verdure, où l'onde
coule, où le torrent bondit, vous tous, pays de la terre,
apprenez que nous marchons aux combats.[91]

(The bones of our brothers whiten the earth, they call
to us; they must be satisfied. Paint yourself with sombre
colours, seize your weapons that bring terror, so that our
war songs and shouts of revenge make the shadows of
the dead rejoice and make the enemy tremble. Let us go
to take prisoners and fight as long as the waters will run
in the rivers, the grass will grow in the fields, the sun and
moon will stay aloft in the firmament. Places that the sun
floods with its light, and that the night whitens with its
pale torch; places where the plants sway, the wave runs, the
torrent leaps, all of you, countries of the Earth, know that
we are marching to battle.)

In reciting this "Chant de guerre chez les Sauvages" (Savages' war song),
the student was making a second type of appropriation. After having
mastered Indigenous people through ethnographic knowledge, *demonized* them in the historical narrative of the battle between civilization
and savagery, and *erased* them thanks to the myth of the dying race,
the educational corpus allowed the student to *appropriate* Indigenous
speech. Taken from an act of Canadian literary ventriloquism that
endeavours to make the Savage "speak," this war song finally enables
the student to *be* the Indian.

The Appropriated Indian

The "imaginary Indian" is an important character in the Canadian literature used by the educational corpus. For francophones, the excerpts in
textbooks and dictations were taken from the works of Benjamin Sulte,
George Dugas, F.-X. Garneau, Octave Crémazie, Arthur Buies, A.B.
Routhier, P.J.O. Chauveau, Joseph Lenoir, Joseph Taché, Hubert Larue,
Thomas Chapais, among others.[92] To a large extent, it was in featuring the
"imaginary Indian" that these writers intended to establish the national
character of their literature. From the ferocious, bloodthirsty Savage
to the dispossessed or dying Indian, a representation of contrasts was
offered to the students' imagination. Contrary to what Daniel Francis
maintains, the school Indian is not homogeneous.[93] Observing the
school in its entirety, with all its subjects and extracurricular activities,
it is not a school Indian who appears but many figures who, together,
form an Indian persona, to borrow Toni Morrison's concept.[94] From
the excerpts of educational materials to three manuscripts for college
theatre found in the archives, they are manifestations of appropriated
Indigenous speech that, in these cases, took shape in a *performance*, a
performance of Indigeneity by French-Canadian middle-class youth
that opened the way to an analysis combining ideas of race, authenticity, and subversion.

Many researchers have addressed the importance and significance
of the "Indian myth," as it is called by Maurice Lemire, in French-
Canadian literature. In his study, Lemire explains that the Canadian
writers of the nineteenth century initially featured a romantic Indian,
inspired by Chateaubriand, in particular. Then, in the second half of the
century, the literary world would tend to cultivate a Manichean vision
of Canadian history, which would be closely linked to religious ideology.
Lemire writes: "From then on, everything would play on the figure
of the missionary and those of the savage, themselves reduced to the
rank of stereotype."[95] Including the literary Indigenous person in these
works, itself a sign of the literature's indigenization, also contributed
to the quest for territorial legitimacy, as Vincent Masse remarks. He

nonetheless explains that ambivalence is a corollary to this national literary autonomy, since it is simultaneously through a distancing from and appropriation of the imaginary Indian that indigenization is confirmed.[96] Like Janet Paterson,[97] Masse alludes to the centre of alterity embodied in the Indigenous character in French-Canadian fiction. The national distinction is developed thanks to appropriating this Other, who is presented as authentic. To understand the phenomenon fully, it is necessary to compare the literature with that of other settler colonies: for instance, the desire to create distance from European models can also be found in American literary criticism.

The Indian Persona

The literary Indian of the school corpus was multifarious in the same way as the imaginary Indian in Canadian literature, from which he had sprung. The conceptualization of the Africanist persona in American literature, as developed by Morrison, is useful to the present analysis. For Morrison, "the fabrication of an Africanist persona is reflexive; an extraordinary meditation on the self; a powerful exploration of the fears and desires that reside in the writerly conscious."[98] Faced with the Africanist presence that shows up in great American literary texts, the analyst encounters many difficulties: "Encoded or explicit, indirect or overt, the linguistic responses to an Africanist presence complicate texts, sometimes contradicting them entirely. A writer's response to American Africanism often provides a subtext that either sabotages the surface text's expressed intentions or escapes them through a language that mystifies what it cannot bring itself to articulate but still attempts to register."[99] Like Africanism in American letters, the Indianism of the French-Canadian school corpus is complex, and therefore so is its analysis. I will provide examples by examining various poems and three theatre pieces. In this study, I will highlight "appropriation" of Indigenous speech throughout the literary field, which began in the mid-nineteenth century.

The history of appropriation of the Indian by French-Canadian letters and, as a result, by some students would be a long one, as confirmed by Corrie Scott in her analysis of nineteenth-century literature.[100] Here, "appropriation" should be understood as a power relationship that allowed the French Canadian to pretend to represent or stage the authentic Indian without recognizing a competing speech to unseat. On this point, I go along with the views of historian Andrew Nurse, who voices a concern about "the ways in which the cultures of marginalized and colonized peoples have been used and treated by 'mainstream' media and Settler society. They see it as part of a set of power relationships that often serve to reinscribe colonialism and marginalization."[101] The discussion of appropriation presented here therefore does not concern a general reflection on artistic inspiration.

The poems "Le dernier Huron" (The last Huron) by François-Xavier Garneau, "Donnacona" by Pierre-Joseph-Olivier Chauveau, and "Chant de mort d'un Huron" (A Huron's death song) by Joseph Lenoir, all reproduced in reading textbooks in the nineteenth century, belong to the genre of the proleptic elegy. This is the label Brantlinger uses to classify the discourse about the dying races: "Proleptic elegy is thus simultaneously funereal and epic's corollary—like epic, a nation-founding genre."[102] And so, rather than considering as Lemire does that these maudlin poems constitute "une certaine condamnation de la colonisation blanche sans respect pour un mode de vie tout à fait original" (a certain condemnation of White colonization with no respect for a completely original way of life),[103] we must read them as equivalents of the European epics for the national construction of the settler colonies. The proleptic elegy allows the colonial culture to distance itself from European literature and to locate the myth of the dying race at the foundation of a national and colonial literature.

To account properly for the proleptic elegies of Garneau, Chauveau, and Lenoir, it is necessary to step outside the Canadian and francophone framework. The theme these writers were exploiting effectively constituted common ground, at that time, for the literature of settler colonies such as Australia, South Africa, and the United States. As Francis notes, the myth of the dying race managed to last for more than a century, beginning with the early decades of the nineteenth century, because it made it possible to express a guilty conscience without ordering any remedial action.[104] The deed was done, it was too late. All the White colonists and their descendants could do was to appropriate Indigenous speech and recount the dispossession. This appropriation also made it possible to put distance between denouncing the disappearance and the French Canadians. It was not the French Canadian who denounced the state of dispossession, it was the Indian himself. By putting the lamentation into the Indian's mouth, the poet did not entirely make it his own.

One interpretive trend focused on the mimetic symbolism of representing the "last Huron" in the French-Canadian discourse—for example, in the case of Garneau's poem. This analysis took the Huron's destiny as a foreshadowing of what would happen to the French Canadians if British and anglophone assimilation succeeded. A poet and historian, Garneau was also involved in politics. He composed his poem following the defeat of the Patriots. While the interpretation might be credible that Garneau had thus used the image of the "last Huron" to suggest the possible fate of the French Canadians, it is important to reinsert the poem into the context of colonial literature it was part of, that of the proleptic elegy. It is also essential to analyze the significance that the poem might have assumed in the minds of French-Canadian students who read it many decades after the Act of Union had been passed. While it is probable that equating the Huron's destiny with that of the Canadian was raised, it is more likely that the poem was understood as seen through the prism of the battle between civilization and savagery. As Denys Delâge remarks, "According to Garneau, a radical difference still separates the 'Savage' from the French Canadian. The latter is civilized, but not the former."[105] We would add that the latter is White, but not the former. Although the poems do not all emphasize racial identity, the Indian is often associated with darkness, and his soul, which then haunts the territory, is a shadow. In Chauveau's

"Donnacona," the Indian lives in a black forest replaced by the colonists with the "white walls" of Quebec.

The ventriloquist poets of the nineteenth century thus made an appropriation of Indigenous speech that is complex. Both proleptic elegies and reflections of a destiny that their authors refuse for their own people, "Le dernier Huron," "Donnacona," and "Chant de mort d'un Huron" were manifestations of a national literature and consecrated by inclusion in the educational corpus, which was gaining independence thanks to an Indian persona.

The archives sometimes contain happy surprises. Exploring the fonds of the teaching religious congregations allowed me to get hold of three unpublished manuscripts for stage plays. All three were written by a member of the congregation and had not enjoyed a long career. They were nonetheless part of a certain tradition of the performance of Indigeneity by nineteenth-century schoolboys and schoolgirls. Written over a period of thirty years, they feature Indians as key characters and surprisingly take up the same themes. Here are the details:

1) "Coaïna" or "Rose des Algonquins,"[106] an operetta composed by Sister Ste. Providence, cnd. It was performed twice before an audience by the schoolgirls at Villa Maria in Montreal, once in April 1869 in French, and again in June of the same year in English. It was likely written in 1868 or 1869. The action takes place in Ville-Marie when the colony was first being established. It features Marguerite Bourgeoys and Jeanne Leber, as well as the "filles françaises éleves de M. Bourgeoys" (French girls pupils of M. Bourgeoys). Nonetheless, the principal roles are three Indigenous characters. The operetta tells the story of an Algonquin orphan, Coaïna; the daughter of an Iroquois chief, Winouah; and her aunt, Altoutinou. Winouah wants the White girls to accede to all her wishes. The girls prefer Coaïna, an innocent who is ready to do

anything to make herself loved by the "White Christ."
Altoutinou does not like to see Winouah with the Whites
and tells her that they will make her their slave. To
take revenge on her enemies, on the advice of her aunt,
Winouah tricks Coaïna, who is then seen as a thief by her
French friends. The play ends with the exposure of the
guilty party and Coaïna's forgiving her. Winouah is then
convinced of the kindness of the Whites' religion, because
it allows such forgiveness.

2) "Donnacona,"[107] a drama in three acts written by Father
Filiatrault, sj, was performed on 28 January 1881 by the
students of the Collège Sainte-Marie in Montreal as part of
a celebration for the rector. The performance was open to
the public, and the newspapers published notices the next
day. The play tells the story of a plot by a group of "Savages"
against Jacques Cartier and his sailors. Fed falsehoods by their
Medicine Man, they want to exterminate the French. Alerted
to the plot by Domagaya, a Christian savage, Cartier thwarts
their plan by capturing them before they can carry it out. He
reveals the Medicine Man's deceit to Donnacona, who regrets
having wanted to eliminate the French, those "le grand Esprit
[lui] envoyait pour [lui] apprendre à le connaître et à le servir"
(the Great Spirit sent to teach him to know and serve him).
The play ends with the departure of the French, along with
Domagaya, Taiguragny, and Donnacona, who follow Cartier
to France to learn more about the Great Spirit. The principal
roles are those of the people called Savages.

3) "Dollard,"[108] a historical drama in five acts and verse
written by Frère Symphorien-Louis, fec, in 1899. It was
performed at Mont-Saint-Louis, in Montreal, on 25

April 1900 during a gathering presided over by Bishop
Bruchési to raise funds for a monument in honour of
Bishop Bourget. The piece tells the story of a plot by the
Iroquois-Agniers against the French colony and Dollard's
mobilization to defend it. It concluded with Dollard's
death at the end of the battle with the Iroquois. Aside
from the characters of De Maisonneuve and Dollard, the
principal parts were that of Tessouat, Grand Chief of
the Iroquois; Taiquoi, the Onondaga chief; Anahotaha,
Chief of the Algonquins; Nikoua, the Agnier chief; and a
Medicine Man. The first two acts take place in the forest
and outline the Iroquois conspiracy, with a juggling scene.
These two acts represent almost half of the entire script.

The educational discourse about the Indians, whether through
ethnographical study or the national history, did not give them any
agency. Revenge was often the only motivation given for their actions.
How is it, then, that the plays "Coaïna," "Donnacona," and "Dollard"
feature individualized Indian characters, given a name and true agency?
First of all, we must appreciate the effect of the form imposed by the
theatrical discourse. So, as writes Roger Chartier, it is that "[the deter-
minations at work in the process of constructing meaning] depend
on writing and publishing strategies, but also on the possibilities and
constraints proper to each of the material forms that support the
discourse, and the skills, practices and expectations of each community
of readers (or spectators)."[109] For example, the theatrical discourse does
not depend on the same discursive modes or the same ideologies as the
geographical discourse. In contrast to geography, which essentializes
peoples by representing them through the intermediary of a generic,
depersonalized individual, the theatre offers characters who are individuals in their own right. Including a substantial, active alterity is in
fact necessary to the plot; otherwise, how much interest would it hold

for the student actors and the spectators? And how much depth could the narrative framework have?

Obviously, the agentivity granted to Indian characters does not prevent the authors from keeping them within a stereotypical horizon. It must also be said that in two of the three scripts (C; Don),[110] the dénouement prevents the acts and decisions of these characters from being carried out. Still, the individuality that they are allowed, in particular during the big council scenes (Don; Dol), humanizes the Indigenous populations by giving them a certain depth and justified concerns.

How is the story of dispossession told? Let the playwrights speak:

Donnacona — [. . .] Depuis que les visages pâles ont attaché leurs pirogues aux arbres de la [forêt], l'ours s'est enfui vers les régions de l'étoile immobile; l'élan, le caribou, le chevreuil ne se montrent plus qu'à de rares intervalles, le poisson lui-même échappe sans peine à nos filets; enfin la maladie moissonne nos guerriers, et le bocage de la mort se remplit de leurs ossements. Pour comble de malheurs nous sommes menacés de devenir esclaves, comme si la servitude était faite pour le chasseur habitué à parcourir librement des forêts sans limites. Oui, une croix a été dressée sur notre rivage, en face de notre bourgade, pour être un monument de notre esclavage. (Don)

(*Donnacona* — [. . .] Since the palefaces tied their boats to the trees of the [forest], the bear has fled towards the regions of the unmoving star; the elk, caribou, deer show themselves only rarely, even the fish easily escapes from our nets; finally, sickness mows down our warriors, and the grove of death is filling up with their bones. And the greatest of our misfortunes, we are threatened with becoming slaves, as if servitude had been made for the hunter used to running freely in a forest without limits.

Yes, a cross has been raised on our riverside, in front of our village, to be a monument to our slavery.) (Don)

Altoutinou — Il y a quelques années la fumée de nos wigwams s'élévait [*sic*] de chaque vallée; nos chants de victoire et notre cri de guerre résonnaient à travers les montagnes. Nos guerriers étaient couverts de gloire; nos jeunes gens prêtaient l'oreille aux chants de joies [*sic*] d'autrefois, pendant que nos vieillards reposaient leurs têtes fatiguées, attendaient avec calme l'heure à laquelle le Grand-Esprit devait les admettre à ses chasses perpétuelles par-delà les Cieux! Maintenant tout est passé! L'homme [blanc] est sur notre talon; il nous suit pas à pas et son contact communique un poison qui mène à une ruine prochaine. Bientôt nos villages, nos jeunes gens, nos familles, nos chasseurs, nos guerriers, tous auront disparu, et les vents de l'Océan et la brise des grands lacs ne caresseront plus un seul morceau de terre que nous pourrons appeler *nôtre*. Et c'est l'homme blanc qui accomplira cette œuvre de destruction. (C)

(*Altoutinou* — A few years ago the smoke from our wigwams rose from every valley; our victory songs and war cries sounded across the mountains. Our warriors were covered in glory; our young people listened to songs of long-ago joy, while our elders rested their tired heads, waiting calmly for the time when the Great Spirit would admit them to his endless hunts beyond the Heavens! Now all that has passed! The [White] man is on our heels; he follows us step after step and his contact communicates a poison that leads to impending ruin. Soon our villages, our young people, our families, our hunters and warriors, all will have vanished, and the winds of the Ocean and the

breeze from the great lakes will no longer caress a single
piece of land that we could call *ours*. And it's the White
man who will accomplish this work of destruction.) (C)

Tessouat — [. . .] Sous les coups de canon qui jettent l'épouvante
Au milieu de nos bourgs. La forêt est mourante
Depuis que l'on entend cette voix retentir
Sous nos dais de sapins; tout semble ici périr!
Le chevreuil aux abois s'enfuit de la contrée,
La biche aux pas légers s'est aussi retirée,
Les poissons de nos lacs craignent l'hameçon,
On entend rarement le doux chant du pigeon,
Le canard n'ose plus caqueter sur la mare,
Le doux mets des perdrix devient beaucoup plus rare,
La gaîté disparaît devant le bruit des forts
Qui ne laisse pas même en paix dormir les morts.
Ah! Frères, dites-moi, voulez-vous l'esclavage? (Dol)

(*Tessouat* — [. . .] Under cannon shots that belch terror
In the middle of our towns. The forest is dying
Since we've heard this voice resounding
Under our pine canopy; here all seems to perish!
The desperate buck flees the place,
The lightfooted doe has also withdrawn,
The fish in our lakes fear the hook,
We seldom hear the pigeon's soft song,
The duck no longer dares to quack on the pond,
The sweet dish of partridge becomes something rare,
Gaiety vanishes before the noise from the forts
That lets not even our dead sleep in peace.
Oh, brothers, tell me, do you want slavery?) (Dol)

The primary theme common to all three scripts is that of dispossession—or future dispossession. While the texts have certain features of the proleptic elegy, the discourse of the Indian characters is rather prophetic, given the era in which the action takes place. The strong resemblance between the three scripts suggests a common influence. It would not be surprising if it had come from the American theatre industry. In fact, beginning in the 1820s, stages in the United States were flooded with "Indian dramas" to such a point that certain critics would call them a nuisance.[111] In those plays, of which *Metamora: or the Last of the Wampanoags* would be a prototype, the Indian is presented as a "nationalist" attached to his native soil.

The three texts also have a strong racial dimension in common. Race is not illustrated in a White/Red opposition but in keeping with a much more powerful symbolic binary: White/Black. While in American literature it is Blackness that is specified through the Africanist persona, in "Coaïna," "Donnacona," and "Dollard," it is Whiteness that is constantly named. These plays each contain dozens of instances pointing to the whiteness of the French: "*les blancs,*" "*chiens de blancs,*" "*visages pâles,*" "*hypocrites blancs,*" "*les enfants blancs,*" and "*l'homme blanc*" (the Whites, white dogs, pale faces, White hypocrites, the White children, and White man). These texts mark an absolute alterity between the so-called Savages and the "*maudite race*" (cursed race) whose blood is "aussi clair, pur, limpide et vermeil que la rose écarlate" (as clear, pure, limpid and red as the scarlet rose) (Dol). Two scales are thus united: that of race, where French Canadians occupied the very top position, given the racial ideology presented in the preceding chapter; and that of civilization, where those called Savages were ranked at the very bottom.

Although the characters named as Savages are not explicitly racialized, the vocabulary and the plot elements place them on the dark side. For example, the two scenes of the Savages' council meetings and the Indians' betrayal are set at night. By contrast, the principal scenes for the White characters take place during the day.

"*Sombre forêt*" (gloomy forest) (C); "*lugubres pas*" (sombre steps), "*horizons noirs*" (black horizons) (Dol); "*nuit du paganisme*" (night of paganism) (Don): all these expressions relate to the people known as Savages. The darkness associated with the Indian characters is manifested in two ways, each one having a symbolic resonance in the plot: slavery and paganism.

In the three scripts, the Savages fear that the Whites will make them slaves, and it is for this reason that they plot to exterminate them. In "Dollard," which is the play that leans least heavily on this theme, Tessouat, the Iroquois chief, nonetheless delivers this speech:

> Ah! Frères, dites-moi, voulez-vous l'esclavage?
> Ce mot couvrant vos fronts d'un sinistre nuage
> Me livrent [*sic*] vos secrets! Ah! Vous avez raison,
> Tous les traités de paix sont de la trahison.
> Les blancs, par ce moyen posséderaient nos terres,
> Et seraient nos tyrans au lieu d'être nos frères.

> (Oh, brothers, tell me, do you want slavery?
> This word casting a sinister cloud on your foreheads
> Reveals your secrets to me! Oh, you are right,
> All the peace treaties betray us.
> The Whites, by this means would possess our land,
> And be our tyrants instead of our brothers.)

Later, the warriors sing in chorus:

> La haine dans le cœur,
> Maudissons l'esclavage;
> Répandons la terreur
> De rivage en rivage.
> [. . .]
> Aimons la liberté
> Conquise par nos pères;

Mourons avec fierté
Pour conserver nos terres.

(With hatred in our hearts,
Let us curse slavery;
And spread terror
From shore to shore.
[. . .]
Let us love the liberty
Won by our fathers;
And die with pride
To preserve our lands.)

"Dollard," which was written in 1899, is the most "nationalist" of the plays, and the Iroquois chief's words echo the patriotism that the French-Canadian people should cultivate. But should slavery be understood in relation to the history of Canada alone? The way in which it is treated in "Coaïna" and "Donnacona" leads us to think rather of an influence exerted by the American context.

Written shortly after the American Civil War, these scripts demonstrate a relationship between the practice of slavery and the Whites, as clearly stated in the following lines of dialogue:

Altoutinou — Winouah est dupe des visage pâles. Veut-elle savoir pourquoi ces jeunes filles la traitent avec tant de bonté? C'est pour en faire leur esclave. . . .

Winouah — Leur esclave! . . . Winouah! l'orgueilleuse fille du grand chef Iroquois! . . . esclave des visages pâles . . . Winouah périra plutôt! . . . (C)

(*Altoutinou* — Winouah is being taken in by the palefaces. Does she want to know why these girls are being so kind to her? It's to make her their slave. . . .

Winouah — Their slave! . . . Winouah! the proud daughter
of the Iroquois Grand Chief! . . . slave of the palefaces . . .
Winouah would rather perish! . . . [C])

Le Jongleur — Donnacona, les manitous n'exigent pas qu'un
guerrier libre abandonne sa hutte à l'étranger et que se
jetant à ses pieds, il lui dise: "Voici ton esclave."

Donnacona — Je ne suis pas esclave; je ne le serai jamais!
(Don)

(*The Medicine Man* — Donnacona, the manitous do not
require a free warrior to give up his lodge to the foreigner
and, throwing himself at his feet, tell him: "Here is your
slave."

Donnacona — I am not a slave; I never will be! [Don])

Le Jongleur — [. . .] Oui, c'est l'esclavage que les blancs
vous préparent. Cette croix n'est pas comme le prétend [*sic*]
un signe de religion, mais une marque de servitude, car on y
a gravé une inscription où il est dit que ce pays n'appartient
plus à Donnacona et à ses guerriers, mais au grand chef des
Français. [. . .] Guerrier de Stadaconé consentirez-vous à
devenir esclave? (Don)

(*The Medicine Man* — [. . .] Yes, it is slavery that the
Whites are preparing for you. This cross is not as they
claim a sign of religion, but a mark of servitude, because on
it they have carved an inscription saying that this country
no longer belongs to Donnacona and his warriors, but to
the great chief of the French. [. . .] Warrior of Stadacona,
would you consent to becoming a slave? [Don])

On reading these texts, it is hard not to think of the very recent
history of slavery in the United States at that time. Then again, it is

striking to see that "Coaïna," written between 1868 and 1869, is the
text that most strongly emphasizes the Whiteness of the French. At
a time when the White/Black opposition has been shaken by the
abolition of slavery, Sister Sainte-Providence's play, acted out by young
girls from Montreal's élite, seems to be intended as a reminder that
Canadians belong to the White race. The texts can thus be understood both as a claim to White status by people of French descent in
Canada and as a fantasy affirming French-Canadian colonialism with
the stain of slavery removed.

The Indians refused to be reduced to slavery. For their part, the
French considered them already to be slaves, due to their heathen condition. The Whites want to save them from that second form of slavery
by converting them to the faith of the "White Christ" (C).

> *Cartier* [. . .] La croix dont tu parles, indique, il est vrai que
> le Dieu des chrétiens doit prendre possession de cette terre,
> c'est-à-dire de vos âmes, quand, éclairées par la lumière du
> ciel, elles seront prêtes à recevoir les dons de la grâce; mais
> il s'agit d'une royauté toute spirituelle et intérieure qui te
> laissera la propriété de tes forêts et le gouvernement de ta
> tribu. (Don)

> (*Cartier* [. . .] The cross of which you speak indicates, it's
> true, that the God of the Christians must take possession
> of this land, that is, of your souls, when, lit by heaven's
> light, they will be ready to receive the gifts of grace; but it
> means a royalty, completely spiritual and internal, that will
> leave you with ownership of your forests and government
> of your tribe. [Don])

Ironically, the "converted" characters in all three plays (Coaïna,
Domagaya, and Anahotaha) act exactly like slaves; they are devoted and

voluntarily submissive to the French. The devoted behaviour of these characters is similar to that of the Black slaves presented in the school stories. Slavery is played in accordance with two symbolic representations in which issues of race, slavery, and religion are tightly interwoven. On the one hand, the Indians refuse to be reduced to slavery by the French; on the other, the French consider the Indians already to be slaves since they are ignorant of the Christian religion. In both of these scenarios, slavery is associated with Black populations, as the multiple references to darkness show us.

In the end, it is religion that triumphs, and the speech given to Indian characters supports the religious ideology. What Toni Morrison writes about the Africanist persona applies in large part to the Indian characters who intend to convert at the end of the scripts under study: "Serviceable to the last, this Africanist presence is permitted speech only to reinforce the slave-holders' ideology [in our case Catholic evangelism], in spite of the fact that it subverts the entire premise of the novel. Till's voluntary genuflection [in our case those of Donnacona and Winouah] is as ecstatic as it is suspicious."[112] In the end, the Indian persona has led the authors—and consequently the actors and spectators—onto ground that is out of bounds to other forms of discourse. Religion, for its part, guarantees a dénouement for the play that will agree with the national history and the confessional nature of education in that era.

Performing the Indian

Let us return for a moment to our little boy disguised as an Indian in 1915, featured in the magazine *L'Enseigement primaire*. This illustration perfectly, and powerfully, expresses the long-standing Euro-American tradition of "playing Indian," or, as Paul says in his conversation with the schoolmaster, "playing savage." The possibility of *performing* the Indian was open to several French-Canadian students in the nineteenth century, notably thanks to the roles of Winouah, Donnacona, Tessouat, and company. Having been unable to find substantive educational

sources from the society's lower-class schools, I cannot draw a comprehensive portrait of this performance within the nineteenth-century
educational institution. My research nonetheless allows me to state
that middle-class youth were able, on different occasions, to experience
the practice of the theatrical *performance* of Indigeneity at the *collège*
or the convent. Otherwise, the more ample sources from the twentieth
century tend to confirm that this practice was not only maintained
but also democratized.[113]

Looking at the table of dramatic or academic "séances"[114] presented
at convents, *collèges,* and normal schools in the nineteenth century (see
Appendix), it is striking to see how the speeches of various Indian
chiefs recited by students at the Séminaire de Québec in the 1830s were
replaced, by the end of the 1850s, by the performance of a much more
Canadian Indigeneity, that is, one that is located in Canada's historical
narrative. In its notice about the *séance académique* held at the Séminaire
de Québec on 5 February 1860, the newspaper *Le Canadien* wrote: "Les
deux bouches qui interprétèrent si heureusement le chef Donacona
[*sic*], dans sa lettre écrite de France à sa tribu, et les Algonquins au
parloir des Ursulines, garderont aussi leur place distinguée dans la
mémoire des assistants."[115] (The two mouths so pleasingly interpreting
Donnacona's letter from France to his tribe and the Algonquins in the
Ursulines' parlour, will also hold a place of distinction in the memory
of those in attendance.) Recitations by C. Baillargeon and W. Couture
were emotionally charged and the audience was not unmoved.[116] The
presumed authenticity of these interpretations, as for most of the performances of Indigeneity inventoried, was what most strongly captured the
spectator's imagination. Regarding this practice, Rayna Green writes:
"The taste, in fact, for Indian speeches, whether produced by actual
Indians or not, is already a part of the dramatic repertoire, and these
'dying Indian speeches' (only to culminate in the 19th century passion
for the speech of Seattle) join the songs, the dramatic presentations,
complete with costumes, formalized speech and gestures (facing East

or West, raising the arms upwards towards the sun) so familiar in the later Western movies."[117]

The authenticity of a performance of Indigeneity is closely linked to its racial dimension. The "authentic" Indian is a White person; that is what the journalists who review the student actors' interpretations seem to be saying. And perhaps they were not wrong. In fact, authenticity had nothing to do with historical accuracy or fidelity. It was a question of power and representation. As a rhetorical construction, Indigeneity was authentic as soon as the spectator (or actor) judged it to be so. The eternal modern quest for the authenticity of the primitive was thus doomed to fail, because it was always part of a power relation. This authenticity was at issue in a review of "Donnacona" when the play was performed in 1881 at the Collège Sainte-Marie:

> Que dire du conseil des sauvages où le naturel était scrupuleusement respecté? La voix, le geste, la pose tout enfin dénotait le guerrier brandissant le tomahawh [sic]. M. Mainville était chez lui dans le rôle de Donnacona, chef de la tribu de Stadaconé, M. Tremblay, faisait le jongleur à la perfection. MM. Letondal comme Aouétaté, Lachapelle comme Anahoteha, Merrill comme Taiguragny sauvage apostat et M. May, comme Damagaya sauvage chrétien, ont été admirables.[118]

> (What to say about the savages' council meeting, in which naturalness was scrupulously respected? The voice, the gesture, the pose, finally, everything denoted the warrior brandishing the tomahawk. Mr. Mainville was at home in the role of Donnacona, chief of the Stadacona tribe, Mr. Tremblay played the medicine man to perfection. Mssrs Letondal as Aouétaté, Lachapelle as Anahoteha, Merrill as Taiguragny apostate savage and Mr. May, as Damagaya Christian savage, were admirable.)

On the strength of the ethnographic and historical "knowledge" transmitted in school, the journalist could write that "naturalness was scrupulously respected," as the interpretation conformed to the era's racial discourse.

The authenticity of the performed Indian was even stronger when the costume worn by the student was picturesque and contrasted with those of the White characters. A journalist from the *Montreal Gazette* reviewed a presentation of "Coaïna" at Villa Maria in 1869 as follows:

> The part of the entertainment, however, which seemed to
> enlist most fully the interest of the audience, and which
> called forth the most animated and repeated applause
> was a Charming Operette composed for the occasion,
> and founded on a page from the early annals of the
> Congregational Convent. The personages in this latter
> piece were the Misses Desbarats, Leprohon and Migneault,
> three very attractive looking squaws, in faultless Indian
> costume, forming a most piquant contrast to their pale-face
> sisters, the Misses Leblanc, Kinton, Judah, Vennor, Orr,
> Clerk, Mullarky, Leveille, Murphy, Cunningham, Walsh
> and Chrystal, who attired in spotless white, took part in the
> same Operette. The music, vocal and instrumental, as well
> as the declamation, were really faultless.[119]

The juxtaposition of the Indian costumes and the white dresses of the young French girls makes the performance's racial dimension highly visible. The Sœurs de la congrégation Notre-Dame had produced the same contrast a few years previously: "Un dialogue d'un caractère semi-musical mit en relief la condition de l'instruction dans ce pays au 17me siècle; une des élèves portait le costume des indigènes et les deux autres vêtues de blanc, jouaient le rôle d'élèves."[120] (A semi-musical dialogue accentuated the condition of education in this country in the seventeenth century; one of the students was wearing an Indian costume and the two others dressed in white played the role of the students.) Indeed, disguise is indispensable if one wants to "play Indian" properly, as Philip J. Deloria explains.[121]

In the case of the *collèges* and convents, the importance given to disguise was significant (Figure 20). A drama based on the novel *Les anciens Canadiens* (The Canadians of old) was staged in 1865 and 1868 at the Collège de l'Assomption. For the two productions, through the intercession of Nazaire Piché, the parish priest at Lachine, the *collège* borrowed costumes from the "savage chiefs" of the Caughnawaga Indians (Mohawks of Kahnawà:ke).[122] The trouble taken by the *collège* was even greater in 1868, when the missionary Richot "a consenti à exercer les bandes sauvages qui [figurent dans la pièce] pour rendre la peinture de mœurs plus naturelle" (consented to rehearse the savage bands who [appeared in the play] to render the portrayal of their customs more natural).[123] The intention was to use the missionary's ethnographic knowledge in order to come as close as possible to the expression of the so-called Indian customs. What did it matter that his knowledge concerned the First Peoples of the Red River in the 1860s and not those of the St. Lawrence Valley in the eighteenth century!

But were these measures really necessary to produce the desired authenticity? Wasn't the performance of Indigeneity in itself an ethnographic monstration? In 1865, *La Minerve* wrote:

> Tantôt, c'est le langage et l'accent de l'habitant; tantôt c'est l'approche d'une tribu sauvage qui salue par des cris; c'est le spectacle de ces Indiens, tatoués, bigarrés, couronnés de plumes, qui se glissent dans les broussailles, les yeux ardents, le corps souple comme le serpent et s'élançant sur leur victime avec des cris épouvantables; c'est leur danse et leur chant de mort. Nous apprenons plus dans ces quelques heures de représentation qu'en plusieurs années de simples lectures.[124]

Figure 20. "Actors in the play 'Father Isaac Jogues, S.J. or the Gospel preached to the savages' in June 1874," AJC, Fonds Collège Sainte-Marie, C-0001/S7/SS3/D3, "Le P. Isaac Jogues, S.J. ou l'Evangile prêché aux sauvages," 30 June 1874.

(Now, it's the habitant's language and accent; now it's the approach of a savage tribe, shouting out their greetings; it's the spectacle of these Indians, tattooed, colourful, crowned with feathers, who glide through the bushes, eyes shining and bodies as supple as a snake's, and rushing at their victim with frightful cries; it's their dancing and their death song. We learn more in these few hours of performance than in many years of simply reading.)

Backed up by the racial register and the importance of the physical appearance in both dress and posture, some French-Canadian students thus well and truly succeeded in embodying the "authentic" Indian.

The fantasy and transgression into the forbidden allowed by the performance of Indigeneity provide many avenues for subverting social norms to both the actors and the audience. As Paterson rightly writes: "The Other character, precisely because they are Other, is a way for fiction to express what is unspoken, passionate and forbidden. [. . .] That is undoubtedly why the figure of the Other so often represents freedom from social convention, the attraction to adventure and the power of unreason. The Other is seductive and differs from the norm insofar as they respond to our hidden desires and echoes our unrealized dreams."[125] In a Catholic world where theatre and superstition are not always welcome, the scene in "Dollard" of "le sorcier évoquant l'Esprit des Ténèbres" (the sorceror summoning the Spirit of Darkness) violated the norms. At the same time, it was disguise—therefore theatre—that allowed the forbidden to express itself. By virtue of its exogenous position, the simulated Other could summon Satan and produce, by this very act, strong emotions in the audience; in fact, thanks to "un jeu de scène impressionnant" (impressive stage acting), this sequence was "une des plus remarquables de l'ouvrage" (one of the most remarkable in the work),[126] according to *La Patrie*. A few years previously, the actors at the Collège Saint-Marie who embodied the *"sanguinaires bourreaux"* (bloodthirsty executioners) of Father Jogues had received congratulations from the journalist at *La Minerve:* "Les acteurs se sont acquittés de leur tâche d'une façon irréprochable."[127] (The actors acquitted themselves impeccably.)

These representations of Indian customs were adroitly cloaked in an aura of mystery and enchantment. While it was secondary to the plot, as in *Les anciens Canadiens* or *La conspiration de Champlain* (Champlain's conspiracy), the performance of Indigeneity lent a touch of fantasy to the historical reconstruction. As well, it is remarkable that the newspapers, whether in 1874 or 1902, always considered these scenes to be very important, as this 1902 article in *La Patrie*:

Vers la fin de l'acte, il y a le supplice du chef indien qui mérite une mention. Ici, nous tombons dans la féerie du drame wagnerien: des squelettes sortent de leurs tombes et se tiennent rigides comme des mannequins: les indiens brandissent des haches sur la tête du supplicié qui voit son crâne lacéré, mais n'en continue pas moins son discours: enfin, Champlain, pris de pitié, prend son mousquet, l'épaule et fracasse le crâne du supplicié, afin de le libérer; le corps pend inerte au poteau qui fume: une odeur acre se répand dans la salle. C'est effrayant.[128]

(Toward the end of that act there is the torture of the Indian chief, which deserves notice. Here, we fall into the magic of Wagnerian drama: skeletons rise from their graves and stand as rigidly as dummies: the Indians swing their hatchets at the head of the tortured man, who sees his skull slashed, but still carries on with his speech: finally, Champlain, moved by pity, takes his musket, shoulders it and shatters the skull of the torture victim, to liberate him; the body hangs inert from the stake, which is smoking: an acrid smell fills the auditorium. It is frightening.)

While the proleptic elegy was a component of the epic genre, the historical reconstructions acted out in school theatres tended to call on the genres of fantasy and the supernatural.

The adult audience therefore appreciated the scenes evoking fairy tales. But what about the children and the young actors? The staging of Indigeneity very likely had a pedagogical character. By providing young spectators with a fantastic universe drawn from the national history itself, the playwrights were making a patriotic contribution, as stated by Alphonse Christin:

La magie des décors, comme [. . .] les voix mystérieuses des forêts vierges, les silhouettes fantastiques des jongleurs

et des manitous se glissant au milieu des féroces indigènes
pour les exciter au massacre et au carnage, les chants de
mort, les danses de guerre, les luttes corps à corps, avec
accompagnement de casse-tête et de tomahawk, etc., etc.
Tout ce tremblement contribue beaucoup à l'imagination
des petits, et à leur graver profondément dans la mémoire
les combats et les hauts faits de nos aïeux.

À côté des scènes terrifiantes dont ces drames abondent,
il y a de bien consolants tableaux qui font heureusement
contraste.

Les chants pieux des marins, les prières ardentes des
marins, leur foi inébranlable, [...], etc., etc., reposent l'esprit
des horribles spectacles diaboliques auxquels l'auteur vient
de nous faire assister.[129]

(The magic of the set, like [. . .] the mysterious voices of
virgin forests, fantastic silhouettes of the medicine men
and manitous gliding among the ferocious natives to
incite them to massacre and carnage, the death songs, war
dances, wrestling bodies, with accompaniment of war club
and tomahawk, etc., etc. All this agitation helps greatly to
feed the little ones' imagination and etch deeply in their
memory the battles and heroic feats of our ancestors.

Alongside the terrifying scenes that abound in these
dramas, there are many comforting tableaux that thankfully
provide contrast.

The pious songs of the sailors, the heartfelt prayers of the
sailors, their unshakeable faith, [. . .], etc., etc., give the
mind respite from the horrible, diabolical spectacles that
the author has just given us to watch.)

It was once again good versus evil, the French sailors' piety versus the diabolical spectacle of Indigeneity. The young spectators were certainly fond of these moving entertainments. While the story of the martyrs' torture might strike the imagination of young readers, what can be said of the emotions inevitably produced by watching these terrifying scenes? And what can be said about the intensity of experience for young people who performed these diabolical wonders!

The subversive impact of this performance of Indigeneity by students at the *collèges* and convents is real. As Jeff Bowersox reminds us, the condition that makes this subversion possible is the acceptance of the colonial order: "But doing so depended on accepting the generally received notions of civilized and uncivilized used to justify European expansion; this binary was essential to developing exciting and adventurous, even subversive worlds."[130] Whether it was Winouah or the Medicine Man in "Donnacona," Indian roles allowed the young actors to engage in a performance that subverted the ideals of masculinity and femininity that the educational institution otherwise instilled in them. In her doctoral dissertation on the possibilities offered by "domestic" (home-based) theatre to young girls in Victorian society, Heather Fitzsimmons Frey remarks, "Although violence and the grotesque have an allure for adults, playing with theatrical violence may be especially appealing to children because it allows them to embody what adult civilizing influences try so hard to repress."[131] The same applies to pagan ideas. What could be more subversive and exciting for H. Babin, a young student at a Catholic institution, than to play the role of Satan? The expression of undisciplined violence, the act of speaking in the "Indian" idiom and performing war songs provided opportunities for boys to transgress the social expectations that weighed on them. Moreover, the Indigeneity performed by young girls had a nonconformist dimension that went even further.

After having devised their plan to betray the young Algonquin girl, the two convent pupils who play Altoutinou and Winouah in the operetta "Coaïna" launch into this war song:

Guerre à mort! Poursuivons de notre haine
Et l'Algonquin et l'homme aux blanches mains
Guerre à mort! Que la vengeance indienne
Suive son cours; c'est là tous nos destins
Du caribou la plaine est dévastée
Nos braves guerriers sont sans nom
De l'Indien, la tente est sans fumée
Pour l'homme blanc, point de pardon
Comme un souffle de feu sur les flots, vogue
Avec le dard au poing, la rage au cœur
Le cruel Iroquois. Et sa pirogue,
Jette aux échos ses soupirs de malheur
Guerre à mort!

(War to the death! Let's pursue with our hatred
Both the Algonquin and the man with white hands
War to the death! Let the Indian revenge
Follow its course; there lie all our destinies
The plain is devoid of caribou
Our brave warriors are without a name
The Indian's tent is without smoke
For the White man, no forgiveness
Like a whiff of fire on the waves, sails
With the dagger in his fist, rage in his heart
The cruel Iroquois. And his canoe
Throws to the echoes his sighs of woe
War to the death!)

In the nineteenth century, for a young girl from Montreal's élite, the opportunities to express such violence must have been rare. Similarly, the tableau about Mother Bourgeoys, performed at a private event at the convent, must have allowed a girl to violate the ideas of maternity and femininity she had been taught. The tableau, probably inspired by an image in the reading textbook by the Sœurs de la congrégation de Notre-Dame (Figure 21), shows Marguerite Bourgeoys taking a young Indian child into her arms after the little girl has run away from her mother, "a dark furious looking squaw [. . .] shaking her fist menacingly at Mother Bourgeoys."[132] The speech read by Miss Nault in July 1864 was of a very different nature, but also far from social convention. It was "le discours qu'un chef huron adressa aux Religieuses Ursulines lors du premier incendie de leur couvent" (the speech addressed by a Huron chief to the Ursuline nuns following the first fire at their convent).[133] As Fitzsimmons Frey writes: "For girls expected to exhibit self-control in all aspects of their lives, indulging in big, highly performative emotional displays could have been both challenging and liberating, not to mention fun."[134] For a few hours, these rare female performances of Indigeneity would offer young actors the possibility of embracing a fundamentally other identity.

Like the experience of young Victorian girls playing with the universe of Orientalism brought to light by Fitzsimmons Frey, the performance of Indigeneity by young French Canadians is "potentially *both* empowering and oppressive."[135] The brief escape these activities provided to students and spectators hid the genocide of First Nations taking place at that same time. As Green explains, "the living performance of 'playing Indian' by non-Indian peoples depends upon the physical and psychological removal, even the death, of real Indians." She adds, "In order for anyone to play Indian successfully, real Indians have to be dead. Americans have to believe them dead or kill them off."[136] A few years before the Canadian authorities said they wanted to "kill the Indian in the child"[137] with their program of residential schools, paradoxically, young Whites "played" Indian with the approval of moral and educational authorities. At the very time that Indian authenticity was being claimed by the French Canadians, the government was striving to eradicate the Indigenous peoples and their culture. The paradox is only apparent. The eradication of the real alterity and the appropriation of a fantasy alterity point to the same intention.

Figure 21. "A small savage girl leaves her mother and throws herself into the arms of a sister of the congregation," Sœurs de la congrégation de Notre-Dame, *Lecture à haute voix . . . Cours élémentaire*, 1895, 100.

The multiple forms taken by the representation of the Indian, or the Savage, in the educational corpus of the nineteenth century constitute a hegemonic discourse that is very close to the discursive structure of Orientalism as defined by Edward Said.[138] Taken together, the American, Canadian, and European texts concerning North America's First Nations thus provide a striking parallel with those dealing with Orientalism. In both cases, it is a matter of a relation of domination founded on the authority of European and American speech. Reality comes to be obscured by a bookish authority. As manifestations of the multiple links between knowledge and power at the heart of the colonial and imperial history of the nineteenth and twentieth centuries, the two discourses blurred the contemporary reality. In this framework, the cult of the "last Indian" corresponds to the quest for an eternal or dreamt-of Orient. The two myths serve as antidotes to modernity for the Western imagination. The literary and theatrical performances of these myths finally made it possible for the European and American audience to get off lightly.

Ethnographic knowledge, colonial history, proleptic elegy: these various components of representing the Indian in school were completely interwoven in—and indeed essential to—the performances of Indigeneity constituted by the stage plays and the magazine engraving of the young boy "playing Indian." Appropriating the Indian identity in performance had meaning only once the knowledge had been assimilated by those French-Canadian children. Orientalism does not act otherwise, as Fitzsimmons Frey notes: "*How* girls acquired their 'knowledge' about the 'other' and 'other places' is part of why the performances could be so potent for the imagination, and also why it is reasonable to assume girls held a common orientalist perspective, which ultimately obliterated the human beings in the 'Orient' even as it gave strength to white Victorian girls."[139] The Indian in school similarly reveals a power structure based on a knowledge and desire of the Other that itself, in the same movement, erases the real presence of Indigenous people.

5.

The Other Observed or "Teaching through the Eyes"

A picture can replace a thousand words, but it is never innocent,
empty of situated knowledges, or isolated from one thousand
other words and pictures.

KAREN STANWORTH[1]

Why devote an entire chapter to the role of images in the school's representation of alterity in the nineteenth century? What role do they fulfill
and why should they be analyzed separately from the other discursive
processes that construct otherness? The importance of visuality in the
*re*cognition of alterity is crucial. Throughout this chapter, I will insist on
the idea that observing images of the Other enables a *re*cognition, that
is, the activation of cognition or knowledge acquisition in the student's
mind by observing an image. Moreover, in the nineteenth century,

instilling the image of the Other was both a rhetorical process and a pedagogical imperative. In that regard, it is essential to look at how these illustrations were part of an educational context in which image *and* alterity were both favoured pedagogical instruments of public education.

The gaze directed at the Other and that directed at the Self are fundamental to the development of individual and collective identities. In fact, visuality is a critical element in building social relationships. The impact of seeing others and being seen by them is a key factor in the development of interpersonal encounters. In this regard, it is essential to analyze the act of observing—and consequently the images that are its medium—with the same degree of seriousness as that given to written discourses.

Visual recognition, which is essential to the Self's existence, is always part of a power relationship. As a vehicle of social differentiation, visuality is fundamental in representing otherness. For example, the rhetorical construction of race is based on body differences that are *visible* and therefore *legible*. Sociologist Stuart Hall offers a very accurate comparison between seeing a racialized body and reading a text. For him, these bodies are texts:

> The body is a text. And we are all readers of it. And we
> go around, looking at this text, inspecting it like literary
> critics. Closer and closer for those very fine differences,
> such small these differences are, and then when that does
> work we start to run like a true structuralist, we start to
> run the combinations. Well, if I perm, you know, not so big
> nose, with rather fuzzy hair and a sort of largish behind and
> goodness knows what, I might sort of come out. We are
> readers of race, that what we are doing, we are readers of
> social difference. [. . .] The very obviousness of the visibility
> of race is what persuades me that it functions because it is
> signifying something; it is a text, which we can read.[2]

For schoolchildren to be able to *read* the signifier that is race, they had to be visually "literate." It was in observing the pictorial representation of the "Arab," "Indian," or "Chinaman" that the student would be able to *re*cognize and imagine them. Thus, before students have even been taken on an imaginary voyage, the pictorial representation of the Other obliges them to observe the image and *re*cognize the Other it represents.

In his essay "Showing Seeing. A Critique of Visual Culture," William J.T. Mitchell explains that research on visual culture seeks to reveal what is, at first sight, invisible: the gazer gazing. Mitchell writes, "My aim in this teaching has been to overcome the veil of familiarity and self-evidence that surrounds the experience of seeing, and to turn it into a problem for analysis, a mystery to be unraveled."[3] According to the theory Mitchell developed, analyzing images goes hand in hand with studying the act performed by the observer. In a similar vein, visual studies methodology has combined the study of visual representations of the world (the social construction of the visual) with that of the pedagogical use of images (the visual construction of the social).

Fantasy or optical projection, how does one recognize an image? In an introductory handbook, Martine Joly suggests a very practical, comprehensive definition: "[The word 'image'] indicates something that, while it does not always refer to the visible, borrows certain features from the visual and, in any case, depends on the production of a subject: imaginary or concrete, the image passes through someone who produces or recognizes it."[4] The image is, in its essence, mediated. The mental images that are essential to students in *imagining* "other places" are the result of a lengthy socialization, consisting mostly of observing graphic images, such as engravings, projections, and so on. This process then allows them to imagine a thing or a person through the simple mention of a word, for example, the word "Negro."

The gaze directed at the world as it appears in visual representations is never neutral. It takes place in a specific socio-cultural context. The analyst must pay attention to various actors who come into contact with the image, since the image's context of production does not always tell us much about its utilization. As Peter Burke remarks, the importance of the observer (eyewitness) is considerable. Therefore, we must know about the context of reception in order to understand how images were perceived at a given time.[5]

The connection between the text and the image is the second element to consider when making an iconological analysis. According to Mitchell, texts and images co-respond, and "understanding of one seems inevitably to appeal to the other."[6] We can illustrate this fundamental principle by using an example. In September 1914, the magazine *L'Enseignement primaire* published an English lesson that was modelled on the "rédaction d'après image" (composition based on a picture); students were asked to describe and comment on an image (Figure 22). In the fictional conversation he supplied for the teacher, pedagogue John Ahern suggested starting with an identification exercise: How many characters are there? Are they adults or children? men or women? boys or girls? Then came the question: What colour is the man? As the pedagogical dialogue proceeds, we learn that after age and gender, the skin colour of one character was an important marker in describing him: "What color is he? He is black. A black is what? A black is a negro."[7] The conversation continues. The image's smallest details are examined:

> On the negro's face what is there? There is a broad smile on the negro's face. While smiling what does the black cook show? While smiling he shows his teeth.
>
> Are they small teeth? They are big teeth.
>
> Are they white or black? They are very white.
>
> Is it not strange that a blackman should have very white teeth? No, it is no more strange that a blackman should have very white teeth than that a black cow should give white milk.

In describing the Black man's facial expression, Ahern makes a direct comparison between Black people and cows. Without the text, the analogy would not have arisen. Nothing in the image supports it. In this example, the stereotype is activated by the text, by that very fact attesting to its importance. Ahern was not able to describe the image of a Black man without making a connection to animality.

One last methodological observation is necessary. Images are polysemic. In addition to being attentive to the socio-cultural and textual contexts in which an image appears, the analysis must raise other questions: Are the images observed typical or unusual? In what learning situations are they exposed to the gaze? Are they isolated images, or are they part of a consistent series? Which details reveal themselves only after prolonged observation? Taking these questions into consideration is essential to interpreting the school's images of the Other in the nineteenth century.

A Pictorial Turn in the Nineteenth Century: Image, Science, and Imperialism

One of the fundamental concepts in Mitchell's theory of iconology is that of the pictorial turn. According to Boily and Roth, as cited by Mitchell, this shift is "a recurring phenomenon, correlative of numerous practical or technical renewals in the structures of the visible, from the adoration of the Golden Calf to the advent of photography, by way of the revolution of perspective in the Renaissance."[8] In the West, the nineteenth century saw a significant pictorial turn. Beyond the advent of photography and the technical changes in reproducing images, the era saw a transformation of visual culture that exceeded the simple material nature of the images. Scientific knowledge and popular entertainments such as expositions, shows, and parades then entered the domain of sight: you must *see*. In this connection, the anthropologist Johannes Fabian very correctly insists on the fact that we must "get away from attributing the development of the Western scientific mind

Figure 22. Untitled, *L'Enseignement primaire,* 36th year [September 1914], 43.

mainly to literacy or, at any rate, to our kind of literacy."[9] Learning
through images was as important as being taught through what was
written. Moreover, the ascendancy of images in public education and
the centrality of vision in the expansion of European imperialism are
two features of the nineteenth-century pictorial turn, and together they
constitute the particular context for the appearance of images of alterity
in the educational corpus.

The development of public education coincided with the preoccu-
pation with visual pedagogy in the nineteenth century. The advent of
illustrated school textbooks was evidence of a paradigm shift in social
thinking about children's instruction and public education. With utter-
ances like "Que distinguez-vous dans la gravure ci-dessous?" (What do
you see in the picture above?) or "Indiquez les personnages et les objets
que vous découvrez dans la gravure" (Point out the people and objects
you find in this picture), the authors of school textbooks asked the
children to observe the pictures and identify the things they recognized.
The school exercises called *rédaction d'après image* required students
to write a composition based on the observation of an image. Then
again, these didactic practices show how the pedagogues linked the
faculty of observation to knowledge. In the pedagogical method called
l'enseignement par les yeux (teaching through the eyes), the image was
not only an accessory to illustrate the text, it was the central learning
tool. A program of studies run by the Sœurs de la congrégation de
Notre-Dame confirmed the use of this pedagogical practice in the nineteenth century. Explaining images was featured in the program for the
second primary year (age eight), and the *rédaction d'après image* was
practised in the fourth year.[10] The pedagogical journals began to write
about the importance of the image in teaching in the 1850s. "Pictures!
pictures! hang your walls with pictures!" wrote the *Journal of Education*
in December 1857.[11] That same year, the prospectus of McGill College's
High School Department explained that the teaching of history and
geography was enhanced by the choice of "judicious illustrations."[12] In

1871, the writers of the *Journal de l'instruction publique* published an article on this topic:

> Des cinq sens par lesquels notre intelligence perçoit les choses extérieures, le sens de la vue est sans contredit celui qui grave le plus facilement et le plus permanemment les objets dans la mémoire. [. . .] C'est, de plus, celui des sens qui, pour ouvrir l'esprit à la compréhension, exige le moins de raisonnement. D'où il suit que la vue, surtout lorsqu'il s'agit de l'enfance, doit jouer un rôle considérable dans l'enseignement.[13]

> (Of the five senses through which our intelligence perceives things outside ourselves, the sense of sight is undeniably that which most easily and permanently engraves objects on our memory. [. . .] In addition, it is the one sense that requires the least reasoning to open the mind to understanding. It follows that sight, since it is active from childhood, should play a considerable role in teaching.)

According to these writers, the pedagogy of observation is useful for two reasons. First, it makes it possible to "[faire] parvenir l'enfant à la connaissance des faits" ([have] the child reach an awareness of the facts) by showing facts to them. Then, since children enjoy images, they help to hold their attention.

The concrete material response to this pedagogical imperative was first seen among the anglophones. In the 1860s, many publishers addressing Protestant students as well as Catholics included engravings in the school textbooks they were producing. For the francophones, aside from a few illustrated alphabet books published earlier, it was not until the 1870s that images began to appear in certain textbooks for geography and reading. In 1875, in the preface to their first illustrated

French-language geography book, the Frères des écoles chrétiennes explained that "les illustrations ou vignettes [contribuent] à dévelop-per l'intelligence de l'élève, tout en charmant et réjouissant ses yeux" (the illustrations and inserts help to develop the student's intelligence, all while charming and delighting his eyes).[14] Moreover, according to the brothers, it was an "innovation" for Canada "en ce qui concerne les écoles françaises" (where the French schools are concerned). In a book published three years later, in their foreword, the brothers again underlined the usefulness of illustrations, but this time as a standard feature rather than a novelty. They wrote that "les illustrations, de nos jours fort recommandées, peuvent donner un enseignement d'intuition aussi instructif qu'intéressant" (the illustrations, highly recommended at this time, can contribute to teaching of intuition that is as instructive as it is interesting).[15] This timing coincides with the advent of illustrated textbooks in France.

For many decades, actors in the pedagogical communities insisted on the importance of "*l'enseignement par les yeux.*" Thirty-two years after publication of the article in the *Journal d'instruction publique* mentioned above, the magazine *L'Enseignement primaire* reprinted part of it, without giving credit, and headed it up with the same title. Despite the proliferation of school images in the early twentieth century, advocating the importance of illustrations was still necessary. In 1901, in the foreword to his geography textbook, J.N. Miller wrote that "une image, en un instant, dit plus qu'une longue explication; et le souvenir en est beaucoup plus persistant" (one image, in an instant, says more than a lengthy explanation; and its memory is far more lasting).[16] On his side, Father Magnan addressed the children directly:

Cher enfant, c'est pour toi que j'ai préparé ce premier Livre de Lecture. En l'ouvrant tu chercheras naturellement les images et tu les étudieras. C'est bien, elles sont placées là pour te faire mieux aimer ton livre et graver plus aisément

et profondément dans ton esprit les choses qu'elles
représentent.[17]

(Dear child, it is for you that I prepared this first Reader.
On opening it you will naturally look for pictures and study
them. That's good, they were put there to make you love
your book even more and to etch in your mind more easily
and deeply the things they represent.)

Magnan's comments echoed the two pedagogical motives already stated
by the writers of the *Journal d'instruction publique* in 1871: the knowledge and pleasure gained from looking at illustrations.

The children of the nineteenth and early twentieth centuries were
put into contact with a multitude of images. Those analyzed in this
chapter are taken, without exception, from illustrated school textbooks
and from pedagogical periodicals. It was images that were most often
preserved by archivists. If textbooks were not the only material supports
that allowed students of that time to exercise their faculty of observation,
they were probably among the most widely distributed and democratic.
Wall maps were also among the favoured tools for "teaching through
the eyes." Large-size illustrations took different forms, and photographs from that time show the variety of objects hung on classroom
walls: religious images, maps of the world, natural history charts, and
scenes from the Bible.

The Québécois student's visual culture was also shaped by screenings of "*vues lumineuses*" (luminous views). Magic lanterns started to be
used in Quebec's educational institutions in the nineteenth century. The
archives we consulted made it possible to track the "extracurricular" use
of this projection device back to the 1840s. In a series of articles about
the history of Canadian *collèges* that appeared in the *Journal of Education*
in 1857, Pierre J.O. Chauveau recalled the pedagogical work of John
Holmes at the Séminaire de Québec. He wrote: "During play hours in
the long winter evenings he gave lectures which were more sought after,
even by the youngest pupils, than any other kind of recreation. They

were accompanied by illustrations with the aid of the magic lantern, and experiments in natural philosophy and chemistry."[18] However, there are few clues about the use of magic lanterns in a school context during the following decades, and the projector at the Séminaire de Québec seems to be an exception. Nonetheless, at the turn of the twentieth century, many prestigious teaching institutions owned projection equipment. For example, the annual prospectus for Montreal High School and Montreal High School for Girls repeatedly featured the students' interest in illustrated lectures given during school hours and at special events. At that time, students at the convent of Mont Sainte-Marie had use of a botanical room equipped with projection equipment. The students of the Frères des écoles chrétiennes at the Collège de Longueuil had access to a very large collection of "views" thanks to Brother Marie-Victorin. Despite the popularity of "luminous view" screenings in the nineteenth century, it was not until after the turn of the century that the use of such projectors in schools became widespread.[19]

Images used by the schools are to be found mostly in textbooks. Before looking at the provenance of textbook images, it is important to understand the economy of school images in general: What was the context of utterance that determined them? Do they illustrate a text or stand alone? Are they engravings or photographs? Which Others are visually represented and which are not?

Not surprisingly, the geographical atlases are the textbooks in which we find the greatest number of images of the Other. In these books, there is an average of one to two images per page. Some, like those of J.N. Miller (1901), have as many as four on a page. Their engravings feature the world's great cities and their monuments, each country's principal industries, and the animals native to the different continents. Most frequent are images presenting the inhabitants of the Earth. They show individuals engaged in a traditional activity or exhibited in an ethnographic pose. There are also many illustrations in reading textbooks, but representations of the Other are not as present as in geography textbooks. The ethnographic images heading up certain scientific readings appear next to "narrative" illustrations (Figure 23). We also found many engravings representing Indigenous peoples in books of Canadian history. Images of the Other and the pedagogical texts they accompany are connected in various ways, depending on the textbooks in which they are found. In reading textbooks, engravings generally illustrate a specific lesson. In the atlases, they appear with greater independence from the text; in some cases, the "ethnographic types" represented are even completely unrelated.

In the 1860s and 1870s, textbook publishers seldom used photogravure, a process that made it possible to reproduce photographic images on etched plates. At that time, illustrations of the different peoples of the Earth were still strongly influenced by Orientalist painting and sketches reproduced in travel accounts. Compared with the photogravures featured in textbooks by the end of the century, these depictions of humans lacked realism. The way in which the groups of characters were arranged also changed considerably from the time of the first pictorial representations to the early twentieth century. The science of the "ethnological types" was very popular at the end of the nineteenth century and greatly influenced the presentation of human diversity in geography textbooks (Figure 24). Writers Gilles Boëtsch and Jean-Noël Ferrié maintain that it was the realistic quality of photography that changed the representation of physical alterity at the end of the nineteenth century: "Painting and engraving were generally considered to be coloured by their authors' subjectivity while photography was seen, at least in its early stages, as an objective way to reproduce reality. This innovation introduced an essential shift in the way of knowing the body and culture of other people."[20]

All the peoples of the Earth were not visually represented in Canadian school textbooks. Certain "types" very often recurred, such as the Arabs and the Indians. Conversely, although texts in the books provided ample information about the Hottentots and Australia's Indigenous peoples, none of them were presented to the student's gaze. How to interpret this visual absence? We must remember that

Supplice du P. de Brébeuf.

TYPES AFRICAINS

Egyptien. Tunisien. Kabyle. Algérien. Marocain. Nègre. Cafre.

the Hottentots and the Australian Blacks were among the "peoples" described as the most repugnant of the human species, while the visual representation of alterity is linked to desire and aestheticism. That being the case, in the pedagogical context proper to the textbooks, what interest could there be in visually exhibiting hideous people? The absence of images of the Hottentots calls to mind the importance of what the images include and what they exclude: the act of omission (the Hottentots) or exclusion (the women) is as eloquent as the act of exhibition.

To knowledge of the pedagogical discourse on the image must be added analysis of the ideological context of which these images are a part, as Annie Renonciat aptly puts it: "Examining the various pedagogical supports—both for the schools (textbooks and imagery) and for instructive recreation (books as gifts and prizes)—reveals the ambiguity of the didactic image when it is intended for young readers. On the one hand, it contributes to the increasingly rigorous training and structuring of a child's intelligence [. . .]. On the other, it does not escape the determination of the powers and institutions to govern, through it, the minds of future soldiers, citizens and consumers."[21]

Transnational Circulation of Visual Stereotypes: Same Images, Different Contexts

In the eighteenth century, the Europeans' accounts of their voyages to America, Africa, and Oceania were adorned with ethnographic engravings: the images gave the "best idea" of the objects, scenes, and human beings encountered by the explorers and described in their texts. These ethnographic illustrations played an important role for metropolitan

Figure 23. "Torture of Father de Brébeuf," Magnan, *Cours français de lectures graduées. Degré supérieur,* 1902, 356.

Figure 24. "African Types," Frères maristes, *Atlas-géographie,* 1908, 49.

LA CROIX OPÈRE LA VRAIE CIVILISATION.

Figure 25. "La croix opère la vraie civilisation" (The cross brings the true civilization), Frères des écoles chrétiennes, *Nouvelle géographie illustrée*, 1875, 5.

readers; they allowed them to *know* the countries explored and then conquered by "their" explorers. In the nineteenth century, the beginnings of photography were also intimately linked to the scientific process and the desire to popularize human diversity and make it accessible for everyone to see.

Anthropologist Johannes Fabian clearly explains the close connection established between the precedence of sight, aesthetico-pictorial visualism, and the production of knowledge about the Other. This tendency to favour visuality in knowing other cultures amplified the effect of their being located out of time; the reifying visual representation of the primitive and the barbarian reinforced their allochronic position. Elizabeth Edwards adds that the transition from engravings to photographs in representing the Other also increased this allochronic effect.[22]

The ethnographic portraits included in school textbooks (re)produced the expulsion of conquered populations from history.

Let us now look at how the modes of domination instituted by European imperialism appeared in the images in school textbooks. A perfect example is the engraving entitled "La croix opère la vraie civilisation" (Figure 25), which was reproduced in two geography textbooks by the Frères des écoles chrétiennes, in French and in English. The image presents ten men who have at their feet the instruments of the geographer-explorer, with the cross surmounting all. The men representing the New World are grouped to the left of the cross and those of the Old World to the right. A knowledge of the racial typology of the time makes it possible to *re*cognize most of the featured individuals. In the centre, two White men, one European and the other American, are shaking hands. A Chinese man and an "Oriental" (Turkish, Persian, or Hindu?) are standing beside the European. On the left, two "Indians" can be seen behind the White man, likely representatives of the northern and southern hemispheres of America. The four individuals in the background are probably an "Eskimo" and a "Patagonian" on the left, a "Malay" and a Black inhabitant of Africa on the right. The figures chosen by the engraver to illustrate human diversity demonstrate his detailed knowledge of racial thinking and the archetypes of otherness.

What does this image still teach us? What ideology does it transmit? The two Whites embody the civilizing action of the Euro-American nations; their handshake signals the agency granted by the artist—they are the only "active" characters in the image. The deal they seem to be closing also evokes the fact that the fate of the world is in the hands of the "civilized" nations: the details included, such as the instruments for navigation, the landscapes, and "Natives," denote the imperial aim of their agreement. The fact that all of the individuals except the Whites and Chinese are armed refers to the image's title: the savages and barbarians wage war with weapons; civilization fights with the cross. The other characters are more or less passive. There are first of all the four men who surround the two Whites: they are on their feet and seem to be watching the Whites' action with interest—and concern? Do these men represent obstacles to civilization's expansion? In fact, at the time the engraving was published there were many international conflicts: the conquest of the West in Canada and the United States, the Opium Wars in China (1856 to 1860), the Sepoy Mutiny (1857), the Second Franco-Mexican War (1861 to 1867), and so on.

The four characters in the background are completely deprived of agency. The position of the two seated men suggests a state of domination. As for the two smaller characters at the back, they are watching the scene as if it does not really concern them. In any case, these four cast members are not interlocutors. The breakdown of this engraving reveals the racialized and hierarchized world view transmitted at that time through teaching geography.

The preceding analysis deals with what is present in the engraving. But who is strikingly absent from this geopolitical vision of the world? Women. On the one hand, White women did not decide the fate of the world, and, conversely, on the other hand, the image suggests that the colonial conquest was not directed at racialized women. Making geography the purview of men reinforces the gender separation between the private and public spheres that children were taught about in school. The analysis of "La croix opère la vraie civilisation" also reminds us of the importance of images in justifying colonial expansion. To borrow from Martin Jay, "the role of visuality in creating, sustaining, justifying, and undermining imperial power is impossible to deny."[23]

Images of the Other circulated freely among the various Canadian pedagogical publications. Analyzing the schools' corpus makes it possible to document the recycling of engravings of alterity. In 1861, in Montreal, two publications intended for a young readership were released that reproduced the same engravings. They were the first edition of the geography textbook written by Hodgins and published by Lovell and the "Compte rendu de la Sainte Enfance en Canada, 1860" (Report on the Holy Childhood in Canada, 1860). The two documents reproduced more than ten identical engravings. First, we can find illustrations of Canadian

Man of Bethlehem.   Sheik of Mount Lebanon.   Woman of Nazareth.

SYRIANS IN THEIR NATIVE COSTUME.

Figure 26. "Syrians in Their Native Costumes," Hodgins, *Lovell's General Geography*, 1861, 84.

BUDDHIST PRIEST AND ATTENDANTS, CEYLON.

Figure 27. "Buddhist Priest and Attendants, Ceylon," Hodgins, *Lovell's General Geography*, 1861, 89.

cities by Montreal engraver John Henry Walker. And then, images from "other places" used in the Holy Childhood's report[24] can also be found in the geography textbook (Figures 26 and 27): "Jerusalem," "Infidels," "Syrians," "Chinese Mandarins," and "Shanghai, in China." The captions sometimes differ; for example, the "Infidels" in the report are identified as "Buddhist Priest and Attendants, Ceylon" in Hodgins's textbook. The coincidence of their publication in Montreal at the same time supports the idea that the publishers went to the same sources and drew from the same image bank. One question remains: Who chose those images first, Lovell or the editor of the report? The random nature of the illustrations selected for the Holy Childhood report—the images from "other places" do not necessarily refer to the text—leads to speculation that the editor drew on the images used by publisher Lovell, whose textbook, moreover, displays a greater consistency between the text and the images.

The circulation Canada-wide of images from "other places" is indicated by another example involving the country's two language communities. The very same engraving depicting the Egyptian city of Cairo appears in both the *Fifth Book* of André-Napoléon Montpetit's series of readers and in the geography textbook of Nova Scotian John Burgess Calkin (Figure 28). As in the previous case, the image is not used for the same narrative purposes. While the engraving represents urban Egypt in the geographical atlas, in Montpetit's book it illustrates a lecture on Napoleon's expedition to Egypt. The reproduction of the same images in different pedagogical documents speaks to a high degree of homogeneity in Canada's visual representations of otherness.

The origin of certain images used by Canadian publishers can be traced. These discoveries make it possible to show how the circulation of images often went beyond national boundaries.[25] We find many foreigners among the engravers whose work was reprinted by the textbook publishers. For example, the images that illustrate Calkin's geography are credited to at least four French engravers or illustrators: Laly, Sargent, Monnet, and Pannemaker. The same applies to the textbooks published

773. CAIRO.

THE PAPUAN ISLANDS.

HEAD-DRESSES OF THE NATIVES OF NEW GUINEA.

Figure 28. "Cairo," Calkin, *Calkin's New Introductory Geography*, 1898, 78.

Figure 29. "Head-Dresses of the Natives of New Guinea," Hodgins, *Lovell's General Geography*, 1967, 99.

by Lovell, whose engravings bear an assortment of international signa-
tures: Walker, Jackson, Massey, Thomas, Williams, among others.

The engravings in the textbooks are sometimes reproductions of
ethnographic sketches made during the Europeans' voyages of exploration. From 1822 to 1825, Jules-Isidore Duperrey of France completed
an exploratory voyage to Oceania. A few years later, he published seven
volumes of his *Voyage autour du monde* (Voyage around the world), which
was illustrated with ethnographic drawings by Jules-Louis Le Jeune.
What was the fate of the illustration of the "Naturels de la Nouvelle-
Guinée" (Native of New Guinea)? The research did not allow me to trace
the career of this image before it appeared in Hodgins's geography in
1867, but the fact remains that the Anglo-Canadian textbook carried
an adaptation of Le Jeune's illustration (Figure 29). The same travel
account also seems to have inspired the engraving of the Patagonians
in the textbook by Calkin (Figure 30). As well, the "Tatooed [*sic*]
New-Zealand [*sic*] Chief" in Hodgins's textbook is adapted from an
image in a travel account by American Charles Wilkes.[26] These two
illustrations in Anglo-Canadian textbooks attest to the transimperiality
of the Other's representation. They also evoke the lasting influence of
travel accounts on ethnographic knowledge in the nineteenth century.

Aside from illustrations whose sources we can find in the travel
accounts, we can see that other images are identical to those contained
in American didactic books. It remains difficult to trace their itinerary.
Did the Canadian authors deliberately copy the American textbooks,
as was the case for certain portions of the text? Nothing indicates it.
The publishers of pedagogical materials perhaps had access to the same
image banks on either side of the border. Some images to be found in the
geography textbooks of American author Samuel Augustus Mitchell,
which were very popular in the United States, can also be found in a
geography book by the Frères des écoles chrétiennes and in an atlas by
the Sœurs de la congrégation de Notre-Dame (Figures 31 to 33). The
sisters' textbook also includes a scene of "Esquimaux dans leur hutte"
(Eskimos in their lodge), which was used in the textbook by American

397. PATAGONIANS.

Figure 30. "Patagonians," Calkin, *Calkin's New Introductory Geography*, 1898, 43.

Vue générale

de

l'Afrique.

Figure 31. "Vue générale de l'Afrique," Sœurs de la congrégation de Notre-Dame, *Géographie. Cours moyen et cours supérieur*, 1897, 409.

Alexis Frye, as noted in the article by researchers Lisa L. Zagumny and Lydia Mihelic Pulsipher on American geography textbooks.[27] The engraving representing the various human races in Hodgins's textbook can also be seen in an American textbook of the same era.[28]

Was the fonds of available images that limited? Or was there in this transnational and transimperial circulation of images a determination to make the representation uniform in order to produce a stereotype and make the alterity *recognizable*? Was Canada a special case with greater circulation here because the publishers went to American,

British, and French sources? Whatever the case, the transnationality of images is striking, and it attests to the homogeneity in Western representation of the Other. The invention of photography would do little to change this reality.

The first series of colonial photographs were inspired, in large part, by Orientalist painting. The staging, models' postures, and set elements imitated those of the great painters following that trend—Delacroix, Gérôme, Benjamin-Constant, and so on. The evolution of anthropological theories and consolidation of imperial domination later made a profound change in the nature of colonial photographs, as Bancel and Blanchard write:

> The connections between this scientific development
> of the theory of races, making pictures of the colonized
> and disseminating representations of the races to the
> general public were evident from the turn of the century.
> At that time, series of postcards called "Scènes et Types"
> were widely distributed, featuring "exotic" populations
> *in situ*. The photographs' captions led to such a definite
> identification that the series eventually became a genre of
> postcard in and of itself. The cards at once constituted an
> othering and a fusion of anthropological and ethnological
> perspectives with the appeal of exotism. Through a
> process of popularizing and simplifying, it was primarily
> the physical or cultural alterity that was sought in these
> images. The "Scènes et Types" series played the role of an
> iconic vector of difference in the guise of ethnography,
> the spectacular and the strange: a fascination mixed with
> repulsion for other peoples, directly descended from the
> exotic mode popularized by voyagers' accounts [. . .].
> By highlighting the stigmas of these differences, they
> broadcast the theory of the hierarchy of races for use by the
> greatest number.[29]

38   NOTIONS PRÉLIMINAIRES.

population de l'Amérique. Elle comprend les Européens en général ; les Turcs, les Arabes, les Persans, en Asie; les Egyptiens, les Berbères, en Afrique. Elle compte environ 640 millions d'individus.

Où habite la race jaune?

La *race jaune* habite l'Asie orientale et septentrionale. Elle comprend les Chinois, les Japonais, les Sibériens, et compte environ 620 millions d'individus.

Où habite la race noire?

La *race noire* habite l'Afrique centrale et méridionale ainsi que l'Australie ; elle a été transportée en esclavage en Amérique. Elle comprend les Nègres en général, et compte plus de 150 millions d'individus.

RACE BLANCHE—Soldat romain.

RACE JAUNE—Chinois.   RACE NOIRE—Cafre.

La *race brune* habite l'Asie méridionale, l'Afrique cen-

ETHNOGRAPHIE.   39

trale et l'Océanie. Elle comprend les Indous, les Indo-Chinois, les Abyssins et les Malais, et compte plus de 280 millions d'individus.

La *race rouge* forme la population indigène de l'Amérique, désignée sous le nom d'Indiens et de Peaux-

RACE BRUNE—Malais.   RACE ROUGE—Indien.

Rouges. Elle compte à peine 10 millions d'individus, et ce nombre diminue graduellement, tandis que celui des autres races augmente plus ou moins rapidement.

Langues.—*Quelles sont les langues les plus répandues?*

La langue chinoise est parlée par un plus grand nombre d'hommes ; la langue anglaise est la plus répandue, elle est parlée dans toutes les parties du monde ; la langue française est plus parlée en Europe, c'est la langue diplomatique, et la première des langues littéraires.

Qu'appelle-t-on langue mère, langue sœur, langue vivante, langue morte?

On appelle *langue mère* celle qui est la source de plusieurs autres ; le latin est une langue mère par rapport au français, et le français est une langue dérivée.

Figure 32. Untitled, Sœurs de la congrégation de Notre-Dame, *Géographie . . . Cours moyen et cours supérieur*, 1897, 38–39.

We therefore must not underestimate the impact of colonial photographs reproduced on postcards, in illustrated magazines, and in Canadian school textbooks. By virtue of its aura of objectivity, the ethnographic photograph pretends to offer an "authentic" portrait of the colonized native.

For the metropolitan observer, photography of the Indigenous type was a real, authentic visual representation. Furthermore, the transnational circulation of these images increased the effect of disconnection between the colonial reality and how it was understood by Western readers: "If the postcard is 'an illustrated version of the colonialist discourse,' it is because it shows us a reality of the vanquished, a pacified

THE RACES OF MANKIND.   33   34   CIVIL AND POLITICAL GEOGRAPHY.

139. What may be said of the Caucasian race?

The Caucasian race are of fair complexion, with finely-formed features and well-developed forms.

They are the most improved and intelligent of the human family, and seem capable of attaining the highest degree of progress and civilization. The nations of Europe, Western Asia, Northern Africa, with the white inhabitants of America, are included in this division of mankind. This is also called the European race.

140. What is known of the Mongolian or Mongol race?

The Mongolian race are of a yellow complexion, with the eyes set obliquely in the face.

In disposition they are patient and industrious, but limited in genius and slow in progress. The Chinese and Japanese comprise a large portion of the Mongol race. The Finns and Laplanders of Europe, also, are said to belong to it.

141. What is said of the Black or Negro race?

The Black race are of a dark complexion, varying from a coffee color to deep coal-black.

THE CAUCASIAN RACE.

THE MONGOL RACE. (A Chinese Laborer.)   THE BLACK RACE. (A Negro Chief.)

Generally, they are strong and active in body, but indolent in habit, and have not attained to any high degree of civilization. They inhabit nearly all the districts of Africa south of the Great Desert, and are found also in America, whither they were carried as slaves. A peculiar race, called Papuan negroes, are found in New Guinea and Australia.

THE MALAY RACE. (A New Zealand Chief.)   THE RED RACE. (An Indian Chief.)

142. What is said of the Malay race?

The Malay race are of a dark brown complexion, fierce and revengeful in disposition, and have made but little progress in civilization.

This race is found in most of the islands of the Pacific Ocean near the coast of Africa. There are many and in the peninsula of Malacca south of Farther India. pirates among the Malays.

143. What is said of the American or Red race?

The American or Red race are of a copper color, with straight black hair, tall and well formed, but revengeful and warlike.

They are fast disappearing before the progress of white civilization. This race comprises the Indians of both North and South America. The Esquimaux, who inhabit the shores of the Arctic Ocean, have sometimes been confounded with them, but are supposed to be of the Mongol race.

N.B.—A consideration of the races of men according to these divisions is called Ethnography. This forms a science apart from Geography, and, to be thoroughly understood, it must be studied separately.

Figure 33. Untitled, Samuel Augustus Mitchell, *A System of Modern Geography*, 1878, 33–34. Note that among the vignettes, the only difference between Mitchell's textbook and that of the sisters is in the representation of the White race.

reality in which women remain silent, in a play of appearances and illusions. [. . .] From the real colonial scene, not a sound is heard, not even a stifled one. And the colonial postcard competed in popularizing images for a large metropolitan audience that had no awareness of the complexity of the societies in which they were produced."[30] With good reason, Safia Belmenouar and Marc Combier here make a link between the ethnographic photograph and colonial expositions. In both cases, the Euro-American audience believed that it had *seen* an authentic visual representation of the various colonized populations and took from it a real sense of knowing. In addition, the colonial expositions spawned many ethnographic studies with photographic documentation.

In the preface to his geography textbook, Miller wrote that the engravings it contains "are varied and as perfectly executed as possible. These images by themselves will give students a knowledge of the various human races, their habits and customs, type of architecture, means of communication, etc."[31] In 1905, in the preface to the English translation of the book, Miller explained that most of the images came from photographs.[32] The "native weavers of Colombia" (page 95); "Dutch milkmaid" (page 112); "Turkish water bearer" (page 121); "young girl of Burma" (page 130); "Arabs" (page 173): all these vignettes, and many others, attest to the strong hold the ethnographic image had on the visual construction of alterity. But where did the photographs in the Canadian textbook come from? In comparing the composition of the engravings with that of colonial photographs reproduced in certain contemporary works, it seems certain that Miller, or his publisher, drew on an impressive catalogue of ethnographic photographs. The "Arab Woman with Her Child," the "Arab Chief," and the "Tunis Grocery Store" are photographs taken by J. Garrigues of France and were mainly reproduced on postcards at the turn of the century (Figures 34 to 36). As for the "rue du vieux Caire" (Street in old Cairo) (Figure 37), it is from the French photography studio of Bonfils.[33] The engraving of the young "Eskimo" was inspired by a photograph taken at the World's Columbian Exposition in Chicago.[34]

How widespread the circulation of images actually was needs to be better understood. To quote Edwards, "The cornerstone in constructing the image of the Other would rest [. . .] more heavily on the entire visual economy in which these images operate, and on the particular sites of their consumption, since the snapshot is essentially an object fated to be reproduced over time as well as in space."[35] That the same images should have served as postcards in the French colonies and as geographical knowledge in Canadian school textbooks speaks to their fictional authenticity. As it was, their captions often differed, depending on the use being made of them. For example, the "Arab Woman" in

Femme arabe avec son enfant.

Chef arabe.

Figure 34. "Arab Woman with Her Child," Miller, *Nouvelle géographie élémentaire*, 1901, 139.

Figure 35. "Arab Chief," Miller, *Nouvelle géographie élémentaire*, 1901, 139.

Epicerie à Tunis.

Figure 36. "Tunis Grocery Store," Miller, *Nouvelle géographie élémentaire*, 1901, 139.

Rue du vieux Caire.

Figure 37. "Street in Old Cairo," Miller, *Nouvelle géographie élémentaire adaptée*, 1901, 142.

Les sauvages.

Arabes.

THE OTHER OBSERVED 277

Miller's textbooks is a "Bedouin" on Garrigues's photograph. Similarly, the "Arab Chief" is simply an "Arab" on the postcard.

The malleability of captions for ethnographic images was not limited to their use in school materials. In an article on colonial photography in the Maghreb, Boëtsch and Ferrié explain how the French anthropologists illustrated their works with photographs of "natives" that they rarely took themselves. The caption they placed below an image emanated from the photograph, whose authority was accepted from the outset. Nonetheless, Boëtsch and Ferrié demonstrate that the photographers themselves changed the captions of ethnographic photographs according to the needs of the moment and the terminology—sometimes obsolete—established by anthropologists: "[The photographers] could even use ethnographic precision for fantasy purposes, for example, calling the same female subject 'Young Bedouin' and 'Young Daughter of Bou-Saâda' and another subject 'Woman of the South' and then 'Young Kabyle Girl.'"[36] Christelle Taraud, for her part, raises the commercial argument behind this overuse of the same images.[37]

When we trace the multiple Western utilizations of the same images of the Other, in voyagers' accounts, school textbooks, postcards, ethnographic studies, and so on, what shows up is the full import of the stereotype. In order for these images to have an effect on the reader, in order that the reader could eventually come to *re*cognize Cairo, the Arab woman, or the "Eskimo," the visual economy of difference was required to produce a rarefaction of the available images and the subjectivities expressed. In so doing, the culture transmitted in school contributed to constructing the racist field of vision of Canadian society.

Figure 38. "The Savages," Magnan, *Cours français de lectures graduées. Degré supérieur*, 1902, 323.

Figure 39. "Arabs," Miller, *Nouvelle géographie élémentaire*, 1901, 135.

Visual Stereotypes: Observing the Alterity

What is a stereotype? A stereotype is a generalization concerning one social group that has been created and commonly accepted by another group. The stereotype acts in such a way that the trait associated with the stereotyped group should be considered to apply to all members of the group. An individual who does not correspond to the stereotype will be seen as an exception, or even inauthentic, and he will not cause the stereotype to be questioned. What is special about the visual stereotype? It makes it possible to recognize and identify an individual as belonging to a "type" or a "race" at first glance. William J.T. Mitchell defines the visual stereotype as "an especially important case of the living image because it occupies precisely this middle ground between fantasy and technical reality, a more complexly intimate zone in which the image is, as it were, painted or laminated directly onto the body of a living being, and inscribed into the perceptual apparatus of the beholder."[38] Image making also sets up a different relation to politics, particularly in comparison with the text-based stereotype, since the visual has a stronger aesthetic and symbolic dimension. From there, just one step is to be taken before arriving at the idea that the image of the Other often fluctuates between repulsion and desire. In large part, the school framework excluded the repellent and degrading aspects of the Other's visual representation and preserved only the desirable part.

The school fostered the association between the image and the stereotype. For example, when students read the caption "The Savages" below an image (Figure 38), or their teacher told them, "Dans cette image nous voyons des Sauvages" (in this image we see Savages), they associated the illustration's details with the mental image they had made of the people called "Savages": tents, feathers, calumet, squatting, "primitive" weapons, long hair. . . . Images like "The Savages," "Arabs," or "A Turk" allowed children to assimilate an ethnographic knowledge of the "types" that would then be *recognizable* (Figures 38 and 39). The socialization required to make the students able to *re*cognize the stereotype wherever they encountered it was effected through frequent contact with images that repeated the same details.

Images of the Other have great pedagogical importance. While the textual descriptions of otherness can obviously lead students to "know" the Other, by being "conforme[s] à leur naturel et à leur manière de connaître" (true to their nature and their way of knowing), as Magnan noted, images nonetheless have the advantage of substituting themselves for an abstract idea through a physical representation.[39] Like other knowledge transmitted through school imagery, in this context the representation of the Other would have an aura of truth and scientific objectivity. Further, for many Canadian children, the graphic image engraved in the school textbooks—now a mental image—would never be challenged by the reality of a genuine encounter with the Other. And even when an encounter had taken place, the stereotypes learned in school would certainly have mediated the in-person contact.

The number of images of the Other contained in educational materials indicates the interest and fascination stimulated by the fact of *seeing* the alterity. The analyzed corpus in fact contains several hundred images of the Other and of "other places." In general, hypervisibility can provide information about two opposing movements: desire and disgust.[40] An image that is attractive, even exciting, leads to a voyeur's desire, as in the case of Orientalist painting. Conversely, dehumanization most often shows itself in a degrading visual representation; the Other's traits then take on those of the monster or the animal. The Other's hypervisibility can thus originate in hatred or fantasy but also in simple curiosity. Further, historian Peter Burke remarks that the gaze directed at the Other, as he appears in the stereotype, informs us about the desires and fears of the observing society rather than the characteristics of the group being observed.[41]

What does hypervisibility of the Other in school materials tell us? Was it part of a movement of repulsion? Or was it the manifestation of a desire to escape? School images of human diversity and of "other places" in fact had a connection with the interest stimulated by evoking faraway lands. In this sense, with some exceptions, they inspire neither hatred nor repulsion.[42] The school framework thus provided an interesting counterweight to other visual representations of otherness. Think of a caricature, for example. In this case, the Other (usually the internal Other) is often ungainly, even deformed. In the school materials, the distant Other could be vested with desire—desire to escape, aesthetic desire—because he does not constitute an internal threat. The school textbook engraving also differs from caricature in that it offers a representation intended to be authentic. As well, it contains an aesthetic element related to the intention to introduce children to the Beautiful.

The desire to render the Other visible is most clearly expressed in the selection of engravings. Why did Miller show Black people working on plantations in the United States when his text does not mention them (Figure 40)? Why offer the reader a portrait of an "Esclave du Soudan" (Slave from Sudan) (Figure 41) if the students know nothing beyond what his profile tells them? While the choice of engravings may seem random, presenting images that sometimes have no relation to the text, it is more accurate to think that it resulted from a rigorous selection. The "slave from Sudan" and the Black workers were not there by chance. They were exhibited to the gaze because of a fascination with otherness that was linked to racist ideology. Moreover, the paragraph accompanied by the portrait provides a good illustration of the image's ideological import. The student would read, "Depuis ces dernières années, les divers peuples de l'Europe se sont emparés d'une grande partie du territoire de l'Afrique. L'Angleterre, l'Allemagne, la France, l'Italie et le Portugal ont étendu considérablement leurs possessions dans le continent noir, et ouvert ainsi de nouveaux débouchés au commerce et à l'industrie."[43] (In recent years, the various peoples of Europe have taken hold of a large portion of African lands. England, Germany, France, Italy and Portugal have considerably expanded their holdings on the Dark Continent and thus opened up new outlets for commerce and industry.) On the same page, a few paragraphs further down, Miller explained what *"la traite des nègres*" (the slave trade) was and made it clear that the Europeans and the Americans condemned it. The next question is a basic one: Which had more power, the association of the image with the words around it or the knowledge obtained from the text by itself? It is impossible to deny the psychological effect of enclosing the slave's portrait within a paragraph that recounts how African lands were taken over by the European powers. Moreover, this image stood out among the dozens contained in the geography textbook as the only one that allowed the children to see the portrait of an individual without being gazed at in return. The eyes of this man known to be a slave, and therefore by definition the property of someone else, are not looking at the reader. This "Slave from Sudan" is completely reified and at the same time his alterity is radically increased.

Commenting on Frantz Fanon's reflections on the immediacy of the visual in a racist relation, Mitchell writes: "The ocular violence of racism splits its object in two, rending and rendering it simultaneously hypervisible and invisible, an object of, in Fanon's words, 'abomination' and 'adoration.' *Abomination* and *adoration* are precisely the terms in which idolatry is excoriated in the Bible [. . .]. The idol, like the black man, is both despised and worshipped, reviled for being a nonentity, a slave, and feared as an alien and supernatural power."[44]

The Black characters in Figures 40 and 41, who do not exist in the text, are spied on by the eye. Apolitical bodies absent from the geographical explanation, these individuals were presented to the young reader who could adopt, for the length of a gaze, the slave owner's point of view.

In her study "Domesticating Nature, Appropriating Hierarchy: The Representation of European and Non-European Peoples in an Early Nineteenth-Century Schoolbook of Natural History,"[45] Ildikó Kristóf puts forward a series of concepts that are useful in studying visual representations of alterity. First of these is the concept of morphological *invariability*. In order to function, visual stereotypes must be constant so as to be *re*cognized by readers. The Other's morphological invariability is expressed in the longevity of certain school illustrations that survive multiple new editions of textbooks. For example, the vignette presenting the different human races and the image "La croix opère la vraie civilisation," both included in the geography produced by the Frères des écoles chrétiennes in 1875, were still there in the 1915 edition. Considering the lifespan of school textbooks, it means that for more than fifty years, the brothers' pupils were exposed to the same racial representations. This is even more interesting when we know that not all of the illustrations in the brothers' geography books lasted as long; many of the originals were not reproduced in the 1915 edition and new images were added.

According to Kristóf, the analysis should also look at the authors' and publishers' intentions regarding how their texts would be read. A choice of images that would serve to illustrate the student's "journey around the world" through a geography textbook was one of its author's implicit messages. In selecting the engravings to adorn their textbooks, authors offered the children a partial representation of alterity. In fact, these images harbour various "visual strategies of Othering." Kristóf says, "The first of such visual strategies is *simplification* and *uniformization*, that is, reducing the representation of the people (mostly of non-European indigenous people) to some basic features like dark skin and (almost) nakedness, wearing simple clothes like loin-cloths, short skirts, and so forth. The second strategy is *stereotypization* and *commonplacing*, that is, assigning certain activities to or features thought/proposed to be dominant among the people depicted. [. . .] Not unrelated to the second, the third strategy of representation used in the images of Raff is an explicit 'nature-isation' of the human beings depicted."[46] "Nature-isation" consists in associating the Other with nature by placing him, for example, in a forest or close to animals. The corpus analyzed provides a good example of this othering strategy. An Indian is included in an engraving used in two geography textbooks to represent the animals of America (Figure 42).[47] The writers' objective of associating America's Indigenous populations with nature and the animal realm is confirmed by the fact that there is no human presence in engravings illustrating the animals of other continents.

La récolte du coton, Mississipi.

Figure 40. "Picking Cotton, Mississipi [sic]," Miller, Nouvelle géographie élémentaire, 1901, 79.

The last strategies of otherness outlined by Kristóf are ethnologization, gendered representation, and hierarchization. Ethnologization consists in including the elements of a people's material culture in the illustration; for example, the calumet in representations of America's Indigenous peoples. As for gendered representation, it relates to the fact that the majority of human beings visually represented are men. Finally, the strategy of hierarchization functions through matching elements of the visual representation with those of the theory of stages of social evolution. In the textbooks studied, this strategy can be seen particularly in images of "barbarian and despotic" societies that often included their leaders, such as the Japanese Mikado, the Arab chief, and so on. By contrast, illustrations for societies said to be civilized were in the majority images of large urban centres and their middle-class

Esclave du Soudan.

Figure 41. "Slave from Sudan," Miller, *Nouvelle géographie élémentaire*, 1901, 141.

populace. The large corpus of images gathered as part of my study offers a unique opportunity to see and analyze the influence of the visual strategies of otherness identified by Kristóf in how the images of human diversity were made.

Adult women are rarely visible in the illustrations of school text-books. In the images used in reading textbooks, for example, the female characters are mostly children. This was not the case in geography books. First, with few exceptions, the engravings do not feature children. In addition, even if the human beings featured are mostly men, analyz-ing the few images showing women makes it possible to draw certain distinctions between representations of White and racialized women.

With the exception of Miller's selection of engravings,[48] White women who are present are middle class in appearance: they are walking along city streets, picnicking next to waterfalls, contemplating the land-scape, and so on. It is to be noted that they do not figure for their own sake but only to embellish a landscape or a street scene. As well, the engravers never put them in the foreground. Racialized women are more numerous and placed in differing contexts, although certain associations proved to be constant over time. This is the case in particular of images illustrating the cotton harvest. Black women can always be recognized in them. In a variation on the same theme, vignettes depicting the harvest of coffee or of tea in China also feature female workers. Thus, a primary distinction of class and race shows up in the visual representation of women. White women stroll about; Black and Chinese women work. The former seem to be middle class, while the latter are working class.

Women of other cultures sometimes also appear in a maternal role; for example, Indigenous women from North America. Beginning at the turn of the twentieth century, the textbooks were presenting images of families of the "Savages of the Northwest" in which the women were very visible (Figure 43). In contrast to people whose representation illustrated industrial work, Indigenous people were shown in an ethno-logical posture suggesting an association with primitivism: whether sitting on the grass or standing beside their tent, it was the monotony

PRINCIPAL ANIMALS ON THE CONTINENTS OF AMERICA.

of the Indians' daily life that students were given to see. The idea of an anhistorical, stationary existence behind these representations reinforced the belief that the Indigenous people could not become civilized or did not know how to.

Miller's textbook, published in 1901, provided a visual representation of women that was very different from that put forward in other textbooks. In contrast to textbooks published in the nineteenth century and in the first decade of the following century, women were *hypervisible* in his book, and the distinctions of class and race that we have just seen were not to be found. The great majority of engravings included by Miller are ethnographic. On page 107 we can see the "French washerwomen," and on page 10, "a young girl from Burma," and a woman making "corn flour and bread in Mexico" on page 82. When not simply shown head-on, the women, regardless of race, are working. In opposition to the exclusively masculine representation of working shown in other textbooks, Miller offered a more nuanced vision. Women's work was not only positively presented but also normalized, by being present in almost all societies. The Canadian women in cotton mills on page 56; Dutch milkmaids, page 112; Persians weaving a tapestry, page 134—all these women contributed to the world's economic and commercial activity.

What ideology was being disseminated by presenting these female ethnographic "types"? What message was Miller trying to deliver to his readers? As Taraud explains regarding colonial photography, these images transmit a vision of "woman" that hews to the values of the Western middle class: "There is a pedagogic virtue in these profiles of good wives, good mothers and good workers, in which we can nonetheless detect a curious match with the moral and patriarchal values of

Figure 42. "Principal Animals on the Continents of America," *Lovell's Intermediate Geography*, 1879, 27.

Figure 43. "Indians in Their Encampment," Sœurs de la congrégation de Notre-Dame, *Géographie. Cours moyen et cours supérieur*, 1897, 199.

the 19th-century middle class."[49] By making women invisible in their geography textbooks, the pedagogues were transmitting the ideology of the two spheres: a woman's place was in the private sphere (hidden) and not in the world order (public). At the turn of the twentieth century, Miller's textbooks attested to a paradigm shift: by showing women at work, he recognized their contribution to commerce, industry, and progress. The fact remained that their place was still circumscribed by a moral order that had changed very little.

The school corpus also contains Orientalist images in abundance. Combined with the texts analyzed in Chapter 1, they confirm how pervasive and widely disseminated Orientalism was in the nineteenth century. Various Oriental engravings in school imagery attest to this visual culture's accessibility. Because of the public taste for Orientalist works, engravers were likely better trained and more inclined to reproduce scenes from the Orient than those from Oceania, for example. The bank of images they were drawing on certainly contained many images of that type. The process is circular: Oriental engravings inundated the school textbooks because of the popularity of Orientalist painting and, in return, the pedagogical materials shored up the hegemony of the Orientalist imaginary by initiating a new generation.

Which visual Orientalism did the schools disseminate? What do the dozens of images reproduced in school textbooks represent? The desert incontestably recurs the most frequently. The oases, caravans (Figures 44 and 45), and Arab encampments were the principal versions of desert imagery that proved to be so fascinating. A second series of images, related directly to Biblical history and antiquity, represented the lands of Egypt and Palestine: views of Cairo and Jerusalem, scenes on the Nile, and images of the pyramids each summoned up a geography that was Biblical, distant in both space and time, and yet familiar. Finally, some rare images symbolized a contemporary Orient, as in the case of "Rue de [sic] Maroc" [(Street in Morocco) (Figure 46). The Oriental woman—eroticized—was significantly absent in this visual representation of the Orient. No odalisques or harem scenes in textbooks for schools.

Summarizing the work of art historian Linda Nochlin, John M. Mackenzie writes: "According to Nochlin, Europeans are visually absent [from Orientalist painting] but psychologically present because they constitute the all-seeing, all-powerful gaze. Westernising influences are also absent, as the violence and expropriation of the imperial thrust is cloaked in a highly selective and essentially destructive nostalgia. Orientalist images imply timelessness, the absence of the historical dynamic of progress that represents Western superiority. Yet its idealised vision also excludes squalor, disease and low life."[50] The vision of the Orient transmitted by school imagery corresponds exactly to Nochlin's analysis. The Orient is immutable. It is a land frozen in a distant time from which, above all, it must not be extracted. The Orient's inertia, as expressed in school images (Figure 47), was a necessary part of the exotic fascination. The Orient was the land of escape and nostalgic exile. In the religious context that was Quebec's, it was also a territory of origin associated with memories of sacred history. Time therefore did not matter.

Let us now address three illustrations that sum up, by themselves, the racist, dehumanizing representation of Black communities, and that were disseminated by Canadian school culture until the first decades of the twentieth century. "Halte d'une Caravane" (A caravan stops to rest) (Figure 48), an illustration by Montreal engravers Walker and Wiseman, appeared in the geography book published in 1875 by the Frères des écoles chrétiennes and it was still being used in the 1915 edition of their geography-atlas for upper-year students. At first glance, this engraving provides a fine example of Orientalist imagery. The scene presents a group of Arabs breaking their journey at an oasis. Palm trees, camels, hookahs, turbans, veils—it is all there, and it is all that a quick glance would have retained. However, the student who held the book open in front of him while listening to the teacher's lesson would likely have had the time to take a longer look at the engraving. His eyes would then be directed to the details in the foreground. Separate from the

684. A CARAVAN CROSSING THE DESERT TO MECCA.

Rue de Maroc.

other members of the caravan, a slave (as we suppose) is sitting with the animals. But is it really a man? A detail disturbs the eye: the face is not human. This Black slave—because there is no ambiguity about the skin colour—has a simian face. The text on the same page had already made a connection between the Blacks and animality:

> Moins intelligent et moins actif que les autres races,
> le Nègre est resté généralement sauvage, ignorant,
> superstitieux, adorateur de fétiches; il se laisse dominer par
> des chefs absolus et féroces, qui le traitent comme bête de
> somme, le sacrifient à leurs plaisirs ou le vendent à vil prix.[51]

> (Less intelligent and less active than the other races,
> the Negro has generally remained savage, ignorant,
> superstitious, an idolator of fetishes; he allows himself to be
> dominated by fierce, uncompromising chiefs, who treat him
> like a beast of burden, sacrifice him at their pleasure or sell
> him for a low price.)

With this image, the association of Black populations with animality is taken to the limit.

The second image of interest was found among glass plates used by the Sœurs de la congrégation de Notre-Dame to teach geology at the beginning of the twentieth century. It is the forty-first and last plate in a series, and entitled "Manière de produire des ombres avec ses doigts" (Shadows, how to produce them with the fingers) (Figure 49). Did the teacher leave the students to amuse themselves for a few minutes with the projector? The deliberate inclusion of this plate at the end of a geology lesson leads to that supposition. The young girls probably tried

Figure 44. Untitled, Calkin, *Calkin's New Introductory Geography*, 1898, title page.

Figure 45. "A Caravan Crossing the Desert to Mecca," Calkin, *Calkin's New Introductory Geography*, 1898, 69.

Figure 46. "Rue de [*sic*] Maroc," Miller, *Nouvelle géographie élémentaire*, 1901, 143.

La nonchalance de l'Arabe.

HALTE D'UNE CARAVANE.

Figure 47. "La nonchalance de l'Arabe," Magnan and Ahern, *Mon premier livre*, 1900, 52.

Figure 48. "Halte d'une Caravane," Frères des écoles chrétiennes, *Nouvelle géographie illustrée*, 1875, 83.

to produce a swan, an antelope, or even a wolf. That is, if they would not have preferred to produce "le Nègre." Among the twelve examples given on the glass plates, only two did not represent animals: "Père Thomas" and "le Nègre." Again in this case, the association of the "Negro" with animality is obvious. Unlike "Père Thomas," this person has no name or individuality. This illustration speaks not only to the importance of Black raciality as an inescapable figure of alterity but also to the exaggerated essentialization of Black individuals.

A final analysis concerns an image from the textbook *Mon premier livre: lire, écrire, compter* (My first book: reading, writing, counting) (1900), written by Charles-Joseph Magnan and John Ahern and distributed for decades to primary schools in the province by the Government of Quebec. Among the hundreds of engravings the book included, two are of an ethnographical type (in particular Figure 47) and only one depicts a Black person (Figure 50). In the arithmetic lesson "Les nombres et les chiffres de 1 à 9" (Numbers and numerals from 1 to 9), the children are asked to count the number of melons illustrated in the image: "Combien y a-t-il de melons dans la boîte? Combien y a-t-il de melons sur la boîte? [. . .] Combien le négrillon a-t-il de melons dans les bras? Les melons dans la boîte, sur la boîte et dans les bras du négrillon font en tout combien de melons?"[52] (How many melons are there in the box? How many melons are there on the box? [. . .] How many melons does the *négrillon* have in his arms? The melons in the box, on the box and in his arms make how many melons in all?) The image presents a young Black boy carrying a melon in his arms with a small dog at his feet. Is he working? It is not possible to say for certain, but that is the impression given by the engraving. The textbook's illustrations were redrawn for the edition published in 1922. The image had been modified, and the boy's features were more pronounced (Figure 51): thick lips, darker skin over whiter clothes, big white eyes. The modifications made to the drawing document the evolution of racism and the influence of popular visual culture on the school materials, in particular cartoons and caricatures.

Figure 49. "Shadows, how to produce them with the fingers," ACND, Boîte 50, Series on geology, Plaque no. 41 [partial view].

Why did Magnan and Ahern decide that Québécois children would learn to count thanks to the image of a Black child holding a melon in his arms? The authors' choice does not fit with the otherwise very nationalist content of the book, which is in fact characterized by the scarcity of its allusions to human diversity. If understanding the image is not possible in terms of the textbook's internal economy, it becomes clear when *Mon premier livre* is viewed in the larger context of Black representation in Western culture. For more than a century, many Western children have learned to count by making ten Black or Indigenous children disappear via a violently racist verse. As Jan Nederveen Pieterse reminds us: "The counting rhyme 'Ten Little [N. . .]' was allegedly written by an Englishman, Frank J. Green, in 1864; but there was already an earlier rhyme, 'Ten Little [I. . .],' by which American children still learn to count. For more than a hundred years, then, children in the West have been learning to count by making non-western children disappear, usually in not such pleasant ways."[53] The illustration in *Mon premier livre* serves to get children to count up to nine. Although they never asked schoolchildren to eliminate Black children, Magnan and Ahern surely took inspiration from this tradition.

ARITHMÉTIQUE
Les nombres et les chiffres de 1 à 9

ARITHMÉTIQUE
Les nombres et les chiffres de 1 à 9

Figure 50. "Les nombres et les chiffres de 1 à 9," Magnan and Ahern, *Mon premier livre: lire, écrire, compter*, 1900, 43.

Figure 51. "Les nombres et les chiffres de 1 à 9," Magnan and Ahern, *Mon premier livre: lire, écrire, compter*, 1922, 43.

A last detail again reveals the influence of popular culture on the image's composition. Why count melons? At the turn of the twentieth century, Black people became the principal comic figures in the American press's comic strips. The watermelon thief was a recurring character in these cartoons. Far from being harmless, the illustration of the stereotyped Black child and the melons speaks rather to the hold a transnational popular culture had on the minds of two Québécois teachers at the turn of the twentieth century.

The school initiated the student into the visual representation of alterity. The resulting socialization allowed the student to *recognize* the Other wherever he saw him. But is that the only power of imagery for children? Images, purveyors of knowledge, also have a very great evocative power: they make it possible to imagine "other places" and to feel a whole range of emotions. Whether they were friend or foe, the observed Others were certainly of great importance in the children's imagination.

In 1858, the *Rapport de l'Œuvre de la Sainte-Enfance pour le Canada* (Report of the Holy Childhood Association for Canada) reported on the various actions taken by children across the colony to "save" little Chinese children from death and religious infidelity. To convince them to join the association, the promoters used different narrativities with the children. One of the most important was conveyed through images. The chronicler described the situation in the Parish of Champlain in 1858 as follows:

> Un homme, qui s'est dévoué à cette belle œuvre, montrait ordinairement aux petits enfants une image qui représente les petits Chinois dévorés par les chiens et les pourceaux, ou traînés dans un chariot, ou noyés, etc. "Combien de fois," dit-il, "n'ai-je pas vu couler des larmes des yeux de ces petits enfants, tandis que d'autres déchiraient, avec les ongles, et chiens et Chinois, pour les punir d'ôter la vie à ces pauvres petits."[54]

(A man, who had dedicated himself to this wonderful
work, usually showed the children an image of little
Chinese children being devoured by dogs and swine, or
dragged by a trolley, or drowned, etc. "How many times,"
he said, "have I seen tears streaming from the eyes of these
children, while others, with their fingernails, tore them
apart, both dogs and Chinese people, to punish them for
having taken the life away from these poor little children.")

This example tells us that, in particular during the nineteenth century,
it was entirely possible for Canadian children to cry at the sight of an
alterity that was nonetheless very far away. That these children should
have wanted to punish the Chinese "with fury" from the simple observation of an image speaks to an emotional charge that is fuelled by alterity.

6.

Of Missions and Emotions: Children and the Missionary Mobilization

Early on the afternoon of 18 April 1872, nearly 3,000 children were marching in the streets of Quebec City. They all converged on the main auditorium of the Académie de musique on rue Saint-Louis.[1] Why were they going there? And what was the significance of the Chinese characters on the multicoloured banners they held up? Admission was free but limited to the children and the adults accompanying them. The crowd rushed in to hear the Reverend Father Vasseur, an apostolic missionary to China, who was in Quebec City to raise funds for the Oeuvres des orphelins chinois auxiliaires, a charity for Chinese orphans, of the Society for the Propagation of the Faith.[2] Over the afternoon, Father Vasseur told his young spectators at length about Chinese customs and the new crusade he was inviting them to join. The lecture had barely ended when the children rushed to the Ursulines' church to have their banners blessed. "Ainsi se termina cette journée" (And so the day ended), reported the *Courrier du Canada*. "Elle vivra de longues années dans les coeurs de nos petits enfants de Québec."³ (It will live for many long years in the hearts of our little children in Quebec City.)

A mesmerizing preacher and outstanding pedagogue, Father Vasseur allied exoticism with religious zeal and military imagery to win the Québécois children to his cause. From the outset, he leaned on the link that would connect his audience to the Chinese children: love. In soliciting this emotion, he reminded the young Associés de la Sainte-Enfance (Holy Childhood Association), who probably made up most of his audience, of the existence of the "millions of little children in China" watching over them: "Les troupes innombrables de ces petits innocents volent au-dessus de vous, ils vous regardent avec amour, ils vous remercient de leur avoir ouvert le ciel, ils prient l'enfant Jésus de vous donner une magnifique place dans sa gloire!" (The countless troops of these little innocents fly over you, look at you with love, thank you for having opened Heaven to them, they pray to the Infant Jesus to give you a magnificent place in his glory.) Their love was only equalled by that of the Catholic child members of the Sainte-Enfance:

> Comptez-les, vous verrez qu'ils forment par tout le monde
> la plus grande et la plus belle de toutes les armées, trois
> ou quatre millions de petits enfants de tous les pays et de
> toutes langues, tous s'aimant entr'eux, tous aimant l'enfant
> Jésus de tout leur cœur, et lui envoyant des millions de
> petits anges autour de son trône!⁴

> (Count them and you'll see that throughout the world
> they make up the biggest and most beautiful of all armies,
> three or four million small children of all countries and
> all languages, all loving one another, all loving the Infant
> Jesus with all their heart, and sending him millions of small
> angels to surround his throne!)

Love soon gave way to horror, fear, and courage. "Dites-moi, voulez-vous être des chevaliers de l'Enfant-Jésus?," Vasseur asked the children. (Tell me, do you want to be the knights of the Infant Jesus?) "*Oui! oui!*" they answered. What were these modern-day knights? Vasseur explained, "Des chevaliers, ce ne sont pas des soldats ordinaires, ce sont des soldats plus nobles et plus généreux, hardis, prêts à tout, pour arrêter les méchants. De notre temps, il faut beaucoup de soldats comme cela, même parmi les enfants, parce que de notre temps les soldats timides sont sans nombre."[5] (Knights are not ordinary soldiers, they are more noble and generous, bold, and ready to do anything to stop the wicked. In our day, we need many soldiers like that, even among children, because in our day the timid soldiers are without number.) Depicting a perverted European Christendom and stimulating a romantic, adventurous imaginary, Father Vasseur asked the children of Quebec for their help. Not only must these young knights bring charming women and girls back to the straight and narrow but perhaps even die to keep faith with Jesus Christ. By moving rapidly from a superficial concern to the possibility of martyrdom, the missionary no doubt created a great stir among the children:

> Et si pour être fidèles à l'enfant Jésus, il fallait mourir, êtes-vous prêts à mourir?
> (Les enfants: oui! oui!)
> (Le missionnaire tire de son fourreau le sabre Japonais posé sur la table.) Tenez, voilà un de ces sabres avec lesquels on coupait, au Japon, la tête des martyrs. Pendant douze ans, il y eut au Japon soixante mille martyrs. On les crucifiait, on les empaillait, on les brûlait, on les décapitait. Il y avait parmi eux des petits enfants de quatre à cinq ans, et des petites filles, et ils n'avaient pas peur. Eh bien, vous, si on vous menaçait de ce sabre pour vous faire offenser le bon Dieu, seriez-vous comme eux? N'auriez-vous pas peur?
> (Les enfants: non, non!)[6]

(And if to be faithful to the Infant Jesus, you had to die, are
you ready to die?
[The children: Yes! Yes!]
[The missionary unsheathes the Japanese sword that was
lying on the table.] Look, here is one of the swords they
use in Japan to cut off the heads of martyrs. In twelve years,
there were sixty thousand martyrdoms in Japan. They
crucified them, impaled them, burned them, cut off their
heads. Among them were small children four and five years
old, and little girls, and they weren't afraid. And you, if
they threatened you with a sword to make you offend God,
would you be like them? Wouldn't you be afraid?
[The children: No, no!])

In luring them with the possibility of martyrdom, Father Vasseur gave
the listening children a feeling of power and a capacity for action that
they were seldom granted. In short, as Michelle King remarks, "Vasseur's
lecture attested to both intense curiosity about Chinese customs and
popular religious fervor for the Catholic missionary cause."[7]

Throughout the second half of the nineteenth century, Canadian
children, both Catholic and Protestant, maintained a special connection
to the "pagan" world and the Christian missions established there. Far
from being an exception, Father Vasseur's lecture is part of a long history
of the missionary mobilization of children, more particularly schoolchildren and most particularly schoolgirls. Between the pedagogical
exploitation of adults and the hijacking of entertainments for children,
this discourse also provoked certain criticisms and protests. But one
thing is certain: central to this missionary rhetoric was an alterity that
had been instrumentalized for the benefit of the emotional education
of Christian children.

The Missions, the Children, and the Schools

In the nineteenth century, European and American societies underwent a religious revival. This took various forms. Relaunching missionary activity and taking charge of children "at risk" were two of its manifestations. The issue of children in difficulty sparked numerous historical works dealing with specific national or local situations. The Western nature of this inquiry was expressed in many transnational surveys. The concern for having children in need of "protection" or "salvation" was paralleled by moral and philosophical reflections on childhood that resulted, in the early nineteenth century, in its being conceptualized in terms of innocence. In that context, it is not surprising to see that, as the missionary renewal came together at that time, a good part of its discourse was devoted to the idolatrous child to be "saved." The specificity of this movement in favour of "infidel children" resided in the involvement of Christian children. In this regard, it was considered a key factor that Catholic children judged to be "at risk" should contribute to the redemption of "pagan children." Furthermore, it seems that, for the missionary movement, involving children in the mission's organization was the most critical factor. The missionary charities were also the first philanthropic organizations with an interest in recruiting children as donors.[8]

Recent historical works clearly show the importance given to involving Protestant children in the funding of foreign missions in the nineteenth century. The missionary renewal created a new form of religious activism, one conceived in terms of the interests and power of children.[9] While a truly comparative study of the Protestant and Catholic communities has not yet been produced, reading the historiography and consulting the Canadian archives have enabled me to state that the two groups went about involving children in missionary activity in similar circumstances and using the same arguments. As well, the success of these religious activities would not have been possible without the institutional support of the educational community, whether through the Sunday schools in Protestant communities or the expansion of religious teaching communities among the Catholics. Analysis that deals with the historiographic fields of childhood, missions, emotions, and world history could therefore be enriched with a new perspective, that of education.

Before presenting the particular forms these initiatives took in Quebec, two of the movement's characteristics should be mentioned. First, the initiatives shared a dimension that was not only transnational but also transdenominational and transsectarian, made possible by the universalistic nature of the "civilizing mission." By insisting on the importance of Christendom in European imperialism's expansion, the missionary discourses managed to reach a very broad audience. The various missionary magazines intended for Protestant children crossed national and denominational boundaries. In the Catholic case of the Holy Childhood Association, known in French Canada as the Association de la Sainte-Enfance, the transnational appeal was backed up, on occasion, by a transsectarian aspect. In fact, many reports stated that the Muslims in the Middle East and Protestants, particularly in Canada, made financial contributions to the Holy Childhood. Aside from the importance of ensuring a Christian imperialism, to what did these organizations owe their transnational success? According to Sophie Heywood, it resided in the mobilization of two groups at the centre of the nineteenth century's religious revival—women and children.[10] I would add that it is also because of their use of a radical, distant alterity that these missionary works were able to become such powerful transnational movements.

The second characteristic of children's mobilization for the missionary cause was the rhetorical use of "humanist" ideas. A special notice published by the Sainte-Enfance in Montreal in 1859 stated the conditions to be fulfilled in order to be admitted as a member: "Pour être de la Ste. Enfance, il n'est pas nécessaire d'être chrétien, il suffit d'être humain."[11] (To be part of the Holy Childhood, it is not necessary to be Christian, it is enough to be human.) Enthusiasm for saving and redeeming pagan children even gave rise to the first large transnational humanitarian enterprises. On this topic, historian Katharina Stornig writes: "Attempting to mobilise support for children who did not belong to their own religious, social or national group, Catholic philanthropists, going beyond an inner-confessional language and practice of solidarity, appealed to their readers' sense of human solidarity with distant children, whom they constructed as the most helpless, needy and innocent part of humankind."[12] The humanity claimed for them by these organizations was precisely what cemented relations of the children of Europe and America to their Chinese or African counterparts. In that regard, the idea of common humanity rested in large part on that of childhood, while the children's "barbaric" and "pagan" parents were often qualified as inhuman.

Sunday schools, founded in England at the end of the eighteenth century, were schools sponsored by the Protestant churches. In addition to religious instruction, they offered a basic education to working-class children. They were also important outlets for the missionary propaganda campaign that was organized in the nineteenth century. According to Frank Prochaska, the missionary mobilization of English children through Sunday schools went back to the early nineteenth century. However, it was not until the 1840s that the links between the Sunday schools and the foreign missions became institutionalized, in particular thanks to missionary magazines intended for children.[13] The launch in Montreal in 1849 of the magazine *The Missionary and Sabbath School Record* shows that initiatives were taken simultaneously in the metropolis and in the British colony.

Although the children's mobilization had been in operation since mid-century, it really became relentless after 1870, as much in the United States as in Canada and New Zealand. Between the middle of the century and the First World War, transnational interest in the missions would gradually make way for a more national and denominational dynamic. The timing of this shift to "nationalist" missionary propaganda coincided with changes observed in representations of alterity in the schools. At the turn of the twentieth century, teaching was increasingly patriotic, and identifying with the nation gradually supplanted a sense of belonging to a broader civilization and culture.

In 1893, at the annual convention of the Brome County Sunday School Association, Miss Georgia Taber stressed the importance of missionary teaching in Quebec's Sunday schools. On 11 October, the convention's second day, she and her colleague Miss Bertha Castle successively discussed temperance and the missions in the work of Sunday schools. The convention's report states: "These two papers on two of the most important topics were presented in a manner which not only reflected credit upon the young ladies who gave them but which also gave much pleasure and inspiration to those who listened."[14] A few years later, a speech on "How to Make Missions Interesting to our S.S. [Sunday School]" was delivered by the Reverend James Pletts at another convention.[15] Finally, in 1912, at the association's twentieth annual meeting, the topic was again on the agenda when the Reverend Hayden of Sutton addressed the audience "on missionary Education in the Sunday School."[16]

Sunday school clergy and teachers were not the only ones to have an interest in missionary work. On 6 November 1906, the members of the Montreal High School Literary and Debating Society congratulated their colleague Skelton "on the way he spoke [on the missionary work in the West]."[17] Two years later, students from the high school attended an illustrated lecture on the missions delivered by Ralph E. Diffendorfer, Secretary of the Missionary Education Movement of the United States and Canada.[18] At the same time, the young girls at the prestigious Dunham Ladies' College also involved themselves in the missionary effort. During the 1910–11 school year, they sponsored Mary Martin, "the little Indian girl in Miss Soraby's school in India." The next year, following a visit from the president of the Women's Auxiliary for the Diocese of Montreal, the students decided to support a Chinese girl in Ku-cheng. That same year they also received a visit from two missionaries who told them about their work at Hudson Bay and in China.[19] A study of the missionary mobilization of Protestant children and its link to the history of education remains to be completed, but the proposed overview shows that there was a Protestant correlative to the representation of the world disseminated in the Catholic missionary discourses to be analyzed below.

The Œuvre de la Sainte-Enfance/Holy Childhood Association was founded in 1843 by the Bishop of Nancy, Mgr de Forbin-Janson, and its purpose was the "rachat des Enfants indifèles en Chine, et dans les autres pays idolâtres" (redemption of infidel children in China, and in the other idolatrous countries).[20] The Sainte-Enfance adopted an associative model and was, according to the notice sent to Bishop Bourget, the first association dedicated especially to Catholic children. Children were "associates" until their First Communion and could then remain "*agrégés*" (qualified) until their twenty-first birthday. From that age on, the *agrégé* must become a member of the Society for the Propagation of the Faith, another association supporting missions, in order to remain a member of the Sainte-Enfance.[21] Each month, members would contribute one penny as a membership fee. The association operated at the grass-roots level through the constitution of series of twelve young members presided over by a "chief," whose responsibilities were to ensure that membership fees were collected and the *Annales* were distributed. In addition to the obligation of making a monthly offering, members were required to recite an Ave Maria each day, with the following invocation: "O Marie et St. Joseph, priez pour nous et pour les pauvres petits enfants infidèles."[22] (Oh, Mary and St. Joseph, pray for us and for the poor little infidel children.) Introduced into the Diocese of Montreal in 1851, the association rapidly received the support of the bishops of Quebec City, Saint-Hyacinthe, and Trois-Rivières. To those who remembered the preaching done in the colony in the early 1840s by Mgr de Forbin-Janson, the enthusiasm that greeted the Holy Childhood in Canada probably came as no surprise. By the end of that decade, the association was well established in Canada and the United States, as stated in the various reports and accounts published between 1858 and 1860 by the director for North America, François Daniel.

The history of Catholic children's missionary involvement is closely linked to the history of education. As Heywood explains in her article about the association:

> One of the first aims of Mgr de Forbin-Janson was that
> the Holy Childhood work hand in hand with schools and
> support their work. It is therefore no surprise that the rapid
> development of the Holy Childhood Association between
> the 1840s and the 1880s coincided with the expansion
> of Catholic teaching congregations during the religious
> revival. The development of children's missions in Europe
> was closely linked to the growth of formal systems of
> education. Just as the British Protestant missions relied
> upon Sunday schools to fill their ranks, so the Catholic
> schooling sector provided a natural recruiting ground for
> the Holy Childhood. The bulk of the Holy Childhood's
> members were recruited from schools and other
> institutions that worked with children.[23]

This phenomenon could also be seen in Canada. Throughout the nineteenth century, the Holy Childhood's success was due in large part to the convents, *collèges*, and primary schools.[24] For example, according to the fundraising figures for 1895, 70 percent of the entries from "Montreal and surroundings" were identified as coming from teaching establishments; in the case of rural parishes, 50 percent of contributions were attributed to school institutions.[25] The schools' support for the missionary effort is not only to be seen in relation to the Holy Childhood. In 1868, Bishop Bourget sent the teaching congregations a circular inviting them to inform their students about "les maux qui pèsent à l'heure qu'il est, sur les infortunés Arabes de l'Afrique" (the evils weighing, at this very moment, on the unfortunate Arabs of Africa). As well as asking their pupils to pray for "ce peuple qui meurt de faim" (this populace dying of hunger), the teachers should also beg them for "une obole,

afin de contribuer au salut des orphelins que les Sœurs de l'Algérie
recueillent avec l'espérance d'en faire des Chrétiens" (an offering, so as
to contribute to the salvation of the orphans taken in by the Sisters of
Algeria in the hope of making Christians of them).[26]

Over time, the links grew stronger between the missionaries' funding
and the educational institutions. From the outset, the religious congregations had been the natural allies of the Holy Childhood, and the lay
teaching body rapidly joined their own zeal to that of the missionaries.
In July 1904, at their annual convention, Quebec's primary schoolteach-
ers received a visit from Father Forbes, one of Canada's first missionaries
to Africa. One of the teachers summed up the lecture in this way:

> À la séance de 2 heures, le rév. Père Forbes, supérieur des
> Pères Blancs des missions d'Afrique, nous entretint de
> ses missions Kabyles du Nord et de celles des nègres de
> l'Afrique équatoriale. Ce bon Père a beaucoup intéressé
> son auditoire par l'explication de la langue arabe et de celle
> des nègres, ainsi que par la récitation de leurs prières et
> l'exécution de leurs chants. Ce voyage en Afrique a été très
> expéditif et surtout très intéressant. Nous serons désormais
> portés à prier et à faire prier nos élèves pour le salut de ces
> arabes et de ces nègres si malheureux, ainsi que pour les
> dévoués Pères et Sœurs missionnaires pour que Dieu leur
> envoie de nouveaux missionnaires.[27]

(At the 2:00 session, the Reverend Father Forbes, Superior
of the Pères Blancs of the African missions, told us about
his Kabyle missions in the North and those with the
Negroes in Equatorial Africa. The good father held the
interest of his audience by explaining the Arabic language
and that of the Negroes, as well as by reciting their prayers
and performing their songs. This journey to Africa was
very rapid and particularly interesting. From now on we

will be more inclined to pray and have our students pray
for the salvation of these unfortunate Arabs and Negroes
as well as for the devoted missionary Fathers and Sisters so
that God will send them new missionaries.)

After having lost momentum at the turn of the twentieth century,
the Holy Childhood experienced a revival during the 1910s. As in
the Protestant communities, the association's relaunching then took
on a national cast. In 1914, Bishop Bruchési wrote to Mgr de Teil, the
association's president-general, to assure him of his support: "Tous les
élèves de nos collèges, de nos pensionnats [sic] de nos écoles primaires
seront heureux et fiers d'y contribuer généreusement. Les maîtres et
les maîtresses, laïques aussi bien que religieux et religieuses, se feront
un devoir de stimuler leur ardeur."[28] (All the students in our collèges,
boarding schools, and primary schools will be proud and happy to make
a generous contribution. The teachers, lay as well as religious, will make
it a duty to stimulate their ardour.) In order to ensure the enterprise's
success, Bruchési entrusted a young French-Canadian missionary
congregation, the Sœurs de l'Immaculée-Conception, with visiting the
schools of Montreal to stoke the children's zeal:

L'Œuvre de la Sainte Enfance a toujours été en faveur
dans nos écoles. J'aime à croire que les Sœurs missionnaires
de l'Immaculée-Conception dont on connaît les œuvres
si belles en Chine seront admises par Messieurs les
Commissaires, les principaux, les maîtres et les maîtresses,
pour intéresser les élèves à cette grande Œuvre et recueillir
leurs aumônes.[29]

(The Holy Childhood's work has always been in favour in
our schools. I like to think that the Sœurs missionnaires
de l'Immaculée-Conception, whose very good work in
China we know, will be accepted by the Commissioners,

principals, and schoolmasters, to interest the students in
this great Work and collect their alms.)

But what are the rhetorical elements underlying the missionary
discourse? As Bancel and Blanchard write: "Figures of the Other are
indispensable, driving elements of all forms of social mobilization:
summoned up, instrumentalized, they initiate or consolidate networks
of sociability, structure or restructure groups, and forge relationships,
whether of opposition or unity, among social factions."[30] The missionary
propaganda of the nineteenth century used alterity as an engine of
profound social change. Invoking a faraway Other to "save" also served
the purposes of Christian society's religious revival.

But first we should take a little time to consider the characteristics
appropriate to an Other who is invoked specifically to serve missionary propaganda. The discourse's longevity depended on summoning a
mysterious, exotic alterity that must be reached by apostolic effort. Given
their "humanist" nature, the missionary discourses did not propose a
biologically hierarchized world view; that is, the racial stereotypes they
disseminated were not supported by a scientific discourse. This "softer"
racism, as Brian Stanley maintains,[31] nonetheless contributed to racial
thinking and the discrimination that proceeded from it. Moreover, we
must not confuse the report of an encounter between the missionaries
and the missioned populace with a discourse delivered for fundraising
purposes. The missionaries' writings were often modified before appearing in the propaganda publications intended for the metropolis. I am
of the same opinion as historians Felicity Jensz, Henrietta Harrison,
and Frank Prochaska, who have all underscored the importance of the
missionary discourse in the construction of non-European, non-White,
and non-Christian alterity. However, even if the missionary discourses
were not proposing a strongly racialized vision of the Other, they actively
contributed to the construction of Whiteness. In the mid-nineteenth
century, it was not only the child who was seen as innocent but childhood itself that became the incarnation of innocence. And yet, "this

innocence was raced white,"[32] specifies Robin Bernstein. The idealization of Whiteness manifested itself in the same way as did the performance of Indigeneity analyzed in Chapter 4. For celebrations of the Holy Childhood, the young people representing Chinese children wore costumes, while those who played a role in the celebration were often "vêtu[s] de blanc, ce qui, en donnant un air d'innocence à tou[s], ajout[e] encore à l'éclat de la Fête" (dressed in white which, by giving them all an air of innocence, adds to the splendour of the event).[33] This racialization, which could be termed "moderate," changed in the twentieth century, when the racist import of the missionary content aimed at young people was unequivocal. The change was surely related to growing attention to the missionary discourse regarding Africa as the new century began.

Who are the Others in the Catholic missionaries' discourse delivered to French-Canadian children in the nineteenth century? Obviously, paganism was the real target of Christian evangelism, taking in "toutes les tribus, [tous] les peuples, [toutes] les nations" (all the tribes, [all] the peoples, [all] the nations). As mentioned in a publication by the Sainte-Enfance in 1893, the children "*envoyés en paradis*" (sent to heaven) thanks to the associates' alms came from "tous les pays où règne encore l'infidélité, et où ont pénétré des Missionnaires: de la Chine, des Indes orientales, des Indes occidentales, de toutes les régions de l'immense Continent africain" (all the countries where infidelity still reigns, and which the Missionaries have penetrated: from China, the East Indies, the West Indies, from all regions of the immense African Continent).[34] However, owing to the Holy Childhood's enduring rhetoric about China, the Chinese remained the principal figure of alterity in the missionary discourse.[35] America's Indigenous nations were also often mentioned, particularly in the *collèges classiques*, Quebec's grammar schools.[36] At the turn of the twentieth century, the Arabs and Black Africans were added to those two populations.

On 2 May 1854, some students at Montreal's Collège Sainte-Marie were competing for the role of series leader in the Society for the Propagation of the Faith. To win the title, each candidate had to deliver a speech. In his address, young Alary neatly summed up the conception of pagan peoples transmitted in the religious discourse:

> L'existence de ces êtres est comme celle de la brute, ils sont remplis de férocité, ils admettent toute licence, ils exercent la poligamie [*sic*] ils cultivent le fétichisme; ils sont donc. perdus sans ressources n'ayant personne pour les instruire. [. . .] N'ayant que la croix d'une main et l'Évangile de l'autre et les trésors de la Foi dans son cœur, le missionnaire se rend inconnu au milieu de ces hommes beaucoup plus rapprochés de l'état animal que de la condition humaine. Il obtient enfin accès auprès de ses boureaux [*sic*]. Il les apaise par des paroles qui ne respirent que la douceur, il les charme par la persuasion des vérités qu'il leur prêche, il les humanise par ses conseils et l'exemple de sa conduite. Il est enfin parvenu à les civiliser et désormais, il communiquera avec eux, comme avec des frères. [. . .] Vous avez un cœur sensible et compatissant, ne restez pas sourds aux cris d'infortune que poussent ces pauvres malheureux pour vous appeler à leur secours. [. . .] Et ainsi emportant les regards de votre sollicitude sur ces peuples éloignés, et en subvenant à leur secours, vous montrez par votre zèle et votre générosité que vous chérissez les intérêts de la religion et de l'humanité.[37]

> (These beings lead the existence of ruffians, they are filled with ferocity, they allow all licence, they practise polygamy, they cultivate fetishism; they are therefore lost people without resources, having no one to teach them. [. . .] With nothing but the cross in one hand and the Gospel in the other and the treasures of the Faith in his heart, the missionary arrives as an unknown among these men much closer to the animal state than the human condition.

He finally obtains access to these murderers. He pacifies
them with words that breathe only gentleness, he charms
them by persuading them of the truths he preaches, he
humanizes them with his counsel and the example of his
behaviour. He finally manages to civilize them and from
that moment on he will communicate with them as with
brothers. [. . .] You have a tender, merciful heart, don't be
deaf to the cries of misfortune these poor unhappy people
send out to call you to their rescue. [. . .] And thus casting
the gaze of your concern on these distant peoples, and by
supporting their rescue, you show through your zeal and
your generosity that you care deeply about the interests of
religion and humanity.)

This address is a prime example of missionary rhetoric in the nineteenth
century. First of all, the young man starts and finishes his speech by
alluding to humanity. The pagan person is not really human, but has only
a "potential" humanity that the Christian should awaken. These "beings"
like "ruffians" are "much closer to the animal state." What should be
done? The missionary, playing the pivotal role in the narrative, arrives
and "humanizes" them. The change is dramatic, almost miraculous. The
argument finally stated by Alary concerns the emotions and agency
of his audience. While ably written, this student's argument contains
nothing original but borrows the background from accounts of conversion. Regarding the Christianization of African populations thanks to
the Holy Childhood's contributions, a notice from 1893 explains: "Ce
sont pourtant les petits Associés de la Sainte-Enfance qui ont opéré
par l'aumône de leurs petits sous, cette transformation merveilleuse."[38]
(However, the little Associates of the Holy Childhood are the ones who,
with the alms of their pennies, produced this marvellous transformation.)

Beyond the argument of the battle to be waged against paganism that was broadcast in the missionary publications, the children's
mobilization was implemented mostly through staging parent/child

relationships associated with idolatry. In fact, the Holy Childhood's success was entirely due to the exaggerated opposition between the inhumane cruelty of Chinese parents and the tender love of childhood among the Catholics. In this regard, it is very relevant to point out, like Michelle King and like Katharina Stornig here, the total absence of any resemblance being drawn between abandoned children in China and those in Europe: "What all texts shared was the fact that authors largely ignored the existence of social phenomena such as child abandonment or infanticide in Christian Europe but rather located them in what they constructed as 'heathen' parts of the globe."[39] In 1853, *L'Abeille*, the student newspaper of the Petit Séminaire de Québec, informed its readers about the charitable organization that was new to the diocese. Before outlining the Holy Childhood Association's rules, the author devotes a lot of space to the barbarity of Chinese parents:

> Là, le père barbare étouffe son enfant dans un bassin d'eau chaude ou le jette dans la rivière sans que les cris de cette innocente créature puissent toucher son cœur; plus loin, la mère dénaturée jette dans la rue son fils qui lui sourie [*sic*] et qui tend vers elle ses petites mains.[40]

> (There, the barbaric father drowns his child in a basin of hot water or throws her into the river while the cries of the innocent creature leave his heart untouched; further on, the unnatural mother puts her son out into the street, while he smiles at her and reaches out to her with his little hands.)

Far from being the exception, this denigration of Chinese parents is constantly repeated. In 1855, in a pastoral letter recommending the association, Bishop Bourget wrote:

> Associez vos enfants à la Sainte Enfance, cette admirable Association, qui est spécialement pour eux, et qui fait

baptiser par année, plus de deux cent mille enfants, dans le
vaste empire de la Chine, où des parents barbares jettent
dans les rues et laissent manger par les pourceaux, ceux de
leurs enfants qu'ils ne veulent pas élever.[41]

(Subscribe your children in the Holy Childhood, that
admirable association that is especially for them, and that
each year allows more than two hundred thousand children
to be baptized in China's vast empire, where children
whose barbaric parents choose not to raise them are thrown
into the streets or eaten by swine.)

Bishop Prince of Saint-Hyacinthe also inspired zeal by condemning
the supposed deficiencies of Chinese parents: "La Société de la Sainte
Enfance en l'honneur du Saint-Enfant-Jésus, est établie en Europe pour
le rachat des pauvres enfants chinois que leurs parents barbares livrent
tout vivants aux chiens et aux pourceaux ou qu'ils jettent à la rivière."[42]
(The Holy Childhood Association, in honour of the Holy Infant Jesus,
was established in Europe to redeem poor Chinese children whose
barbaric parents deliver them still alive to dogs and swine or throw
them into the river.)

In the nineteenth century, many phenomena contributed to the
increasingly uncontested belief that infanticide was a Chinese custom.
The Holy Childhood was in part responsible for that prejudice.
A comparison of the geography textbook written by Father Holmes
in 1833, before the Holy Childhood came on the scene, with that of
François-Xavier Toussaint, published in the late 1860s, tellingly illustrates a change in perception. While Holmes mentioned that "l'usage
cruel d'exposer les enfans dans les rues ou sur l'eau, est fort ancien,
quoique assez rare aujourd'hui" (the cruel practice of exposing their
children to death in the streets or in the water goes back a very long
way, although it is quite rare today), Toussaint baldly stated that "l'infanticide est commun chez les Chinois" (infanticide is common among

the Chinese).[43] Reading the Holy Childhood publications, which are unambiguous, helps us to understand how this belief came to be so strong. On the one hand, the holy pictures distributed by the association very often featured the abandonment of Chinese children by their parents; on the other, the texts described the barbarities in meticulous detail. For instance, in 1859, Sulpician Father François Daniel wrote:

> Ici, c'est un père dénaturé qui ensevelit son enfant toute vivante avec sa femme qui vient de mourir; là c'est une mère cruelle qui enfonce son enfant dans un bourbier, sans se laisser émouvoir par ses cris; ailleurs, c'est le père et la mère qui, d'un commun accord, écrasent sous une pierre leur enfant sous prétexte qu'elle est maladive, etc.[44]

> (Here, an unnatural father is burying his child, still alive, with his wife who has just died; there, a cruel mother pushes her child down into a quagmire, without being moved by her cries; elsewhere, the father and mother, by common accord, crush their child under a stone on the pretext that she is sickly, and so on.)

The Chinese were certainly not the only people accused of parental indifference. At the turn of the century, the association extended this accusation to include Africans:

> Pendant assez longtemps, notre compassion s'était comme concentrée sur les petits Chinois, que l'on expose en si grand nombre et que les Missionnaires, grâce aux aumônes de la Sainte-Enfance, recueillent et baptisent par centaines de mille. Mais depuis que le Continent africain, demeuré si mystérieux jusqu'à nos jours, a ouvert ses portes aux diverses nations d'Europe, on a constaté que les pauvres petits Africains ne sont pas traités avec moins de cruauté et

de barbarie que le sont les petits Chinois. Laissez-moi vous citer quelques faits à l'appui de cette assertion.[45]

(For quite a long time now, it seems that our compassion has been focused on the little Chinese children, who are exposed to death in such large numbers and whom the Missionaries, thanks to the alms of the Holy Childhood, take in and baptize by the hundreds of thousands. But since the African Continent, which has remained so mysterious until the present day, has opened its doors to Europe's various nations, we have seen that the poor little Africans are not treated with any less cruelty or barbarity than the little Chinese. Allow me to quote you some facts in support of this claim.)

The governments of colonial settlements would use the same argument regarding the First Peoples. In that discourse, the adults, being judged "inhumane," were represented as Others. But the children, considered to be innocents, were for that reason not the same. Missionary propaganda took as its own the conceptualization of childhood as innocence. If guilty, the "little Chinese children" or the "poor Indians" would not arouse the compassion of Canadian children. The Holy Childhood publications made a connection between the innocence of the Catholic child and that of the pagan child. In this way, the little pagans' innocence was established through the actions of Catholic children. The difference in race or civilization made way for a difference between the "saved" child and the child "to be saved." It was no accident that the missionary rhetoric used the child to drive its discourse. The concept of childhood in Western thinking evolved considerably in the nineteenth century. In addition to creating a lasting association between childhood and innocence, the sciences also came to see the "savage" in the child. The use of childhood in the representation of alterity was not the same where the Chinese and Indigenous peoples were concerned.

On the one hand, there were the Chinese, among whom newborns were mainly represented as innocents to be saved. In fact, it would have been impossible to represent the Chinese as a "childlike" people, given the centuries-long history of China's civilization, as taught in the educational materials. Conversely, regarding the Indigenous peoples, the innocence associated with childhood was extended to the entire populace. As a "savage" people, the rhetoric of the child-people applied perfectly to them. Thus, on the one hand, evangelism aimed to save the innocents, whether they were Chinese newborns or Indigenous peoples; and on the other, it helped to "straighten up" and "civilize" the Catholic child.

The *Rapport de l'Œuvre de la Sainte-Enfance pour le Canada, la province d'Halifax et les États-Unis* published in 1858 includes a hymn to be sung by the children at the annual Holy Childhood celebrations held each year in certain parishes. In addition to restating the passive innocence of the Chinese children and the cruelty of their parents, the lyrics celebrate the empowerment of Catholic children:

Petits chinois, dans vos misères
Nous voulons vous soulager tous.
Nous en parlerons à nos mères:
Jeunes frères, consolez-vous! [. . .]
Des enfants nouveau-nés implorent le baptême;
Ils meurent, étouffés par leur mère elle-même,
Enfants chrétiens! dans un espoir suprême,
Ils vous tendent leurs petits bras!
Ne les sauverez-vous pas? [. . .]
Mais loin d'ici, sur les plages lointaines
Que le démon tient encor dans ses chaînes,
A l'ombre de la mort!
Combien d'enfants, au jour de leur naissance,
Sont exposés, malgré leur innocence,
Au plus funeste sort!

Plus inhumain que le pâtre sauvage
Qui va ravir, cachés sous le feuillage,
Les petits des oiseaux,
Parfois leur père, étouffant la nature,
Les fait servir de vivante pâture
Aux plus vils animaux. [. . .]
Assez longtemps à vos cris lamentables
Sont restés sourds les cœurs impitoyables
De vos persécuteurs
Oui, dès ce jour, vous deviendrez nos frères
Et, chers petits, si vous êtes sans mères,
Vous aurez des sauveurs.
Nouveaux croisés, jeunes, mais intrépides,
Nous mettrons fin aux efforts homicides
De vos cruels parents;
L'Enfant-Jésus guidera notre enfance,
Et par sa croix brisera la puissance
De vos lâches tyrans.[46]

(Little Chinese, in your misery,
We want to relieve you all.
We will tell our mothers:
Little brothers, be consoled! [. . .]
Newborn children plead for baptism:
They die, suffocated by their own mother,
Christian children! in supreme hope,
They hold out their little arms to you!
Will you not save them? [. . .]
But far from here, on faraway sands,
That the devil still holds in his chains,
In the shadow of death!
How many children, on the day of their birth,
Are exposed, despite their innocence,

To the most deadly fate!
Less humane than the wild predator,
Hidden in the leaves, who steals
The birds' little ones,
At times their father, stifling nature,
Makes them into living feed
For the most vile animals. [. . .]
Long enough your pitiful cries
Have fallen unheard on the flinty hearts
Of your persecutors
Yes, from this day, you will become our brothers
And, dear little ones, if you have no mothers
You will have saviours.
New crusaders, young, but intrepid,
We'll stop the homicidal acts
Of your cruel parents;
The Child Jesus will guide our childhood,
And with his cross he will break the power
Of your cowardly tyrants.)

In the missionary rhetoric, Chinese children were represented as innocents and in this respect the "equals" of Christian children. And yet this
equality was only apparent, because a new dichotomy was immediately
set up. Chinese children were presented as innocent, passive victims
waiting to be saved. Conversely, privileged Christian children shared
with their brothers and sisters of the Catholic and Protestant worlds
the ability to intervene in the fate of these innocent victims.

The materials produced by the Holy Childhood—the images,
hymns, texts, and stage plays—were saturated with an emotionality
whose fulcrum was the suffering of others. The reader or spectator was
asked to remedy it. The compassion summoned up by these accounts
from a mysterious, threatening "other place" was not the only emotional

reaction elicited by the missionary rhetoric. The fate of the "petits chinois" allowed Canadian children to experience a wide range of emotions: from horror and pity, they moved quickly to joy and happiness.

"None deserve the compassion of the entire Catholic world like the poor children of China": The Emotional Uses of Alterity

The history of emotions is now a well-established field of research. As constituents of the real, emotions have many social and political implications. Their study enables a better understanding of the motivations that guide human actions. For many years, strong connections have been built between the history of emotions and the history of childhood.[47] Once the historical dimension of emotions had been confirmed, specialists wanted to understand how they had shaped individuals and communities. From this point of view, childhood constitutes a special field of study. Presumed to be malleable, children have long been the target of emotional socialization and education.

In the history of the Holy Childhood Association of the nineteenth century, emotions were crucial. First, the broader emotional context in which this pious association functioned must be clarified. On the one hand, as Sophie Heywood remarks, the association's history contributed to the emotional freight attributed to childhood in the nineteenth century, and which I have briefly addressed in dealing with the issue of innocence.[48] On the other hand, by playing a part in the history of humanitarianism, the Holy Childhood contributed to the sweeping change that occurred between the end of the eighteenth and middle of the nineteenth centuries in the Euro-American countries' regime of sympathy. Compassion then became an important emotional component.

In her book *The Cultural Politics of Emotion*, Sara Ahmed analyzes how emotions circulate among individual and collective bodies. Rather than adopting the theories of "inside out" and "outside in," Ahmed proposes a sociality of emotions that does not consider them to be possessed by individuals or societies: "In other words, emotions are not 'in' either the individual or the social, but produce the very surfaces and boundaries that allow the individual and the social to be delineated as if they are objects. [. . .] My argument still explores how emotions can move through the movement or circulation of objects. Such objects become sticky, or saturated with affect."[49] According to Ahmed, individuals and communities are objects that accumulate an affective value through history. They are then saturated with emotions. She illustrates her theory by analyzing various situations; in particular, she explains how racialized bodies become the surface on which fear circulates, or how the relationship with the nation is defined by love.

Ahmed's theorization associates the bodies that are invaded and affected by emotions with the texts that contribute to the emotions' circulation:

> So I am not discussing emotion as being "in" texts, but as
> effects of the very naming of emotions, which often works
> through attributions of causality. The different words for
> emotion do different things precisely because they involve
> specific orientations towards the objects that are identified
> as their cause. As such, my archive is full of words. But
> the words are not simply cut off from bodies, or other
> signs of life. I suggest that the work of emotion involves
> the "sticking" of signs to bodies: for example when others
> become "hateful," then actions of "hate" are directed against
> them.[50]

Ahmed's thinking is very useful in analyzing the history of the Holy Childhood in Canada. Her conceptualization of emotions as circulating between bodies, accumulating on certain objects, and being activated by certain texts makes it possible to address the complexity of the emotions involved in missionary work. In fact, this history (re)produces the association, still ongoing, between the suffering body of the distant Other and the redemptive action of the Western/White/Christian philanthropists.

For this association to be effective, an emotional connection must be made between the two bodies, one acting and the other submitting.

In a circular letter dated 2 August 1855, Bishop Bourget wrote the following to his clergy:

> Le fruit de cette dévotion (à St. Innocentius) sera infailliblement un intérêt tout surnaturel pour les enfants infortunés, parmi lesquels nuls ne méritent LA COMPASSION DU MONDE CATHOLIQUE TOUT ENTIER, COMME LES PAUVRES ENFANTS DE LA CHINE. Si vous faites vibrer cette corde si sensible, vous arriverez tout droit au cœur des parents, comme au cœur des enfants; et alors le succès de la Sainte-Enfance est assuré.[51]

> (The result of this devotion [to St. Innocentius] will infallibly be a completely supernatural interest in the unfortunate children, among whom none deserve THE COMPASSION OF THE ENTIRE CATHOLIC WORLD LIKE THE POOR CHILDREN OF CHINA. If you make this very sensitive string vibrate, you will reach straight into the heart of the parents, as into the heart of the children; and then the Holy Childhood's success is assured.)

The emotion of compassion is central to the charity discourse. Bishop Bourget understood that completely. Moreover, his letter is exemplary: it shows how the emotion (compassion) is inscribed on the bodies of the "poor children of China," as echoed in the text. Compassion does not emanate from the parishioners, it is in motion, produced and put into circulation by evoking the "poor children of China" and through the intermediary of the parish priest, who should "make this very sensitive string vibrate."

The emotional link between the Canadian and Chinese children was based, first and foremost, on compassion. For it to be established and to function, there had to be a relationship established between the Canadian children and those faraway Others, thanks to an intermediary with whom they could identify. According to Daniel Brückenhaus, "Children could see non-Europeans through the eyes of the (mostly white) protagonists of the stories, and they could share the characters' emotional bond (or lack thereof) with non-white peoples."[52] The missionary story's power of persuasion was necessary for compassion to exist. The emotional involvement of the Associates of the Holy Childhood depended on the figure of the missionary. In that regard, and to apply Ahmed's theory once more, emotions were activated by the stories. The particularity of compassion, in comparison with sympathy or empathy, for example, is that it establishes a power relationship. To "be compassionate," one must be in a position of privilege relative to the object of compassion. In the case of the Holy Childhood, the children were constantly reminded of their good luck in having been born to Catholic parents. As well, in the chain of emotions provoked by the association's story, it was the Catholic children who had the ability to act, thanks to these emotions; the Others always remained passive.

The centrality of compassion in the charity discourse masked much more important emotions that were involved: sadness, anger, and joy. This is well illustrated by the history of the Holy Childhood. In fact, the compassion emphasized in the propaganda constituted the pivotal point between the emotions felt on hearing the missionary's story (sadness, anger, hatred) and that occasioned by charitable action (joy). Compassion cemented the link from the unknown, distant Other to the missionary's story and to the Catholic child who is *moved* by that story.[53] The transition between sadness, pity, powerlessness, and joy can easily be read in a letter addressed to the Holy Childhood's director by the "smallest pupils" at the Villa Maria boarding school in 1851:

Monsieur,

Nos petites amies, nos chères compagnes viennent
de rendre compte à Monseigneur le président de la

Sainte-Enfance de leurs sentiments au sujet de cette œuvre;
permettez nous [*sic*] de vous exprimer aussi les nôtres.
Nous sommes petites, petites, mais nous ne laissons pas
d'avoir un cœur et ce cœur est bien sensible.

O Monsieur, comme nous avons été émues de pitié en
entendant parler des maux qui pèsent sur les malheureux
enfans de la Chine! nos yeux étaient gros de larmes.
Pauvres petits enfans! Il nous semblait les voir arrachés
des bras de leurs mères, abandonnés, rejetés de leurs mères
elles-mêmes. Il nous semblait les voir se débattre contre les
angoisses de la mort, les uns au milieu des flots, les autres
sous la dent d'animaux immondes. Il nous semblait les
voir, tendre leurs petites mains, jeter des regards mourans,
comme pour appeler au secours. Il nous semblait entendre
leurs cris déchirans. infortunées [*sic*] petites créatures que
ne sommes nous plus rapprochées de vous! nous irions
vous arracher à la mort. C'est en voyant un si affreux
délaissement que nous avons compris tout ce que nous
devons à la religion catholique! C'est en contemplant un
si lamentable spectacle que nous nous sommes estimées
heureuses d'être nées de parens nourris aux inspirations
de la Foi. O religion Sainte, de quels maux tu nous as
préservés.[54]

(Sir,

Our little friends, our dear companions have just reported
to Monsignor the president of the Holy Childhood on
their feelings about this work; please allow us to express
our own as well. We are little, little, but we are not without
a heart and that heart is very sensitive.

Oh, Sir, how moved we were by pity on hearing about
the evils that weigh on the unhappy children in China!
Our eyes were swollen with tears. Poor little children! It
seemed that we could see them torn from the arms of their
mothers, abandoned, rejected by their mothers themselves.
It seemed that we could see them struggling against the
fear of death, some in the middle of the waves, others
under the teeth of foul animals. It seemed that we could
see them, holding out their little hands, casting dying
glances, as if calling for help. It seemed that we could hear
their wrenching cries. Unfortunate little creatures if only
we could be closer to you! We would go and tear you away
from death. It is in seeing such horrible abandonment
that we have understood all that we owe to the Catholic
religion! It is in contemplating such a pitiful sight that
we considered ourselves fortunate to have been born to
parents nourished by the inspirations of the Faith. O Holy
Religion, from what evils you have preserved us.)

From the second sentence on, the young girls emphasize the emotional
power of the Holy Childhood. Knowing the fate of the "unhappy
children in China" has aroused their feelings. "Moved by pity," they
were affected *in their bodies* by the fate of these "unfortunate creatures."
Despite the fact that a short time before nothing connected them to
the children of China, they could now *see* and *hear* them.

"Unhappy," "poor," "unfortunate," "abandoned": it is the passivity of
the Chinese children that the young girls declare. Their own agency is
its corollary. They effectively emphasize that only distance prevents them
from "tearing them away from death." The emotional transition shows
up at the end of the paragraph—gaining awareness of the privilege of
being born Catholic takes them from sadness to joy. They continue:

Nous étions accablées sous le froid de ces pénibles impressions quand pour nous consoler, on nous a fait savoir qu'une Association avait été formée pour venir au secours de ces enfans et que cette association était composée presque toute d'enfans catholiques. Oh! avec quel *plaisir* nous avons accueilli cette bonne nouvelle! Il ne faut pas demander si nous avons voulu nous mettre de cette œuvre. Toutes nous avons voulu en être. À l'instant même nous avons donné notre petit sou et chaque jour nous disons un petit Ave Maria pour les enfans de la Chine.[55]

(We were overwhelmed by the chill of these painful impressions when to console us, we were told that an Association had been formed to come to the rescue of these children and that the association was made up almost entirely of Catholic children. Oh, with what *pleasure* we greeted this good news! We did not have to be asked whether we wanted to join in this work. We all wanted to. At that very moment we donated our little penny and each day we say a little Ave Maria for the children of China.)

This part of the letter shows us how the representation of the Other is instrumentalized for the happiness of young Catholics. The Other allows the young girls of Villa Maria to be empowered. It is the condition of possibility for their agency. Ahmed's analysis of the charity discourse can successfully be applied to the students' letter: "The negative emotions of anger and sadness are evoked as the reader's: the pain of others becomes 'our,' an appropriation that transforms and perhaps even neutralized their pain into our sadness. [. . .] The pain of the other is overcome, but it is not the object of hope in the narrative; rather the overcoming of the pain is instead a means by which the reader is empowered."[56]

By focusing on the "saved" souls, the Holy Childhood's publications highlight those who made the "saving" of these souls possible. By directing the text to the saving actions of the associates, the partisans of the Holy Childhood set up a power relationship that resides in the fact that saving the pagans cannot be carried out without the young Catholics' help. In a letter addressed to the Holy Childhood's director in 1866, Villa Maria's students sum up in a few lines what their predecessors had explained at length:

> La pensée qu'au moyen d'une modique contribution nous avons le bonheur d'ouvrir le Ciel à bon nombre de pauvres petits infidèles, fait palpiter nos cœurs d'une joie bien douce. Ces pauvres petits enfants, exposés si cruellement à une double mort, excitent en nous les sentiments de la compassion la plus vive. Nous avons voulu faire partager notre bonheur à nos petits frères et sœurs, en consacrant de grand cœur l'argent de nos menus plaisirs pour payer leur souscription, afin qu'eux aussi contribuassent au salut éternel de ces êtres malheureux.[57]

> (The thought that with a modest contribution we have the happiness of opening Heaven to a large number of poor little infidels, makes our hearts throb with a sweet joy. These poor little children, so cruelly abandoned to a dual death, excite in us the liveliest feelings of compassion. We wanted to share our happiness with our little brothers and sisters, with a wholehearted sacrifice of the money for our small pleasures to pay their fees, so that they can also contribute to the eternal salvation of these unhappy beings.)

The words used by these students are revealing. They speak to the dichotomy between the passive Other and the acting Self. On the one hand, there is the emotional state of the donors (joy, happiness, excitement) and their power to act (opening, sharing), and, on the other, the inactivity of the little infidels (poor, unhappy, abandoned). Finally, this letter also indicates that positive emotions are the most significant aspect of the Holy Childhood's history in Quebec.

The love felt by the Catholic children for the Chinese children was part of a *movement* and a hierarchical relationship. The Holy Childhood's publications and first-person accounts show that the "saved souls" became, for the associates, so many little angels who watched over them in heaven. The supposed love between the donors and the "saved" was based on the fact that the latter must love their saviours back. Ahmed puts it this way: "Importantly, if our hope is a gift, then the other remains indebted of us. The position of indebtedness is the position of gratitude."[58] To convince the children to give for distant people with whom they had no real ties, they had to be persuaded of a relationship and its reciprocity: the love they gave to the young infidels would be returned in the prayers of the "saved." The reciprocal relation was expressed by Elvina, a boarder at the Sault, in 1866: "Maintenant, nous ne formons plus qu'un désir; c'est que notre offrande parvienne bien vite aux Missionnaires, afin qu'ils envoyent au ciel de petits anges qui prieront pour nous."[59] (Now, we have but one desire; it is that our offering will very quickly reach the Missionaries, so that they can send little angels to heaven who will pray for us.)

Another example is also revealing. It concerns a conversation between a parish priest and a parishioner in Quebec and was reported by Bishop Henri Têtu on the occasion of the Sainte-Enfance's Golden Anniversary in Quebec City:

Oui, lui répondis-je, oui, je crois que je pourrais faire passer de l'argent en Chine. Mais, expliquez-vous, pourquoi me demandez-vous cela?—Monsieur le curé, voici l'affaire: Il y a quelque temps, j'ai lu dans les *Annales de la Propagation de la Foi*, la lettre d'un évêque qui demandait de l'argent pour acheter et faire baptiser des petits enfants infidèles; ils meurent presque tous et vont tout droit au ciel. Là-dessus,

j'ai réfléchi, et je me suis dit: Il me faudra partir pour
le grand voyage; ce serait une bonne chose, si j'envoyais
devant moi quelques-uns de ces petits innocents pour me
recevoir, quand j'arriverai là-haut. [. . .] Eh bien! Monsieur
le curé, voilà cent piastres, mais vous allez me donner un
reçu sur lequel vous marquerez que cet argent sera employé
à racheter les petits enfants et à leur procurer le Baptême:
je veux que mes enfants le sachent.[60]

(Yes, I answered him, yes, I believe that I could get money
sent to China. But, please explain, why are you asking me
this?—Father, here's what it's about: A while ago, I read
in the *Annales de la Propagation de la Foi* a letter from a
bishop who was asking for money to buy and baptize little
infidel children; almost all of them die and go straight to
heaven. I thought about it, and I said to myself: I will have
to leave on the great journey; it would be a good thing, if I
sent ahead of me some of these little innocents to welcome
me, when I arrive up there. [. . .] So, well, Father, here's
a hundred dollars, but you're going to give me a receipt
on which you write that this money will be used to save
the little children and get them the Baptism: I want my
children to know it.)

The end of the letter written in 1851 by the boarders at Villa Maria
confirms the debt owed by the "saved" children to the donors:

Dans quelques semaines nous enverrons les noms de celles
d'entre nous qui ont été désignées par le sort pour être
donnés aux enfans à baptiser. Quel bonheur d'apprendre
ensuite que parmi ces enfans désormais nos protégés nous
avons des protecteurs, et que plusieurs sont allés au ciel où
ils prieront pour nous!

O monsieur que ne nous envoyez nous donc pour nous
encourager, une de ces innocentes créatures! nous en
aurions bien soin. [P]lusieurs fois l'année on nous procure
la satisfaction de donner à de pauvres enfans des habits
faits de nos mains. Mais [si] ce n'est possible, envoyez
nous du moins des annales, nous vous [sic] en servirons
pour nous animer et animer les autres à propager la Ste
Enfance.[61]

(In a few weeks we will be sending the names of those
among us who have been chosen by the lottery for the
children to be baptized. It made us so happy to then learn
that among these children who are now our protégés we
have protectors, and that many have gone to heaven, where
they will pray for us.

Please, Sir, therefore send us to encourage us one of these
innocent creatures! We will take very good care of them.
Many times a year we have the satisfaction of giving poor
children the clothes we make with our own hands. But
[if] this is not possible, at least send us the annals, we will
use them to motivate ourselves and motivate others to
propagate the Holy Childhood.)

The final lines also show us the close relation between the pleasure
elicited by the Holy Childhood and its consumerist aspect. The associates consume the annals, own the images of welcome, and accumulate
"saved souls." Which brings us back to Ahmed's theory. The emotions
were not *inside* the children, they were rather activated through the
bodies (if only they could "possess" one of those "innocent creatures")
and objects (annals and images) that conveyed them. In this way, joy
and happiness, the most important emotions for the Associates of the

Holy Childhood, were again reinforced by the pleasure prompted by the act of possession.

For its charitable and religious purposes, the Holy Childhood used methods that are reminiscent of consumerist and capitalist logic. Focusing on a faraway Other to save, the missionary discourse had to be convincing. This selling aspect can also be seen in the association's structure—the chiefs have more advantages than mere associates—as well as in the importance given to accumulating saved souls. The Holy Childhood thus followed a seller's logic in which the act of "buying" is central, as Michelle King so justly states it: "At the other end of the transaction, the idea of 'purchasing' a Chinese child in order to save it was repeated so often in Holy Childhood literature that it shaped the attitudes of Holy Childhood contributors in Europe, who came to see a helpless Chinese child as Henrietta Harrison suggests, as a kind of desirable 'consumer item.'"[62] The ultimate argument, the associates' "purchasing power," was used in 1860 by the writer of the *Petit manuel des associés de la Sainte-Enfance* (Little handbook for Associates of the Holy Childhood) to kindle their zeal:

> Que les uns et les autres se souviennent, pour s'encourager, non seulement des travaux des Missionnaires,—du zèle des enfants catholiques,—des grâces et des récompenses qui seront le prix de leurs efforts, etc.; mais encore, mais surtout qu'ils se souviennent du malheur des enfants infidèles, de la facilité si grande qu'ils ont de les sauver. Avec 100 f., on peut acheter 400 enfants; avec 20 sous, on peut en acheter trois ou quatre. Souvent même, les Missionnaires pourraient en acheter à moins; mais les ressources leur manquent.[63]

> (Let everyone remember, for encouragement, not only the work of the missionaries—the zeal of Catholic children— the grace and rewards that will crown their efforts, etc.; but more, but most of all that they remember the unhappiness

of the infidel children and the very great ease with which
they can save them. With 100 f., you can buy 400 children;
with 20 cents, you can buy three or four. Even, often, the
Missionaries could buy them for less; but they lack the
resources.)

Moreover, the cause's legitimacy had to be unassailable—and therein
lay the importance of the religious context—if a rhetoric so close to
that of slavery could be used in this way.

The importance of emotions in the history of the Holy Childhood
was much more complex than it appears to be at first glance. Not only
do the emotions that circulate thanks to this discourse maintain a hierarchical relationship between the acting Self and the submissive Other,
but they also introduce a consumerist logic that must be considered in
the global context of Canadian society's industrialization at that time.

Motivations of Adults, Motivations of Children: The Mission's Pedagogical Use

The missionary discourse was used by the clergy and other pedagogical
actors to achieve specific ends. The infidels' fate often served as the
pretext for a regulatory action that was much more local and politi-
cally oriented. But were the children completely taken in by the clergy
and the teachers? It is not possible to tell by consulting the sources
what proportion of the young people resisted the missionary discourse.
However, it is possible to analyze the motivations that led numerous
children to embrace the missionaries' work. In that regard, the children's
own interests fit with the adults' determination to regulate.

The Holy Childhood was introduced into Canada in the early
1850s. To ensure the association's propagation and sustainability, its
defenders not only had to convince the children to join but also to
plead their cause to bishops, parish priests, religious congregations,

and Canadian families. What arguments did they use? In the arena of
charities, financing foreign missions competed with local good works
that directly affected Catholic Canadians. The advantages of missionary
work had to go beyond saving infidels. And so, to the fate of Chinese
children, the apostles of the Holy Childhood quickly added a more
immediate objective: to regenerate the Catholic society.

Published in 1860, the *Petit manuel des associés de la Sainte-Enfance*
lists the association's advantages. Aside from itemizing the strictly spiritual benefits, the author clarified that:

> En s'y associant, et en y associant les autres, on détourne
> la colère de Dieu; on régénère la jeunesse par les beaux
> sentiments que l'Œuvre lui inspire; [. . .] on remplace
> les plaisirs sensuels, par les plaisirs purs [. . .]. En s'y
> associant, et en y associant les autres, on donne le bon
> exemple, et on répare ainsi bien des scandales; on procure
> à la Propagation de la Foi, dans un avenir prochain, des
> auxiliaires nombreux; on donne une nouvelle impulsion à
> toutes les bonnes œuvres, en stimulant l'ardeur des grandes
> personnes, par le spectacle de la charité des enfants; on
> accoutume ces enfants eux mêmes à faire le bien; on
> paralyse les efforts du démon, de l'impiété et de l'hérisie
> [*sic*]; on conserve la Foi à son pays, en contribuant à la
> répandre dans les autres, etc., etc.[64]

> (By joining, and by recruiting others, we turn away the
> wrath of God; we regenerate young people through the
> beautiful feelings the Association inspires; [. . .] we replace
> sensual pleasures with pure ones [. . .]. By joining, and by
> recruiting others, we give a good example, and in this way
> we make amends for many scandals; we secure numerous
> helpers for the Propagation of the Faith in the near future;
> we give new impetus to all the good works, by stimulating
> the ardour of grown-ups at the sight of the children's

charity; we accustom the children themselves to doing
good; we paralyze the efforts of the devil, of godlessness
and heresy; we preserve the Faith in our country, by
helping to spread it to others, etc., etc.)

In this discourse, the figure of the Other is used to benefit the vitality of
the French-Canadian society's religious and patriotic spirit. The annual
report for 1860 provides a good illustration: the fate of infidel children
is not mentioned until page 26. Moreover, one of the objections that
the Holy Childhood's advocates often had to counter was that it would
impair other good works, an argument checked by that of the mission's
power of global regeneration:

> Et qu'on ne craigne pas de faire tort aux autres œuvres!
> La Ste. Enfance, en mettant dans tous les cœurs plus de
> charité, plus de commisération, en est le plus ferme appui,
> comme elle en est le plus doux espoir. Ne remarque-t-on
> pas en effet pièces justificatives en main, que là où la Ste.
> Enfance est établie, la jeunesse est meilleure, les bonnes
> œuvres plus nombreuses et plus florissantes?[65]

> (And let us not fear doing harm to other good works! The
> Holy Childhood, in putting in all hearts more charity,
> more commiseration, is their staunchest support, as it is
> the sweetest hope. Have we not indeed noted, supporting
> documents in hand, that wherever the Holy Childhood
> becomes established, the younger generation is better and
> good works are more numerous and thriving?)

The directors of the Holy Childhood counted on the children to be
the agents of social regeneration. In "Emotions and the Global Politics
of Childhood," Karen Vallgårda, Kristine Alexander, and Stephanie
Olsen explain how the modern history of childhood is marked by the

emotional enterprises that have targeted it: "Because children have often been considered particularly malleable, parents, educators and even other young people have frequently sought to promote in them a programme of feeling that accorded with a particular set of moral standards and relationship of power."[66] The missionary rhetoric used by the Holy Childhood was part of this history. In a notice from 1860, the importance of childhood's emotional education to the future of the society is stated as follows:

> On s'est beaucoup préoccupé de réformes en ces derniers temps: on voulait régénérer la société. On a essayé divers moyens plus ou moins heureux. De tous ces moyens, quel a été, quel est encore le plus efficace? N'est-ce pas celui qui consiste à élever bien la jeunesse? Qui pourrait le nier? personne. C'est un fait acquis, que c'est par les enfans, et les enfans seulement, qu'on peut changer la face d'un pays, détruire les abus, faire fleurir toutes les vertus. Ceux qui ont voulu procéder autrement, ont perdu leur temps et leurs peines.[67]

> (People have been very concerned about reforms lately: they wanted to regenerate the society. They tried out various means that worked more or less well. Of all of them, which one was, which still is the most effective? Is it not the one that consists in raising young people properly? Who could deny it? No one. It is a given that it is through the children, and only the children, that we can change the face of a country, stamp out the abuses, and make all the virtues bloom. Those who wanted to proceed otherwise wasted their time and effort.)

The moral training of children was the first step in revitalizing the society. According to its Montreal director, for that reason the Holy

Childhood was best equipped to manage this moral training through the emotional involvement it generated.

The actors in the pedagogical community were convinced that the missionary charity had an important regulatory power over children. First, the alms given periodically to the "poor children in China" taught charity. That argument was used by François Daniel when he wrote to Bishop Bourget in 1862, urging him to relaunch the Holy Childhood: "En la faisant progresser, les enfans qui sont l'espoir de la société, n'en seront que meilleurs, et plus disposés à entrer dans un âge avancé dans les autres œuvres de zèle. Votre Grandeur connaît trop bien ces choses, pour qu'elles ne soient pas de quelque considération dans son esprit si élevé."[68] (By moving it forward, the children who are the hope of society can only become better and more inclined at an older age to take up other zealous works. Your Greatness knows these things too well for them to be given no consideration in his exalted mind.) The clerics and pedagogues then reiterated on many occasions that the practice of charity transformed a child's deepest nature; the infidel's conversion matched the Catholic child's transformation. Contact with the Other's unhappy fate would not only make the latter more religious but also more docile:

> Ici, c'est un enfant qui était léger, paresseux, indocile;
> depuis qu'il est de la Ste. Enfance, il est plus refléchi [sic],
> plus soumis, moins indolent. [. . .] Des enfans jusques là
> indifférents, irréligieux même, en devenant membres de la
> Ste. Enfance, deviennent tout à coup pieux, reconnaissants.
> Ils n'ont plus que des sentiments d'amour pour Dieu, pour
> sa religion sainte, qui les a soustraits à des traitements
> barbares. [. . .] Telle est l'influence de la Ste. Enfance sur
> le cœur des enfans! Elle les transforme, elle en fait d'autres
> enfans.[69]

> (Here is a child who was thoughtless, lazy, unruly; since
> he joined the Holy Childhood, he is more thoughtful and
> submissive, less indolent. [. . .] Children who until then

were indifferent, even irreligious, on becoming members of
the Holy Childhood suddenly become pious, grateful. They
have only feelings of love for God, for his holy religion,
which has shielded them from barbarous treatment. [. . .]
Such is the influence of the Holy Childhood on the heart
of children! It transforms them, it makes them other
children.)

The Holy Childhood's advocates invoked the mission's power to regulate
in order to convince teachers and mothers that there was an advantage
to making their pupils or children members.

From the point of view of the actors involved in missionary propaganda, children were the subjects to a social, moral, and emotional regulation based on charity for the benefit of a distant, unhappy Other. From
the children's point of view, it could be said that they were also agents
for the cause. They had many reasons to embrace the charitable mission.
A study of the missionary charity reveals the various avenues for the
children's agency, beyond a feeling of empowerment inspired by the fact
of "saving" innocent children who lived on the other side of the world.

For some children, the missionary discourse primarily took on
an important religious value. Several years after the Holy Childhood
was introduced in Saint-Hyacinthe, the students at the convent of the
Congrégation de Notre-Dame wrote the following to the association's
director: "Comblées des bienfaits de la Providence [. . .] nous n'avons pu
comparer notre condition à celle de ces jeunes infortunés sans remercier
Dieu de nous avoir fait naître au milieu d'un pays où la religion nous
adoucit les peines de la vie, en nous montrant une éternité de bonheur."[70]
(Filled with the blessings of Providence [. . .] we cannot compare our
condition to that of the young unfortunates without thanking God for
having granted us birth in the middle of a country where religion allays
the troubles of life, by showing us an eternity of goodness.) Stimulating
a fervent piety, the spiritual connection to the "saved" children also

took on a very private dimension. This happened to a young associate from Saint-Henri de Lévis who, at the bedside of her unwell mother, pledged to donate to the Sainte-Enfance in exchange for curing her mother of her illness:

> Je me disais: "Comment se fait-il que moi, qui suis depuis si longtemps zélatrice de la Sainte Enfance, je n'ai pas pensé encore à m'adresser à ces anges qui, grâce au sou des associés de l'Œuvre, jouissent du bonheur du ciel?" Ma mère s'associa à ma promesse, et, dès lors, le mal diminua sensiblement.[71]

> (I said to myself, "How is it that I, who have been a zealot for the Sainte-Enfance for such a long time, have not yet thought of addressing the angels who, thanks to the pennies from the Sainte-Enfance associates, are benefiting from heaven's goodness?" My mother joined me in my pledge and since then the pain has noticeably diminished.)

The religious importance of the missionary discourse in the life of young Catholics is also revealed in the vocations it prompted. In 1857 and 1858, the Sœurs de Sainte-Anne were visited by Mgr Demers, a missionary bishop in New Caledonia, the name used until 1858 to designate part of today's British Columbia. On his first visit, a number of sisters "s'offr[ent] pour les missions lointaines" (offered to work in the far-off missions). The following year, it was the students who were expressing their missionary zeal: "Cette fois, les élèves du pensionnat elles-mêmes, prises d'un beau zèle, sollicitèrent l'honneur d'aller faire le catéchisme aux sauvages. Le prélat leur conseilla d'attendre à plus tard. De fait, quelques-unes devaient dans la suite mettre à exécution leur pieux projet."[72] (This time, the students at the boarding school, inspired by a beautiful zeal, themselves sought the honour of going to teach the catechism to the savages. The bishop advised them to wait. In fact, some of them later proceeded to carry out their pious project.) The missionary vocation of Délia Tétreault, founder of the Sœurs de l'Immaculée Conception, had a direct connection to the Holy Childhood. As a child, Délia would often take refuge in her attic to read the *Annales de la Sainte-Enfance* and *Annales de la Propagation de la Foi* stored there.[73] Contact with the missionary's reality, whether through lectures, reading annals, or looking at holy pictures, left a lasting imprint on the children's spirituality, as evidenced by these childhood memories.

Nonetheless, a vocational response to the Holy Childhood's activities was the exception. More often, children were enthusiastic about the recreational opportunities the association offered. Bazaars, lotteries, celebrations, theatrical presentations, collecting images, reading the *Annales*—the association provided the students with many leisure activities. It is therefore not surprising to conclude that it was often these extraordinary events that sustained the young associates' zeal. For the celebrations, it was not unusual for the children to dress up "in Chinese" to tell adults about the sad fate of the infidel children. The pleasure of performing alterity, added to the fact that the children appeared front and centre in these religious services, explains in large part why the events were so popular with the young associates.

The convent students were the zealots who derived the greatest benefit from recreational activities related to the Holy Childhood. The bazaars and lotteries organized for the sake of the "poor children in China" relieved the monotony of life in a boarding school. The Holy Childhood even allowed young women to lighten up a bit under the normally weighty rules of propriety, as expressed in this account of a lottery held in a convent:

Que veut dire ce bruit? Que signifie ce va et vient?
Pourquoi tout ce monde? Et c'est dans un couvent; dans un
asile ordinairement si silencieux, que tout cela se passe! Ne
soyez pas scandalisé. C'est aujourd'hui jour de Loterie en
faveur de la Sainte-Enfance. Toute permission est donnée

de parler et de faire le plus d'argent possible. Comme on
en profite! De petites marchandes sont installées à de jolies
tables chargées d'objets charmants. Elles provoquent les
acheteurs. [. . .] Ainsi se passe la journée. Chacun se retire
joyeux. Quand tout le monde est parti, on compte les écus.
Quel bonheur alors, si le résultat a dépassé les espérances!
Pendant le sommeil, on n'a que de riantes images sous les
yeux: ce sont des milliers d'anges à qui on a ouvert les cieux
en se divertissant, et qui viennent vous remercier.[74]

(What can this noise mean? What about all the coming
and going? Why all these people? And it's in a convent;
a refuge usually so silent, that all this is going on! Don't
be shocked. Today is the day of the Lottery to benefit the
Holy Childhood. Permission is given to talk and make as
much money as possible. And we take full advantage! Small
vendors have set themselves up at pretty tables loaded with
charming objects. They beckon the buyers. [. . .] And so
goes the day. Each one goes away filled with joy. When
everyone has left, the coins are counted. How good it feels
then, if the results surpass your hopes! When you sleep,
you see only merry images under your lids: they are the
thousands of angels for whom you opened the heavens while
entertaining yourselves, and who are coming to thank you.)

Theatrical performances to benefit charitable works also provided
the means to get around certain interdictions, as Julie Plourde explains
when she interrogates the practice of theatre in the convents: "Does
the presence of young girls on stage at public events pose a moral
problem? The fact that this presence is part of fundraising for charitable causes goes some way to legitimizing and rendering acceptable a
practice that remains problematic for some. The theatrical events are
tolerated when they help to carry out charitable works, a value defined as

being particularly feminine."[75] As early as in 1858, the Holy Childhood annalist reported that the boarders of the Sœurs de la congrégation de Notre-Dame were performing for the benefit of Chinese orphans. The experience was repeated, notably in 1889 and 1894.[76]

The most frequent and frequently solicited benefits for children remained receiving the annals and holy images. Many of the Sœurs de la congrégation de Notre-Dame who wrote to Father Daniel about the Holy Childhood asked for images in order to maintain the interest of students and teachers, or simply to reward their zeal. According to the sisters, receiving images was the occasion of great joy, as reported to Father Daniel by Sister St-Clarisse:

> Comment puis-je assez vous remercier, vous prouver ma gratitude pour votre magnifique envoi d'images?. . . Vraiment j'admire votre générosité à notre égard. Nos petites enfants étaient ivres de joie, jamais si belles gravures ne leur avaient été présentées. Et nous donc, nous nous croyions presqu'en paradis, contemplant déjà à loisir la Cour Céleste . . . en un mot, c'est vous dire que tout le monde en a été charmé.—Merci, donc, Bon père, de nous procurer ainsi tant de jouissances ici bas.[77]

> (How can I thank you enough, prove my gratitude to you for your magnificent parcel of images? . . . Truly I admire your generosity to us. Our little children were drunk with joy, never have they been presented with such beautiful engravings. And we, therefore, we believe ourselves to be almost in paradise, already contemplating at leisure the Celestial Court . . . in a word, this is to tell you that everyone has been charmed.—Therefore, thank you, Good Father, for having thus provided us with such enjoyment down here.)

In other cases, the sisters attest directly to the students' materialistic motives:

Sans doute vous allez être fière [*sic*] des Sœurs de la Cong. de Notre Dame à St Albans et plus particulairement [*sic*] de leurs chères élèves qui se sont dévouées à cette œuvre si chère à votre cœur. Elles ont hâte de voir les belles images que vous allez envoyer. Je crois vraiment que c'est l'espoir d'une récompense qui les [a] rendues si zélées.[78]

(No doubt you will be proud of the Sœurs de la Congrégation de Notre-Dame in St. Albans and more particularly of their dear pupils, who devoted themselves to this work that is so dear to your heart. They are eager to see the beautiful images you will be sending. I really believe that it is the hope of a reward that made them so zealous.)

Some members of the clergy saw in the Holy Childhood charitable works that were likely to civilize both Chinese and Catholic children at once. The latter found many attractions in the discourses about foreign missions. In addition to taking them on an imaginary journey and affirming their capacity to act, the missionary work's fundraising efforts provided uncommon leisure activities in the children's everyday life.

Challenges and Conflicts

The history of the Holy Childhood in Canada was not exempt from the effects of power relations across the entire society. Not only did the association's activity for the benefit of "little Chinese children" find critics among lay people, but certain religious orders even challenged its presence in the schools. The outbursts of joy that excited the young convent students who wrote to Father Daniel contrast in this regard with the competition that was set up between schools and the sacrifices required of the children least able to afford them. The missionary discourse often showcased making it possible for all children, even the poorest, to contribute to the salvation of Chinese children. However, it should be noted that class differences played a role in the children's involvement. If the children's missionary commitment was able to give young people from the middle class and the bourgeoisie a feeling of empowerment and control over world affairs, it was probably different for the less fortunate children in Quebec society. In many cases, the experience of missionary involvement for lower-class children could have been oppressive, one of having to endure shame or sacrifice.

In October 1881, Father Daniel addressed a long, reproachful letter to the superior general of the Frères des écoles chrétiennes. The reason for his discontent was the absence of the Holy Childhood in the brothers' schools. Father Daniel did not treat them gently. He accused them of being the only congregation that had not encouraged the association's establishment in its schools, in the United States as well as in Canada. He wrote: "Ici même à Montréal, où nos désirs devraient être des ordres, sur dix grandes écoles, c'est à peine si deux s'occupent de la Ste Enfance."[79] (Even here in Montreal, where our desires should be orders, of ten large schools, at most only two concern themselves with the Holy Childhood.) Father Daniel goes so far as to attack the brothers on religious grounds: "Faire avancer les enfants dans les sciences profanes, leur donner quelque instruction religieuse semble tout le but de leur zèle. Pour ce qui est de former les enfants à la charité, ils ne paraissent pas en avoir souci." (To make the children advance in the profane sciences, while giving them some religious instruction, seems to be the entire goal of their zeal. As for training the children in charity, they do not appear to be concerned.) What would happen to these children? They would certainly be good workers, Daniel went on, but they would spend their money immorally rather than on charity.

Such a charge did not go unnoticed. Upon receiving Daniel's letter, Brother Armin-Victor wrote a letter of complaint to the Sulpicians' provincial superior, Joseph-Alexandre Baile. He nonetheless noted that he was aware that the letter he had received involved only Father Daniel, not all of the Sulpicians; moreover, he was familiar with Daniel's temperament and knew that the entire situation had been exaggerated. At the same time, Brother Armin-Victor took the trouble to answer Daniel's letter, patiently challenging each of the accusations. In particular, he reminded him that the brothers' Montreal schools mostly took in the needy, and he was not comfortable obtaining subscription fees from them. Then again, the brothers had introduced the Holy Childhood into their schools, but, following the establishment of Daniel's lists of "winners"—which was hurtful to their institutions—they had preferred to withdraw.[80]

The Frères des écoles chrétiennes were not alone in protesting Daniel's warnings. Many indications lead us to believe that he was performing his role of director of the Holy Childhood in an almost despotic fashion. After having lambasted the Frères, would he dare to scold the Sœurs de la congrégation de Notre-Dame? In January 1882, after some delay, one of the congregation's sisters replied to a letter from Daniel in which he wrote that he hoped to receive "some documentary evidence" from her. Daniel must have expressed dissatisfaction with the fundraising at some of the convents, because the sister replied:

> Je me ferai un devoir de vous [faire connaître les collectes] pour nous donner la satisfaction de les encourager (l'avantage en sera pour les localités elles-mêmes) et, de mon côté, je travaillerai, selon mon pouvoir, auprès de celles qui n'ont rien fait. Vous m'obligeriez en ne faisant à celles-ci d'autres reproches que celui de ne leur rien envoyer.[81]

> (I will make it my duty to inform you about the funds raised, to give us the satisfaction of encouraging them [the advantage will be to the communities themselves] and, on my end, I will work to the best of my ability with those who have done nothing. You will oblige me by delivering

no other reproach to them than that of not sending them anything.)

Daniel's authoritarian enthusiasm for the Holy Childhood was therefore not unanimously shared. The congregations' superiors at times had to temper his ardour and inform him of the internal challenges that prevented the association from prospering.

The excerpt of a dialogue presented as part of the Holy Childhood's Golden Anniversary celebrations nicely stated the argument that the association's partisans were most often called upon to counter: its competition with the needs of local charities.

Léon — Un Ave Maria par jour, et 12 sous par an, voilà ce que demande l'Œuvre de la Sainte-Enfance; est-ce trop?

Joseph — Je ne dis pas. Mais un sou par ici, un sou par là, ça finit par faire une somme. [. . .]

Henri — Sans compter que, chez nous aussi, on ne manque pas de malheureux. Eh bien! mon principe à moi, c'est de faire la charité à ma porte. [. . .]

Joseph — Moi, je suis, comme Henri, pour les œuvres locales. Je suis Canadien; j'aime mon pays avant tout; et je trouve que nous avons bien assez de mal heureux chez nous, sans aller encore en chercher ailleurs.

Auguste — [. . .] Eh bien! Sans oublier les pauvres nécessiteux (je ne parle pas de tous ces fainéants qu'on voit rôder tous les jours, cherchant, comme on dit, de l'ouvrage, et priant le bon Dieu de ne leur en point trouver); eh bien, tout en donnant aux œuvres locales, selon mes faibles moyens, j'estime que les plus malheureux sont les plus dignes de pitié. Et les plus malheureux ne sont-ils pas ces

peuples sauvages, ces nations infidèles qui ne connaissent
point, comme nous, le Dieu qui les a créés?[82]

(Léon — One Ave Maria a day, and 12 cents a year, that's
what the Œuvre de la Sainte-Enfance asks; is that asking
too much?

Joseph — I'd say no. But a cent here, a cent there, it adds
up. [. . .]

Henri — Not counting that here, too, we have no shortage
of unfortunates. You see, my own principle is that charity
starts right outside my front door. [. . .]

Joseph — Like Henri, I'm for the local charities. I'm
Canadian; I love my own country before all else; and I
think that we have plenty of unhappy people here, without
having to go and find more somewhere else.

Auguste — [. . .] Well, without forgetting the needy poor
[I'm not talking about all those layabouts we see roaming
around every day, looking, as they say, for work, and praying
to God not to find them any]; well, while I give to local
charities, as much as my limited means allow, I think that
the most unfortunate are the most deserving of pity. And
aren't the most unfortunate the savage people, those infidel
nations who unlike us know nothing of the God who
created them?)

To counter this argument, Father Daniel constantly reaffirmed the good
done by the association for the general spirit of charity in the parishes
where it had taken hold. And yet, the competition among charities had
very real effects on children. The children's money—and their sensibility—was coveted not only by François Daniel. As Sister des Anges wrote
to him in 1891, the defenders of the Holy Childhood must "quasi se

battre avec toutes les vieilles filles de la place qui se disputent les sous de nos enfants" (almost do battle with all the old ladies in the place who fight over our children's pennies).[83] When we know that the recreational pleasures of lotteries, bazaars, and dramatic events associated with the Holy Childhood were organized just as often for the benefit of other charities, we can understand that there remained only the mobilization of a distant, wretched alterity to win the children's favour.

In February 1869, Arthur Buies took exception to the Saint-Enfance in his (ephemeral) newspaper *La Lanterne*. With trenchant irony he expanded on the tendency of the Chinese to feed their children to swine. Buies remembered being *"pétrifié d'étonnement"* (petrified with astonishment) when he was told in secondary school "pour la première fois qu'il fallait racheter au Christ les enfants des Chinois *exposés aux pourceaux par leurs pères*" (for the first time that Chinese children who had been *abandoned to the swine by their fathers* had to be saved for Christ).[84] Among his reminiscences, Buies included an argument that he was probably not the only one to state:

> On m'avait bien laissé lire au collège quelques pages de
> *Robinson Crusoë*, où j'avais vu que les Carhaïbes [*sic*], les
> plus féroces des hommes, mangeaient leurs ennemis, mais
> adoraient leurs enfans, (c'est un sentiment du reste naturel
> aux tigres eux-mêmes), mais voilà que tout-à-coup on nous
> apprenait que les Chinois, réputés jusqu'alors le plus ancien
> peuple civilisé de la terre, en étaient venus subitement, sans
> transition, peut-être blasés des jouissances ordinaires, à se
> repaître d'un régal de leurs enfans par des pourceaux.[85]

> (At school they had let me read a few pages of *Robinson
> Crusoe*, where I learned that the Carhaïbes [*sic*], the
> most ferocious of men, ate their enemies but adored
> their children [besides, it's a sentiment natural to tigers
> themselves], but then all of a sudden they were telling

us that the Chinese, until then reputed to be the oldest
civilized nation on Earth, had suddenly, without transition,
perhaps bored with ordinary pleasures, started to take
delight in making their children a treat for swine.)

In Buies's memory, the Holy Childhood—and the image of the devouring swine—was the personification of the "sacrifices [faits par le corps
enseignant] pour imbéciliser les élèves" (sacrifices [on the part of the
teaching profession] to make imbeciles of the students). His critique
also attested to the doubts that many people had surely voiced regarding
the veracity of the stories used to win the hearts of the children.

A few years after Buies published his article, it was the turn of
French journalist Francisque Sarcey to make a charge against the stories
conveyed by the Holy Childhood.[86] In the magazine Le XIXe siècle,
Sarcey recalled his childhood memories of the association:

> À la suite de ce cantique, il y avait quelques fois une
> abondante distribution d'images. L'une d'elles,— je la vois
> encore—représentait une scène de massacre en Chine. Une
> ligne, enluminée du plus bel ocre, figurait le fleuve Jaune.
> Sur les bords de cette rivière maudite, grouillaient des
> multitudes de petits enfants au travers desquels se ruaient
> des porcs immondes pour les dévorer.[87]

> (Following this hymn, on several occasions there was a
> generous distribution of images. One of them—I can still
> see it—presented a scene of massacre in China. A line,
> illuminated in the most beautiful ochre, stood for the
> Yellow River. On the banks of this accursed river crawled
> multitudes of small children, and among them foul pigs
> darted to devour them.)

The voracious pigs were in fact a central point in the imagery and rhetoric of the Holy Childhood. In almost all of the images that I was able to see, there is a swine coveting the children saved by the missionaries and nuns. The menacing pigs left a deep mark on Sarcey's imagination: "Oh! ces cochons! ces farouches cochons! ces cochons dévorants! en ai-je eu l'imagination envahie! Les ai-je vus, dans mes songes, fourrageant dans ces grappes de petits corps nus, que traversait un fleuve jaune d'ocre! Quelle foi ardente j'avais aux cochons en ce temps-là!"[88] (Oh, those pigs! those fierce pigs! those devouring pigs! my imagination was invaded! I saw them, in my dreams, foraging among the clusters of small naked bodies, crossed by an ochre-yellow river! What an ardent faith I then had in pigs!)

Buies's and Sarcey's memories, like the letters from young associates printed in the reports published by Father Daniel, illustrate the influence of these horror stories on a child's imagination. Beyond their inherent criticism, the articles attest above all to the powerful hold that the missionary rhetoric had on the children's sensibilities and faith.[89]

A Gendered Rhetoric: Maternal Feelings and Male Heroism in the Missionary Discourse

From the time that it was first introduced in the 1850s, the Œuvre de la Sainte-Enfance had always made a special appeal to women. According to the clerical propaganda, it was in the women's best interest to enroll their children in the association in order to "*attirer les grâces de Dieu*" (attract God's graces) to them.[90] It was believed that women were much more likely to be moved by the fate of the poor infidel children. As Sara Ahmed remarks, "Emotions are associated with women, who are represented as 'closer' to nature, ruled by appetite, and less able to transcend the body through thought, will and judgment."[91] The gender division was set up in the missionary rhetoric very early on. Further, it was not so much that men were located outside the emotional sphere as that the range of emotions they were allowed differed appreciably from that attributed to women.

The gendered division in the missionary rhetoric was not very present in the propaganda intended for children; however, it was particularly strong in the material for adolescents. In general, the youngest children became involved in the redemption of the Chinese children regardless of gender. Some effort was nonetheless made to interest young boys in particular. First, the association borrowed a hierarchical military structure, which it valorized. The military analogy, directed at boys, could be seen in the objects awarded to children when they were received into the association: "Chaque Associé qui donne sa Contribution (12 sous), a droit à une Image ou à une Médaille, en entrant dans la Société. Ordinairement on donne la Médaille aux garçons, et l'Image aux filles."[92] (Each Associate who makes the Contribution [12 cents] is entitled to an Image or a Medal. Normally the Medal is given to boys and the Image to girls.) In addition, the defenders of the Holy Childhood would sometimes use the heroic figure of the missionary to attract the children's interest. The young men's interest in missionary work was based on their admiration for the missionary figure. Thus, it was probably boys Bishop Têtu was thinking of in 1893 when he wrote:

En étant de la Sainte-Enfance, vous êtes donc tous de petits missionnaires. Missionnaires, oui, mes enfants, de vrais missionnaires [. . .] vous devenez tour à tour missionnaires en Chine, dans les Indes, en Afrique, en Océanie. Jugez maintenant si je suis heureux de pouvoir saluer en vous tous, ici présents, autant de petits missionnaires![93]

(By being a member of the Holy Childhood, you are therefore all little missionaries. Missionaries, yes, my children, real missionaries [. . .] you become missionaries in China, India, Africa, and Oceania in turn. Now think how

happy I am to be able to salute in all of you, present here,
so many little missionaries!)

Despite these efforts, the Holy Childhood would never attract as many
boys as girls. In this regard, the conflict between Father Daniel and the
Frères des écoles chrétiennes was telling. Throughout the nineteenth
century, the fiery defender of the Association of Holy Childhood
was not able to succeed in engaging the brothers' pupils to lasting
effect. This leaves us to wonder about the nature of the interest that
engendered the special commitment to the fate of Chinese children in
girls and young women.

In 1881, the charitable power of women was praised by the author
of a report on the association's status in America:

> Le zèle des particuliers n'est pas moins grand, quand le feu
> de la charité a été allumé dans les cœurs. C'est alors qu'on
> voit ce qu'est capable de faire la femme chrétienne, la jeune
> fille, lorsqu'elle s'est déclarée l'avocate d'une cause, dont elle
> comprend si bien le but et les moyens d'action.[94]

> (The zeal of individuals is no less significant when charity's
> fire is set alight in their heart. That is when we see what
> the Christian woman, the young girl, is capable of doing
> when she has declared herself the advocate for a cause
> whose goal and means of action she so well understands.)

The association of young girls with missionary financing was derived
from a desire for social regulation that was part of the charity world in
general in the nineteenth century. As Father Daniel wrote to students
at the convent of Mont Sainte-Marie in 1886, it was important to raise
young girls in a spirit of charity because they would later be "la providence vivante des indigents, des apôtres de toutes les bonnes oeuvres"
(living providence for the needy, the apostles of all good works).[95] In

a way, the Sulpician father links the fate of Montreal's needy to that of the Chinese children. Twenty-five years later, in the same way, an anonymous "Canadienne" exhorts young girls and women teachers to support a new missionary magazine called *Visite annuelle de Notre-Dame d'Afrique aux foyers canadiens* (Annual visit of Our Lady of Africa to Canadian homes). In her appeals to potential subscribers, the author repeatedly calls on young women: "S'intéresseront aussi, nous le croyons nos lecteurs, nos lectrices surtout, puisqu'elles possèdent le don précieux de la tendresse compatissante, de la constance inlassable qui trouvent un aliment de vie [*sic*] de persévérance, dans la profondeur, dans l'horreur même de l'infortune, de la misère à soulager."[96] (We believe that our readers, and especially our female readers, will also be interested, since they possess the precious gift of compassionate tenderness and tireless patience that find a source of life and perseverance in the depths, even the horror, of misfortune, of misery to be relieved.)

Emotion was always central in the orders to participate directed at young girls, and the authors constantly referred to the woman's "compassionate *nature*." In this context, the school presented an ideal conduit for communication. In 1911, the editors of *L'Enseignement primaire* introduced their readers to another missionary publication. Unsurprisingly, the message was addressed to women teachers:

> La lecture de certaines lettres adressées du centre de l'Afrique par des religieuses canadiennes nous a émus jusqu'aux larmes. Mais cette émotion ne fut pas stérile elle nous inspira la pensée de suggérer à toutes nos institutrices dont le cœur généreux est si bien fait pour aimer toutes les œuvres d'apostolat, de se faire zélatrice de l'œuvre des missions d'Afrique.[97]

> (Reading some of the letters sent from the centre of Africa by Canadian nuns moved us to tears. But this emotion was not sterile, it inspired the thought of suggesting to all our teachers whose generous hearts are so well made for loving

all apostolic works, to make themselves zealots for the
work being done by the African missions.)

By targeting the female teachers from the outset, and not their male
counterparts, the missionary discourse in part conditioned the participation and emotional reaction of girls and young women by presuming and
therefore expecting particularly useful emotional tendencies in them.
By itself this exhortation does not explain the considerable support
given to apostolic work by women. Since the Holy Childhood had been
introduced into Canada in the 1850s, young girls in particular seemed
inclined to embrace the charity with enthusiasm. Without exception,
the reports released in the 1850s and 1860s included the abundant
correspondence addressed to the association's directors by young girls.
In 1860, 87 percent of the 128 chiefs in the city of Montreal were
women. Among them, 61 percent were single (identified by "Delle")
and 39 percent were married or widowed (identified by "Mde").[98] Why
did young girls so promptly, and so intensely, adopt missionary work
with the "little Chinese"? The many recreational activities could have
nurtured their infatuation. The girls could also have been attracted by
the way in which the missionary narratives offered new possibilities, as
much to their imagination as to their piety. Being addressed especially
to them, the narrative of redeeming infidel children constituted in some
way the female equivalent of the adventure narratives so highly regarded
by young boys at that time.

Two expressions of femininity emerge from the Holy Childhood's
missionary discourse: maternity and the religious vocation. By high-
lighting the maternal aspect of redeeming abandoned children, the Holy
Childhood discourse offered girls a course of action that was inextricably
linked to the role they were called upon to play as adults if they chose
to remain lay persons. The Catholic girls learned about the ideals of
maternity in reading how Chinese mothers "cruelly" abandoned their
children. Some were even ready to assume the maternal role: "Que ne

pouvons-nous voler personnellement au secours de ces pauvres enfants! Avec quel plaisir nous les recueillerions! Avec quelle attention nous leur prodiguerions tous les soins!"[99] (If only we could fly to the rescue of these poor children! We would welcome them with such pleasure! What attention we would lavish on them, to meet all their needs!) We should again remember that the convent students at Villa Maria asked Father Daniel to send them, in order to encourage them, "one of these innocent creatures." However, for the youngest girls, the idea of having the care of rescued children in reality could have caused anxiety. In this regard, a pupil of the Ursulines in Quebec City reported that a little girl, "qui avait payé pour quatre [petits Chinois] demandait naïvement à sa maman ce qu'elle ferait, si on les lui envoyait" (who had paid for four [little Chinese] naïvely asked her mother what she would do, if they were sent to her).[100]

For some young girls, the redemption of infidel children instead allowed the expression of the intention to be a missionary: "Il y a même plusieurs de nos compagnes qui volontiers consentiraient à s'expatrier pour aller les secourir, si cela dépendait d'elles."[101] (There are even many of our companions who would gladly consent to leave our country and go to their rescue, if it were up to them.) Even if the missionary vocation expressed here was not explicitly promoted in the Holy Childhood's Montreal publications, the fascination with the fate of children in distant lands allowed the young girls to imagine a life of adventure that was far from the marital model. In this regard, they appropriated the works of the Holy Childhood in order to dream of an unanticipated destiny. Among the various charitable works and religious vocations that were offered to young Catholic girls in the nineteenth century, the missionary apostolate also held a special place owing to the exotic universe it evoked. The fervour of the girls' interest speaks to the imagined possibilities it offered. In addition, and in this it is comparable with ethnographic knowledge, missionary work gave girls a capacity for action and a sense of control over an exotic, threatening "other place."

Anne-Marie Gaboury, a pupil of the Sœurs de la congrégation de Notre-Dame in Sherbrooke, introduced an important character from the religious and imperial universe of the nineteenth century in a very simple assignment. To the question "Exercice d'invention. Comment appelez-vous: [. . .] Un prêtre en mission chez les infidèles?" (Invention exercise. What do you call: [. . .] A priest on a mission to the infidels?), Anne-Marie wrote as her answer: "*Un missionnaire.*"[102] The importance acquired by the figure of the heroic missionary at that time came from the fact that it had been constructed simultaneously across an entire range of discourses: church sermons, national historiography, missionary publications, and school textbooks. The missionaries were often themselves the architects of their reputation, as shown in a dictation drawn from the work of Father Dugas: "L'homme qui garde le sentiment de sa noblesse ne se fera jamais sauvage, et s'il embrasse ce genre de vie, ce ne sera que comme le missionnaire, par vertu et par héroïsme, pour gagner des âmes à Jésus-Christ."[103] (The man who keeps a sense of his nobility will never become a savage, and if he embraces this kind of life, it will only be as the missionary, through virtue and heroism, to win souls over to Jesus Christ.) Introduced by the school system for the admiration of girls as well as boys, the missionary was essential to the production of a gendered narrative of apostolate among the "infidels." As well, he represented one of the strongest masculine figures transmitted by the school. That was what Father Casgrain was expressing when he wrote "une des plus grandes figures qu'offre l'histoire du nouveau-monde, après la sublime figure du missionnaire, c'est, à mon avis, celle du pionnier canadien" (one of the greatest figures the history of the new world has to offer, after the sublime figure of the missionary, is, in my opinion, that of the Canadian pioneer).[104]

A document preserved in the archives of the Collège de Montréal attests to the importance of the missionary among the masculine models offered to young men.[105] In the dialogue called "La dispute des vocations" (The argument about vocations), eight boys face off in a verbal sparring match, each one defending his choice of occupation. The various occupations are lawyer, farmer, millionaire, professor, missionary, vicar, journalist, and doctor. After having announced his vocation to his colleagues, André, the future missionary, must run the gauntlet of their responses, because they try to make him renounce it. And so "*Bonne-terre*" (Good-earth [the farmer]) asks: "Tu voudrais nous quitter? / Que dis-tu, cher ami, toi-même t'exiler? . . . / Ton discours il est vrai je l'ai trouvé sublime, / Mais de t'anéantir quelle est donc la maxime / Qui te fait une loi? Nous ne te verrons plus!" (You want to leave us? / What are you saying, dear friend, that you will go into exile? . . . / It's true I found your speech sublime, / But to do away with yourself, where is the maxim / Who is making it a law? We won't see you again!) For his part, "*Guérit-tout*" (Cure-all [the doctor]) reminds him of his filial duties and warns him that his constitution is "too frail" for this type of evangelism. Nothing works and the missionary remains determined. At the very end of the dialogue, voices call upon Mary, and her blessing is intended for the missionary in particular:

> 1er voix (bis) / Notre vocation / Dans cet exil ô Mère! /
> Qui la conservera? Ta bénédiction, / Mais donne la surtout
> au Missionnaire / 2me voix (bis) / À l'ami de la croix / A
> celui qui de Dieu veut faire aimer les lois / Jusqu'au bout de
> la terre. / Et que beaucoup d'élus appelleront mon Père.

> (1st voice [bis] / Our vocation / In this exile O Mother! /
> Who will keep it? Your blessing, / But give it above all to
> the missionary / 2nd voice (bis) / To the friend of the cross
> / To the one who wants to make the laws of God loved /
> Unto the ends of the earth. / And whom many of the elect
> will call my Father.)

This dialogue was featured in an event organized by the division called the Petits of the Collège de Montréal in 1915. Was its purpose to promote the figure of the missionary? The archives are not clear on this point, but "La dispute des vocations" was followed by an oratorio in four acts about the departure of a missionary for Mongolia.[106] The oratorio's text, like the dialogue, stresses the missionary's heroism:

> Leur voix retentira jusqu'aux bornes du monde, / Ils iront, méprisant les colères de l'onde, / Parler d'un Rédempteur à tous les archipels. / Ils verront sans trembler l'apprêt de la torture / Et, rayonnants déjà de la gloire future, / Ils sauront de leur sang cimenter leurs autels.

> (Their voice will resound unto the limits of the world, / They will go, scorning the anger of the waves, / To speak of a Redeemer in all the islands. / They will see without trembling the readying for torture / And, already alight with future glory, / They will with their blood cement their altars.)

Again, note that among the eight masculine models presented in the dialogue, the missionary is the only heroic figure. In a way he embodies the religious equivalent of the masculine figures of the adventurer, explorer, or frontiersman. A line delivered by the professor highlights this heroism: "Au professeur instruit / De former lentement et sans faire de bruit / Médecins, avocats, cultivateurs, vicaire, / Et ces jeunes héros qu'on nomme missionnaires."[107] (To the learned professor / Training slowly and without fuss / Doctors, lawyers, farmers, a vicar, / And these young heroes we call missionaries.)

The missionary's heroism was characterized by a variety of attributes. To begin with, heroism was displayed in confronting a threatening, dangerous natural environment. Physical conditions of the missionary life were often emphasized. Second, it was magnified by the level of cruelty of the "barbarians" he was seeking to convert. This is what the boys of the Collège de Sainte-Marie de Montréal were expressing when they delivered a discourse in 1854 in favour of the Œuvre de la Propagation de la Foi. Young Dubuc wrote: "En effet rien de plus propre et de plus prompt pour civiliser un peuple féroce que les généreux efforts de ces saints missionnaires qui s'exposent à des dangers sans nombre."[108] (In fact nothing could be swifter or more appropriate in civilizing a fierce people than the generous efforts of these holy missionaries, who expose themselves to countless dangers.)

In many narratives, the missionary is seen as a bold, active man with a strong body who is unafraid to die for the cause he is advocating. The importance of the missionary's virile body is highlighted by a young man at the Collège de Sainte-Thérèse in his account of a visit by Bishop Grandin, a missionary in the Northwest:

> Nous avons donc joui, pendant plusieurs heures, de la présence d'un évêque missionnaire, d'un de ces hommes de Dieu, héros de l'Evangile, zélés propagateurs des grandes œuvres patriotiques aussi bien que religieuses, dont les vertus et les quelques traits d'héroïsme, consignés aux *Actes des Apôtres* et dans les *Annales de la propagation de la Foi*, nous étonnent en même temps qu'ils nous font rougir de la timidité de notre foi, et de notre peu de dévouement à la grande cause de notre sainte religion. Mgr Grandin est demeuré assez longtemps au milieu de nous, pour que nous ayons pu le voir et l'entendre à loisir, l'examiner de plus près, et, qu'on nous permette de le dire, l'étudier au physique comme au moral. [. . .] Monseigneur est d'une haute stature; sa charpente osseuse et robuste lui donne une attitude imposante que tempèrent la modestie de son regard et la douceur de sa physionomie.[109]

> (We therefore enjoyed, for several hours, the presence of a missionary bishop, one of those men of God, heroes of the Gospel, zealous propagators of great works that are patriotic as well as religious, whose virtues and signs of heroism, recorded in the *Acts of the Apostles* and the *Annales de la Propagation de la Foi*, astonish us even as they shame

us for the timidity of our faith and our feeble devotion to the great cause of our holy religion. Bishop Grandin stayed among us for a long time so that we would be able to see and hear him at leisure, examine him closely, and, if we may be allowed to say so, study him on the physical as well as the moral level. [. . .] The Bishop is tall; his big-boned, robust build gives him an imposing air that is tempered by his modest gaze and gentle physiognomy.)

Along the same lines, a series of compositions was written for the occasion of the World's Columbian Exposition in Chicago in 1893 by students at the Collège de Montréal. They retell an episode in the life of Father Lacombe, another celebrated Northwest missionary. The texts attest to the calibre of the missionary's personality as a model of masculinity. As the story opens, the missionary spots an encampment of "savages" in the distance. He wants to go to them, but runs up against the fear of the two Indians accompanying him, who were "alléguant que ces sauvages pourraient fort bien être des ennemis" (claiming that these savages could well be enemies). Students J.S. Bilodeau and Edgar David then focus on Lacombe's virile heroism (and at the same time underscore the cowardly, fearful nature of the Indigenous characters): "Enfin le missionnaire leur promit de se jeter au-devant d'eux s'ils avaient affaires [*sic*] à des ennemis et ils consentirent à partir" (Finally the missionary promised to throw himself in front of them if they were dealing with enemies, and they consented to go ahead), and "Ils finirent enfin par céder lorsque le missionnaire leur eût [*sic*] déclaré qu'il leur servirait de rempart, si l'on avait affaire à des ennemis."[110] (They finally agreed when the missionary told them that he would act as their shield, if they were dealing with enemies.) Not only did the missionary "save" lives and souls, but he was also ready to sacrifice his person for the cause of propagating Christianity throughout the world.

Father Lacombe was not identified in these compositions; however, reading his memoirs allows us to make the connections. As well, the students had probably heard this story from the missionary himself. Throughout the nineteenth century, the Northwest missionaries made very frequent visits to the *collèges classiques* when visiting Quebec. Many of their students thus met in person with these "heroes," whom they had also come to know as protagonists in various narratives. In the dialogue "La dispute des vocations," André explains his vocation in this way:

> Un soir, tu t'en souviens le bon père Lacombe / Nous tenait ce discours: "Je suis près de la tombe, / Quarante ans j'ai servi les Indiens Métis, / Je ne veux pas mourir sans leur laisser un gage, / Un père, ainsi que moi, peut-être davantage, / Apte, à tout point de vue, à les servir longtemps / Est-il chez les Petits? Est-ce parmi les Grands? / Je l'ignore; mais Dieu doit parler à son âme! / Qu'il ne résiste pas au but qui le réclame."[111]

> (One night, you remember, the good Father Lacombe / Delivered this speech: "I am nearing the grave, / For forty years I have served the Métis Indians, / I don't want to die without leaving them a keepsake, / A father, along with me, may be more / Able, in all respects, to serve them for a long time / Is he with the Little Ones? Is he among the Big Ones? / I don't know; but God must speak to his soul! / Let him not resist the goal that claims him.")

What is this hero lacking? This is where the emotional dimension of the "new apostle's" masculinity came into play. Appealing to the emotions was crucial in promoting the young people's missionary involvement, whether they were girls or boys, as we have seen. But how the emotional reaction expressed itself differed greatly between the two groups. Contrary to the Holy Childhood's discourse, in which the Other to be saved played an important role in the emotional response of young girls, in the case of the boys, the Other was secondary, part of the stage set in which the hero, that is, the missionary, is acting.

Nothing new in that. A good portion of the emotional content of the "heroic missionary" narrative was revealed even before the "pagans" were encountered. In fact, the emotional charge the narrative sought to produce would reach its peak in the "departure" scene.[112] Here, the emotion had little to do with the distant Other, if not to represent what made the missionary's return uncertain. Above all, it related to the separation of this "exceptional" being from his circle: the parents' sadness and the missionary's withheld tears.

In this case, the emotional dimension of the missionary narrative does not generate a feeling of empowerment in young men. In most cases, its aim was to stimulate their admiration.[113] Did it succeed? How did the young men appropriate the figure of the heroic missionary? The accounts of two secondary students at the turn of the twentieth century make it possible to confirm the missionary figure's domination of young men and their ambivalent emotions toward it. On 6 March 1901, the students at the Collège de Valleyfield received a visit from Father Forbes, a Canadian missionary to Africa. After having listened to his lectures, Erle Bartlett, fourteen years old, confided to his journal his fear of hearing the call of a missionary vocation:

> Je m'attendais à, ou plutôt, je craignais un peu, je l'avoue, qu'en entendant ces conférences, je sentirais en moi quelque désir de me faire missionnaire ou quelque chose de la sorte mais je trouve que cela ne me tente pas du tout. Il est vrai qu'il serait si beau d'aller dans ces lointains pays passer une vie de souffrances, couronnée [*sic*], peut-être, par le martyr mais mon idéal tel qu'il est formé jusqu'ici c'est si jamais j'ai le bonheur de devenir prêtre, de faire tout le bien possible soit dans un collège (ou) soit en d'autres places semblables et je sens que c'est là que Dieu m'appelle.[114]

> (I was expecting, or rather, I was a little afraid, I admit it, that on hearing these lectures, I would feel some desire to become a missionary or something of that kind but I find

that it tempts me not at all. It is true that it would be a very
beautiful thing to go to those distant lands and spend a
life of suffering, perhaps crowned with martyrdom, but my
ideal as it has taken shape so far is, if ever I have the good
fortune to become a priest, to do the most good possible
whether at a collège or in other places like it and I feel that
that is where God is calling me to go.)

The following year, it was the turn of Émile Léger, a student at the
same institution, to secretly admit refusing to embrace the missionary's apostolic career:

Voilà mes rêves: me consacrer à l'éducation de la jeunesse.
Pour elle je me sent [*sic*] prêt à l'immolation. Va pour
d'autre [*sic*] cœurs peut-être plus généreux, l'évangélisation
des nègres ou des chinois. L'œuvre que j'entreprendrai est
sans aucun doute, aussi méritoire, aussi grande; il y a tant à
faire pour le relèvement moral du jeune homme.[115]

(Those are my dreams: to devote myself to teaching young
people. For that, I feel ready for immolation. It is for
other hearts that are perhaps more generous to evangelize
Negroes and Chinese. The good work that I will undertake
is without a doubt just as deserving, just as great; there is so
much to be done for the moral rehabilitation of the young
man.)

By confiding their rejection of the missionary vocation to their journal,
the two young men speak to the pressure the heroization of this model
of masculinity put on boys. Moreover, the way in which Émile Léger
defends choosing to become a teacher also reflects the heightened—even
exaggerated—glorification of the missionary figure.

How did nineteenth-century Canadian children come to be emotionally attached to children living on the other side of the world? In explaining their emotional state to the Holy Childhood director in 1851, the young girls from the boarding school run by the Congrégation de Notre-Dame inaugurated the long-lasting emotional involvement of Canadian children in the fate of "pagan" children. Negotiating the deep waters of the compassion they felt when exposed to the sufferings of others and the joy of contributing to their salvation, the young girls experienced an empowerment that broadened their horizons. On their side, the boys had to deal with the heroic ideal of the missionary vocation. For those who supported missionary works, the objective of associating Catholic children with the fate of a distant Other was, first and foremost, to ensure Canadian society's religiosity and spirit of charity. The "civilizing mission" had two dimensions: civilizing action among pagans strengthened the civilization of Christian communities.

The missionary rhetoric's relationship to alterity is complex. As demonstrated, exposing a cruel, exotic otherness was necessary to justify missionary action. Paradoxically, the ideal of the missionary apostolate aimed to reduce this very otherness; that is, the conversion to Christianity was seen as a way to eliminate the "barbaric" practices of infidels and to civilize them. The desire to evangelize Other peoples points to a drive for homogeneity that tends to obliterate differences. The love Canadian children felt for the "little Chinese" implied a reduction in their alterity into an idealization of the Self and the desire for a transformation of the Other into the Self. And, to this point, the central place occupied by children in this history is instructive, as Ahmed remarks: "To be moved by the suffering of some others (the 'deserving' poor, the innocent child, the injured hero), is also to be elevated into a place that remains untouched by other others (whose suffering cannot be converted into my sympathy or admiration). So it is not a coincidence that it is a child's suffering that touches the nation. The child represents the face of innocence; through the child, the threat of difference is transformed into the promise or hope of *likeness*."[116]

The apostolic discourse was at once spiritual and imperial. It helped to affirm a homogeneity advocated by certain European intellectual trends linked to imperial enterprises. Norman Ajari expresses this idea in an article on the coloniality of being: "Heidegger's example demonstrates it very clearly: there is no fantastical distortion of alterity unless it is against the backdrop of the imaginary of one's own rootedness and one's own indigeneity. [. . .] There is, behind any manifestation of the coloniality of being, not hostility, but quite the contrary, a peaceful and total certainty of self."[117] With regard to these ideologies of the Self, the criticisms expressed by Arthur Buies and Francisque Sarcey are crucial: they accept the existence of Chinese alterity without wishing to abolish it.

Signs still linger of the enormous influence on Euro-American societies of the Holy Childhood and the missionary interest in children of other cultures. Analyzing this history casts light on the strong emotional bond that continues to unite Western audiences and children of the Global South, thanks to the feeling of empowerment gained by a White donor who is moved by the plight of the Other. The history of the Holy Childhood and the empowerment it granted to children are, in my opinion, at the heart of the idea of the "White saviour" that is still very present in Western societies.

Conclusion

The education of the boy is complete: He has been successfully and artfully taught racism and believes he acquired respectability, status. And the illusion of power through the process of inventing an Other.

TONI MORRISON[1]

In this book, I have sought to understand the relation of alterity to Canadian society, particularly French Canadian, of the nineteenth century as expressed and experienced in the school institution. I brought to light the intensity of the transnational circulation of representations and the influence of imperialism on the constitution of school knowledge. In the nineteenth century, pedagogical and disciplinary knowledge circulated in abundance among various European and North American countries, and Canada undoubtedly provides one of the most telling examples of this phenomenon. Canadian educators drew on different European and American sources to assemble the knowledge that they hoped to instill in children. Canadian writers relied on the discourses contained in travel literature, generalist atlases, and school textbooks produced in various countries. Alterity was a favoured pedagogical tool as public education expanded in the nineteenth century.

Within this transnational knowledge, how was the rhetorical construction of Others accomplished? Alterity's contours appeared through frequent use of a play of oppositions, among them civilization/

barbarity and domination/liberty. Alterity also functioned by high-lighting certain specific figures that had been narratively constructed through the vocabulary of difference. In her book *Strange Encounters*, Sara Ahmed suggests using the concept of "particularity" to define the sites of encounter between the Self and the Other. "In this sense, introducing particularity at the level of encounters (the sociality of the 'with') helps us to move beyond the dialectic of self-other and towards a recognition of the differentiation between others, and their different functions in constituting identity, and the permeability of bodily space."[2]

The various figures of the Other were developed through a variety of discourses, in accordance with different characteristics (cultural or corporal), and they fulfilled different functions in the formation of a student's collective identity. Objects of fascination or contempt, Others were reified, objectified, animalized, and erased. In sum, they were dehumanized. This dehumanization was *"constitutive de l'Occident"* (constituent of the West) and of its relation to death.[3] In keeping with what Thierry Hentsch writes regarding the relationship of Western culture to alterity, the representations fashioned, disseminated, and transformed by the school positioned alterity outside history, in a fixed time. It was life—progress, history, the march of civilization—that was opposed to death—the past, barbarity, extinction, the body-machine. Owing to the almost total absence of women in these representations, also involved was a profound reflection on masculinity: the figures of the Arab, the Black, and the Indian, which were all, in general, models of virility, even hypervirility, fed into the definition of White masculinity.

Inherited from a long European tradition, the various representations of otherness evolved so as to respond to political, scientific, and cultural developments that were current in the nineteenth century. The primary school recycled and popularized the knowledge created by imperialism in order to present children with a discourse that divided the world into accessible categories, within everyone's reach. While they occurred in a particular intellectual context, the representations then fed into the thinking and actions of many generations of Canadians.

The reification of the Other on the pages of school textbooks was in part responsible for the preservation and reinforcement of colonialist oppression and incidents of racist violence and discrimination. Far from being harmless, the words copied through dictation, read in textbooks, and delivered on stage had an effect on reality. It is the ethical responsibility of the academic community to recognize this and make it seen, as Emma LaRocque insists: "Are scholars to be exempt from having to address the historical and social consequences of textual dehumanization? Texts do have social consequences; the thought that social scientists can be so alienated from the social purpose of knowledge is not a comfortable one."[4] As I have shown, the entire rhetorical construction of alterity resides in the words used, the repeated qualifiers, the recurring oppositions. These words have had the power to perpetuate and reinforce the modes of domination. But words and narratives can also overturn oppression and establish new avenues for dialogue. It is precisely because of the power of teaching that today many civil society groups stress the importance of education in the battle against intolerance, discrimination, and racism. It therefore comes back to the school in particular to deconstruct and unlearn the ideologies that it has itself taught for such a long time.

During the period under study, children acquired a feeling of authority over the Others, thanks to the school. They "knew," for instance, what the "Indians" were. The knowledge of Others, or, more specifically, the belief in this knowledge, gave them an impression of control. The school also provided a hierarchical vision of the world that led Canadian children to believe, even when they came from a lower-class background, that they belonged to the privileged categories of humanity, that is, to civilization and the White race. Demonstrating that this faith existed is in fact one of the essential contributions made by my research. The children were not first defined as French Canadians when confronted with the Others—for example, in a relation of alterity with the "Anglais"—but rather as White and civilized. The representations of alterity transmitted by the school laid the groundwork for a visual, racist relationality; the "I" did not resemble the Others, who were immediately *re*cognizable in all situations.

Moreover, it seems that the interest in "other places" preceded nation building by the school. It was after having taught children what they *were not* for decades that the school finally became engaged in glorifying the Nation and also initiating the students into it—once again excluding children who were not part of the national group as it was defined. The passage to the twentieth century thus marks a turning point in the representations transmitted by the school institution. Owing to the recentring of pedagogical knowledge on the national space,[5] the interest in other places dwindled in the regular curriculum and the avenues for transmission of figures of alterity in school changed. At that point, representations of alterity were passed along more and more frequently through the missionary propaganda disseminated in the schools. There is every reason to believe that reduced alterity in the regular curriculum did not go hand in hand with a less hierarchical or less racist vision of the world in the twentieth century. Furthermore, the heroization of certain historical characters, paired with broader dissemination of the national story—up until the present day—left the Indian, who became an *Amérindien* along the way, as the principal figure of alterity presented for children's knowledge.

Studying the rhetorical construction of alterity at school shed light on the various scales, regarding civilization and race, on which the Self and the Other were positioned. Although these scales at first served to "understand" and "know" the Other, they allowed students to discover for themselves an identity that went beyond the national identities of "French Canadian," "Canadian," and "British." The encounter between the child and these different figures of the Other took the form of a journey toward knowledge of the self. Owing to a negation of dialogue and recognition of the Other as someone else, the alterity was a projection through which Canadian society voided its fears and desires. Ironically, unveiling this journey exposed the long memory lapse, both historical and historiographical, of which the society was a casualty. An inevitable lapse?

In the groups' fight for recognition, the darker side of the collective identity cannot be held up with pride. But when we try too hard to forget this history, other groups in the society are muzzled and refused recognition. The cultural and political consequences of an atrophied social memory should not be belittled. Given the debates and events that have shaken contemporary Québécois society,[6] it would in fact be ill-advised to underestimate the importance and lasting influence of the stereotypes transmitted in school institutions for over a century. The resurgence of certain prejudices, like those now directed at Arab Muslims, and the long battle of Black and Indigenous communities to expose police violence, often waged amid indifference from non-marginalized groups, remind us that our duty to remember the past dehumanization and the discourses of hatred spread by the school is necessary and urgent.

"My place in the sun."

In his book *Éthique comme philosophie première* (Ethics as the first philosophy), Emmanuel Levinas details his vision of ethics using the expression "my place in the sun":

> Having to respond to one's right to be, not through
> reference to the abstraction of some anonymous law or
> some legal entity, but in fearing for others. My being-in-
> the-world or my "place in the sun," my at-home, have they
> not been a usurpation of places belonging to others I have
> already oppressed or starved, expelled to a third world:
> a pushing away, an excluding, an exiling, a despoiling, a
> killing. [. . .] Fear of everything that my existing—despite
> its intentional, conscious innocence—can accomplish in

violence and murder. [. . .] Fear that comes to me from the
faces of others.[7]

The research I have carried out in recent years has led me to ask myself
many questions: Where does my "place in the sun" come from? From
whom was it usurped? Why have I never had to define myself as
"White"? Why was it not until I had engaged in a deep reflection on
race, halfway through my doctoral studies, that I became aware of my
Whiteness? My journey along the roads of alterity has obliged me to
examine, and accept, the genocidal part of my heritage as a White person
and Québécoise of French-Canadian extraction. I must recognize the
privilege of this Whiteness and understand exactly how it allows me to
ignore or renounce the racist, colonial culture I come from.[8]

Examining the historical construction of alterity presented to children was a way to revisit my own history. Encountering those young
girls who were overwhelmed when told of the misfortune of Chinese
children shed a light on my own youth that I was not expecting. My
adolescence was marked by involvement in such organizations as the
Amnesty Internationals, World Visions, and Oxfams of our world. That
makes me a direct heir to the tradition of imperialism, colonialism, and
the civilizing mission going back, at least, to the nineteenth century.
Thus, from aspiring to a career as an international reporter in the Middle
East to the fascination that for a long time, as an adolescent, I cultivated
for other places, this entire history is a legacy of the representations of
exoticism in modern culture. Today, the Québécois school invents new
ways for young people to play "Indian" or, in the guise of an arithmetic
problem, calculate the costs of a humanitarian mission to Haiti. It is
therefore not only a matter of history.

My research interrogated the roots of the colonial, racist discourse
transmitted through the Canadian educational system in the nineteenth century. It is when we are faced with these representations that
a discourse of resistance, a decolonial discourse, makes itself heard.
Taking the measure of hegemony in the colonial discourse is essential

to understanding the opposition narratives that defy it. Listening to the Other is getting away from sight's primacy; it is recognizing their quality of subject and our belonging to a humanity that is shared and different at the same time. Let us conclude by listening to Emma LaRocque: "How shall 'I' say I am human and at the same time different without resorting to stereotypes or to a return to the past? How shall I say I am different and yet the same as a human? And how shall we claim and develop our literatures and intellects unique to us without having always to juxtapose them against Western portrayals and canonization? Or without always preoccupying ourselves with the colonizer's yearnings for primitivistic authenticity?"[9]

Acknowledgements

The research I completed as part of my doctoral dissertation, which resulted in this book, was motivated by a desire to understand the external sources of Quebec's nation building, and it led me into avenues I had not anticipated. I was able to pursue them to their ends, thanks to the mentoring of leading thinkers and intellectuals: Sara Ahmed, Emmanuel Levinas, Madeleine Ouellette-Michalska, Thierry Hentsch, Toni Morrison, Emma LaRocque, and many others. Inspired by their words, I understood that Quebec's educational archives from the nineteenth century furnished evidence of performances, rhetorical constructions, a visual literacy, and the transmission of a world view that are fundamentally racist and colonialist.

Thanks to help received along the way from numerous archivists, notably Josée Sarrazin of the Congrégation de Notre-Dame and Nancy Lavoie of the Frères des écoles chrétiennes, I was able to locate in history anonymous schoolgirls and schoolboys who have left behind only a handful of class compositions.

It is precisely the gestures of these schoolchildren, the slow, repetitive writing of assignments, the challenging or irresistible reading of schoolbooks, and the boredom relieved by looking at the pictures that trace the deep furrows left by this history of learning racism in Quebec schools.

"They are barbaric," "barbarians," "barbaric and hardly civilized," "despotic," "a less intelligent race," "they feed their children to swine," "the lowest class of humanity," "to be civilized," "assets," "savages," "few of them remain," "disappearing." These words were read, written, recited, and felt. The gestures were repeated generation after generation. Deep furrows.

The years I devoted to this research were marked by inspiring encounters and the beginnings of warm friendships. With Virginie Pineault, whom I met along the way, I felt the power of a genuine meeting with the Other, in all its radical significance. As for Florence Prévost-Grégoire, our friendship allowed me to grow and helped me find myself, an invaluable gift. I thank her for all of it, especially for her intelligent, painstaking reading of this book in original draft form.

And what more can I say about Ollivier Hubert this time? His patient, enthusiastic supervision really took me to another level in my doctoral work. From the very beginning, I felt seen and heard by him. Over the years, our intellectual collaboration has become a friendship and still more in other matters that are so precious to me. The writing of this book owes much to him. I say, thank you, Ollivier.

This book would not have seen the light of day without the contributions of various institutions and many individuals. I thank the Social Sciences and Humanities Research Council of Canada, the Fondation Desjardins, and the University of Montreal, as well as the Prix d'auteurs pour l'édition savante, for their financial support. I am also grateful to editor Nadine Tremblay of the Presses de l'Université de Montréal, her staff, and the assessors of my manuscript for their careful, generous reading. The publication of an English translation of my book has been a goal since the submission of my doctoral thesis. I would like to warmly thank the team at University of Manitoba Press for their openness towards my work. Special thanks to Jill McConkey, Glenn Bergen, David Larsen, and all their team. A huge thank you to Sue Stewart who was able to translate my thoughts into English so well. Her talent and dedication have faithfully conveyed the essence of my work in another language, opening the door to new readers and new opportunities. An incredible privilege.

I would not have been able to complete this project without the support of my family and friends. Special thanks to André, the father of my children, who supported me in our daily life throughout my studies and who continues to share parenthood with me in a spirit of solidarity. A special salute to Marie, Florence, and Louis, who have generously recognized the importance of my research and encourage me to keep speaking out about these issues. They are my hope for the future.

The in-depth reflection on alterity that I began in summer 2011 in dialogue with my master's thesis director at the time, Jean-Marie Facteau, does not end with this book. If there is one thing of which I remain convinced after all these years, it is that we must never cease our questioning about these fundamental topics. To alterity, we should offer receptivity and dialogue. Our ethos for relating to Others cannot proceed by negation, rejection, or the desire to abolish their otherness. Further, the senses at play in encounters must be expanded to include listening and reaching out our hand, in order to understand that our common humanity is a multitude.

Appendix

Performance of Indigeneity (Collèges and Convents)
This partial list has been drawn up by consulting the following documents:

Journal de l'instruction publique, 1857–1879.

Journal of Education, 1857–1879.

Jean Béraux, *350 ans de théâtre au Canada français*, Montreal, Le Cercle du Livre de France, 1958.

Fernand Boulet, *Répertoire du théâtre au Collège de l'Assomption*, L'Assomption, QC, Collège de l'Assomption, 1987.

Jeanne Corriveau, "Jonathas du R.P. Gustave Lamarche et le théâtre collégial," Master's thesis (French Studies), University of Montreal, 1965.

Julie Plourde, "Un genre en construction: le théâtre à la Congrégation de Notre-Dame, 1850–1920," Master's thesis (History), University of Montreal, 2014.

Date	Institution	Title/Description of the Performance	Boys/Girls
1834	Séminaire de Québec	"Exhibition d'un grand nombre d'objets d'histoire nationale, de costumes sauvages, etc.—Discours d'un sauvage du N.O" (Exhibition of a large number of nationally historical objects, savages' costumes, etc.—Speech by a savage from the Northwest)	Boys
11 August 1835	Séminaire de Québec	"Rapports de plusieurs jeunes voyageurs arrivés des États-Unis et du Mexique: discours d'un descendant de Montézuma—Discours d'un chef Apache, etc., etc." (Reports by many young travellers recently arrived from the United States and Mexico: speech by a descendant of Montezuma—Speech by an Apache chief, etc., etc.)	Boys
14 (?) August 1838	Séminaire de Québec	Trois discours anglais: allocution d'un chef Indien à ses guerrier [sic] au moment de combattre les Espagnols (Three speeches in English: address by an Indian chief to his warrior [sic] before a battle with the Spaniards)	Boys
12 August 1839	Séminaire de Québec	"Ataliba, or the last of the Incas, in French, in which last the audience was struck with the gorgeous appearance of the dresses of the Peruvians, almost realizing the fairy tales of those times of gold and silver."	Boys
1859	École normale Laval	"Séance littéraire et musicale à l'École normale Laval [. . .] Parmi les morceaux de musique [. . .] "le Chant de l'Iroquois" (Literary and musical presentation at the École normale Laval [. . .] Among the musical pieces [. . .] the "Song of the Iroquois")	Boys
5 February 1860	Séminaire de Québec – Académie Saint-Denys	"Séance académique (5 February 1860) Discours d'ouverture [. . .] LETTRE écrite de France par Donacona [sic] à sa tribu, M.C. Baillargeon, élève de Seconde, candidat. [. . .] NARRATION—Les Algonquins dans le parloir des Ursulines de Québec,—déclamée par M. W. Couture, élève de Seconde, candidat." (Academic show [5 February 1860] Opening address [. . .] LETTER written in France by Donacona [sic] to his tribe, M.C. Baillargeon, Sophomore, candidate. [. . .] STORYTELLING—The Algonquins in the parlour of the Ursuline nuns of Quebec City,—recited by M.W. Couture, Sophomore, candidate.)	Boys

8–9 July 1861	Ursulines	"La Fille Blanche chez les Abénaquis" (The White girl among the Abenaki)	Girls
14 January 1861	CND–Mont Sainte-Marie	"Sujet pris de l'histoire du Canada 1658" (Topic taken from Canadian history, 1658)	Girls
5 July 1864	CND–Villa Maria	"Dialogue semi-musical: 2 blanches et une sauvagesse (lors des examens de fins d'année. Auditoire sélect)" (Semi-musical dialogue: 2 white women and one sauvagesse [during year-end exams. Select audience])	Girls
6 July 1864	Ursulines	"Un discours, qu'un chef huron adressa aux Religieuses Ursulines lors du premier incendie de leur couvent, fut récité avec beaucoup de succès par Mlle Nault." (A speech, made by a Huron chief to the Ursuline Nuns the first time their convent caught fire, was recited by Miss Nault with great success.)	Girls
11 July 1865	Collège de l'Assomption	"Archibald Cameron of Lochiell, ou épisode de la guerre de 7 ans en Canada, grand mélodrame en 3 acte, [sic] tiré des *Anciens Canadiens* de Ph. Aubert de Gaspé" (Archibald Cameron of Lochiell, or an episode from the 7-year war in Canada, high drama in 3 act [sic], based on *Les Anciens Canadiens* by Ph. Aubert de Gaspé)	Boys
March 1868	Collège de l'Assomption	*Les Anciens Canadiens* (The Canadians of old)	Boys
April 1869	CND– Villa Maria	Rose des Algonquins [Coaïna] (Rose of the Algonquins [Coïana])	Girls
June 1869	CND– Villa Maria	Coaïna	Girls
11 May 1870	Collège Sainte-Marie (Jesuits)	"Le P. Isaac Jogues, S.J. ou l'Évangile prêché aux sauvages" (Father Isaac Jogues. S.J., or the Gospel preached to the savages)	Boys
30 June 1874	Collège Sainte-Marie (Jesuits)	"Le P. Isaac Jogues, S.J. ou l'Évangile prêché aux sauvages" (Father Isaac Jogues. S.J., or the Gospel preached to the savages)	Boys

2 July 1878	Séminaire de Trois-Rivières	*Les Anciens Canadiens* (The Canadians of old)	Boys
20 February 1879	Collège Bourget in Rigaud	*Le Chevalier de Mornac* (The knight of Mornac)	Boys
15 January 1880	Séminaire de Québec	*Les Anciens Canadiens* (The Canadians of old)	Boys
28 January 1881	Collège Sainte-Marie (Jesuits)	"Donnacona"	Boys
20 October 1890	Séminaire de Québec	*Les Anciens Canadiens* (The Canadians of old)	Boys
May 1894	Ursulines, Trois-Rivières	"Tableaux avec Combat contre les Sioux, et Sauvagesses et Métis du nord-Ouest," sur la vie de missionnaire de Laflèche ("Tableaux with Battle against the Sioux, and Sauvagesses and Métis from the Northwest," based on the missionary life of Laflèche)	Girls
12 February 1896	Collège Bourget in Rigaud	*Le Chevalier de Mornac* (The knight of Mornac)	Boys
1 May 1899	CND–Caraquet	"Mother Bourgeoys (tableau)"	Girls
16 February 1899	Mont Saint-Louis	"Découverte du Canada (ou Cartier)" (Discovery of Canada [or Cartier])	Boys
1900	Mont Saint-Louis	"Dollard"	Boys
1902	Mont Saint-Louis	"La conspiration ou Champlain" (The conspiracy or Champlain)	Boys
June 1908	Mont Saint-Louis	"Champlain"	Boys
25 April 1912	Collège Sainte-Marie (Jesuits)	"Dollard"	Boys

List of
Abbreviations

AAM   Archives de l'archidiocèse de Montréal

ACECM   Archives of the Montreal Catholic School Commission

ACND   Archives des Sœurs de la congrégation de Notre-Dame, Montreal

AFEC   Archives des Frères des écoles chrétiennes, Laval

AJC   Archives des Jésuites au Canada, Montreal

AMCQ   Archives du Musée de la civilisation, Quebec

ANQ-M   Archives nationales du Québec, Vieux-Montréal, Montreal

APM   Archives Passe-Mémoire, Montreal

ASGM   Archives des Sœurs grises de Montréal

AUCSS   Archives de l'Univers culturel de Saint-Sulpice, Montreal

AUDM   Archives de l'Université de Montréal

AUM   McGill University Archives, Montreal

CND   Congrégation de Notre-Dame

CRCE   Archives of the Eastern Townships Resource Centre, Lennoxville, QC

Notes

Introduction

1   Ouellette-Michalska, *L'amour de la carte postale*, 14.

2   I use the plural form to underline the plurivocity of otherness and to avoid the concept's "fetishism."

3   The title of the book by Cree and Métis writer Emma LaRocque, *When the Other Is Me*, exactly describes this process. Regarding the education of Indigenous children, see Miller, *Shingwauk's Vision*; and Truth and Reconciliation Commission, *Canada's Residential Schools: The History*, Part 1, *Origins to 1939*, vol. 1. Also of interest is a special issue of *Historical Studies in Education*, "Revisiting the Histories of Indigenous Schooling and Literacies" (2017).

4   Aledejebi, "'Girl You Better Apply"; Lafrance, "Appréhender le monde"; Maynard, *Policing Black Lives*; McCallum, "To Make Good Canadians."

5   LaRocque, *When the Other Is Me*, 7.

6   It is understood that there is a historical link between the construction of these figures of alterity and the shared experience of a group of individuals who have been assigned to or are claiming certain identities.

7   Hartog, *Le miroir d'Hérodote*, 328.

8   Lüsebrink, "La construction de l'Autre," 85–86.

9   Ibid., 87.

10   The great majority of the textbooks analyzed were published in Quebec, with the eleven exceptions published in Toronto. The latter consist of one textbook on Canadian history and ten on reading in English; they were all used by anglophone students in Quebec.

11   The selection of these textbooks relied on multiple criteria. For works published after 1860, in most cases I used textbooks that had been approved by the Conseil de l'Instruction publique, Quebec's public education council, for each of the subjects mentioned above. The selection was made possible thanks to

the catalogue of Québécois school textbooks assembled by Paul Aubin and his team, which is available online on Laval University's website. Regarding textbooks published prior to 1860, they were chosen based on their importance, as determined by the historiography and by consulting the archives of various institutions that mention using them.

12   For the *Journal de l'instruction publique* and the *Journal of Education*, I thoroughly perused the issues from 1857 to 1861, inclusively, as well as those for 1864, 1869, 1874, and 1879. For the other periodicals, I made a digital search of entire documents using the following key words and their English equivalents: arabe, barbare, bizarre, chinois, émotion, esquimau, imagination, indien, indigène, mission, nègre, nos peaux-rouges, nos sauvages, patagon, voyage.

13   ACND, 200/110/13, Exposition de Paris, Daily exercises, 3rd year, cours moyen [1898–1899].

14   "Analyse logique (d'après P. Larousse)," *L'Enseignement primaire*, 18th year (1 May 1897), 407.

15   Leonardo, *Race Framework*; Stanley, "Antiracism Without Guarantees."

16   Ngo, "Racism in Canadian Education," 176.

Chapter 1

1   Ahmed, *Strange Encounters*, 2–4. In studies on French Canada, normally the stranger, "he who is not from here," is English or an immigrant.

2   Sartre, *Being and Nothingness*, 252.

3   In the thinking of these male philosophers, women are the Absent Others, as they are in the Canadian school representations in the nineteenth century.

4   Sartre, *Being and Nothingness*, 280–81.

5   Muyembe, *Le regard et le visage*, 104–5.

6   Ibid., 106.

7   Ibid., 113.

8   Levinas, *Alterity and Transcendence*, 101.

9   Ibid., 103–4.

10   Levinas, "Trace of the Other," 351.

11   Levinas, *Time and the Other*.

12   Ibid., 82–83.

13   Levinas, "Emmanuel Levinas: visage," 136.

14   Sartre, *Anti-Semite and Jew*, 76.

15   Ahmed, *Strange Encounters*, 61.

16 Young, *Justice and the Politics*, 125.

17 Hall, *Identités et cultures*; Hall, "Race, the Floating Signifier," 13.

18 Sartre, *Being and Nothingness*, 261.

19 Levinas, *Autrement qu'être*, 184; Levinas, *Alterity and Transcendence*, 98–101.

20 Ricoeur, *Soi-même comme un autre*, 222.

21 Ouellette-Michalska, *L'amour de la carte postale*, 24. The italics are the author's.

22 Ibid., 138. She adds, "The passion for difference finds less gratification in love for the Indian than in a fascination with the code," 139–40.

23 Ahmed, *Strange Encounters*, 21.

24 Ibid., 3.

25 Pieterse, *White on Black*, 226.

26 Morrison, *Origin of Others*, 3.

27 Pieterse, *White on Black*, 233.

28 Ibid., 233.

29 Morrison, *Origin of Others*, 29–30.

30 Sartre, *Anti-Semite and Jew*, 44.

31 Ouellette-Michalska, *L'amour de la carte postale*, 140.

32 Hall, *Identités et cultures*, 102; Hall, "Race, the Floating Signifier," 10.

33 Butler, *Le pouvoir des mots*; LaRocque, *When the Other Is Me*.

34 Ricœur, *Temps et récit*.

35 Todorov, *La conquête de l'Amérique*, 163.

36 LaRocque, *When the Other Is Me*, 4–5.

37 Ouellette-Michalska, *L'amour de la carte postale*, 129.

38 Lüsebrink, *Identité collective et altérité*, 85–86.

39 Ibid., 81.

40 Ricœur, *La mémoire, l'histoire, l'oubli*, 99.

41 Young, *Justice and the Politics*, 98–99.

42 Sartre, *Anti-Semite and Jew*, 57.

43 Young, *Justice and the Politics*, 123.

44 Hentsch, *Raconter et mourir*, 9–33.

45 Fabian, *Time and the Other*, 154–55; Sartre, *Anti-Semite and Jew*, 84.

46 Hentsch, *Raconter et mourir*, 12.

47 AMCQ, Collection Thomas Chapais, Composition exercise book of Hectorine Langevin, 1867–68.

48　Hentsch, *Raconter et mourir*, 419.

49　Ouellette-Michalska, *L'amour de la carte postale*, 135.

50　Ibid., 62.

51　Ahmed, *Strange Encounters*, 40.

52　Todorov, *Nous et les autres*, 139.

53　Schaub, *Pour une histoire politique*, 48.

54　Hall, *Civilising Subjects*, 18.

55　Emma LaRocque presents the story of civilization in a more dichotomous way (much used by the Euro-Canadians in the nineteenth century), in what she calls the *civ/sav* doctrine (civilization/savagery). See LaRocque, *When the Other Is Me*, 38–47.

56　Delsol, "Politique et altérité," 41.

57　Todorov, *Nous et les autres*, 147–48. Emphasis is in original.

58　Harvey, *American Geographics*, 21.

59　Ahmed, *Strange Encounters*, 10. Emphasis is in original.

60　Pingel, *UNESCO Guidebook*, 9.

61　Pericles Trifonas, "Introduction," in *Pedagogies of Difference*, 2.

62　Ibid., 1.

63　Chalvin and Chalvin, *Comment on abrutit nos enfants*, 9, 47–49; Vincent and Arcand, *L'image de l'Amérindien*; Sugunasiri, *Smarten Up, Indians*; Kenny, "The Middle East in Canadian Social Science."

64　Lebrun, "La figure de l'étranger"; McAndrew, Oueslati, and Helly, *Le traitement de l'islam*.

65　In this regard, the entire oeuvre of Timothy J. Stanley traces a strong connection between Canadian educational history and the importance of anti-racist education today.

66　Two books by Daniel Francis, without dealing solely with educational materials, provide a synthesis of representations of the Canadian national body and its Others since the end of the nineteenth century: *The Imaginary Indian* and *National Dreams*. See also Clark, "Images of Aboriginal People."

67　Provenzo, *Culture as Curriculum*, 6.

68　See Gagnon, *De l'oralité à l'écriture*, 118.

69　See the special edition of the journal *Paedagogica Historica* titled "The Colonial Experience in Education: Historical Issues and Perspectives," *Paedagogica Historica*, Suppl. (1995). See also the special edition "Education and Ethnicity," *Paedagogica Historica* 37, no. 1 (2001).

70　This observation applies only to the anglophone and francophone historiographies.

71   Mangan, *"Benefits Bestowed"?*; Mangan, *Imperial Curriculum.*

72   Mangan, *"Benefits Bestowed"?*, 1.

73   Manceron, "École, pédagogie et colonies"; Bancel and Daniel, "Éduquer." See also Boyer, Clerc, and Zancarini-Fournel, *L'école aux colonies*; Daeninckx, *L'école des colonies.*

74   "'Empires Overseas' and 'Empires at Home': Postcolonial and Transnational Perspective on Social Change in the History of Education," *Paedagogica Historica* 45, no. 6 (2009).

75   For example: Savarèse, "Livres noirs pour petits blancs"; Bérubé, "Le monde raconté"; Morgan, "Over One Hundred Years"; Bell et al., "Empire to Nationhood"; Bowersox, *Raising Germans*, 119–64; Brückenhaus, "Ralph's Compassion."

76   Olsen, *Juvenile Nation*; Olsen, *Childhood, Youth and Emotions*; Vallgårda, *Imperial Childhoods and Christian Mission.*

77   Bowersox, *Raising Germans*, 6.

78   Maddrell, "Discourses of Race"; Wilinsky, *Learning to Divide*; Paasi, "Changing Pedagogies of Space"; Harvey, *American Geographics*, 54–55; Bowersox, *Raising Germans*; Egresi, "Representation of 'Other' Cultures."

79   Wilinsky, *Learning to Divide*, 146.

Chapter 2

1   The convent at Hochelaga was then run by the Sisters of the Holy Names of Jesus and Mary. A native of New York, Agnes Hallock spent some of her school years in Montreal at the Hochelaga convent. (ANQ-M, Fonds Agnes Hallock, School notebook from the Hochelaga convent [c. 1860]).

2   ANQ-M, Fonds Agnes Hallock, School notebook from the Hochelaga convent [c. 1860], 227; Hodgins, *Lovell's General Geography*, 11.

3   "Miscellany," *Journal of Education* (May–June 1879), 94. The *Journal of Education* was the English-language counterpart of the *Journal de l'instruction publique*, both of them published monthly by the Département de l'instruction publique du Canada-Est and then by the Province of Quebec, from 1857 to 1879.

4   H.M., "The Natural Sciences in Common Schools," *Journal of Education* (January 1864): 5.

5   *Journal de l'instruction publique* (September–October 1864): 139.

6   Toussaint, *Géographie moderne*, ii–vi.

7   Holmes, *Nouvel Abrégé de Géographie moderne*, viii.

8   Anonymous, *Lovell's Advanced Geography*, 2.

9   Frères des écoles chrétiennes, "Preface," no pag., *New Illustrated Geography*.

10   "Annual Meeting of the Provincial Association of Protestant Teachers," *Journal of Education* (October–November 1874): 160.

11   Borthwick, *British-American Reader*, vii. Another very "Canadian" reader was published in Toronto in 1867 by James Campbell, *The Fifth Book of Reading Lessons for the Use of Schools in the British-American Provinces*.

12   Frères des écoles chrétiennes, *New Illustrated Geography*.

13   Mitchell, *System of Modern Geography*.

14   Sœurs de la congrégation de Notre-Dame, *Géographie*.

15   Aubin and Simard, *Les manuels scolaires*, 21.

16   AUM, Fonds Montreal High School and High School for Girls, Rector's Memoranda of Former Years, 1897.

17   AUM, Fonds Montreal High School and High School for Girls, High School Prospectus, 1900–1914.

18   Ibid.

19   Martin, "Instruction publique," *Journal de l'instruction publique* (January–February 1879): 14.

20   "Nouvelles et faits divers," *Journal de l'instruction publique* (April 1857): 88.

21   *Twelfth Annual Report of the Colonial Church and School Society*, 9.

22   Anonymous, *Lovell's Introductory Geography*, 13.

23   Frères des écoles chrétiennes, *New Primary Illustrated Geography*, 22.

24   Frères des écoles chrétiennes, *Géographie illustrée, cours moyen*, 2nd ed. of *Géographie intermédiaire illustrée*, 14.

25   Montpetit and Devisme, *Abrégé de Géographie moderne*, 95.

26   Ibid., 274.

27   Frères des écoles chrétiennes, *Lectures choisies, quatrième livre*, 17.

28   "Bulletin des sciences," *Journal de l'instruction publique* (August–September 1861): 160.

29   AFEC, D002/102/03, C503877, "Circulaire aux Séminaires, Collèges et Couvents subventionnés et non-subventionnés, 10 décembre 1877," 2.

30   *L'instruction publique de la province de Québec à l'exposition colombienne de Chicago. Rapport de l'honorable secrétaire provincial*, 5.

31   *Educational Record of the Province of Quebec* (October 1885): 259.

32   "Editorial Notes," *Educational Monthly and School Chronicle* (January 1879): 60.

33   "The Canada Educational Monthly and the Paris Exhibition," *Journal of Education* (January–February 1879): 15–17.

34   Montpetit, *Nouvelle série de livres, troisième livre*, 252–53.

35   Sœurs de la congrégation de Notre-Dame, *Géographie, cours supérieur*, 259–60, 268.

36   Ibid., 270.

37   Pratt, *Imperial Eyes*, 3.

38   De Saint-Martin, "Le Tour du Monde," *Journal de l'instruction publique* (February–March 1864): 20.

39   "Monthly Summary," *Journal of Education* (June–July 1857): 107–8. The Indian Revolt began on 10 May 1857 at Meerut.

40   Edmond Joly, son of Pierre Joly de Lotbinière and brother of Henri-Gustave Joly de Lotbinière, who would become the Quebec premier from 1878 to 1879, was born in 1832. From the early 1850s, he served in India and then in Crimea. Following a brief stay in Canada, he again left for India in 1857. He was killed in September 1857 during the siege of Lucknow.

41   "Editorial," *Journal of Education* (November 1857): 167.

42   Hall, *Civilising Subjects*, 17.

43   "Papers on India," *Journal of Education* (November 1857): 159.

44   *Le Canadien* (25 November 1857), 4. The translation presented by the *Journal of Education* had lightly censored the section in which Joly describes the rape of European women and the massacre of their husbands. "Letters of a Canadian officer," *Journal of Education* (November 1857): 165–66.

45   Luttrell, "The General Exercise Hour," *The Educational Record of the Province of Quebec* (August 1883): 192–95.

46   "Dictée. La fin d'une race," *L'Enseignement primaire*, 13th year (1 September 1891), 6.

47   "The Historical Sciences," *Fifth Book of Reading Lessons*, 288.

48   Fabian, *Time and the Other*, 154.

49   "The Historical Sciences," *Fifth Book of Reading Lessons*, 291.

50   Holmes, *Nouvel Abrégé de Géographie moderne*, 59.

51   Hingston, "Climate of Canada," in Borthwick, *British-American Reader*, 131.

52   Frères des écoles chrétiennes, *New Primary Illustrated Geography*, 6; Frères des écoles chrétiennes, *Nouvelle Géographie illustrée, cours moyen*, 10; Frères des écoles chrétiennes, *New Illustrated Geography*, 4.

53   Calkin, *Calkin's New Introductory Geography*, 15.

54   "The Languages of Our Globe," *High School Magazine* (1 October 1912): 3 (AUM, Fonds Montreal High School and High School for Girls, High School Magazine).

55 Sœurs de la congrégation de Notre-Dame, *Géographie, cours primaire et intermédiaire*, 72, 96.

56 Hartog, *Anciens, modernes, sauvages*, 38–40.

57 Fabian, *Time and the Other*, 63.

58 *Oeuvre de la Sainte-Enfance en Canada*, 23–24.

59 The Reverend gave this "illustrated" speech on Yukon and Alaska at the annual congress of Protestant teachers from the Province of Quebec in 1901. "Editorial Notes," *The Canada Educational Monthly* (November 1901): 353.

60 "Du choix des livres," *L'Enseignement primaire*, 16th year (1 June 1895), 297.

61 Ibid.

62 "Correspondance d'un Inspecteur d'écoles," *L'Enseignement primaire*, 2nd year (2 October 1882), 176–79.

63 Hartog, *Le miroir d'Hérodote*, 536.

64 Holmes, *Nouvel Abrégé de Géographie moderne*, 162.

65 Fabian, *Time and the Other*, 144.

66 Toussaint, *Petit abrégé de géographie*, 77.

67 ACND, 326/200/27 B.60, Daily assignments by students of the Congrégation Notre-Dame, Académie Visitation, Montreal, 1891 to 1892.

68 Frères des écoles chrétiennes, *Nouvelle géographie illustrée*, 19.

69 Holmes, *Nouvel Abrégé de Géographie moderne*, 180.

70 As in the case of many authors of school textbooks, we do not have much information on the life of J.N. Miller, aside from the fact that after completing teacher training, he worked in education for the rest of his life, by turns as a teacher, school inspector, and public servant ("J.N. Miller," *Les manuels scolaires québécois*, http ://www.bibl.ulaval.ca/ress/manscol/auteurs/auteursm.html).

71 Holmes, *Nouvel Abrégé de Géographie moderne*, 185; Miller, *Nouvelle géographie élémentaire adaptée*, 128.

72 Toussaint, *Abrégé d'Histoire du Canada*, 11.

73 Zagumny and Pulsipher, "'Races and Conditions of Men,'" 422.

74 Frères des écoles chrétiennes, *Extrait du cours théorique*, 4.

75 Hartog, *Le miroir d'Hérodote*, 348.

76 Pratt, *Imperial Eyes*, 62.

77 Magnan, *Cours français de lectures graduées, degré moyen*; Magnan, *Cours français de lectures graduées, degré supérieur*.

78 Robert, *Méthode pratique*, 65.

79 Toussaint, *Géographie moderne*, 1868.

80 Frères des écoles chrétiennes, *New Primary Illustrated Geography*, 36.

81   Also referring to the reader's reaction, Toussaint writes that the customs of Asian populations "trigger our surprise" (Toussaint, *Géographie moderne*, 320–21).

82   Calkin, *Calkin's New Introductory Geography*, 53; Anonymous, *Second Reader*, 38.

83   Sœurs de la congrégation de Notre-Dame, *Géographie, cours supérieur*, 228.

84   Miller, *New Elementary Geography*, 15.

85   APM, Fonds Serge Lafrance, Notebooks of daily assignments by Anny Pilon, 1895–1897.

86   Calkin, *Calkin's New Introductory Geography*, 98.

87   Frères des écoles chrétiennes, *Nouvelle géographie illustrée*, 12.

88   Frères des écoles chrétiennes, *New Illustrated Geography*, 6.

89   Frères des écoles chrétiennes, "Introduction," in *Histoire du Canada*.

90   Miller, *Nouvelle géographie élémentaire*, 128.

91   Miller, *New Elementary Geography*, 123.

92   Dumézil, "Introduction," *Les barbares*, xi.

93   Frères des écoles chrétiennes, *Lectures graduées, troisième livre*, 50.

94   Fecteau, *Pauper's Freedom*, 3, 8.

95   Ibid., 38.

96   Toussaint, *Géographie moderne*, 226.

97   Hodgins, *Lovell's General Geography*, 58.

98   Miller, *New Elementary Geography*, 108.

99   Pinnock, *Catechism of Geography*, 55.

100   Zagumny and Pulsipher, "Races and Conditions of Men," 412.

101   Montpetit and Devisme, *Abrégé de Géographie moderne*, 309. The incidence of public opinion being expressed in independent Turkestan is also noted, 291.

102   Frères des écoles chrétiennes, *New Illustrated Geography*, 73.

103   Toussaint, *Géographie moderne*, 109, 210, 213.

104   Holmes, *Nouvel Abrégé de Géographie moderne*, 64.

105   De Brumath, *Précis d'Histoire du Canada*, 5.

106   Sœurs de la congrégation de Notre-Dame, *Lecture à haute voix, cours moyen*, 131.

107   Toussaint, *Abrégé d'Histoire du Canada*, 98.

108   Borthwick, *British-American Reader*, 63.

109   Miller, *Nouvelle géographie élémentaire*, 38.

110   Garneau, *Abrégé de l'Histoire du Canada*, 24.

111   Montpetit and Devisme, *Abrégé de Géographie moderne*, 181.

112   Roy, "Expeditions of Champlain," in Borthwick, *The British-American Reader*, 34.

113   Toussaint, *Géographie moderne*, 126.

114   Frères des écoles chrétiennes, *Nouvelle géographie illustrée*, 77, 83; Calkin, *Calkin's New Introductory Geography*, 66; Frères des écoles chrétiennes, *New Primary Illustrated Geography*, 34.

115   Calkin, *Calkin's New Introductory Geography*, 66–67.

116   ACND, 312/922/6, École Notre-Dame-des-Anges, Montréal, Competitive assignments for students in 1st, 3rd and 4th grades, June 1883.

117   ACND, 309/700/13, Daily homework assignments of Séraphine Marchand, Académie Saint-Joseph, Montreal [1892–1893].

118   Egyptian army soldiers who had rebelled under the direction of Ahmed Urabi.

119   *Fourth Reading Book, Royal Canadian Series*, 342.

120   Garneau, *Abrégé de l'Histoire du Canada*, 226.

121   Hentsch, "L'altérité dans l'imaginaire occidental," 350.

122   De Brumath, *Précis d'Histoire du Canada*, 10.

123   Hentsch, "L'altérité dans l'imaginaire occidental," 351. Emphasis is in original.

124   Garneau, *Abrégé de l'Histoire du Canada*, 54; Frères des écoles chrétiennes, *Nouvelle géographie illustrée*, 74.

125   Hodgins, *Lovell's General Geography*, 23.

126   Frères des écoles chrétiennes, *Nouvelle géographie illustrée*, 74.

127   Montpetit and Devisme, *Abrégé de Géographie moderne*, 321.

128   Miller, *New Elementary Geography*, 103, 133.

129   AJC, Fonds Collège Sainte-Marie, C-0001/S7/SS3/D3, Students' performances, 1864–1869; ACND, 326/000/347, Programmes, "Esther, drame en trois actes [Esther, drama in three acts]," n.d.

130   ACND, 200/110/11, Exposition de Paris, Daily assignments, Cours moyen, 1re classe [1898–1899].

131   See Hentsch, *Imagining the Middle East*, 128. The dictation is drawn from Volney's book *Ruines ou Méditations sur les révolutions des Empires*, published shortly after the French Revolution.

132   Ibid., 128–29.

133   ACND, 200/110/11, Exposition de Paris, Daily assignments, Cours moyen, 1re classe [1898–1899].

134   AFEC, 509372, "Frère Flamian."

135   "Nouvelles et faits divers," *Journal de l'instruction publique* (December 1861):
       212. See also Millard, *Félicien David*, 85–92.

136   AJC, Fonds Collège Sainte-Marie, C-0001/S7/SS3/D3, Students' perfor-
       mances, 1870–1879.

137   "Mgr Langevin au Mont Saint-Louis," *La Minerve*, 1 May 1895, 3.

138   Frères maristes, *Méthode pratique de style*, 21.

139   "Synonymes," *L'Enseignement primaire*, 1st year (15 April 1881), 93.

140   "L'Arabe et son cheval," in Montpetit, *Nouvelle série, quatrième livre*, 17–18.

141   "Dictée," *L'Enseignement primaire*, 5th year (15 September 1885), 174.

142   ACND, 660/055/7, Exercices d'orthographe, n.d., 65.

143   "Dictée. La Fantasia," *L'Enseignement primaire*, 17th year (15 October 1895),
       65.

144   Said, *L'Orientalisme*; Hentsch, *Imagining the Middle East*.

Chapter 3

1   "Bulletin géographique," *L'Enseignement primaire*, 14th year, no. 3 (1 October
       1892), 47; "Bulletin géographique," *L'Enseignement primaire*, 14th year, no. 6
       (15 November 1892), 95.

2   Le Breton, "Notes sur les imaginaires," 54.

3   Miller, *Nouvelle géographie élémentaire*, 13.

4   Le Breton, "Notes sur les imaginaires," 59.

5   Fabian, *Time and the Other*, 121.

6   "Grammar," *Journal of Education* 1, no. 7 (September 1857): 131.

7   Perreault in Montpetit, *Nouvelle série, quatrième livre*, 66.

8   Duclos, *Leçons de style*, 58.

9   Holmes, *Nouvel Abrégé de Géographie moderne*, 267–68.

10   Frères des écoles chrétiennes, *New Illustrated Geography*, 18.

11   Anonymous, *Lovell's Advanced Geography*, 138.

12   Calkin, *New Introductory Geography*, 83.

13   Miller, *Nouvelle géographie élémentaire*, 147. The English version of his textbook
       makes the same statement in a slightly different form.

14   Sœurs de la congrégation de Notre-Dame, *Géographie, cours supérieur*, 260.

15   Toussaint, *Géographie moderne*, 37.

16   Frères des écoles chrétiennes, *New Illustrated Geography*, 11.

17   De Bourbourg, in Sœurs de la congrégation de Notre-Dame, *Lecture à haute voix, cours élémentaire*, 82–83.

18   Montesquieu, in *Nouvelle série, quatrième livre*, 132–33.

19   Miller, *New Elementary Geography*, 15.

20   CRCE, Fonds Education, Students File, Student related materials (1854–1900) [from 1853 to 1857].

21   Calkin, *Calkin's New Introductory Geography*, 62.

22   *Journal de l'instruction publique* 1, no. 12 (December 1857): 233.

23   Hodgins, *Lovell's General Geography*, 96, 99.

24   Holmes, *Nouvel Abrégé de Géographie moderne*, 272–75.

25   Duvernay-Bolens, *Les géants patagons*, 12–13.

26   Fauvelle-Aymar, *L'invention du Hottentot*, 365.

27   Ibid., 88.

28   Holmes, *Nouvel Abrégé de Géographie moderne*, 257.

29   Fauvelle-Aymar, *L'invention du Hottentot*, 91.

30   Toussaint, *Géographie moderne*, 298.

31   Sœurs de la congrégation de Notre-Dame, *Géographie, cours supérieur*, 34.

32   Duvernay-Bolens, *Les géants patagons*, 14.

33   Pigeon, *Géographie à l'usage des écoliers*, 4, 6.

34   Holmes, *Nouvel Abrégé de Géographie moderne*, 86–87.

35   Duvernay-Bolens, *Les géants patagons*, 63.

36   Calkin, *Calkin's New Introductory Geography*, 43.

37   Sœurs de la congrégation de Notre-Dame, *Géographie, cours primaire et inter-médiaire*, 63.

38   Anonymous, *Éléments de Géographie moderne*, 19.

39   Holmes, *Nouvel Abrégé de Géographie moderne*, 35. At that time, the term "mediocre" signified "that which is between big and small, good and bad," *Dictionnaire de l'Académie française* (Paris: Paul Dupont, 1835), 85.

40   Montpetit and Devisme, *Abrégé de Géographie moderne*, 36.

41   Borthwick, *British-American Reader; Fifth Book of Reading Lessons*. The fifth reading textbook in Montpetit's series, published in 1877, also contains a fifteen-page passage on the "polar regions" (Montpetit, Nouvelle série, cinquième livre, 74–88).

42   Toussaint, *Géographie moderne*, 152.

43   "Miscellany," *Journal of Education*, no. 6–7 (June–July 1874): 108.

44   *Fifth Book of Reading Lessons*, 289–90.

45   Frères des écoles chrétiennes, *New Illustrated Geography*, 6.

46   Gayon, "Le corps racialisé," 292.

47   Toussaint, *Géographie moderne*, 18.

48   Frères des écoles chrétiennes, *Nouvelle géographie illustrée*, 10–11.

49   Anonymous, *Modern School Geography*, 5.

50   Frères maristes, *Atlas-géographie*, 11.

51   Hodgins, *Lovell's General Geography*, 10.

52   "The Presbyterian College, Montreal," *Journal of Education* [April 1874]: 59.

53   Frères des écoles chrétiennes, *New Primary Illustrated Geography*, 8.

54   Frères des écoles chrétiennes, *Géographie illustrée*, 8.

55   Miller, *Nouvelle géographie élémentaire*, 16; Miller, *New Elementary Geography*, 13; Sœurs de la congrégation de Notre-Dame, *Géographie, cours supérieur*, 33.

56   Frères des écoles chrétiennes, *Nouvelle géographie illustrée*, 49.

57   Frères maristes, *Atlas-géographie*, 15.

58   Frères des écoles chrétiennes, *Nouvelle géographie illustrée*, 10.

59   Ibid., 20–21.

60   Anonymous, *Lovell's Intermediate Geography*, 21.

61   Miller, *Nouvelle géographie élémentaire*, 14.

62   Calkin, *Calkin's New Introductory Geography*, 18.

63   Ibid., 23.

64   Miller, *Nouvelle géographie élémentaire*, 27.

65   Ibid., 12.

66   Ibid., 13–14.

67   Frères maristes, *Atlas-géographie*, 15.

68   Scott, *De Groulx à Laferrière*, 67.

69   Gingras, in *Lectures graduées, troisième livre*, 77–78; Casgrain, *Nouvelle série de livres de lecture . . . troisième livre*, 171–74.

70   Miller, *New Elementary Geography*, 13; see also 141, 148.

71   Ibid., 154.

72   Ibid., 123.

73   Ibid., 130. In 1907, the question of "Asiatic labor" was twice debated by the Montreal High School's Debating Club (AUM, Fonds Montreal High School and High School for Girls, Minutes of High School Literary and Debating Society, 1906–1908).

74   Frères des écoles chrétiennes, *Nouvelle géographie illustrée*, 81; Montpetit and Devisme, *Abrégé de Géographie moderne*, 367.

75   Young, *Colonial Desire*, 96.

76   Calkin, *Calkin's New Introductory Geography*, 39–40; Pinnock, *Catechism of Geography*, 39–40.

77   Frères des écoles chrétiennes, *Nouvelle géographie illustrée*, 87.

78   Frères maristes, *Atlas-géographie*, 100.

79   Anonymous, *Éléments de Géographie moderne*, 85.

80   Holmes, *Nouvel Abrégé de Géographie moderne*, 221.

81   Toussaint, *Géographie moderne*, 223.

82   "Dictation," *L'Enseignement primaire*, 5th year (15 September 1885), 174.

83   Montpetit and Devisme, *Abrégé de Géographie moderne*, 317; Itti, *L'image des civilisations*, 80.

84   Frères des écoles chrétiennes, *Nouvelle géographie illustrée*, 77.

85   Stoler, *Race and the Education of Desire*; Young, *Colonial Desire*; Lane, *Ruling Passion*.

86   Lane, *Ruling Passion*, 6.

87   Sœurs de la congrégation de Notre-Dame, *Géographie, cours moyen et cours supérieur*, 342, 366.

88   Stoler, *Race and the Education of Desire*, 174.

89   Young, *Colonial Desire*, 175–77.

90   Holmes, *Nouvel Abrégé de Géographie moderne*, 54; Hodgins, *Lovell's General Geography*, 44.

91   Clyde, "Characteristics of New World," in *The Fifth Book of Reading Lessons*, 29.

92   Panese, "La fabrique du 'Nègre,'" 59.

93   ACND, 312/560/119, Compositions de Berthe Girard, élève du Mont Sainte-Marie, 1899–1907.

94   Frères des écoles chrétiennes, *Nouvelle géographie illustrée*, 20.

95   Toussaint, *Géographie moderne*, 266.

96   Holmes, *Nouvel Abrégé de Géographie moderne*, 244.

97   Toussaint, *Géographie moderne*, 266, 292.

98   Montpetit and Devisme, *Abrégé de Géographie moderne*, 355.

99   Frères des écoles chrétiennes, *Nouvelle géographie illustrée*, 83–84.

100   Pieterse, *White on Black*, 43.

101   Frères des écoles chrétiennes, *New Illustrated Geography*, 77.

102   Holmes, *Nouvel Abrégé de Géographie moderne*, 252–53.

103   Toussaint, *L'Enseignement primaire,* 1st year (15 March 1881), 70.

104   Holmes, *Nouvel Abrégé de Géographie moderne,* 250.

105   *L'Enseignement primaire,* 1st year (1881), 70.

106   Ibid.; *L'Enseignement primaire,* 2nd year (1 September 1882), 152.

107   Itti, *L'image des civilisations,* 56.

108   *Second Reading Book* (Royal Canadian Series), 70–73. The same story was published in *Le Couvent* in 1895 (D'Arlincourt, "Les deux nègres," *Le Couvent,* 11th year, no. 3 [November 1895], 44–47]).

109   AUDM, Fonds Rodolphe Lemieux, P1114, Cahier de collège, "L'esclave noir" (13 October 1880), 133.

110   "Partie pratique," *L'Enseignement primaire,* 13th year, no. 6 (16 November 1891), 87.

111   Sœurs de la congrégation de Notre-Dame, *Géographie, cours primaire et intermédiaire,* 15; Sœurs de la congrégation de Notre-Dame, *Géographie, cours moyen et cours supérieur,* 32.

112   ACND, Fonds du Bureau des études, Pedagogical notes for teaching Geography by Sœur S. Fabien [from 1899 to 1903].

113   Pieterse, *White on Black,* 53.

114   "Séminaire de Québec," *Le Canadien,* 15 August 1838, 3.

115   Holmes, *Nouvel Abrégé de Géographie moderne,* 254.

116   Ibid., 47; Anonymous, *Éléments de Géographie moderne,* 24. Regarding erasure from history of the memory of slavery in Quebec, see Mackey, *L'esclavage et les Noirs.*

117   Hodgins, *Lovell's General Geography,* 37.

118   Toussaint, *Géographie moderne,* 85. Regarding Canadian support of the Confederate cause, see Winks, *Blacks in Canada,* 270–71, 288–89; and Lamonde, *Histoire sociale des idées au Québec,* 396.

119   Pieterse, *White on Black,* 64.

120   Toussaint, *Géographie moderne,* 266–67.

121   Miller, *Nouvelle géographie élémentaire,* 141.

122   Toussaint, *Géographie moderne,* 293.

123   "Langue française," *L'Enseignement primaire,* 23rd year, no. 6 (February 1902), 365.

124   ACND, 200/110/13, Exposition de Paris, Daily assignments, Cours moyen, 3e classe [1898–1899].

125   Sœurs de la congrégation de Notre-Dame, *Lecture à haute voix, cours élémentaire,* 246.

126 "Langue française," *L'Enseignement primaire*, 30th year, no. 6 (February 1909), 357.

127 Magnan, *Cours français de lectures graduées, degré moyen*, 43.

128 Toussaint, *Géographie moderne*, 97.

129 Anonymous, *Second Reader*, 97.

130 "Orthographie, idées et grammaire," *L'Enseignement primaire*, 20th year, no. 9 (May 1899), 558.

131 Boëtsch and Villain-Gandossi, "Introduction," Hermès, *La Revue* 30 (2001/2): 20.

Chapter 4

1 Auclair, "Formation nationale à l'École primaire," *L'Enseignement primaire*, 33rd year, no. 8 (April 1912), 508–9.

2 Francis, *Imaginary Indian*.

3 ACND, 200/110/25, Exposition de Paris, Daily assignments, Cours élémentaire, 7e classe [1898–1899].

4 Magnan, *Cours française, supérieur*, 322–25; Garneau in Montpetit, *Nouvelle série, deuxième livre*, 85–88; De Bourbourg in Sœurs de la congrégation de Notre-Dame, *Lecture à haute voix, cours élémentaire*, 82–83.

5 ACND, 326/000/317, Daily assignments—Histoire du Canada, Pensionnat de Villa Maria [between 1899 and 1900].

6 Clyde, "Characteristics of New World," in *The Fifth Book Reading Lessons*, 25–29.

7 Garneau in Montpetit, *Nouvelle série, deuxième livre*, 85–88; Garneau, *Abrégé de l'Histoire du Canada*, 23.

8 Toussaint, *Abrégé d'Histoire du Canada*, 11. Emphasis is the author's.

9 Magnan and Ahern, *Mon premier livre*, 109.

10 LaRocque, *When the Other Is Me*, 62.

11 Magnan, *Cours français, supérieur*, 322.

12 LaRocque, *When the Other Is Me*, 53.

13 Magnan, *Cours français, supérieur*, 322.

14 Assikinack, "Indian Fasting," in Borthwick, *British-American Reader*, 197–99.

15 For a short biography of Francis Assikinack, see Leighton, "Assikinack, Francis."

16 Borthwick, *British-American Reader*, 199. The same kind of exceptionalization of an Indigenous individual can be found in Hodgins, *A School History of Canada*, 115–16.

17   Truth and Reconciliation Commission of Canada, *Final Report, Vol. 1, Canada's Residential Schools*, 219–41.

18   Miles, *Histoire du Canada pour les enfants*, 20–25; Frères des écoles chrétiennes, *Histoire du Canada*, 11–12; De Brumath, *Précis d'Histoire du Canada*, 8–9.

19   Gélinas, *Les Autochtones dans le Québec*, 59.

20   Hodgins, *School History of Canada*, 99. Hodgins was the only writer to make studying the Indigenous ethnography optional.

21   Frères des écoles chrétiennes, "Introduction," *Histoire du Canada*, n.p.

22   Miles, *Child's History of Canada*, 22.

23   Borthwick, "Preface," *British-American Reader*.

24   LaRocque, *When the Other Is Me*, 54.

25   Calkin, *Calkin's New Introductory Geography*, 27.

26   ACND, 315/850/106, Daily assignments, 4e et 6e année du cours [St-Roch, Quebec, half-boarding], 1882.

27   Frères des écoles chrétiennes, *Nouvelle géographie illustrée*, 30.

28   Frères des écoles chrétiennes, *Lectures choisies*, 367; Montpetit and Devisme, *Abrégé de Géographie moderne*, 78.

29   ACND, Guide pour les leçons orales de géographie (2 lessons of 20 minutes per week), Montreal, 1915, 51.

30   Jeffers, *History of Canada*, 7.

31   Ibid.

32   Mrs. Moodie, "The Maple Tree," in Borthwick, *British-American Reader*, 100–102.

33   Taché, "Le géant des Méchins," in Montpetit, *Nouvelle série de livres de lecture, quatrième livre*, 73–79.

34   Anonymous, "Our Trip to the Country," in *Second Reading Book* (Royal Canadian Series), 12.

35   Brantlinger, *Dark Vanishings*, 3.

36   "Character and Decay of the North American Indians," in Borthwick, *British-American Reader*, 200.

37   De Nadaillac, "Dictée. La fin d'une race," *L'Enseignement primaire*, 13th year, no. 1 (September 1891), 6.

38   Brantlinger, *Dark Vanishings*, 2.

39   Bouvier and Allard, "Introduction," *L'histoire nationale à l'école québécoise*, 9–14.

40   Allard, "L'enseignement de l'histoire nationale (1831–1873)," *L'histoire nationale à l'école québécoise*, 49.

41   Brian Gettler presented his concept of the term in a presentation entitled "Recolonizing Confederation: Indigenous Policy and the Making of Canada" at the study day "The Other 60s: A Decade That Shaped Canada and the World," held at the University of Toronto on 22 April 2017.

42   On this point, the considerable work of Patrice Groulx must be mentioned. He demonstrated the central role of Indigenous people in building the myth of Dollard (Groulx, *Pièges de la mémoire*).

43   LaRocque, *When the Other Is Me*, 68.

44   Ricoeur, *La mémoire, l'histoire, l'oubli*, 96–97.

45   Bouvier and Allard, *L'histoire nationale à l'école québécoise*, 14.

46   Toussaint, *Abrégé d'Histoire du Canada*, 55–56.

47   Bell, *Cult of the Nation in France*, 94–95.

48   Brantlinger, *Dark Vanishings*, 62.

49   CECM, Fonds Direction générale, Bureau du directeur général, Reports, Philippe Perrier, 1907–1909, 68.

50   Coates and Morgan, *Heroines and History*, 4.

51   Montpetit, *Nouvelle série de livres de lecture, deuxième livre*, 97–100.

52   ASGM, Fonds École Notre-Dame des Neiges, Daily exercise notebooks of Marie-Louise Sarrazin, 1899.

53   Brisebois, "Quatre-vingt-dix-septième conférence de l'Association des Instituteurs de la circonscription de l'école normale Jacques-Cartier, tenue le 26 mai 1893," *L'Enseignement primaire*, 15th year, no. 7 (2 December 1893), 104.

54   Gélinas, *Les Autochtones dans le Québec post-confédéral*, 76.

55   Garneau, *Abrégé de l'Histoire du Canada*, 12.

56   Ibid., 46.

57   Bishop Laflèche, "Les Canadiens-Français sont réellement une nation," in Frères des écoles chrétiennes, *Lectures choisies*, 57.

58   ANQ-M, Fonds P, Couvent de Saint-Antoine, Magog, Dictation notebook of Emma Comtois, maternal grandmother of Jacques Fauteux, [188x].

59   Ibid.

60   Sœurs de la congrégation de Notre-Dame, *Le syllabaire gradué*, 75–76.

61   Frères des écoles chrétiennes, *Extrait du cours théorique*, 61.

62   Gélinas, *Les Autochtones dans le Québec post-confédéral*, 71.

63   ACND, 309/420/4, Daily assignments, Cours moyen, Saint-Jean [1909].

64   ACND, 326/000/317, Daily assignments—Canadian history, Pensionnat de Villa Maria [from 1899 and 1900].

65   Magnan and Ahern, *Mon premier livre*, 127.

66   Toussaint, *Abrégé d'Histoire du Canada*, 28.

67   Toussaint, *Géographie moderne*, 40.

68   Frères des écoles chrétiennes, *Extrait du cours théorique*, 61.

69   Lagacé, *Cours de lecture à haute voix . . . écoles modèles et élémentaires*, 102–3.

70   LaRocque, *When the Other Is Me*, 43.

71   Garneau, *Abrégé de l'Histoire du Canada*, 45.

72   AMCQ, Fonds du Séminaire de Québec, Société St-Louis de Gonzague et Société Laval, "Miscellaneous," 1858–1877, 17.

73   Marquis, "Procès-verbal de la 157e conférence de l'Association des Instituteurs de la circonscription de l'École normale Laval," *L'Enseignement primaire*, 36th year (September 1914), 25.

74   Nansot, "La rédaction à la petite école," *L'Enseignement primaire*, 36th year, no. 10 (June 1915), 596–600.

75   Emphasis is the author's.

76   Deloria, *Playing Indian*.

77   Magnan, "Le programme officiel," *L'Enseignement primaire*, 12th year (1 January 1981), 3–4.

78   Frève, "La géographie," *L'Enseignement primaire*, 17th year (15 November 1895), 94.

79   Blais, "L'*Histoire du Canada* à l'École primaire," *L'Enseignement primaire*, 30th year (March/April 1909), 402.

80   "The Value of Literature in Moral Training," *Educational Record of the Province of Quebec* 13, no. 6/7 (June–July 1893): 172.

81   "Grand Concours," *La Patrie*, 9 May 1908. See also the issues for 6, 13, and 20 June 1908.

82   One of the winners was unable to choose among all of Canada's heroes, among them the Patriots.

83   "Notre Concours—Les réponses des Lauréats," *La Patrie*, 20 June 1908, 6.

84   Ibid.

85   "La joie de nos Petits Lauréats," *La Patrie*, 11 July 1908, 2.

86   "Notre Concours—les réponses," *La Patrie*, 6 June 1908, 6.

87   Raymond-Dufour, "Le Canada français face à sa destinée," 73.

88   Frères des écoles chrétiennes, *Extrait du cours théorique*, 67 and 69.

89   Sœurs de la congrégation de Notre-Dame, *Lecture à haute voix, cours supérieur*, 121.

90   Lagacé, "Avant-propos [Preface]," in *Cours de lecture à haute voix*, 103.

91   Garneau, "Chant de guerre chez les Sauvages [Savages' war song]," in Lagacé, *Cours de lecture à haute voix*, 174–75.

92   The assumption that this figure disappeared from the anglophone corpus beginning in the 1880s should be confirmed by further research into the English-Canadian educational corpus. For this reason, the last section of this chapter will focus only on the francophone corpus.

93   Francis, *Imaginary Indian*, 158.

94   Morrison, *Playing in the Dark*.

95   Lemire, "Le mythos indien," in *Formation de l'imaginaire littéraire au Québec*, 184.

96   Masse, "L'Amérindien 'd'un autre âge,'" 114.

97   Paterson, *Figures de l'Autre*, 172; Destrempes, "Mise en discours."

98   Morrison, *Playing in the Dark*, 17.

99   Ibid., 66.

100   Scott, *De Groulx à Laferrière*, 34.

101   Nurse, "Thanking God for . . . ?"

102   Brantlinger, *Dark Vanishings*, 3.

103   Lemire, *Formation de l'imaginaire littéraire*, 184.

104   Francis, *Imaginary Indian*, 57.

105   Delâge, "La peur de 'passer pour . . . ,'" in *Les Cahiers des Dix*, 29.

106   ACND, 660/600/7, Notebook of short plays, including "Coaïna" and "La Bergère de Pibrac" [n.d.]. The other information was found in the annals of the Villa Maria boarding school (ACND, 326/000/271, Journal du pensionnat de Villa Maria de 1866 à 1874, 153). This operetta was likely inspired by the novel *Coaina, the Rose of the Algonquins* by Anna Hanson Dorsey, published in 1866.

107   AJC, Fonds Collège Sainte-Marie, C-0001/S7/SS3/D4, Actes et prologues, "Donnacona," 1881.

108   AFEC, Symphorien-Louis (FÉC), "Dollard," 1899 (manuscript).

109   Chartier, *Au bord de la falaise*, 15.

110   The scripts are identified by the abbreviations Coaïna–C; Donnacona–Don; Dollard–Dol.

111   Jones, "First But Not the Last," 13.

112   Morrison, *Playing in the Dark*, 28.

113   Un demi-siècle au Mont-Saint-Louis, 1888–1938, 226, 442; Faubert, *Orphelinat Saint-Arsène*, 13.

114   A séance académique was a public or private event during which students performed dramatic plays or skits with musical interludes.

115   "Séance académique," *Le Canadien*, 6 February 1860, 4.

116   AMCQ, Fonds du Séminaire de Québec, Académie Saint-Denys, Séances de l'Académie Saint-Denys (1858–1880), Séance académique on 5 February 1860.

117   Green, "Tribe Called Wannabee," 35.

118   The excerpt is drawn from a newspaper clipping dated 29 January 1881 and inserted into the manuscript of the play "Donnacona" (AJC, Fonds Collège Sainte-Marie, C-0001/S7/SS3/D4, Actes et prologues, Donnacona, 1881).

119   *Montreal Gazette*, 31 June [*sic*] 1869, quoted in the *Journal of Education* 8–9 (August–September 1869): 161.

120   *La Minerve*, 7 July 1864, 2.

121   Deloria, *Playing Indian*, 6.

122   *La Minerve*, 14 July 1865, 2; *La Minerve*, 20 March 1868, 1; *La Minerve*, 27 March 1868, 2.

123   *La Minerve*, 20 March 1868, 1. The importance of ethnography in this practice is outlined by Deloria in *Playing Indian*, 117.

124   *La Minerve*, 14 July 1865, 2.

125   Paterson, *Figures de l'Autre*, 168.

126   Colonnier, "Au Mont St-Louis," *La Patrie*, 26 April 1900, 10.

127   *La Minerve*, 1 July 1874, 3.

128   "Champlain," *La Patrie*, 30 April 1902, 2. See also *Le Journal des Trois-Rivières*, 8 July 1878, 2.

129   Christin, "Lettre ouverte [Open letter]," *La Patrie*, 14 May 1900, 6.

130   Bowersox, *Raising Germans*, 21.

131   Frey, "Victorian Girls," 169.

132   ACND, 200/110/11, Exposition de Paris, Daily assignments, Cours moyen, 1re classe [1898–1899].

133   "Examens Publics et Distributions de Prix dans les Universités, les Collèges, Académies et Écoles Modèles," *Journal de l'instruction publique*, no. 8 (August 1864): 112.

134   Frey, "Victorian Girls," 174.

135   Ibid., 235.

136   Green, "Tribe Called Wannabee," 49.

137   Rousseau, "Mémoires et identités blessées," 11.

138   Said, *L'Orientalisme*, 25.

139   Frey, "Victorian Girls," 205.

Chapter 5

1   Stanworth, *Visibly Canadians*, 16.

2   Hall, "Race, the Floating Signifier," 15.

3   Mitchell, *What Do Pictures Want?*, 337.

4   Joly, *Introduction à l'analyse de l'image*, 9.

5   Burke, *Eyewitnessing*, 14.

6   Mitchell, *Iconology*, 45.

7   Ahern, "Leçon d'anglais d'après la méthode naturelle," *L'Enseignement primaire*, 36th year (September 1914), 41.

8   Boily and Roth, "Avant-propos," in Mitchell, *Que veulent les images?*, 9.

9   Fabian, *Time and the Other*, 112.

10   ACND, 660/310/14, Program of studies [n.d.].

11   "Monthly summary," *Journal of Education* 10 (December 1857): 188.

12   AUM, Fonds Montreal High School and High School for Girls, High School Department of McGill College, 1857–1858.

13   "L'enseignement par les Yeux," *Journal de l'instruction publique* 10 (Octobre 1871): 131–32.

14   Frères des écoles chrétiennes, *Nouvelle géographie illustrée*, iii.

15   Frères des écoles chrétiennes, *Nouvelle géographie primaire illustrée*.

16   Miller, *Nouvelle géographie élémentaire*, 3.

17   Magnan, *Cours français de lectures graduées, degré inférieur*, xiv.

18   Chauveau, "Laval University," 109.

19   AUM, Fonds Montreal High School and High School for Girls, High School Prospectus, 1900–1914; ACND, 312/560, Mont Sainte-Marie, Montréal [likely dating from the first decade of the 20th century]; AFEC, Fonds Frère Louis Roland (Rolland-Germain), N50106/507128, Lettre du Frère Marie-Victorin à Rolland-Germain, 8 January 1915.

20   Boëtsch and Ferrié, "Du daguerréotype au stéréotype," 169.

21   Renonciat, *L'image pour enfants*, 5–6.

22   Edwards, "La photographie ou la construction," 324.

23   Jay, "A Parting Glance," 613.

24   I sometimes shorten the name of the Œuvre de la Sainte-Enfance to "Sainte-Enfance" and of the Association of the Holy Childhood to "Holy Childhood."

25   Hodgins, *Lovell's General Geography*, 4. In his book's preface, Hodgins thanks "Messrs. Blackie & Sons, of Glasgow [. . .] for the copies of some of the better

class of engravings which appear in their admirable work, the Imperial Gazetteer, and which have been chiefly taken from recent books of travel."

26   Wilkes, *Narrative of the United States*, vol. 2, 396–97.

27   Zagumny and Pulsipher, "'Races and Conditions of Men,'" 420.

28   *Colton's Common School Geography*, 1872, 16.

29   Bancel and Blanchard, "De l'indigène à l'immigré," 13.

30   Belmenouar and Combier, *Bons baisers des colonies*, 12–13.

31   Miller, *Nouvelle géographie élémentaire*, 4.

32   Miller, *New Elementary Geography*, 4.

33   According to information in the Library of Congress inventory, the photograph of the street in Old Cairo was taken between 1867 and 1899.

34   Blanchard, Boëtsch, and Snoep, *Exhibitions*, 190.

35   Edwards, "La photographie ou la construction," 323.

36   Boëtsch and Ferrié, "Du daguerréotype au stéréotype," 170.

37   Taraud, *Mauresques*, 94.

38   Mitchell, *What Do Pictures Want?*, 295.

39   Magnan, "Les difficultés que rencontrent les institutrices," *L'Enseignement primaire*, no. 8 (April 1906), 463.

40   Burke, *Eyewitnessing*, 125–30. The term "hypervisibility" comes from W.J.T. Mitchell's essay "What Do Pictures Want?" in *What Do Pictures Want?*, 34.

41   Burke, *Eyewitnessing*, 125–26.

42   The engravings illustrating the martyrdom of Father Bréfeuf exemplify this argument. The Indians represented in the images do not look like ferocious demons. The value of making an independent pictorial analysis is once again confirmed.

43   Miller, *Nouvelle géographie élémentaire*, 141.

44   Mitchell, *What Do Pictures Want?*, 34.

45   Kristóf, "Domesticating Nature," 40–66.

46   Ibid., 49–50.

47   See also Hodgins, *Lovell's General Geography*, 16. In the same spirit, one of the textbooks by the Frères des écoles chrétiennes features an engraving of the animals of America in which a canoe is visible. (Frères des écoles chrétiennes, *Géographie illustrée, cours moyen*, 12.)

48   In addition to Miller's treatment, there are three other exceptions: an engraving of Queen Victoria and two illustrations of Western "pioneers" depicting a family of immigrants.

49   Taraud, *Mauresques*, 72.

50   MacKenzie, *Orientalism*, 46.

51   Frères des écoles chrétiennes, *Nouvelle géographie illustrée*, 83.

52   Magnan and Ahern, *Mon premier livre*, 43.

53   Pieterse, *White on Black*, 166.

54   *Rapport de l'Œuvre*, 57.

Chapter 6

1   The auditorium was the largest in the city at that time and was also reputed to be one of the most beautiful in North America; Lebel, "La nuit où périt," 66.

2   *Iu-Chien-Tchou-Iom: Trois entretiens illustrés sur la Chine donnés à Québec, Avril 1872 par le R.P. Vasseur, S.J.*, n.p., n.d. I learned of this source on reading Michelle King's book *Between Birth and Death: Female Infanticide in Nineteenth-Century China*. My thanks to Professor King for having generously shared this source, of which the only copy is in the Shanghai Library Bibliotheca Zi-ka-wei; King, *Between Birth and Death*, 111–14.

3   "Lecture aux petits enfants de Québec (suite et fin)," *Le Courrier du Canada*, 22 May 1872, 1.

4   *Iu-Chien-Tchou-Iom*, 10, 11.

5   Ibid., 30.

6   Ibid., 30–31.

7   King, *Between Birth and Death*, 112.

8   Prochaska, "Little Vessels," 103; Moruzi, "'Donations Need Not Be Large,'" 190–213.

9   Stanley, "Missionary Regiments," 391–403; Jensz, "Firewood, Fakirs and Flags," 167–91; Morrison, "'Impressions Which Will Never Be Lost,'" 388–93; Heywood, "Missionary Children," 451.

10   Heywood, "Missionary Children," 449.

11   *Œuvre de la Sainte-Enfance. Notice spéciale* (1859), 15.

12   Stornig, "Between Christian Solidarity," 249–50.

13   Prochaska, "Little Vessels,"112.

14   CRCE, Fonds Mansonville United Church, Brome County Sunday School Association, F. Minutes, 1891–1899.

15   Ibid.

16   Ibid.

17   AUM, Fonds Montreal High School and High School for Girls, "Minutes of High School Literary and Debating Society, 1906–1908."

18   AUM, Fonds Montreal High School and High School for Girls, High School Prospectus, 1900–1914, "Prospectus for Session 1909–1910," 58.

19   CRCE, Fonds Dunham Ladies' College, Yearbooks, 1879–1964.

20   Œuvre de la Sainte-Enfance ou Association des Enfants chrétiens, pour Le rachat des Enfants infidèles en Chine, et dans les autres pays idolâtres. Sous la protection spéciale de NN. SS. Les évêques, E.-J. Bally, Place Sorbonne, n.d. This notice was addressed to Mgr Ignace Bourget, Bishop of Montreal, probably between the late 1840s and 1851; AAM, Œuvre de la Sainte-Enfance [1845–1923].

21   Extrait de la notice de Mgr. De Forbin-Janson, évêque de Nancy et de Toul, sur l'Œuvre de la Sainte-Enfance, pour le rachat des enfants infidèles en Chine, et dans les autres pays idolâtres. Sous la protection spéciale de NN. SS. les évêques, n.p., n.d. (AAM, Œuvre de la Sainte-Enfance [1845–1923]).

22   *Rapport de l'Œuvre*, 19.

23   Heywood, "Missionary Children," 452.

24   *État présent de la Sainte-Enfance*, 9.

25   Œuvre de la Sainte-Enfance, Collectes de 1895. For rural parishes, 39 percent of entries were in the name of a parish. It is possible that the rural schools played a big part in these contributions.

26   ACND, 326/000/270, Journal du pensionnat de Villa Maria de 1854 à 1868. Bourget's request relates to a visit to Canada by two priests from Algeria in spring 1868.

27   A primary school teacher, "Association des institutrices," *L'Enseignement primaire*, no. 1 (September 1904), 21.

28   AAM, Œuvre de la Sainte-Enfance [1845–1923], "Lettre de Mgr Bruchési à Mgr de Teil," 28 October 1914.

29   AAM, Œuvre de la Sainte-Enfance [1845–1923], "Lettre de sa grandeur Monseigneur Paul Bruchési, Archevêque de Montréal, autorisant les Sœurs missionnaires de l'Immaculée-Conception à faire le travail de la Sainte-Enfance dans les Écoles de son Diocèse," 20 May 1916.

30   Bancel and Blanchard, "Civiliser," 149.

31   Stanley, "From the 'poor heathen,'" *International Bulletin of Missionary Research*, no. 1 (2010): 4, cited in Morrison, "The 'joy and heroism,'" 174.

32   Bernstein, *Racial Innocence*, 4.

33   *Œuvre de la Sainte-Enfance*, 44. See also *Rapport de l'Œuvre*, 27–28.

34   *Noces d'or de la Sainte Enfance*, 28.

35   The representation of China's inhabitants circulating in the missionary propaganda differed noticeably from the stereotypes associated with the ideology of the "yellow peril" in North America at the end of the nineteenth century. About this, see Kuo Wei Tchen and Yeats, *Yellow Peril!*

36   During the 1860s, the associates of Montreal's Holy Childhood believed that they were redeeming the "little Chinese" with their alms, but their donations

were in fact sent to the Red River region in present-day Manitoba; AAM, Œuvre de la Sainte-Enfance [1845–1923], "Lettre de M. De Girardin à Bourget," 29 May 1861.

37 AJC, Fonds Collège Sainte-Marie, C-0001/S7/SS4/D10, Association de la Sainte Enfance et de la Propagation de la foi, 1854–1863.

38 *Noces d'or de la Sainte Enfance*, 31.

39 Stornig, "Between Christian Solidarity and Human Solidarity," 255.

40 "La Sainte-Enfance," *L'Abeille* 36 (9 June 1853): 3.

41 *Rapport de l'Œuvre*, 14.

42 Ibid., 15.

43 Holmes, *Nouvel abrégé*, 185; Toussaint, *Géographie moderne*, 255.

44 *Œuvre de la Sainte-Enfance*, Notice spéciale, 8.

45 *Noces d'or de la Sainte-Enfance*, 1893, 29.

46 *Rapport de l'Œuvre*, 45–48.

47 Olsen, "History of Childhood"; Olsen, *Childhood, Youth and Emotions*; Frevert et al., *Learning How to Feel*; Vallgårda, *Imperial Childhoods*; Olsen, *Juvenile Nation*.

48 Heywood, "Missionary Children," 461.

49 Ahmed, *Cultural Politics of Emotion*, 10–11.

50 Ibid., 10–11.

51 *Rapport de l'Œuvre*, 14.

52 Brückenhaus, "Ralph's Compassion," 75.

53 The English verb "move," as in the expression "I am moved," very effectively expresses the corporality and the movement inherent in emotion. It takes place on a body in response to another body.

54 AUCSS, Fonds Œuvre de la Sainte-Enfance, P1/35.32/02, Lettres de la congrégation de Notre-Dame, 1851–1878.

55 Ibid. The emphasis is the author's.

56 Ahmed, *Cultural Politics of Emotion*, 21.

57 *Rapport de l'Œuvre*, 24.

58 Ahmed, *Cultural Politics of Emotion*, 193.

59 *Rapport de l'Œuvre*, 33.

60 Mgr Têtu, *Noces d'or de la Sainte-Enfance*, 8.

61 AUCSS, Fonds Œuvre de la Sainte-Enfance, P1/35.32/02, Lettres de la congrégation de Notre-Dame, 1851–1878.

62 King, *Between Birth and Death*, 126.

63   *Petit manuel des associés de la Sainte-Enfance*, 50.

64   Ibid., 23.

65   *Rapport de l'Œuvre*, 20.

66   Vallgårda, Alexander, and Olsen, "Emotions and the Global Politics," 21; See also Olsen, "Introduction," in *Childhood, Youth and Emotions*, 3.

67   *Notice sur la Ste Enfance*, 16.

68   AAM, Œuvre de la Sainte-Enfance [1845–1923], "Lettre de Daniel à Bourget," 20 January 1862.

69   *Notice sur la Ste Enfance*, 16–17.

70   *Rapport de l'Œuvre*, 39.

71   *Annales de l'Œuvre de la Sainte-Enfance* 46, no. 282 (February 1895): 422–23.

72   Auclair, *Histoire des Sœurs de Sainte-Anne*, 86.

73   Langlois, *Délia*, 23–25.

74   *Notice sur la Ste Enfance*, 31–32.

75   Plourde, "Un genre en construction," 45.

76   *Rapport de l'Œuvre*, 24; Plourde, "Un genre en construction," 44; ACND, 326/000/347, Programmes, Séance, 17 March 1894. The young men at the *collèges classiques* also occasionally organized bazaars and events for the benefit of the missions; AUCSS, Fonds Collège de Montréal, i2/7.3/2 Bazars, 1873–1893.

77   AUCSS, Fonds Œuvre de la Sainte-Enfance, P1/35.32/02, Lettres de la congrégation de Notre-Dame, 1888–1897.

78   Ibid.

79   AUCSS, Fonds Correspondance, P1/21.74/5/02, Correspondance de Joseph Alexandre Baile, p.s.s, Copy of the letter sent by François Daniel. Daniel was talking principally about his own desires, since the Sulpicians' archives do not indicate permission to state a real interest in the association on the part of the priests of Saint-Sulpice.

80   AUCSS, Fonds Correspondance, P1/21.74/5/02, Correspondance de Joseph Alexandre Baile, p.s.s, Letter from Frère Armin-Victor, f.é.c, 10 October 1881.

81   AUCSS, Fonds Œuvre de la Sainte-Enfance, P1/35.32/02, Lettres de la congrégation de Notre-Dame, 1880–1885.

82   *Noces d'or de la Sainte Enfance*, 39–40.

83   AUCSS, Fonds Œuvre de la Sainte-Enfance, P1/35.32/02, Lettres de la congrégation de Notre-Dame, 1888–1897.

84   Buies, *La Lanterne* 1, no. 2 (4 February 1869): 340. Emphasis is author's.

85   Ibid.

86   Sarcey would then be sued by the association's director in Paris for damages and required to pay compensation; see *La Gazette des familles canadiennes: journal religieux, agricole et d'économie domestique* 7, no. 3 (January 1876), 86. His critique extended over several issues of the newspaper in November and December 1875.

87   Sarcey, "Les petits chinois," *Le XIXe siècle* (30 November 1875), 2.

88   Ibid.

89   The Sainte-Enfance's hold on children's sensibility lasted for many decades. In a personal account from 2002, Québécois author Michel Tremblay talks about the attachment he had, as a child, to the missionary work for the "little Chinese"; see Tremblay, "Petit chinois à vendre," 165–75.

90   *Rapport de l'Œuvre,* 19.

91   Ahmed, *Cultural Politics of Emotion,* 3.

92   *Petit manuel des associés de la Sainte-Enfance,* 20.

93   *Noces d'or de la Sainte Enfance,* 31.

94   *État présent de la Sainte Enfance,* 6.

95   ACND, 312/560/2a, Annales du Mont Sainte-Marie, 1878–1889, 185.

96   A Canadian Woman, "Une nouvelle Revue Africaine mensuelle," *L'Enseignement primaire,* 33rd year, no. 3 (November 1911), 186.

97   "Les religieuses de N.-D. D'Afrique," *L'Enseignement primaire,* 32nd year, no. 10 (June 1911), 635.

98   *Petit manuel des associés de la Sainte-Enfance,* 51–53.

99   *Rapport de l'Œuvre,* 24. The relations established between "saving" Chinese newborns and maternity provide interesting parallels with the idea of "maternal colonialism." See Jacobs, "Maternal Colonialism" 453–76; Turkyilmaz, "Maternal Colonialism."

100 *Rapport de l'Œuvre,* 15.

101 Ibid., 25.

102 ACND, 200/110/23, Exposition de Paris, Daily assignments, Cours élémentaire, 5e classe [1898–1899].

103 "Dictée. Cours supérieur," *L'Enseignement primaire,* 37th year, no. 1 (September 1915), 43.

104 Father Casgrain, "Le pionnier canadien," in Montpetit, *Nouvelle série de livres de lecture graduée, troisième livre,* 171.

105 AUCSS, Fonds Collège de Montréal, i2/7.3/5, Théâtre, 1898–1959, "La dispute des vocations." The document seems to be a composition by students. The dialogue was performed at least twice in the twentieth century, once in 1915.

106   AUCSS, Fonds Collège de Montréal, i2/7.3/3, Recreational séances, 1875–[1969?].

107   AUCSS, Fonds Collège de Montréal, i2/7.3/5, Théâtre, 1898–1959, "La dispute des vocations," 13.

108   AJC, Fonds Collège Sainte-Marie, C-0001/S7/SS4/D10, Association de la Sainte Enfance et de la Propagation de la foi, 1854–1863.

109   Eduardus, "Mgr Grandin," 205.

110   AUCSS, Fonds Collège de Montréal, i2/6.3.3/41, Collected classwork in Method, Literature and Versification, 1892–1893.

111   AUCSS, Fonds Collège de Montréal, 7.

112   "Les adieux du missionnaire," *L'Opinion publique* (21 June 1877), 298.

113   Anthos, "Chroniques," *Annales térésiennes*, 3rd year (March 1883), 194.

114   ANQ-M, CLG49, Fonds Erle G. Bartlett, A1, "Journal de Erle G. Bartelet," 1900–1901, 31–32. Thanks go to Pierre Gauthier, who drew my attention to these two sources. Thanks to Pierre also for having shared his transcription of the two journals with me.

115   ANQ-M, CLG43, Fonds Émile Léger, S1, D3, "Journal d'Émile Léger," 1900–1901, 26.

116   Ahmed, *Cultural Politics of Emotion*, 192. Emphasis is author's.

117   Ajari, "Être et race."

Conclusion

1   Morrison, *The Origin of Others*, 24.

2   Ahmed, *Strange Encounters*, 144.

3   Giroux, "Thierry Hentsch/Proche-Orient," 245–46.

4   LaRocque, *When the Other Is Me*, 62.

5   Daniel, *National Dreams*, 11.

6   We need only think, for example, of the Idle No More, Black Lives Matter, and Québec inclusif movements, the debates of the Quebec Consultation Commission on Accommodation Practices Related to Cultural Differences, the proposed Charter of Quebec Values, the Quebec City mosque shooting in January 2017, the Commission of Inquiry into relations between Indigenous people and certain public services in Quebec in 2019, Quebec's Bill 21, and the death of Joyce Echaquan.

7   Levinas, *Éthique comme philosophie première*, 93.

8   Honeck, "Innocent Ignorance."

9   LaRocque, *When the Other Is Me*, 169.

Bibliography

Primary Sources

School Textbooks (in chronological order)

GEOGRAPHY

Pigeon, François-Xavier. *Géographie à l'usage des écoliers du Petit Séminaire de Québec.* Quebec: J. Neilson, printers, 1804.

Holmes, Jean. *Nouvel abrégé de géographie moderne, suivi d'un appendice and d'un abrégé de géographie sacrée, à l'usage de la jeunesse.* 2nd ed. Quebec: Neilson and Cowan, 1833.

Pinnock, William. *A Catechism of Geography: Being an Easy Introduction to the Knowledge of the World, and Its Inhabitants; the Whole of Which May Be Committed to Memory at an Early Age.* 1st Canadian ed. Montreal: W. Greig, 1839.

Anonymous. *Éléments de géographie moderne. Imprimé sous la direction de la Société d'éducation du district de Québec. À l'usage des écoles élémentaires.* Quebec: Fréchette, 1841.

Mitchell, Samuel Augustus. *A System of Modern Geography, Comprising a Description of the World, and Its Five Great Divisions, America, Europe, Asia, Africa, and Oceanica, with Their Several Empires, Kingdoms, States, Territories, etc. Adapted to the Capacity of Youth.* Philadelphia: Thomas, Cowperthwait, 1852.

Anonymous. *Modern School Geography and Atlas Prepared for the Use of Schools in the British Provinces.* Montreal and Toronto: J. Campbell; Saint John: J. and A. M'Millan; Halifax: A. and W. Mackinlay; Charlottetown: Laird and Harvi; St. John's: J. Graham, 1865.

Hodgins, John George. *Lovell's General Geography: For the Use of Schools, with Numerous Maps, Illustrations, and Brief Tabular Views*. Montreal: John Lovell; Toronto: Robert and Adam Miller, 1870 [1867].

Toussaint, François-Xavier. *Géographie moderne à l'usage des étudiants de la puissance du Canada*. Quebec: Léger Brousseau, 1868.

Toussaint, François-Xavier. *Petit abrégé de géographie moderne à l'usage des écoles élémentaires*. Quebec: Léger Brousseau, 1870.

Montpetit, André-Napoléon, and Léopold Devisme. *Abrégé de géographie moderne à l'usage de la jeunesse. D'après une nouvelle méthode raisonnée*. Quebec: Léger Brousseau, 1870.

Toussaint, François-Xavier. *An Abridgment of Modern Geography for the Use of Elementary Schools*. Translated by the Ursuline ladies. Quebec: C. Darveau, 1871.

Colton's Common School Geography. New York: Sheldon and Company, 1872.

Mitchell, Samuel Augustus. *A System of Modern Geography, Physical, Political, and Descriptive: Accompanied by a New Atlas of Forty-Four Copperplate Maps, and Illustrated by Two Hundred Engravings*. Philadelphia: J.H. Butler, 1874.

Frères des écoles chrétiennes. *Nouvelle géographie illustrée à l'usage des écoles chrétiennes de la puissance du Canada*. Montreal: Frères des écoles chrétiennes, 1875.

Frères des écoles chrétiennes. *The New Intermediate Illustrated Geography for the Use of the Christian Schools in the Dominion of Canada*. Montreal: J. Chapleau, 1876.

Frères des écoles chrétiennes. *The New Primary Illustrated Geography for the Use of the Christian Schools in the Dominion of Canada*. Montreal: J. Chapleau, 1876.

Frères des écoles chrétiennes, *Géographie illustrée. Cours moyen, 2e éd. de la Géographie intermédiaire illustrée*, Montréal, s. é., 1876.

Frères des écoles chrétiennes. *The New Illustrated Geography for the Use of Christian Schools for the Dominion of Canada*. Montreal: J. Chapleau, 1877.

Frères des écoles chrétiennes. *Nouvelle géographie primaire illustrée à l'usage des écoles chrétiennes de la puissance du Canada*. Montreal: Frères des écoles chrétiennes, J. Chapleau [1878].

Mitchell, Samuel Augustus. *A System of Modern Geography, Physical, Political, and Descriptive: Accompanied by a New Atlas of Forty-Four Copperplate Maps and Illustrated by Two Hundred Engravings*. Philadelphia: J.H. Butler, 1878.

Anonymous. *Lovell's Intermediate Geography: With Maps and Illustrations: Being Introductory to Lovell's Advanced Geography*. Montreal: John Lovell, 1879.

Anonymous. *Lovell's Advanced Geography for the Use of Schools and Colleges: With Maps, Illustrations, Statistical Tables, &c.* Montreal: John Lovell, 1880.

Sœurs de la congrégation de Notre-Dame. *Cartographie*. Montreal: Congrégation de Notre-Dame, 1891.

Sœurs de la congrégation de Notre-Dame. *Géographie à l'usage des élèves de la congrégation de Notre-Dame. Cours primaire et intermédiaire*. Montreal: C.O. Beauchemin [1891].

Sœurs de la congrégation de Notre-Dame. *Géographie à l'usage des élèves de la congrégation de Notre-Dame. Cours supérieur*. Montreal: C.O. Beauchemin [1891].

Frères des écoles chrétiennes. *Géographie illustrée. Cours moyen*. Second edition of *Géographie intermédiaire illustrée*. Montreal: n.p., 1894.

Sœurs de la congrégation de Notre-Dame. *Géographie à l'usage des élèves de la congrégation de Notre-Dame. Cours moyen et cours supérieur*. Montreal: C.O. Beauchemin et Fils, 1897.

Calkin, John Burgess. *Calkin's New Introductory Geography with Outlines of Physiography*. London, Edinburgh, and New York: Thomas Nelson; Halifax: A. and W. Mackinlay, 1898.

Miller, J.-N. *Nouvelle géographie élémentaire adaptée aux écoles canadiennes*. Quebec: Dussault et Proulx, 1901.

Miller, J.-N. *New Elementary Geography Adapted for Use in Canadian Schools*. Montreal: F.E. Grafton [1905].

Frères maristes. *Atlas-géographie comprenant 40 cartes polychromes, 90 gravures et de nombreux devoirs*. Iberville, QC: Procure des Frères maristes, 1908.

Anonymous. *Lovell's Introductory Geography: With Maps and Illustrations: Being Introductory to Lovell's Intermediate Geography*. Montreal: John Lovell, 1911.

CANADIAN HISTORY

Garneau, François-Xavier. *Abrégé de l'histoire du Canada, depuis sa découverte jusqu'à 1840. À l'usage des maisons d'éducation.* Quebec: A. Côté, 1856.

Hodgins, John George. *A School History of Canada, and of the Other British North American Provinces.* Montreal: John Lovell; Toronto: Adam Miller, 1865.

Miles, Henry Hopper. *The Child's History of Canada: For the Use of the Elementary Schools and of the Young Reader.* 2nd ed. Montreal: Dawson, 1876.

Jeffers, James Frith. *History of Canada.* Toronto: Canada Publishing Company, 1879.

Sœurs de la congrégation de Notre-Dame. *Abrégé de l'histoire du Canada en rapport avec l'arbre historique.* Montreal: Eusèbe Sénécal, 1882.

Miles, Henry Hopper. *Histoire du Canada pour les enfants. À l'usage des écoles élémentaires.* Montreal: Dawson, 1888.

Toussaint, François-Xavier. *Abrégé d'histoire du Canada. À l'usage des jeunes étudiants de la province de Québec.* Quebec: N.S. Hardy, 1890.

Leblond de Brumath, Adrien. *Précis d'histoire du Canada. À l'usage des écoles primaires.* Montreal: Librairie Saint-Joseph, Cadieux et Derome, 1895.

READING—FRENCH

Anonymous. *Le livre des enfans.* Quebec: T. Cary, 1834.

Bransiet, Frère Philippe (FPB). *Lectures instructives et amusantes sur diverses inventions, découvertes, etc.* Montreal: J.B. Rolland, 1864.

Juneau, Félix-Emmanuel, and Napoléon Lacasse. *Alphabet ou syllabaire gradué. D'après une nouvelle méthode.* Quebec: C. Darveau, 1872.

Lagacé, Pierre. *Cours de lecture à haute voix, ou Leçons pratiques de lecture française et de prononciation, préparées spécialement pour les écoles canadiennes. À l'usage des écoles modèles et élémentaires.* Quebec: A. Côté, 1875.

Lagacé, Pierre. *Cours de lecture à haute voix, ou Leçons pratiques de lecture française et de prononciation, préparées spécialement pour les écoles canadiennes. À l'usage des écoles normales et des pensionnats.* Quebec: A. Côté, 1875.

F.J.-O.P. *Syllabaire ou premiers exercices de lecture en rapport avec la méthode d'écriture des Frères des écoles chrétiennes.* Quebec: Elzéar Vincent, 1875.

Montpetit, André-Napoléon. *Nouvelle série de livres de lecture graduée, en langue française, pour les écoles catholiques. Seule série approuvée par le Conseil de l'Instruction publique de la province de Québec. Premier livre.* Montreal: J.B. Rolland, 1876.

Montpetit, André-Napoléon. *Nouvelle série de livres de lecture graduée, en langue française, pour les écoles catholiques. Seule série approuvée par le Conseil de l'Instruction publique de la province de Québec. Deuxième livre.* Montreal: J.B. Rolland, 1876.

Montpetit, André-Napoléon. *Nouvelle série de livres de lecture graduée, en langue française, pour les écoles catholiques. Seule série approuvée par le Conseil de l'Instruction publique de la province de Québec. Troisième livre.* Montreal: J.B. Rolland, 1876.

Montpetit, André-Napoléon. *Nouvelle série de livres de lecture graduée, en langue française, pour les écoles catholiques. Seule série approuvée par le Conseil de l'Instruction publique de la province de Québec. Quatrième livre.* Montreal: J.B. Rolland, 1877.

Montpetit, André-Napoléon. *Nouvelle série de livres de lecture graduée, en langue française, pour les écoles catholiques. Seule série approuvée par le Conseil de l'Instruction publique de la province de Québec. Cinquième livre.* Montreal, J. B. Rolland, 1877.

Frères des écoles chrétiennes. *Lectures choisies en prose et en vers. Quatrième livre.* Quebec: Elzéar Vincent, 1891 [1880].

Sœurs de la congrégation de Notre-Dame. *Le syllabaire gradué, ou Le premier livre des enfants.* Montreal: C.O. Beauchemin, 1890.

Frères des écoles chrétiennes. *Syllabaire. Premier livre.* Montreal: n.p., 1891.

Frères des écoles chrétiennes. *Lectures graduées. Troisième livre.* Montreal: n.p., 1891.

Sœurs de la congrégation de Notre-Dame. *Lecture à haute voix. Lectures et récitations précédées d'une étude théorique et pratique de la prononciation française d'après la méthode de M.V. Delahaye. Cours élémentaire.* Montreal: Beauchemin, 1895.

Sœurs de la congrégation de Notre-Dame. *Lecture à haute voix. Lectures et récitations précédées d'une étude théorique et pratique de la prononciation française d'après la méthode de M.V. Delahaye. Cours supérieur.* Montreal: Beauchemin, 1898.

Magnan, J.-Roch. *Cours français de lectures graduées. Degré inférieur.* Montreal: Beauchemin, 1902.

Magnan, J.-Roch. *Cours français de lectures graduées. Degré moyen.* Montreal: C.O. Beauchemin, 1902.

Magnan, J.-Roch. *Cours français de lectures graduées. Degré supérieur.* Montreal: Beauchemin, 1902.

Tremblay, Nérée. *Ab*écé. *Nouvelle méthode de lecture par l'image et l'ancienne épellation. Premier livret.* Montreal: Compagnie d'imprimerie moderne, 1902.

Rochon, T. *Méthode pratique de lecture-écriture. Première partie.* Montreal: Beauchemin, 1902.

Rochon, T. *Méthode pratique de lecture-écriture. Deuxième partie.* Montreal: Beauchemin, 1904.

Rochon, T. *Deuxième livre de lecture: contenant, sous forme de conversation et d'historiettes mises à la portée des enfants, des notions élémentaires de morale, d'histoire sainte, d'histoire du Canada, de géographie, de grammaire et de composition.* Montreal: Beauchemin, 1905.

Sœurs de la congrégation de Notre-Dame. *Lecture à haute voix. Lectures et récitations précédées d'une étude théorique et pratique de la prononciation française d'après la méthode de M.V. Delahaye. Cours moyen.* Montreal: CND, 1909.

OTHERS—FRENCH LANGUAGE

Frères des écoles chrétiennes. *Extrait du cours théorique et pratique.* Montreal: J. Chapleau, n.d.

Robert, E. *Méthode pratique et raisonnée de style et de composition. Première année.* n.p., 1878.

Lippens, Bernard. *Recueil de devoirs. Exercices sur l'application des règles grammaticales, exercices, exercices sur l'orthographe et la dérivation, devoirs d'invention, exercices préparatoires de style, sujets de composition d'un genre simple.* Quebec: J.A. Langlais, 1890.

Germain, A. *La lettre, ou Leçons de style épistolaire à l'usage des écoles primaires.* Quebec: J.A. Langlais, 1890.

Duclos, J. *Leçons de style spécialement destinées aux jeunes garçons: conformes aux nouveaux programmes. Cours préparatoire et élémentaire.* Montreal (Mile End): Institution des sourds-muets, 1891.

Constans, Stanislas. *Le style enseigné par les leçons de choses et la pratique conforme aux nouveaux programmes officiels. Cours élémentaire et moyen.* Montreal (Mile End): Clercs de Saint-Viateur, 1892.

Frères maristes. *Méthode pratique de style et de composition littéraire. Cours élémentaire.* Lévis: Mercier, 1892.

Frères du Sacré-Cœur. *Mes premières leçons de rédaction.* Montreal: Institution des sourds-muets, 1914.

READING—ENGLISH

Goodrich, Samuel G. *Goodrich's Sixth School Reader.* Louisville: Noble Butler, 1857.

Borthwick, John Douglas. *The British-American Reader.* Montreal and Toronto: R. and A. Miller, 1860.

Barber, Jonathan. *The Elements of Elocution: Designed for the Use of Schools.* Montreal: John Lovell, 1860.

Anonymous. *The National Third Reader: Containing Exercises in Articulation, Emphasis, Pronunciation, and Punctuation.* New York: Richard G. Parker and J. Madison Watson, 1865.

Gillespie, Angela. *The Metropolitan Third Reader: Carefully Arranged in Prose and Verse for the Use of Schools.* New York, Boston, and Montreal: D. and J. Sadlier, 1866.

Gillespie, Angela. *The Metropolitan First Reader: Carefully Arranged in Prose and Verse for the Use of Schools.* New York, Boston, and Montreal: D. and J. Sadlier, 1867.

Gillespie, Angela. *The Metropolitan Second Reader: Carefully Arranged in Prose and Verse for the Use of Schools.* New York, Boston, and Montreal: D. and J. Sadlier, 1867.

Anonymous. *The Fifth Book Reading Lessons: For the Use of Schools in the British American Provinces.* Toronto: James Campbell and Son, 1867.

Frères des écoles chrétiennes. *The First Reader Carefully Arranged for the Use of Schools: Part First*. Montreal: Printed for the Brothers of the Christian Schools by Eusèbe Senécal, 1872.

Anonymous. *First Reading Book*. Toronto: Canada Publishing Company [1883].

Anonymous. *Second Reading Book (Royal Canadian Series)*. Toronto: Campbell [1883].

Anonymous. *Third Reading Book (Royal Canadian Series)*. Toronto: Campbell [1883].

Anonymous. *Fourth Reading Book (Royal Canadian Series)*. Toronto: Campbell [1883].

Anonymous. *First Reader: Part I*. Toronto: W.J. Gage [1884].

Anonymous. *First Reader: Part II*. Toronto, W.J. Gage [1884].

Anonymous. *Second Reader*. Toronto: W.J. Gage [1884].

Anonymous. *Third Reader*. Toronto: W.J. Gage [1884].

Anonymous. *Fourth Reader*. Toronto: W.J. Gage [1884].

SECOND LANGUAGE—ENGLISH AND FRENCH

Duval, N. *Lectures choisies pour la jeunesse. Contenant une foule d'anecdotes amusantes, d'historiettes, de contes et de fables, etc. Avec un dictionnaire des mots français*. Translated into English. Montreal: Dawson, 1875.

Nantel, Antonin. *Nouveau cours de langue anglaise selon la méthode d'Ollendorff à l'usage des écoles, académies, pensionnats, collèges*. Montreal: Beauchemin et Valois, 1868.

Robert, E. *Méthode de langue anglaise. Première année*. Montreal: Institution des sourds-muets, 1884.

OTHERS

Cloutier, Jean-Baptiste. *Le premier livre des enfants, ou Méthode rationnelle de lecture*. Quebec: A. Côté, 1875.

Dunn, Oscar. *Manuel de dessin industriel à l'usage des maîtres d'écoles primaires, d'après la méthode de Walter Smith, accompagné de cartes-modèles à l'usage des élèves. Deuxième livre*. Montreal: Duvernay et Dansereau, 1878.

MacVicar, Donald Harvey. *A Complete Arithmetic, Oral and Written: Designed for the Use of Common and High Schools and Collegiate Institutes.* Montreal: Dawson, 1879.

Magnan, Charles-Joseph, and John Ahern. *Mon premier livre: lire, écrire, compter. Éducation, instruction. Manuel des commençants.* Quebec: n.p., 1900.

Archival Sources

Archives nationales du Québec, Vieux-Montréal Branch, Montreal, Canada

Archives of the Anglican Diocese of Montreal, Montreal, Canada

Archives of the Archidiocèse de Montréal, Montreal, Canada

Archives of the Eastern Townships Resource Centre, Lennoxville, Canada

Archives of the Frères de l'instruction chrétienne, La Prairie, Canada

Archives of the Frères de Saint-Gabriel, Montreal, Canada

Archives of the Frères des écoles chrétiennes, Laval, Canada

Archives of the Montreal Catholic School Commission, Montreal, Canada

Archives of the Musée de la civilisation, Quebec, Canada

Archives of the Sœurs de la congrégation de Notre-Dame, Montreal, Canada

Archives of the Sœurs grises de Montréal, Montreal, Canada

Archives of the Univers culturel de Saint-Sulpice, Montreal, Canada

Archives of the Université de Montréal, Montreal, Canada

Archives Passe-Mémoire, Montreal, Canada

McGill University Archives, Montreal, Canada

Pedagogical Periodicals

Journal de l'instruction publique (1857–1879)

Journal of Education (Quebec) (1857–1879)

L'Enseignement primaire (1881–1955)

The Educational Record of the Province of Quebec (1881–1965)

Le Couvent (1886–1899)

L'Abeille, student newspaper of the Petit Séminaire de Québec

Other Sources

Iu-Chien-Tchou-Iom: Trois entretiens illustrés sur la Chine donnés à Québec, Avril 1872 par le R.P. Vasseur, S.J., Missionnaire Apostolique en Chine, Directeur de l'Œuvre Chinoise de St. Luc pour la Propagation de la Foi. n.p., n.d.

Duperrey, Louis Isidore. *Voyage autour du monde, exécuté par ordre du roi, sur la corvette de Sa Majesté, La Coquille, pendant les années 1822, 1823, 1824 et 1825: sous le ministère de S.E.M. le marquis de Clermont-Tonnerre et publié sous les auspices de son excellence M. le cte de Chabrol, ministre de la Marine et des colonies.* 9 vols. Paris: Arthus Bertrand, 1826–1830.

Dictionnaire de l'Académie française. Paris: Paul Dupont, 1835.

Immediate Emancipation: The Speech of Lord Brougham in the House of Lords, on Tuesday, February 20th, 1838, on Slavery and the Slave-Trade. London: Printed for the Central Emancipation Committee, 1838.

Wilkes, Charles. *Narrative of the United States Exploring Expedition during the Years 1838, 1839, 1840, 1841, 1842.* 2 vols. London: Wiley and Putnam (printed by C. Sherman, Philadelphia), 1845.

Circulaire de l'Archevêché de Québec. 10 December 1855.

Le Canadien, 25 November 1857.

Rapport de l'Œuvre de la Sainte-Enfance pour le Canada, la province d'Halifax et les États-Unis. n.p., 1858.

Œuvre de la Sainte-Enfance, *Notice spéciale.* n.p., 1859.

Petit manuel des associés de la Sainte-Enfance. n.p., 1860.

Compte-Rendu de la Sainte-Enfance en Canada. 1860.

Notice sur la Sainte-Enfance. 1860.

Twelfth Annual Report of the Colonial Church and School Society. Montreal: Lovell, 1865.

Œuvre de la Sainte Enfance en Canada. Montreal: Eusèbe Sénécal, 1866.

La lanterne. 4 février 1869.

Le Courrier du Canada. 22 May 1872.

L'Opinion publique. 21 June 1877.

Département de l'Instruction publique. *Exposition scolaire de la province de Québec, Canada: Catalogue.* 1878.

Quelques documents relatifs à l'organisation pédagogique des écoles de la province de Québec (Canada) offerts aux instituteurs de France à l'occasion de leurs visites d'études à l'exposition universelle de 1878. 1878.

Devoirs d'écoliers étrangers recueillis à l'exposition universelle de Paris (1878) et mis en ordre par MM. De Bagnaux, Berger, Brouard, Buisson et Defodon. 1879.

Exposition du Canada, Montréal, 1880. Exposition scolaire de la province de Québec. Catalogue. 1880.

État présent de la Sainte Enfance en Amérique. 1881.

La Sainte-Enfance dans le diocèse de Québec. Quebec: C. Darveau, 1883.

Annales térésiennes, 3rd year, March 1883.

Œuvre de la Sainte-Enfance—Collecte de 1887. 1888.

Faucher de Saint-Maurice. *Loin du pays. Souvenirs d'Europe, d'Afrique et d'Amérique.* vol. 1. Quebec: A. Côté, 1889.

des Écorres, Charles (pseud.). *Au pays des étapes. Notes d'un légionnaire.* Paris and Limoges: Henri Charles Lavauzelle, 1892.

Noces d'or de la Sainte Enfance, 1893. n.p., n.d.

Annales de l'Œuvre de la Sainte-Enfance. 1895.

L'instruction publique de la province de Québec à l'exposition colombienne de Chicago. Rapport de l'honorable secrétaire provincial. Quebec: Charles-François Langlois, 1895.

La Minerve, 67th year, 1 May 1895.

Cycle of Prayer of the General Missionary Society, the Woman's Missionary Society, Epworth Leagues and Sunday Schools for the Methodist Church, Canada: Copied Largely from the Cycle of Prayer of the Student Volunteer Movement for Foreign Missions. 2nd ed. Toronto, 1896.

Têtu, Mgr Henri. *Noces d'or de la Sainte-Enfance à Québec*. Quebec: Compagnie d'imprimerie de Québec, 1901.

"Editorial Notes." *Canada Educational Monthly* 23 (November 1901).

Hixson, Martha B. *Missions in the Sunday School: A Manual of Methods*. Toronto: Methodist Young People's Forward Movement for Missions, 1906.

With the Boys and Girls in Our Mission Fields: A Study Book for Mission Bands and Young People. Toronto: The Woman's Foreign Missionary Society of the Presbyterian Church in Canada, 1911.

Priest, H.C. *Canada's Share in World Tasks*. Toronto: The Canadian Council of the Missionary Education Movement, 1920.

Houston, Mary I. *Talks on the Maple Leaf in Many Lands: For Leaders of Mission Bands and Other Junior Organizations*. Toronto: Canadian Council of the Missionary Education Movement, 1920.

Auclair, Élie-J. *Histoire des Sœurs de Sainte-Anne: les premiers cinquante ans, 1850–1900*. Montreal: Imprimerie des Frères des écoles chrétiennes, 1922.

Gauthier, Henri. *Sulpitiana*. Montreal: Au Bureau des Œuvres paroissiales de St-Jacques, 1926.

Un demi-siècle au Mont-Saint-Louis, 1888–1938. L'album jubilaire. Montreal: Imprimerie De-La-Salle, 1939.

Secondary Sources
Monographs and Anthologies

Abu-Laban, Baha, and Faith Zeadey, eds. *Arabs in America: Myths and Realities*. Wilmette: Medina University Press International, 1975.

Ahmed, Sara. *The Cultural Politics of Emotion*. Edinburgh: Edinburgh University Press, 2014.

———. *Strange Encounters: Embodied Others in Post-Coloniality*. London and New York: Routledge, 2000.

Alatas, Syed Hyssein. *The Myth of the Lazy Native: A Study of the Image of the Malays, Filipinos and Javanese from the 16th to the 20th Century and Its Function in the Ideology of Colonial Capitalism*. London: Cass, 1988.

Anderson, Benedict. *L'imaginaire national. Réflexions sur l'origine et l'essor du nationalisme*. Poche Series. Paris: La Découverte, 2002.

Arnold, David. *Colonizing the Body: State Medicine and Epidemic Disease in Nineteenth-Century India*. Berkeley and Los Angeles: University of California Press, 1993.

Asor Rosa, Alberto, ed. *En marge. L'Occident et ses "autres."* Paris: Éditions Aubier-Montaigne, 1978.

Atroshchenko, Olga, Inessa Kouteinikova, and Patty Wageman. *Russia's Unknown Orient: Orientalist Paintings 1850–1920*. Groningen: Groningen Museum; Rotterdam: NAI Publishers, 2010.

Aubin, Paul. *Les communautés religieuses et l'édition du manuel scolaire au Québec, 1765–1964*. Sherbrooke: Ex Libris, 2001.

———. *L'État québécois et les manuels scolaires au XIXe siècle*. Sherbrooke: Éditions Ex Libris, 1995.

Aubin, Paul, ed. *300 ans de manuels scolaires au Québec*. Montreal: Bibliothèque et Archives nationales du Québec; Quebec: Presses de l'Université Laval, 2006.

Aubin, Paul, and Michel Simard. *Les manuels scolaires dans la correspondance du Département de l'instruction publique 1842–1899: inventaire*. Sherbrooke: Éditions Ex Libris, 1997.

Axelrod, Paul. *The Promise of Schooling. Education in Canada, 1800–1914*. Toronto: University of Toronto Press, 1997.

Bancel, Nicolas, Pascal Blanchard, and Gilles Boëtsch, eds. *Zoos humains. Au temps des exhibitions humaines*. Poche Series. Paris: La Découverte, 2004.

Bancel, Nicolas, Thomas David, and Dominic Thomas, eds. *L'invention de la race. Des représentations scientifiques aux exhibitions populaires*. Paris: La Découverte, 2014.

Barnett, Michael. *Empire of Humanity: A History of Humanitarianism*. Ithaca: Cornell University Press, 2011.

Beaulieu, Alain, and Stéphanie Chaffray, eds. *Représentation, métissage et pouvoir. La dynamique coloniale des échanges entre Autochtones, Européens et Canadiens (XVIe–XXe siècle)*. Quebec: Presses de l'Université Laval, 2012.

Bell, David A. *The Cult of the Nation in France: Inventing Nationalism, 1680–1800*. Cambridge, MA: Harvard University Press, 2001.

Belmenouar, Safia, and Marc Combier. *Bons baisers des colonies. Images de la femme dans la carte postale coloniale*. Paris: Éditions Alternatives, 2007.

Berger, Stefan, and Chris Lorenz, eds. *The Contested Nation: Ethnicity, Class, Religion and Gender in National Histories*. Writing the Nation Series. London: Palgrave Macmillan, 2011.

Bernstein, Robin. *Racial Innocence: Performing American Childhood from Slavery to Civil Rights*. New York: New York University Press, 2011.

Bird, S. Elizabeth. *Dressing in Feathers: The Construction of the Indian in American Popular Culture*. Boulder: Westview Press, 1996.

Blanchard, Pascal, Nicolas Bancel, and Sandrine Lemaire, eds. *Culture impériale 1931–1961*. Mémoires/Histoire Series. Paris: Autrement, 2004.

Blanchard, Pascal, Gilles Boëtsch, and Nanette Jacomijn Snoep, eds. *Exhibitions. L'invention du Sauvage*. Paris: Actes Sud and Musée du Quay Branly, 2011.

Blondin, Denis. *L'apprentissage du racisme dans les manuels scolaires*. Montreal: Agence d'ARC, 1990.

Boëtsch, Gilles, Christian Hervé, and Jacques J. Rozenberg, eds. *Corps normalisé, corps stigmatisé, corps racialisé*. n.p.: De Boeck Supérieur, 2007.

Bouchard, Gérard. *La pensée impuissante. Échecs et mythes canadiens-français (1850–1960)*. Montreal: Boréal, 2004.

Bouvier, Félix, Michel Allard, Paul Aubin, and Marie-Claude Larouche, eds. *L'histoire nationale à l'école québécoise. Regards sur deux siècles d'enseignement*. Quebec: Septentrion, 2012.

Bowersox, Jeff. *Raising Germans in the Age of Empire: Youth and Colonial Culture, 1871–1914*. Oxford: Oxford University Press, 2013.

Boyer, Gilles, Pascal Clerc, and Michelle Zancarini-Fournel, eds. *L'école aux colonies, les colonies à l'école*. Lyon: ENS Éditions, 2013.

Brantlinger, Patrick. *Dark Vanishings: Discourse on the Extinction of Primitive Races, 1800–1930*. Ithaca: Cornell University Press, 2003.

———. *Rule of Darkness: British Literature and Imperialism, 1830–1914.* Ithaca: Cornell University Press, 1988.

Brosseau, Marc. *Les manuels de géographie québécois. Images de la discipline, du pays et du monde—1800–1960.* In collaboration with Vincent Berdoulay. Quebec: Presses de l'Université Laval, 2011.

Brown, Kathleen H. *Schooling in the Clearings: Stanstead 1800–1850.* Stanstead: Stanstead Historical Society, 2001.

Brunn, Stanley D., Anne Buttimer, and Ute Wardenga, eds. *Text and Image: Social Construction of Regional Knowledges.* Leipzig: Institut für Länderkunde, 1999.

Burke, Peter. *Eyewitnessing: The Uses of Images as Historical Evidence.* London: Reaktion Books, 2001.

Burnett, Michael. *Empire of Humanity: A History of Humanitarianism.* Ithaca: Cornell University Press, 2011.

Butler, Judith. *Le pouvoir des mots. Discours de haine et politique du performatif.* Paris: Éditions Amsterdam, 2004. [*Excitable Speech: A Politics of the Performative.* London and New York: Routledge, 2021].

Cabanel, Patrick. *Le tour de la nation par des enfants. Romans scolaires et espaces nationaux (XIXe–XXe siècles).* Paris: Belin, 2007.

Chalvin, Solange, and Michel Chalvin. *Comment on abrutit nos enfants: la bêtise en 23 manuels scolaires.* Montreal: Éditions du Jour, 1962.

Charland, Jean-Pierre. *L'entreprise éducative au Québec, 1840–1900.* Saint-Nicolas: Presses de l'Université Laval, 2000.

Chartier, Roger. *Au bord de la falaise. L'histoire entre certitudes et inquiétude.* Paris: Albin Michel, 2009.

Coates, Colin M., and Cecilia Morgan. *Heroines and History: Representations of Madeleine de Verchères and Laura Secord.* Toronto: University of Toronto Press, 2001.

Colley, Linda. *Britons.* New Haven: Yale University Press, 1992.

Commission de vérité et réconciliation du Canada. *Pensionnats du Canada: l'histoire. Partie 1: des origines à 1939. Rapport final de la Commission de vérité et réconciliation du Canada.* Vol. 1. Montreal and Kingston: McGill-Queen's University Press, 2016.

Corbin, Alain, ed. *Histoire du corps*. Vol. 2, *De la Révolution à la Grande Guerre*. Paris: Seuil, 2005.

Corbin, Alain, Jean-Jacques Courtine, and George Vigarello, eds. *Histoire de la virilité*. Vol. 2, *Le triomphe de la virilité. Le XIXe siècle*. Paris: Seuil, 2011.

Curtis, Bruce. *Ruling by Schooling Quebec: Conquest to Liberal Governmentality—A Historical Sociology*. Toronto: University of Toronto Press, 2012.

Daeninckx, Didier. *L'école des colonies*. Paris: Hoëbeke, 2015.

Dagnoslaw, Demski, Kamila Baraniecka-Olszewska, and Ildikó Sz. Kristóf, eds. *Competing Eyes: Visual Encounters with Alterity in Central and Eastern Europe*. Budapest: L'Harmattan, 2013.

De Cock, Laurence, and Emmanuelle Picard, eds. *La fabrique scolaire de l'histoire. Illusions et désillusions du roman national*. Paris: Agone, 2009.

Deloria, Philip J. *Playing Indian*. New Haven: Yale University Press, 1998.

Demeulenaere-Douyère, Christiane, and Liliane Hilaire-Pérez, eds. *Les expositions universelles. Les identités au défi de la modernité*. Rennes: Presses universitaires de Rennes, 2014.

Deslandres, Dominique, John A. Dickinson, and Ollivier Hubert, eds. *Les Sulpiciens de Montréal. Une histoire de pouvoir et de discrétion (1657–2007)*. Montreal: Fides, 2007.

Droit, Roger-Pol. *Généalogie des barbares*. Paris: Odile Jacob, 2007.

Dufour, Andrée. *Histoire de l'éducation au Québec*. Montreal: Boréal, 1997.

———. *Tous à l'école. État, communautés rurales et scolarisation au Québec de 1826 à 1859*. LaSalle: Hurtubise HMH, 1996.

Dumézil, Bruno, ed. *Les barbares*. Paris: Presses universitaires de France, 2016.

Dumont, Fernand. *Genèse de la société québécoise*. Montreal: Boréal, 1993.

Dupont-Bouchat, Marie-Sylvie, Jacques-Guy Petit, Éric Pierre, Bernard Schnapper, Françoise Tétard, Jean-Marie Fecteau, and Jean Trépanier, eds. *Enfants corrigés, enfants protégés. Genèse de la protection de l'enfance en Belgique, en France, aux Pays-Bas et au Québec, 1820–1914*. Paris: Ministère de la Justice, 1995.

Duvernay-Bolens, Jacqueline. *Les géants patagons. Voyage aux origines de l'homme*. Paris: Éditions Michalon, 1995.

Este, David, Liza Lorenzetti, and Christa Sato, eds. *Racism and Anti-Racism in Canada*. Halifax and Winnipeg: Fernwood Publishing, 2018.

Etherington, Norman, ed. *Missions and Empire*. Oxford: Oxford University Press, 2005.

Fabian, Johannes. *Time and the Other: How Anthropology Makes Its Object*. New York: Columbia University Press, 2014.

Faubert, Adélard, s.g. *Orphelinat Saint-Arsène*. Montreal: L'Institut des Frères de Saint-Gabriel au Canada, 1989.

Fauvelle-Aymar, François-Xavier. *L'invention du Hottentot. Histoire du regard occidental sur les Khoisan (XVe–XIXe siècle)*. Paris: Publications de la Sorbonne, 2002.

Fecteau, Jean-Marie. *The Pauper's Freedom: Crime and Poverty in Nineteenth-Century Quebec*. Translated by Peter Feldsteins. Montreal and Kingston: McGill-Queen's University Press, 2017.

Fitzpatrick, Matthew P. *Liberal Imperialism in Germany: Expansionism and Nationalism, 1848–1884*. New York: Berghahn Books, 2008.

Fougères, Dany, ed. *Histoire de Montréal et de sa région*. Vol. 1, *Des origines à 1939*. Quebec: Presses de l'Université Laval, 2012.

Francis, Daniel. *The Imaginary Indian: The Image of the Indian in Canadian Culture*. Vancouver: Arsenal Pulp Press, 1992.

———. *National Dreams: Myth, Memory, and Canadian History*. Vancouver: Arsenal Pulp Press, 1997.

Franklin, John Hope. *Reconstruction after the Civil War*. Chicago: University of Chicago Press, 1966.

Frevert, Ute, Bettina Hitzer, Pascal Eitler, Stephanie Olsen, Uffa Jensen, Margrit Pernau, Daniel Brückenhaus, Magdalena Beljan, Benno Gammerl, and Anja Laukötter, eds. *Learning How to Feel: Children's Literature and Emotional Socialization, 1870–1970*. Oxford: Oxford University Press, 2014.

Furstenberg, François. *In the Name of the Father: Washington's Legacy, Slavery, and the Making of a Nation*. New York: Penguin Press, 2006.

Gagnon, Serge. *De l'oralité à l'écriture. Le manuel de français à l'école primaire 1830–1900*. Quebec: Presses de l'Université Laval, 1999.

Gallagher, Catherine. *The Body Economic: Life, Death, and Sensation in Political Economy and the Victorian Novel*. Princeton: Princeton University Press, 2006.

Garavaglia, Juan Carlos, Jacques Poloni-Simard, and Gilles Rivière, eds. *Au miroir de l'anthropologie historique. Mélanges offerts à Nathan Wachtel*. Rennes: Presses universitaires de Rennes, 2013.

Gélinas, Claude. *Les Autochtones dans le Québec post-confédéral, 1867–1960*. Quebec: Septentrion, 2007.

Gordon, Allan. *The Hero and the Historians: Historiography and the Uses of Jacques Cartier*. Vancouver: University of British Columbia Press, 2010.

Greelee, James G., and Charles M. Johnston. *Good Citizens: British Missionaries and Imperial States, 1870–1918*. Montreal and Kingston: McGill-Queen's University Press, 2014.

Groulx, Patrice. *Pièges de la mémoire. Dollard des Ormeaux, les Amérindiens et nous*. Gatineau: Vents d'Ouest, 1998.

Guillaume, Isabelle. *Regards croisés de la France, de l'Angleterre et des États-Unis dans les romans pour la jeunesse, 1860–1914. De la construction identitaire à la représentation d'une communauté internationale*. Paris: Honoré Champion, 2009.

Hall, Catherine. *Civilising Subjects: Metropole and Colony in the English Imagination, 1830–1867*. Cambridge, UK: Polity, 2002.

Hall, Donald E., ed. *Muscular Christianity: Embodying the Victorian Age*. Cambridge, UK: Cambridge University Press, 1994.

Hall, Stuart. *Identités et cultures*. Vol. 2, *Politiques des différences*. Prepared for publication by Maxime Cervulle. Paris: Éditions Amsterdam, 2013.

Hardy, René. *Contrôle social et mutation de la culture religieuse, 1830–1930*. Montreal: Boréal, 1999.

Hartog, François. *Anciens, modernes, sauvages*. Paris: Galaade, 2005.

———. *Le miroir d'Hérodote. Essai sur la représentation de l'autre*. Paris: Gallimard, 2001.

Harvey, Bruce A. *American Geographics: U.S. Narratives and the Representation of the Non-European World, 1830–1865*. Stanford: Stanford University Press, 2001.

Heaman, Elsbeth A. *The Inglorious Arts of Peace: Exhibitions in Canadian Society during the Nineteenth Century*. Toronto: University of Toronto Press, 2000.

Henri, Jean-Robert, and Lucienne Martini, eds. *Littératures et temps colonial. Métamorphoses du regard sur la Méditerranée et l'Afrique*. Aix-en-Provence: Édisud, 1999.

Hentsch, Thierry. *Imagining the Middle East*. Translated by Fred. A. Reed. Montreal: Black Rose Books, 1992.

——. *Raconter et mourir. Aux sources narratives de l'imaginaire occidental*. Montreal: Presses de l'Université de Montréal, 2002.

Hily, Marie-Antoinette, and Marie-Louise Lefebvre, eds. *Identité collective et altérité. Diversité des espaces/spécificité des pratiques*. Paris and Montréal: L'Harmattan, 1999.

Hobsbawm, Éric, and Terence Ranger, eds. *L'invention de la tradition*. Paris: Éditions Amsterdam, 2006.

Honneth, Axel. *La lutte pour la reconnaissance*. Paris: Éditions du Cerf, 2007.

Hurbon, Laënnec. *Le barbare imaginaire*. Paris: Cerf, 1988.

Itti, Eliane. *L'image des civilisations francophones dans les manuels scolaires. Des colonies à la francophonie*. Paris: Publibook, 2006.

Jacobs, Margaret D. *White Mother to a Dark Race: Settler Colonialism, Maternalism, and the Removal of Indigenous Children in the American West and Australia, 1880–1940*. Lincoln: University of Nebraska Press, 2009.

Jaumain, Serge, and Paul-André Linteau, eds. *Vivre en ville. Bruxelles et Montréal (XIXe–XXe siècle)*. Bruxelles: P.I.E. Peter Lang, 2006.

Jay, Martin, and Sumathi Ramaswamy, eds. *Empires of Vision: A Reader*. Durham: Duke University Press, 2014.

Joly, Martine. *Introduction à l'analyse de l'image*. 3rd ed. Paris: Armand Colin, 2015.

Kastoryano, Riva, ed. *Les codes de la différence. Race, origine, religion. France, Allemagne, États-Unis*. Paris: Presses de la Fondation nationale des sciences politiques, 2005.

King, Michelle. *Between Birth and Death: Female Infanticide in Nineteenth-Century China*. Stanford: Stanford University Press, 2014.

Klose, Fabian, and Mirjam Thulin, eds. *Humanity: A History of European Concepts in Practice from the Sixteenth Century to the Present*. Göttingen: Vandenhoeck and Ruprecht, 2016.

Kramer, Lloyd, and Sara Maza. *A Companion to Western Historical Thought*. Oxford: Blackwell, 2006.

Kuo Wei Tchen, John, and Dylan Yeats, eds. *Yellow Peril! An Archive of Anti-Asian Fear*. London and Brooklyn: Verso, 2014.

Lacombe, Sylvie. *La rencontre de deux peuples élus. Comparaison des ambitions nationale et impériale au Canada entre 1896 et 1920*. Quebec: Presses de l'Université Laval, 2002.

Lamonde, Yvan. *Allégeances et dépendances. Histoire d'une ambivalence identitaire*. Quebec: Nota bene, 2001.

———. *Histoire sociale des idées au Québec, 1760–1896*. Montreal: Fides, 2000.

———. *Historien et citoyen. Navigations au long cours*. Montreal: Fides, 2008.

Lane, Christopher. *The Ruling Passion: British Colonial Allegory and the Paradox of Homosexual Desire*. Durham: Duke University Press, 1995.

Langlois, Yvon. *Délia. L'audace des frontières inconnues*. Montreal: Self-published, 1999.

LaRocque, Emma. *Defeathering the Indian*. Agincourt: The Book Society of Canada, 1975.

———. *When the Other Is Me: Native Resistance Discourse, 1850–1990*. Winnipeg: University of Manitoba Press, 2010.

Lebrun, Monique, ed. *Le manuel scolaire, d'ici et d'ailleurs, d'hier à demain*. Quebec: Presses de l'Université du Québec, 2007. CD-ROM.

Lemaire, Sandrine, and Pascal Blanchard, eds. *Culture coloniale 1871–1931*. Paris: Autrement, 2003.

———, eds. *Culture impériale 1931–1961. Les colonies au cœur de la République*. Paris: Autrement, 2004.

Lemire, Maurice. *Formation de l'imaginaire littéraire au Québec, 1764–1867*. Montreal: L'Hexagone, 1993.

Lennon, Joseph. *Irish Orientalism: A Literary and Intellectual History*. Syracuse: Syracuse University Press, 2004.

Leonardo, Zeus. *Race Framework: A Multidimensional Theory of Racism and Education*. New York and London: Teachers College Press, 2013.

Létourneau, Jocelyn. *Le Québec entre son passé et ses passages*. Montreal: Fides, 2010.

———. *Passer à l'avenir. Histoire, mémoire, identité dans le Québec d'aujourd'hui.* Montreal: Boréal, 2000.

Levinas, Emmanuel. *Alterity and Transcendence.* Translated by Michael B. Smith. New York: Columbia University Press, 1999.

———. *Autrement qu'être ou Au-delà de l'essence.* Paris: LGF Livre de Poche, 1990.

———. *Éthique comme philosophie première.* Paris: Rivages, 1982.

———. *Le temps et l'autre.* Quadrige Series. Paris: Presses universitaires de France, 1991.

Löhr, Isabella, and Roland Wenzlhuemer, eds. *The Nation State and Beyond: Governing Globalization Processes in the Nineteenth and Early Twentieth Century.* Heidelberg and New York: Springer, 2013.

Loomba, Ania. *Colonialism/Postcolonialism.* London and New York: Routledge, 2005.

Maynard, Robyn. *Policing Black Lives: State Violence in Canada from Slavery to the Present.* Winnipeg: Fernwood, 2017.

McAndrew, Marie, Béchir Oueslati, and Denise Helly. *Le traitement de l'islam et des musulmans dans les manuels scolaires québécois de langue française.* Montreal: Centre Métropolis du Québec, 2010.

McDiarmid, Garnet, and David Pratt. *Teaching Prejudice: A Content Analysis of Social Studies Textbooks Authorized for Use in Ontario.* Toronto: Ontario Institute for Studies in Education, 1973.

MacKenzie, John M., ed. *European Empires and the People: Popular Responses to Imperialism in France, Britain, the Netherlands, Belgium, Germany and Italy.* Manchester: Manchester University Press, 2011.

———, ed. *Imperialism and Popular Culture.* Manchester: Manchester University Press, 1986.

———. *Orientalism. History, Theory and the Arts.* Manchester: Manchester University Press, 1995.

Mackey, Frank. *L'esclavage et les Noirs à Montréal, 1760–1840.* Montreal: Hurtubise, 2013.

Malaurie, Jean. *Ultima Thulé. De la découverte à l'invasion.* Paris: Éditions du Chêne, 2000.

Mangan, James A., ed. *"Benefits Bestowed"?: Education and British Imperialism.* Manchester: Manchester University Press, 1988.

———, ed. *The Imperial Curriculum: Racial Images and Education in the British Colonial Experience.* London: Routledge, 1993.

Marchand, Suzanne L. *German Orientalism in the Age of Empire: Religion, Race, and Scholarship.* Washington, DC: German Historical Institute; Cambridge, UK: Cambridge University Press, 2009.

Mastasci, Damanio. *L'école républicaine et l'étranger. Une histoire internationale des réformes scolaires en France, 1870–1914.* Lyon: ENS Éditions, 2015.

Matt, Susan J., and Peter N. Stearns, eds. *Doing Emotions History.* Urbana: University of Illinois Press, 2014.

Michaud, Stéphane, Jean-Yves Mollier, and Nicole Savy, eds. *Usages de l'image au XIXe siècle.* Grâne: Créaphis, 1992.

Michel, Pierre. *Un mythe romantique. Les Barbares, 1789–1848.* Lyon: Presses universitaires de Lyon, 1981.

Millard, Arlette. *Félicien David et l'aventure saint-simonienne en Orient.* Paris: Presses Franciliennes, 2005.

Miller, Carman. *Painting the Map Red: Canada and the South African War 1899–1902.* Montreal and Kingston: McGill-Queen's University Press, 1993.

Miller, James R. *Shingwauk's Vision: History of Native Residential Schools.* Toronto: University of Toronto Press, 1996.

Mitchell, William J.T. *Iconology. Image, Text, Ideology.* Chicago: University of Chicago Press, 1987.

———. *What Do Pictures Want? The Lives and Loves of Images.* Chicago: University of Chicago Press, 2005.

———. *Que veulent les images? Une critique de la culture visuelle.* Paris: Presses du réel, 2014.

Mitchie, Helena, and Ronald R. Thomas, eds. *Nineteenth-Century Geographies: The Transformation of Space from the Victorian Age to the American Century.* New Brunswick, NJ: Rutgers University Press, 2003.

Monchalin, Lisa. *The Colonial Problem: An Indigenous Perspective on Crime and Injustice in Canada.* Toronto: University of Toronto Press, 2016.

Morrison, Hugh, and Mary Clare Martin, eds. *Creating Religious Childhoods in Anglo-World and British Colonial Contexts, 1800–1950.* London and New York: Routledge, 2017.

Morrison, Toni. *The Origin of Others.* Cambridge, MA: Harvard University Press, 2017.

———. *Playing in the Dark: Whiteness and the Literary Imagination.* Cambridge: Harvard University Press, 1992.

Moussa, Sarga, ed. *L'idée de "race" dans les sciences humaines et la littérature (XVIIIe et XIXe siècles).* Paris: L'Harmattan, 2003.

Mrinalini, Sinha. *Colonial Masculinity: The "Manly Englishman" and the "Effeminate Bengali" in the Late Nineteenth Century.* Manchester: Manchester University Press, 1995.

Munono Muyembe, Bernard. *Le regard et le visage. De l'altérité chez Jean-Paul Sartre et Emmanuel Levinas.* Berne, Frankfurt, New York, and Paris: Peter Lang, 1991.

Münster, Arno, ed. *La différence comme non-indifférence. Éthique et altérité chez Emmanuel Levinas.* Paris: Éditions Kimé, 1995.

Nelles, Henry V. *L'histoire spectacle. Le cas du tricentenaire de Québec.* Montreal: Boréal, 2003.

Nowicky, Joanna, and Czeslaw Porebski, eds. *L'invention de l'Autre.* Paris: Sandre, 2008.

Olsen, Stephanie, ed. *Childhood, Youth and Emotions in Modern History: National, Colonial and Global Perspectives.* Houndmills: Palgrave Macmillan, 2015.

Olsen, Stephanie. *Juvenile Nation: Youth, Emotions and the Making of the Modern British Citizen, 1880–1914.* London: Bloomsbury, 2014.

Orchard, Stephen, and John H.Y. Briggs, eds. *The Sunday School Movement: Studies in the Growth and Decline of Sunday Schools.* Bletchley: Paternoster Press, 2007.

Otter, Chris. *The Victorian Eye: A Political History of Light and Vision in Britain, 1800–1910.* Chicago: University of Chicago Press, 2008.

Ouellette-Michalska, Madeleine. *L'amour de la carte postale. Impérialisme culturel et différence.* Montreal: Amérique, 1987.

Paterson, Janet. *Figures de l'Autre dans le roman québécois.* Quebec: Nota bene, 2004.

Peltre, Christine. *Dictionnaire culturel de l'orientalisme.* Paris: Hazan, 2008.

Pericles Trifonas, Peter, ed. *Pedagogies of Difference: Rethinking Education for Social Change*. Falmer Series. New York and London: Routledge, 2003.

Pierre, Éric, and Marie-Sylvie Dupoint-Bouchat, eds. *Enfance et justice au XIXe siècle. Essais d'histoire comparée de la protection de l'enfance 1820–1914 (France, Belgique, Pays-Bas, Canada)*. Paris: Presses universitaires de France, 2001.

Pieterse, Jan Nederveen. *White on Black: Images of Africa and Blacks in Western Popular Culture*. New Haven: Yale University Press, 1992.

Pingel, Falk. *UNESCO Guidebook on Textbook Research and Textbook Revision*. Paris: UNESCO; Braunschweig: Georg Eckert Institute for International Textbook Research, 2010.

Porter, Andrew. *Religion versus Empire? British Protestant Missionaries and Overseas Expansion, 1700–1914*. Manchester: Manchester University Press, 2004.

Pratt, Mary Louise. *Imperial Eyes: Travel Writing and Transculturation*. 2nd ed. London and New York: Routledge, 2008.

Provenzo, Eugene F. Jr. *Culture as Curriculum: Education and the International Expositions (1876–1904)*. New York: Peter Lang, 2012.

Prud'homme, Claude. *Missions chrétiennes et colonisation, XVIe–XXe siècles*. Paris: Les Éditions du Cerf, 2004.

Prudhomme, Claude, ed. *Une appropriation du monde. Mission et missions, XVIe–XXe siècles*. Paris: Publisud, 2004.

Renonciat, Annie, ed. *L'image pour enfants: pratiques, normes, discours (France et pays francophones, XVIe–XXe siècles)*. Poitiers: UFR Langues et Littératures, Maison des Sciences de l'Homme et de la Société, 2003.

Ricœur, Paul. *La mémoire, l'histoire, l'oubli*. Paris: Seuil, 2000. [*Memory, History, Forgetting*. Chicago and London: University of Chicago Press, 2004.]

———. *Soi-même comme un autre*. Paris: Seuil, 1990.

———. *Temps et récit*. Vol. 3, *Le temps raconté*. Paris: Seuil, 2005.

Rudin, Ronald. *L'histoire dans les rues de Québec. La célébration de Champlain et de Mgr de Laval, 1878–1908*. Saint-Nicolas: Presses de l'Université Laval, 2005.

Saïd, Edward. *Culture et impérialisme*. Paris: Fayard and Le Monde diplomatique, 2000.

———. *L'orientalisme. L'Orient créé par l'Occident*. Paris: Seuil, 2013.

Salah-Eddine, Myriam, ed. *L'école et la diversité culturelle: nouveaux enjeux, nouvelles dynamiques. Actes du colloque national des 5 et 6 avril 2006*. Paris: Documentation française, 2006.

Sartre, Jean-Paul. *Anti-Semite and Jew*. Translated by George J. Becker. New York: Shocken Books, 1995 [1948].

———. *Being and Nothingness*. Translated by Hazel E. Barnes. London and New York: Routledge Classics, 2003.

———. *L'être et le néant. Essai d'ontologie phénoménologique*. Paris: Gallimard, 2004.

Schaub, Jean-Frédéric. *Pour une histoire politique de la race*. Paris: Seuil, 2015.

Schilinger, Jean, and Philippe Alexandre, eds. *Le barbare. Images phobiques et réflexions sur l'altérité dans la culture européenne*. Bern: Peter Lang, 2008.

Scott, Corrie. *De Groulx à Laferrière. Un parcours de la race dans la littérature québécoise*. Montreal: XYZ éditeur, 2014.

Scott, Joan Wallach. *The Politics of the Veil*. Princeton, NJ, and Oxford: Princeton University Press, 2007.

Sèbe, Berny. *Heroic Imperialists in Africa: The Promotion of British and French Colonial Heroes (1870–1939)*. Manchester: Manchester University Press, 2013.

Smith, Donald B. *Le "Sauvage" pendant la période héroïque de la Nouvelle-France (1534–1663) d'après les historiens canadiens-français des XIXe et XXe siècles*. Ville LaSalle: Hurtubise HMH, 1979.

Stanworth, Karen. *Visibly Canadians*. Montreal and Kingston: McGill-Queen's University Press, 2014.

Stevens, Laura M. *The Poor Indians: British Missionaries, Native Americans, and Colonial Sensibility*. Philadelphia: University of Pennsylvania Press, 2004.

Stitou, Rajaa, and Gérard Laniez, eds. *L'étranger et le différent dans l'actualité du lien social*. Nantes: Pleins feux, 2007.

Stoler, Ann Laura. *Race and the Education of Desire: Foucault's History of Sexuality and the Colonial Order of Things*. Durham: Duke University Press, 1995.

Sugunasiri, Suwanda. *Smarten Up, Indians, and Go Western: A Content Analysis of Ontario's Secondary School Social Studies Texts in Relation to India*. Toronto: Published for the Indian Students' Association at University of Toronto by Indian Immigrant Aid Services, 1978.

Swain, Shurlee, and Margot Hillel. *Child, Nation, Race and Empire: Child Rescue Discourse, England, Canada and Australia, 1850–1915*. Manchester: Manchester University Press, 2010.

Taraud, Christelle. *Mauresques. Femmes orientales dans la photographie coloniale 1860–1910*. Paris: Albin Michel, 2003.

Thiesse, Anne-Marie. *La création des identités nationales. Europe XVIIIe–XXe siècles*. Paris: Seuil, 1999.

Todorov, Tzvetan. *La conquête de l'Amérique. La question de l'autre*. Paris: Seuil, 1991.

———. *Nous et les autres. La réflexion française sur la diversité humaine*. Paris: Seuil, 1989.

Truth and Reconciliation Commission of Canada. *Canada's Residential Schools*. Part 1, *Final Report of the Truth and Reconciliation Commission of Canada*. Vol 1. Montreal and Kingston: McGill-Queen's University Press, 2016.

Tutiaux-Guillon, Nicole, and Didier Nourrisson, eds. *Identités, mémoires, conscience historique*. Saint-Étienne: Publications de l'Université de Saint-Étienne, 2003.

Vallgårda, Karen. *Imperial Childhoods and Christian Mission: Education and Emotions in South India and Denmark*. New York: Palgrave Macmillan, 2015.

Venayre, Sylvain. *Les origines de la France. Quand les historiens racontaient la nation*. Paris: Seuil, 2013.

Vigneault, Louise. *Zacharie Vincent. Une autohistoire artistique*. Wendake: Éditions Hannenorak, 2016.

Vincent, Sylvie, and Bernard Arcand. *L'image de l'Amérindien dans les manuels scolaires du Québec, ou Comment les Québécois ne sont pas des sauvages*. LaSalle: Hurtubise, 1979.

Wilinsky, John. *Learning to Divide the World: Education at Empire's End*. Minneapolis: University of Minnesota Press, 1999.

Winks, Robin W. *The Blacks in Canada: A History*. Montreal: McGill-Queen's University Press; New Haven and London: Yale University Press, 1971.

Wood, Diana, ed. *The Church and Childhood*. Oxford: Blackwell, 1994.

Young, Iris Marion. *Justice and the Politics of Difference*. Princeton: Princeton University Press, 1990.

Young, Robert J.C. *Colonial Desire. Hybridity in Theory, Culture and Race*. London: Routledge, 1995.

Articles

Ajari, Norman. "Être et race. Réflexions polémiques sur la colonialité de l'être." *Revue d'études décoloniales* 1 (2016). https://etudesdecoloniales.press/wp-content/uploads/2022/08/Numero-1-RED-Construction-des-savoirs-decoloniaux.pdf.

Baillette, Frédéric. "Figures du corps, ethnicité et génocide au Rwanda." *Quasimodo* 6 (2000): 7–37.

Bancel, Nicolas, and Pascal Blanchard. "Civiliser: l'invention de l'indigène." In *Culture coloniale, 1871–1931*, edited by Sandrine Lemaire and Pascal Blanchard, 149–61. Paris: Autrement, 2003.

———. "De l'indigène à l'immigré, images, messages et réalités." *Hommes et Migrations* 1207, no. 1 (1997): 6–30.

Bancel, Nicolas, and Denis Daniel, "Éduquer: comment devient-on 'Homo imperialis.'" In *Culture impériale 1931–1961. Les colonies au cœur de la République*, edited by Sandrine Lemaire and Pascal Blanchard, 93–106. Paris: Autrement, 2004.

Bell, Avril, Lesley Patterson, Morgan Dryburgh, and David Johnston. "Empire to Nationhood: Heroism in Natural Disaster Stories for Children." *History of Education Review* 41, no. 1 (2012): 20–37.

Bienvenue, Louise. "L'Église et l'enfance dans les écrits de Jean-Marie Fecteau (1949–2012)." *Bulletin d'histoire politique* 25, no. 1 (Fall 2016): 53–67.

Boëtsch, Gilles, and Jean-Noël Ferrié. "Du daguerréotype au stéréotype: typification scientifique et typification du sens commun dans la photographie coloniale." *Hermès, La Revue*, 30 (2001/2): 169–75.

Boëtsch, Gilles, and Christiane Villain-Gandossi. "Introduction. Les stéréotypes dans les relations Nord-Sud: images du physique de l'Autre et qualifications mentales." *Hermès, La Revue*, 30 (2001/2): 17–23.

Brückenhaus, Daniel. "Ralph's Compassion." In *Learning how to Feel: Children's Literature and Emotional Socialization, 1870–1970*, edited by Ute Frevert, Bettina Hitzer, Pascal Eitler, Stephanie Olsen, Uffa Jensen, Margrit Pernau, Daniel Brückenhaus, Magdalena Beljan, Benno Gammerl, and Anja Laukötter, 74–93. Oxford: Oxford University Press, 2014.

Bruter, Annie. "L'enseignement de l'histoire nationale à l'école primaire avant la IIIe République." *Histoire de l'éducation* 126 (2010): 11–32.

Burguière, André. "L'historiographie des origines de la France." *Annales. Histoire, Sciences Sociales* 58, no. 1 (2003): 41–62.

Cambron, Micheline. "La société récitée. Sur la fécondité du concept d'identité narrative." *Fabula* (May 2013). http://www.fabula.org/colloques/document1926.php.

Chen, Shih-Wen Sue. "'Give, Give; Be Always Giving': Children, Charity and China, 1890–1939." *Papers. Explorations into Children's Literature* 24, no. 2 (2016): 5–32.

Chevrefils, Yves. "John Henry Walker (1831–1899), Artisan-Graveur." *Journal of Canadian Art History / Annales d'histoire de l'art canadien* 8, no. 2 (1985): 178–225.

Clark, Penney. "Images of Aboriginal People in British Columbia Canadian History Textbooks." *Canadian Issues* (Fall 2006): 47–51.

Cordier, Gérard. "Le marquis de Nadaillac et l'Amérique préhistorique [compte-rendu]." *Journal de la Société des américanistes* 82, no. 1 (1996): 325–30.

Deane, Bradley. "Imperial Barbarian: Primitive Masculinity in Lost World Fiction." *Victorian Literature and Culture* 36 (2008): 205–25.

Delâge, Denys. "La peur de 'passer pour des Sauvages.'" *Les Cahiers des Dix* 65 (2011): 1–45.

Delsol, Chantal. "Politique et altérité." In *L'invention de l'Autre,* edited by Joanna Nowicky and Czeslaw Porebski, 39–48. Paris: Sandre, 2008.

Destrempes, Hélène. "Mise en discours et parcours de l'effacement: une étude de la figure de l'Indien dans la littérature canadienne-française au xixe siècle." *Tangence* 85 (Fall 2007): 29–46.

Dubinsky, Karen. "Children, Ideology, and Iconography: How Babies Rule the World." *Journal of the History of Childhood and Youth* 5, no. 1 (Winter 2012): 5–13.

Edwards, Elizabeth. "La photographie ou la construction de l'image de l'Autre." In *Zoos humains. Au temps des exhibitions humaines,* edited by Nicolas Bancel, Pascal Blanchard, and Gilles Boëtsch, 323–30. Paris: La Découverte, 2004.

Egresi, Istvan. "The Representation of 'Other' Cultures in the Romanian Geography Textbooks Published during the First Half of the 20th Century." *European Journal of Educational Studies* 5, no. 1 (2013): 63–71.

Fecteau, Jean-Marie. "La troublante altérité de l'histoire. Réflexion sur le passé comme 'Autre' radical." *Revue d'histoire de l'Amérique française* 59, no. 3 (2006): 333–45.

Fecteau, Jean-Marie, Sylvie Ménard, Véronique Strimelle, and Jean Trépanier. "Une politique de l'enfance délinquante et en danger: la mise en place des écoles de réforme et d'industrie au Québec (1840–1873)." *Crime, Histoire et Société* 2, no. 1 (1998): 75–110.

Gayon, Jean. "Le corps racialisé. Le philosophe et la notion de race." In *Corps normalisé, corps stigmatisé, corps racialisé*, edited by Gilles Boëtsch, Christian Hervé, and Jacques J. Rozenberg, 273–97. De Boeck Supérieur, 2007.

Gettler, Brian. "Les autochtones et l'histoire du Québec. Au-delà du négationnisme et du récit 'nationaliste-conservateur.'" *Recherches amérindiennes au Québec* 46, no. 1 (2016): 7–18.

Giroux, Dalie. "Thierry Hentsch/Proche-Orient. Désarticulation amoureuse de la puissance du négatif." *Cahiers de l'idiotie* 2 (2009): 221–66.

Gossage, Peter. "Les enfants abandonnés à Montréal au 19e siècle: la Crèche d'Youville des Sœurs grises, 1820–1871." *Revue d'histoire de l'Amérique française* 40, no. 4 (1987): 537–59.

Green, Rayna. "The Tribe Called Wannabee: Playing Indian in America and Europe." *Folklore* 99, no. 1 (1988): 30–55.

Hall, Stuart. "Race, the Floating Signifier, Featuring Stuart Hall—Transcript." Media Education Foundation, 1997. https://www.mediaed.org/transcripts/Stuart-Hall-Race-the-Floating-Signifier-Transcript.pdf.

Harrison, Henrietta. "'A Penny for the Little Chinese': The French Holy Childhood Association in China, 1843–1951." *American Historical Review* 113, no. 1 (2008): 72–92.

Hentsch, Thierry. "L'altérité dans l'imaginaire occidental: fonction manifeste, fonction occulte." *Revue d'histoire de l'Amérique française* 59, no. 3 (2006): 347–56.

Heywood, Sophie. "Missionary Children: The French Holy Childhood Association in European Context, 1843–c. 1914." *European History Quarterly* 45, no. 3 (June 2015): 446–66.

Honeck, Mischa. "Innocent Ignorance: Whitewashing an Empire with the Boy Scouts of America." *History of Knowledge. Research, Resources, and Perspectives,* 4 May 2017. https://historyofknowledge.net/2017/05/04/innocent-ignorance-whitewashing-an-empire-with-the-boy-scouts-of-america/.

Igartua, José E. "The Genealogy of Stereotypes: French Canadians in Two English-Language Canadian History Textbooks." *Journal of Canadian Studies* 42, no. 3 (Fall 2008): 106–32.

Jacobs, Margaret D. "Maternal Colonialism: White Women and Indigenous Child Removal in the American West and Australia, 1880–1940." *Western Historical Quarterly* 36, no. 4 (November 2005): 453–76.

Jay, Martin. "A Parting Glance: Empire and Visuality." In *Empires of Vision: A Reader,* edited by Martin Jay and Sumathi Ramaswamy, 609–20. Durham: Duke University Press, 2014.

Jensz, Felicity. "Firewood, Fakirs and Flags: The Construction of the Non-Western 'Other' in a Nineteenth Century Transnational Children's Missionary Periodical." *Schweizerische Zeitschrift für Religions- und Kulturgeschichte, Sonderheft Missiontransnationale Perspektiven* 105 (2011): 167–91.

Jones, Sally, L. "The First but Not the Last of the 'Vanishing Indians': Edwin Forrest and Mythic Re-creations of the Native Population." In *Dressing in Feathers. The Construction of The Indian in American Popular Culture,* edited by S. Elizabeth Bird, 13–27. New York: Routledge, 1996.

Kenny, L.M. "The Middle East in Canadian Social Science Textbooks." In *Arabs in America: Myths and Realities,* edited by Baha Abu-Laban and Faith Zeadey, 131–47. Wilmette: Medina University Press International, 1975.

Kristóf, Ildikó Sz. "Domesticating Nature, Appropriating Hierarchy: The Representation of European and Non-European Peoples in an Early Nineteenth-Century Schoolbook of Natural History." In *Competing Eyes: Visual Encounters with Alterity in Central and Eastern Europe,* edited by Dagnoslaw Demski, Kamila Baraniecka-Olszewska, and Ildikó Sz. Kristóf, 40–66. Budapest: L'Harmattan, 2013.

Lacasse, Germain. "Le phare du train ou le son de la lanterne. Oliver Buell et l'imagerie coloniale au Québec." *Nouvelles Vues—Revue sur les pratiques et les théories du cinéma au Québec* 15 (Winter 2013–14). https://nouvellesvues.org/wp-content/uploads/2021/07/Oliver_Buell_imagerie_coloniale.pdf.

Lafrance, Mélanie. "Appréhender le monde selon la théologie naturelle: l'enseignement des sciences au pensionnat des Ursulines de Québec (1830–1910)." *Historical Studies in Education/Revue d'histoire de l'éducation* 32, no. 2 (2020): 27–48.

Larochelle, Catherine. "L'Orient comme miroir: les altérités orientale et autochtone dans les récits de voyage des Canadiens français au xixe siècle." *Histoire sociale/Social History* 50, no. 101 (May 2017): 69–87.

Lebel, Jean-Marie. "La nuit où périt le Music Hall. . . ." *Cap-aux-Diamants* 52 (1989): 66.

Le Breton, David. "Notes sur les imaginaires racistes du corps." *Quasimodo* 6 (2000): 53–59.

Lebrun, Monique. "La figure de l'étranger dans les manuels québécois de français langue maternelle." In *Le manuel scolaire, d'ici et d'ailleurs, d'hier à demain*, edited by Monique Lebrun, 1–31. Québec: Presses de l'Université du Québec, 2007.

Leighton, Douglas. "Assikinakc, Francis." *Dictionary of Canadian Biography* 9, University of Toronto/Université Laval, 2003–. http://www.biographi.ca/en/bio/assikinack_francis_9E.html.

Levinas, Emmanuel. "Emmanuel Levinas: visage et violence première (phénoménologie de l'éthique). Une interview." In *La différence comme non-indifférence. Éthique et altérité chez Emmanuel Lévinas*, edited by Arno Münster, 129–43. Paris: Éditions Kimé, 1995.

———. "The Trace of the Other." In *Deconstruction in Context*, edited by Mark Taylor, 345–59. Chicago: University of Chicago Press, 1986.

Liebersohn, Harry. "Introduction: The Civilizing Mission." *Journal of World History* 27, no. 3 (September 2016): 383–87.

Lüsebrink, Hans-Jürgen. "La construction de l'Autre. Approches culturelles et socio-historiques." In *Identité collective et altérité. Diversité des espaces/spécificité des pratiques*, edited by Marie-Antoinette Hily and Marie-Louise Lefebvre, 79–92. Paris and Montréal: L'Harmattan, 1999.

Maddrell, Avril. "Discourses of Race and Gender and the Comparative Method in Geography School Texts, 1830–1918." *Environment and Planning D: Society and Space* 16 (1998): 81–103.

Manceron, Gilles. "École, pédagogie et colonies." In *Culture coloniale 1871–1931*, edited by Sandrine Lemaire and Pascal Blanchard, 93–103. Paris: Autrement, 2003.

Manzo, Kate. "Imaging Humanitarianism: NGO Identity and the Iconography of Childhood." *Antipode* 40, no. 4 (September 2008): 632–57.

Martin, Michèle. "L'image, outil de lutte contre l'analphabétisme: le rôle de la presse illustrée au xixe siècle dans l'éducation populaire." *Historical Studies in Education / Revue d'histoire de l'éducation* 19, no. 2 (Fall 2007): 37–52.

Masse, Vincent. "L'Amérindien 'd'un autre âge' dans la littérature québécoise au xixe siècle." *Tangence* 90 (Summer 2009): 107–33.

Matasci, Damiano. "Les missions pédagogiques françaises en Allemagne: un exemple de circulation transfrontière des modèles scolaires (1860–1914)." *Trajectoire* 3 (2009). http://journals.openedition.org/trajectoires/235.

———. "Le système scolaire français et ses miroirs. Les missions pédagogiques entre comparaison internationale et circulation des savoirs (1842–1914)." *Histoire de l'éducation* 125 (2010): 5–26.

McAndrew, Marie, Béchir Oueslati, and Denise Helly. "Islam and Muslim Cultures in Quebec French-language Textbooks over Three Periods: 1980s, 1990s, and the Present Day." *Journal of Educational Media, Memory, and Society* 3, no. 1 (2011): 5–24.

Mitchell, W.J.T. "Showing Seeing: A Critique of Visual Culture." *Journal of Visual Culture* 1, 2 (2002): 165–81.

Morgan, Hani. "Over One Hundred Years of Misrepresentation: American Minority Groups in Children's Books." *American Educational History Journal* 38, no. 2 (2011): 357–76.

Morrison, Hugh. "'Impressions Which Will Never Be Lost': Missionary Periodicals for Protestant Children in Late-Nineteenth Century Canada and New Zealand." *Church History* 82, no. 2 (June 2013): 388–93.

———. "The 'joy and heroism of doing good': *The New Zealand Missionary* Record and Late-Nineteenth Century Protestant Children's Missionary Support." *Journal of New Zealand Literature* 28 (2010): 158–82.

———. "'Little Vessels' or 'Little Soldiers': New Zealand Protestant Children, Foreign Missions, Religious Pedagogy and Empire, c. 1880s–1930s." *Paedagogica Historica* 47, no. 3 (June 2011): 303–21.

9

Moruzi, Kristine. "'Donations Need Not Be Large to Be Acceptable': Children, Charity, and the Great Ormond Street Hospital in *Aunt Judy's Magazine*, 1868–1885." *Victorian Periodicals Review* 50, no. 1 (Spring 2017): 190–213.

Ngo, Hieu Van. "Racism in Canadian Education." In *Racism and Anti-Racism in Canada*, edited by David Este, Liza Lorenzetti, and Christa Sato, 175–200. Winnipeg: Fernwood Publishing, 2018.

Nurse, Andrew. "Thanking God for. . . ? Historical Perspectives on Cultural Appropriation." *Active History* 13 (June 2017). http://activehistory.ca/2017/06/. thanking-god-for-historical-perspectives-on-cultural-appropriation/.

Olsen, Stephanie. "The History of Childhood and the Emotional Turn." *History Compass* 15, no. 11 (November 2017): 1–10.

Olsen, Stephanie, and Rob Boddice. "Styling Emotions History." *Journal of Social History* 51, no. 3 (2018): 476–87.

Paasi, Anssi. "The Changing Pedagogies of Space: The Representation of the Other in Finnish School Geography Textbooks." In *Text and Image: Social Construction of Regional Knowledges*, edited by Stanley D. Brunn, Anne Buttimer, and Ute Wardenga, 226–37. Leipzig: Institut für Länderkunde, 1999.

Panese, Francesco. "La fabrique du 'Nègre' au cap du XIXe siècle: Petrus Camper, Johann Friedrich Blumenbach et Julien-Joseph Virey." In *L'invention de la race. Des représentations scientifiques aux exhibitions populaires*, edited by Nicolas Bancel, Thomas David, and Dominic Thomas, 59–73. Paris: La Découverte, 2014.

Pilarczyk, Ian C. "'So Foul a Deed': Infanticide in Montreal, 1825–1850." *Law and History Review* 30, no. 2 (2012): 575–634.

Prochaska, Frank K. "Little Vessels: Children in the Nineteenth-Century English Missionary Movement." *Journal of Imperial and Commonwealth History* 6, no. 2 (1978): 103–18.

Radford, Ian. "Performance, Politics, and Representation: Aboriginal People and the 1860 Royal Tour of Canada." *Canadian Historical Review* 84, no. 1 (March 2003): 1–32.

Ritchie, Thomas. "Bonfils and Son, Egypt, Greece and the Levant; 1867–1894." *History of Photography* 3, no. 1 (1979): 33–46.

Rousseau, Louis. "La construction religieuse de la nation." *Recherches sociographiques* 46, no. 3 (2005): 437–52.

———. "Les missions populaires de 1840–42: acteurs principaux et conséquences." *Sessions d'étude—Société canadienne d'histoire de l'Église catholique* 53 (1986): 7–21.

Savarèse, Éric. "Livres noirs pour petits blancs. Constructions littéraires et usages idéologiques de l'altérité radicale." In *Littératures et temps colonial. Métamorphoses du regard sur la Méditerranée et l'Afrique*, edited by Jean-Robert Henri and Lucienne Martini, 209–23. Aix-en-Provence: Édisud, 1999.

Stamp, Robert M. "Empire Day in Schools of Ontario: The Training of Young Imperialists." *Journal of Canadian Studies* 8, no. 3 (August 1973): 32–42.

Stanley, Brian. "From the 'poor heathen' to 'the glory and honour of all nations': Vocabularies of Race and Custom in Protestant Missions, 1844–1928." *International Bulletin of Missionary Research* 34, no. 1 (2010): 3–10.

———. "Missionary Regiments for Immanuel's Service: Juvenile Missionary Organization in English Sunday Schools, 1841–1865." In *The Church and Childhood*, edited by Diana Wood, 391–403. Oxford: Blackwell, 1994.

Stanley, Timothy J. "Antiracism Without Guarantees: A Framework for Rethinking Racisms in Schools." *Critical Literacy: Theories and Practices* 8, no. 1 (2014): 4–19.

Stornig, Katharina. "Between Christian Solidarity and Human Solidarity: Humanity and the Mobilisation of Aid for Distant Children in Catholic Europe in the Long Nineteenth Century." In *Humanity: A History of European Concepts in Practice from the Sixteenth Century to the Present*, edited by Fabian Klose and Mirkam Thulin, 249–66. Göttingen: Vandenhoeck and Ruprecht, 2016.

Topdar, Sudipa. "The Corporeal Empire: Physical Education and Politicising Children's Bodies in Late Colonial Bengal." *Gender and History* 29, no. 1 (April 2017): 176–97.

Turgeon, Andréanne. "La littérature normative est-elle un frein à l'analyse des transformations socioreligieuses? L'exemple du 'réveil religieux' québécois des années 1840." *Laval théologique et philosophique* 70, no. 2 (2014): 241–56.

Turkyilmaz, Zeynep. "Maternal Colonialism and Turkish Woman's Burden in Dersim: Educating the 'Mountain Flowers' of Dersim." *Journal of Women's History* 28, no. 3 (2016): 162–86.

Vallgårda, Karen, Kristine Alexander, and Stephanie Olsen. "Emotions and the Global Politics of Childhood." In *Childhood, Youth and Emotions in Modern History. National, Colonial and Global Perspectives*, edited by Stephanie Olsen, 12–34. London: Palgrave Macmillan, 2015.

Vimalassery, Manu, Juliana Hu Pegues, and Alyosha Goldstein. "On Colonial Unknowing." *Theory and Event* 19, no. 4 (2016). https://muse.jhu.edu/article/633283.

Watts, Ruth. "Education, Empire and Social Change in Nineteenth Century England." *Paedagogica Historica* 45, no. 6 (2009): 773–86.

Zagumny, Lisa L., and Lydia Mihelic Pulsipher. "'The Races and Conditions of Men': Women in Nineteenth-Century Geography School Texts in the United States." *Gender, Place and Culture* 15, no. 4 (2008): 411–29.

Theses and Dissertations

Aledejebi, Funké. "'Girl You Better Apply to Teachers' College': The History of Black Women Educators in Ontario, 1940s–1980s." PhD diss., York University, 2016.

Bauer, Natalee Kehaulani. "(En)gendering Whiteness: A Historical Analysis of White Womanhood, Colonial Anxieties, and 'Tender Violence' in US Schools." PhD diss., University of California, Berkeley, 2017.

Bérubé, Justin. "Le monde raconté aux petits Canadiens français dans trois revues jeunesse, 1921–1947." Master's thesis, University of Quebec at Montreal, 2009.

Dittrich, Klaus. "Experts Going Transnational: Education at World Exhibitions During the Second Half of the Nineteenth Century." PhD diss., University of Portsmouth, 2010.

Frey, Heather Fitzsimmons. "Victorian Girls and At-Home Theatricals: Performing and Playing with Possible Futures." PhD diss., University of Toronto, 2015.

Kmiec, Patricia. "Among the Children: Sunday School Teachers and Evangelical Womanhood in Nineteenth-Century Ontario." Master's thesis, University of Ottawa, 2008.

Larochelle, Catherine. "Les représentations de l'Orient méditerranéen dans les manuels de lecture québécois (1875–1945)." Master's thesis, University of Quebec at Montreal, 2013.

McCallum, Mary Jane. "To Make Good Canadians: Girl Guiding in Indian Residential Schools." Master's thesis, Trent University, 2002.

Plourde, Julie. "Un genre en construction: le théâtre à la Congrégation de Notre-Dame, 1850–1920." Master's thesis, University of Montreal, 2014.

Raymond-Dufour, Maxime. "Le Canada français face à sa destinée. La survivance confrontée au discours nationaliste des manuels scolaires, 1870–1880." Master's thesis, University of Montreal, 2008.

———. "L'Universel et le national. Une étude des consciences historiques au Canada français de la première moitié du xixe siècle." PhD diss., University of Montreal, 2016.

Rousseau, Audrey. "Mémoires et identités blessées en contexte postcolonial: la Commission de vérité et réconciliation du Canada." Master's thesis, University of Quebec at Montreal, 2011.

Journals

Historical Studies in Education/Revue d'histoire de l'éducation 29, no. 1 (Spring 2017).

Paedagogica Historica 31, no. 1 (1995).

Paedagogica Historica 37, no. 1 (2001).

Paedagogica Historica 45, no. 6 (2009).

Online Sources

Desmond, Adrian J. "Thomas Henry Huxley." In *Encyclopaedia Britannica*, https://www.britannica.com/biography/Thomas-Henry-Huxley.

Honeck, Mischa. "Innocent Ignorance: Whitewashing an Empire with the Boy Scouts of America." *History of Knowledge*, https://historyofknowledge. scouts-of-america/.

"J.N. Miller." In *Les manuels scolaires québécois*, https://www.bibl.ulaval.ca/ress/manscol/auteurs/auteursm.html.

Leighton, Douglas. "Assikinack, Francis." In *Dictionary of Canadian Biography*, vol. 9, Sainte-Foy, Laval University, and Toronto, University of Toronto, 2003, http://www.biographi.ca/en/bio/assikinack_francis_9F.html.

"Où sont les femmes ?" *Histoire engagée*, http://histoireengagee.ca/?page_id=5453.

Parmentier, Francis. "Buies, Arthur." In *Dictionnaire biographique du Canada*, 13, Université Laval/University of Toronto, 1994, http://www.biographi.ca/fr/bio/buies_arthur_13F.html.

Purdy, Judson D. "Hodgins, John George." In *Dictionnaire biographique du Canada*, 14, Université Laval/University of Toronto, 2003, graphi.ca/fr/bio/hodgins_john_george_14F.html.

Routhier, Gilles, and Frédéric Laugrand, eds. *L'atlas historique du Québec. Les missions au Québec et du Québec dans le monde*, 2014, xixe-siecle.html, https://atlas.cieq.ca.

Other Sources

Les Autres hommes, directed by Michel Viotte, Arte Vidéo, 2006, 90 minutes.

Reel Injun, directed by Neil Diamond, Rezolution Pictures, 2009, 85 minutes.

Tremblay, Michel. "Petits chinois à vendre." In *Bonbons assortis*, 165–75. Montreal, Leméac/Actes Sud, 2002.

Index

Page numbers in *italics* indicate a figure on the corresponding page.

A

Abyssinians, 68, 72, 145

Acadia, 85, 185–86

Africa. *See also* Algeria; Arabs; Berbers; Black Africans; Black bodies; Cafres; Dahomey; Dutch Guyana; Hottentots (Khoikhoi); Kru people; Pygmies; Sudan; Tunisia: beauty described, 137, 138; cannibals, 147, 148–49; colonial photography in, 277; conquest of, 212, 280–81; death penalty seen as barbaric, 85; denigration of parents, 316–17; description of races in, 128; despotism of, 83–84; ethnographic engravings, 257, 258; in geography textbooks, 55, 66–67; imperialism, 190–91; Kaffirs, 57; missionary work and, 62, 308–9, 311, 313; representations of Blacks, 146–47; student's geographical composition about, 91–92

Africanist persona, 216, 225, 230

African primitivism, 153

Ahern, John, 247, 293–94

Ahmed, Sara, 14, 18, 20, 30, 35, 321–22, 324, 329, 331, 350, 367

Ainu people, 72

Ajari, Norman, 365

Alaska, 63

Alexander, Kristine, 335–36

Algeria, 47, 98, 212. *See also* Berbers; Kabyle

Algerians, *256*

allochrony, 67, 258

alterity. *See also* alterity, construction of; the body; Levinas, Emmanuel; narrative alterity; the Other; otherness; radical alterity; *r*ecognition; Sartre, Jean-Paul: active, 221–22; *Anti-Semite and Jew* (Sartre), 18, 25; *Being and Nothingness* (Sartre), 15–16; Blacks, 18, 168; codes of difference, 29–35; culture as code of difference, 32–34; desire for homogenization, 26; emotional uses of, 321–33; as engine for social change, 310; gaze and, 16, 17–19; imperialism and, 52–59; the Indian, 18, 176–77; *Les codes de la différence* (Kastoryano), 30; the objectifying gaze, 26; politics of differentiation, 21–22; *Soi-même comme un autre* (Oneself like another) (Ricoeur), 19–20; *Strange Encounters* (Ahmed), 20; *Time and the Other* (Fabian), 67; time/temporality, 26–29; universality, 30, 32; the use of childhood, 317–18; uses and functions of, 21–26

alterity, construction of: by discursive techniques, 169–70; the Other and Imperialism, 59–63; rhetorical, 368, 369; by science, 59–60; sexual character of, 87–88; through "civilizing mission," 63, 86

Anderson, Benedict, 184

anthrophagy. *See* cannibalism